INTRODUCING

CHRISTIAN THEOLOGIES

Introducing
Christian Theologies

Voices from Global Christian Communities

VICTOR I. EZIGBO

VOLUME TWO

CASCADE *Books* · Eugene, Oregon

INTRODUCING CHRISTIAN THEOLOGIES
Voices from Global Christian Communities, Volume 2

Cascade Books
An Imprint of Wipf and Stock Publishers
199 W. 8th Ave., Suite 3
Eugene, OR 97401

www.wipfandstock.com

PAPERBACK ISBN 13: 978-1-62032-979-5
HARDCOVER ISBN 13: 978-1-4982-8586-5

Cataloging-in-Publication data:

Ezigbo, Victor

    Introducing Christian theologies : voices from global Christian communities / Victor I. Ezigbo.

    xvi + 366 p. ; 23 cm. —Includes bibliographical references and index.

    ISBN: 978-1-61097-364-9 (v. 1: paper) | ISBN: 978-1-4982-1391-2 (v. 1: hardback)
    ISBN: 978-1-62032-979-5 (v. 2: paper) | ISBN: 978-1-4982-8586-5 (v. 2: hardback)

    1. Theology, Doctrinal. 2. Globalization—Religious aspects—Christianity. I. Title. II. Series.

BX1751.3 .E954 2013

Manufactured in the U.S.A.   01/28/2016

To my parents, Rev. (ISLO) Alfred and Mrs. Bridget Elewechi Ezigbo, who were my first informal theology teachers.

And to my great friends Jon Semke and Debbie Cornett, whose love and generosity made it possible for me to complete my PhD degree in theology at the University of Edinburgh.

Contents

Tables and Charts

Acknowledgments

L ike the first volume, I am indebted to all my students for giving me the initial impetus to write this textbook. My colleagues in the Biblical and Theological Studies department at Bethel University, St. Paul Minnesota, have also helped to sharpen the focus and discussions in each of the chapters. During the writing process, I interrupted several of my colleagues on numerous occasions with questions pertaining to theological and exegetical matters. These colleagues and my students at Bethel University have been great dialogue partners in my theological journey. I want to thank the administration of Bethel University for the sabbatical leave I took in the fall of 2014, during which I completed the manuscript.

I spent a good amount of my sabbatical at the Institute for Advanced Studies in the Humanities (IASH) at the University of Edinburgh (Scotland) as a Visiting Research Fellow. I am thankful for the conversations I had with people at IASH and the School of Divinity (University of Edinburgh). Matthew Eddy, my teaching assistant, read some of the chapters. I am thankful for his suggestions on how to make the materials accessible. As always, Ada Rita Ezigbo (my wife) has been a tremendous source of encouragement to me. I remain grateful for her constant reminder that I must write in a manner accessible to people with no formal theological training. Finally, I would like to express my gratitude to the editorial staff of Wipf and Stock Publishers, especially to Charlie Collier, Jacob Martin, and Ian Creeger.

Abbreviations

ANF	*The Ante-Nicene Fathers*
ESV	English Standard Version
NASB	New American Standard Bible
NIV	New International Version
NPNF	*Nicene and Post-Nicene Fathers*

Introduction

Although I am by birth and theological orientation "Evangelical," I do not teach and write theology only for people of evangelical heritage or people who are sympathetic to it. In the contemporary landscape of "World Christianity," I have never been more convinced that Christian theologies must be truly *global*—that is, they must converse with Christian communities from different parts of the world, most of whom face and tackle unique situations from disparate Christian theological outlooks. Also, Christian theologies should be genuinely *ecumenical*—they must engage the theologies from disparate Christian communities.

Introducing Christian Theologies is a two-volume book. In this second volume, I discuss the following topics: Christian theological anthropology, salvation, Christian theologies of religions, church, Christian eschatological hope, and the Christian life.

For those who may not have read volume 1 of *Introducing Christian Theologies*, I have included below the following introductory comments, which can also be found on pages xiii–xv of volume 1.

Many Christians would prefer to skip the study of theology and get on with sharing their personal beliefs about God. Some of them think that the study of theology is unnecessary for the proclamation of the Christian message. Others believe that theology leads to doubts, which can destroy a person's faith or belief. Studying theology, however, has several benefits. It has an effect on every aspect of a Christian's life. For example, theology can help Christians to deepen their knowledge of Christian doctrines, which are necessary for personal edification (e.g., dealing with doubts) and the proclamation of the Christian message.

The vibrant expansion of Christianity in places outside of Europe and North America, namely in Africa, Asia, and Latin America, raises a question about the "theological face" of Christianity. Should Christianity's theological face remain largely European and North American in the twenty-first century? Like all important questions, the question about the "theological face" of Christianity cannot be ignored. For too long, African, Asian, and Latin American theologians have been left out of mainstream theological discussions. Few standard textbooks on Christian theology acknowledge the unique contributions theologians from these continents have made to global Christianity.

Introducing Christian Theologies: Voices from Global Christian Communities is a two-volume textbook that alters the predominantly European and North American "theological face" of Christianity by interacting with the voices of Christian communities from around the globe. *Introducing Christian Theologies* explores the works of key theologians from these communities, highlighting their unique contributions to global Christianity. This first volume covers the following topics: preliminary issues in Christian theology, God's revelation, Christian Scripture, Trinity, Jesus Christ, Holy Spirit, and divine providence. The second volume will cover the topics of theological anthropology, Christian hope, salvation, church, the Christian life and social problems, and theology of religions.

Intended Audience

Introducing Christian Theologies is primarily designed for undergraduates taking an introductory course in Christian theology. However, the depth of the content also makes it a useful text for seminary students and graduate theology students.

Features of the Book

Accessibility: I taught Christian theology at the undergraduate level in Nigeria and in the United Kingdom. I currently teach theology at the same level in the United States. In my experience, very few introductory textbooks on Christian theology are written in a manner that is accessible to undergraduate students who have no previous knowledge of how to interpret and integrate Christian doctrines. This is a serious problem that *Introducing Christian Theologies* addresses.

Contextualization: This is one of the unique features of this book. Every theology is contextual and ought to be so. Although many theologians, especially in the West, have ignored the contextual nature of theology in their theological discussions, theologians should *intentionally* construct their theologies to befit the contexts of the intended recipients. Theologies must reflect a rigorous and constructive engagement with the social location, religious aspiration, culture, experience, and sociopolitical condition of the communities for which they are intended. The contexts of the theologians whose works are explored here will be highlighted. This will help students to appreciate the contributions of these theologians and also to rethink how to appropriate such theologies in their own contexts.

Diversity of Viewpoints: The textbook presents and discusses several positions on the major Christian doctrines. These positions are described in a manner that highlights their differences, similarities, and unique contributions.

Global and Multidenominational: Unlike the majority of the existing introductory textbooks on Christian theology, *Introducing Christian Theologies* covers a vast range of theological positions written by theologians from Africa, Asia, Latin America, North America, and Europe. The theologians whose works are discussed in this book are Protestant, Roman Catholic, Greek Orthodox, Coptic, or Pentecostal.

Key Terms: The textbook has definitions of theological terms at the end of each chapter.

Charts and Tables: Charts and tables are used to buttress key points or to compare similarities and differences of theological positions.

Primary Sources: Excerpts from primary sources that are keyed to the discussion of the major topics are included at the end of each chapter with the exception of chapter 1.

Exercises: A few assignable exercises have been included in some chapters to help students evaluate their knowledge of the topics discussed.

Review Questions: Several questions have been included at the end of each chapter to help students review the major themes and position discussed.

Texts for Further Reading: A list of important texts on the topics covered is provided at the end of each chapter.

1

Christian Theological Anthropology

Theology transforms. Theology can be one of the easiest ways to turn a person into a ruthless terrorist or crusader who has little or no regard for human life, especially others who do not share his or her theological beliefs and convictions. Theology can also turn a person into a self-giving individual who gives sacrificially to preserve the dignity of all people. Christian theologians have the uttermost responsibility to construct theologies that can transform and turn them into people who uphold and maintain the preciousness of human life and dignity. This chapter focuses on "theological anthropology"—theological reflections on the ultimate origins, identity, significance, way of living, and meaning of human beings in the light of the teaching of the Christian Scriptures.

What is it to be a human being? What should human beings become? For what purpose do human beings exist? These are some of the perennial questions that cannot be ignored in any serious theological discussion on human beings. The ways in which these questions are answered will have significant effects on how people live and also where they derive their self-worth. For example, if a person answers the question of what it is to be a human being only in terms of good health, he or she will most likely fail to see dying as an essential aspect of the biological constitution of human beings.

Questions about the meaning of human life, the human body, and the place of human beings in the world are more pressing in our time, when people's lives can easily be whisked away by curable diseases, incurable diseases, acts of terrorism, poverty, and involuntary starvation. Also, in the wake of the increasing threat of climate change,[1] (*mis*)uses of human bodies for commercial purposes, expansion of human trafficking, and the excitement about the prospect of cloning human beings, Christian theologians are constantly rethinking human beings in the light of God as taught in the Christian Scriptures. David Kelsey has argued that the "context that ultimately defines what and who we are and how we are to be is not the created cosmos." He goes on to argue that the creaturely realm is only "the proximate context into which we are born. It, too, helps define what and who we are and how we are to be. But our ultimate context as creatures is the active creativity of God."[2]

Christian theologians contend that questions about human origins, identity, significance, and purpose cannot be successfully answered in isolation from the concept of a creator—God. For some theologians, defining a human being only in human beings' dynamic relationships is not sufficient for answering questions about human origins, meanings, and significance in the world. For some of these theologians, proposing a creator (God) in the search to understand human existence is one of the most intellectually viable options for the study of human origins, meaning, and significance. Following Augustine of Hippo (354–430 CE) and John Calvin (1509–64), some theologians argue that a "sense of divinity" (*sensus divinitatis* in Latin) is innate in human beings. In the *Confessions* Augustine wrote, "Man is one of your creatures, Lord, and his instinct is to praise you. . . . The thought of you stirs him so deeply that he cannot be content unless he praises you, because you made us for yourself and our hearts find no peace until they rest in you."[3] For John Calvin, the capacity to know God is inherent in hu-

---

1. For a recent discussion on theology and climate change, see Northcott, *A Political Theology of Climate Change*.

2. Kelsey, *Eccentric Existence*, 1:162.

3. Augustine, *Confessions* (Pine-Coffin, 21), 1.1.

man beings' noetic structure or cognitive constitution. He writes, "There is within the human mind, and indeed by natural instinct, an awareness of divinity."[4] Calvin's aim is to show that knowledge of God is part of human natural conditions. Knowledge of God, for Calvin, includes both *epistemic knowing* (intellectual assent) and *relational knowing* that leads human beings to glorify God. "Now, the knowledge of God," Calvin writes, "as I understand it, is that by which we not only conceive that there is a God, but also grasp what befits us and is proper to his glory, in fine, what is to our advantage to know of him."[5]

The major goal of this chapter is to explain and assess the Christian claim that human beings are creatures made in God's image, creatures whose lives have been affected by sin, and creatures whose redemption from the effects of sin and restoration into fellowship with God are based on the account of God's work through Jesus Christ and the Holy Spirit.

Human Beings as God's Image-Bearers

Traditionally, Christians believe that God created the first humans beings. Christian theologians, however, disagree on whether the first human beings were created spiritually *perfect* beings or spiritually *immature* beings. They also agree that human beings are *fallible*—that is, capable of sin-

> FOCUS QUESTION:
> How do human beings image God?

ning. Following the testimony of the Bible, the majority of Christians hold that human beings (excluding Jesus Christ) are in a state of sin on the account of the sin of Adam and Eve (Rom 5:12–19). In some Christian circles, Adam and Eve are believed to be the first human creatures of God.[6] In some other communities, "Adam" and "Eve" are construed as the metaphors or the heuristic devices the author or complier of Genesis used to describe the most common human and animal sexes. In this sense, Adam and Eve may not be the first historical figures created by God. But whether or not Adam and Eve were historically the first human beings God created, the theological truths the author of Genesis aimed to convey remain. The theological truths about human beings expressed in the creation story in Genesis may be summarized as follows. For the author or redactor of Genesis, God has created human beings morally good and with the capacity of choice (Gen 1:31; 2:15–17), human beings have mistrusted and transgressed God's law

4. Calvin, *Institutes of the Christian Religion*, vol. 1, 1.3.1.

5. Ibid., 1.2.1.

6. Grenz, *Theology for the Community of God*, 148.

(Gen 3:2–7), God holds human beings responsible for their mistrust and transgression (Gen 3:8–19), humans' mistrust and disobedience have affected their relationship with God (Gen 3:22–24); and God has not abandoned human beings in their sin of mistrust and disobedience (Gen 3:15; 21).

The claim that human beings are made in "God's image" (*imago Dei* in Latin) is central to Christianity's teaching about human beings. Christians appeal to "being made in God's image" for different purposes. To some, being made in God's image sets human beings apart from other (nonhuman) animals and authorizes human beings to use nonhuman creatures and resources in the world to gratify human desires. Some critics of this understanding of "being made in God's image" blame Christianity for the abuse and destruction of nature. To others, being made in God's image is the ground for confronting the ideas, structures, and acts that dehumanize people. Those who hold this view believe that the task of a Christian theologian is to develop the idea of the *imago Dei* in ways that acknowledge human dignity and at the same time hold human beings accountable as stewards in God's creation. To accomplish this task, a theologian cannot afford to restrict himself or herself only to the theological concept of the *imago Dei*. David Kelsey has noted that a Christian theological anthropology should be grounded in holistic understanding of the scriptural teaching on human beings.[7] I add also that the theologian must engage the findings about human beings that are being discovered in other fields of study such as human genetics, sociology, anthropology, and psychology. In this way, Christian theological anthropology will continue to make relevant contributions to contemporary discourses on human beings.

The ideas of the *imago Dei* are expressed in Gen 1:26–27; 5:1; 1 Cor 11:7–12; and James 3:9. According to Gen 1:26–27, "God said, 'Let us make man in our image, in our likeness, and let them rule over the fish of the sea and the birds of the air, over the livestock over all the earth, and over all the creatures that move along the ground.' So God created man in his own image, in the image of God he created him; male and female he created them" (NIV). Being created in God's image, however, does not imply that human beings have all of God's attributes and properties. Although God has created human beings in God's image, God remains largely distinct from human beings. For example, God does not come into being or existence; God simply *is*, which is to say God is self-existent. Human beings, on the contrary, come into being: they exist because God has called them into existence.

How should we understand the theological concept of the *imago Dei*? The majority of Christian theologians agree that the concept of the *imago*

---

7. Kelsey, *Eccentric Existence*, 2:897.

Dei presupposes human beings' finitude. The *imago Dei* stands in direct opposition to the belief that humanity is self-autonomous and self-explanatory. When Christians confess that human beings are made in the "image of God," they express humanity's dependence upon God for their existence, dignity, and meaning. The Apostle Paul expressed this understanding of human beings in his speech at Athens in the presence of Epicureans and Stoic philosophers. "For in him [God]," Paul says, "we live and move and have our being" (Acts 17:28 NIV). Human beings' dependence on God for their existence, dignity, and meaning is not the result of divine judgment; it is rather the consequence of their ontological existence as God's creatures. Theologically, the *imago Dei* also entails that human worth and dignity are not contingent upon how human beings fare in their survival skills in a treacherous world of competition. Human achievements (education, wealth, etc.) and physical appearance do not (and *ought not* to) determine human beings' worth and dignity. Human beings' dignity and worth derive from God who creates, loves, forgives, disciplines, and provides for them.

While the majority of Christian theologians do not dispute that the *imago Dei* implies humanity's finitude and dependence on God and also that the *imago Dei* presents God as the maker of human beings, the exact nature of the *imago Dei* is a matter of dispute. Genesis 1:26 uses two words to express the idea of the *imago Dei*—namely, "image" and "likeness." The meanings of "image" (*tselem* in Hebrew) and "likeness" (*demut* in Hebrew) are debated. Some theologians see these two words as different qualifiers used by the author of Genesis to express two aspects of human beings. To these theologians, "likeness" refers to the spiritual and moral conditions (or "original righteousness") of human beings whereas "image" refers to the cognitive constitution of human beings. For some of these theologians, human beings lost the *likeness of God* after Adam and Eve sinned but retained the *image of God*. Human beings can regain the likeness of God only through the "renewing activity of the Holy Spirit."[8] Irenaeus of Lyons (ca. 130–ca. 202 CE) was perhaps the earliest theologian who articulated this view of "image" and "likeness." For Irenaeus, only those in whom the Holy Spirit dwells can regain the likeness of God. Those who do not have the Holy Spirit remain spiritually dead even though they continue to possess the image of God.[9] Most biblical scholars and theologians see "image" and "likeness" as essentially synonymous, a sort of Hebrew parallelism. They nonetheless differ on the precise meaning the author of Genesis aimed to communicate with the words "image" and "likeness." In what follows, I will

8. McGrath, *Christian Theology*, 441.

9. Irenaeus, *Against Heresies* 5.6.1 (*ANF* 1:532).

discuss the major theological interpretations of the *imago Dei*. Note that some of these views may share similar ideas .

Major Theological Interpretations of the *Imago Dei*

Constitutive View

The *constitutive* view of the *imago Dei*, known also as the "structural view" or the "substantialist view," poses the question, of what are human beings composed? It answers this question by arguing the *imago Dei* refers to the essential properties or characteristics human beings *possess* that may be similar to or analogous to God's properties. For the representatives of the constitutive view, the *imago Dei* defines what it is to be a human being. This view of the *imago Dei* was held by many theologians prior to the Reformation era. Justin Martyr (ca. 100–165), Irenaeus of Lyons (ca. 130–202),[10] Clement of Alexandria (died ca. 205),[11] Augustine (354–430),[12] and Thomas Aquinas (1225–74) held the constitutive view of the *imago Dei*, although with some modifications. Some versions of the constitutive view of the *imago Dei* emphasize spiritual resemblance, some physical or corporeal resemblance, and others cognitive resemblance. All versions of the constitutive view teach that the *imago Dei* refers to what a human being *is* and not what a human being *does*.[13] The cognitive version of the constitutive view of the *imago Dei* focuses on the rational ontological constitution of human beings—that is, human beings' capacity for rational thought. Some theologians point out that rationality and self-determination are the properties human beings *possess* that separate them from other animals but liken them to God. Based on some biblical texts such as (Matt 10:28 and 1 Thess 5:23), some supporters of the constitutive view argue that human beings have both material (body) and immaterial parts (soul and/or spirit). The cognitive properties of human beings (e.g., rationality, freedom of the will, etc.) are part of the immaterial aspect of humanity.[14] In the substantive view, human rationality reigns supremely. It is the possession of rational capacity that sets humanity apart from other animals.

10. See ibid., 5.6.1–2 (*ANF* 1:531–32).

11. Like other theologians of his era, Clement believed that "image" and "likeness" were not used interchangeably by the author of Genesis. While Adam continued to bear God's image after the fall, he lost the divine likeness (that is, moral resemblance). See Clement, *Exhortation to the Heathen* 12 (*ANF* 2:206).

12. See Augustine, *Confessions of St. Augustin* 13.32 (*NPNF*[1] 1:206).

13. Erickson, *Christian Theology*, 532.

14. Tertullian, *Treatise on the Soul* 38 (*ANF* 3:219).

Thomas Aquinas was one of the medieval theologians who articulated the constitutive view of the *imago Dei*. For Aquinas, the *imago Dei* is intrinsically connected to the nature of God, which human beings (with the exception of Jesus Christ) imperfectly reflect or bear in their nature. Aquinas also made a distinction between (*a*) *being made according to the image of God* and (*b*) *being the image of God*—that is, one who *is* the image of God. For Aquinas, only Jesus Christ is the image of God. All other humans, including Adam, are made according to the image of God. The excerpt below highlights key themes in Aquinas' view of the *imago Dei*.

As Augustine says, *where an image exists, there forthwith is likeness; but where there is likeness, there is not necessarily an image.* Hence it is clear that *likeness* is essential to *image*; and that an image adds something to likeness—namely, that it is copied from something else. For an image is so called because it is produced as an imitation of something else; and so an egg, however much like and equal to another egg, is not called an image of the other egg, because it is not copied from it.

But equality does not belong to the essence of an image, for, as Augustine says in the same place, *where there is an image there is not necessarily equality,* as we see in a person's image reflected in a glass. Yet equality is of the essence of a perfect image, for in a perfect image nothing is wanting that is to be found in that of which it is a copy. Now it is manifest that in man there is some likeness to God, copied from God as from an exemplar; yet this likeness is not one of equality, for such an exemplar infinitely excels its copy. Therefore there is in man a likeness to God, not, indeed, a perfect likeness, but imperfect. And Scripture signifies the same thing when it says that man was made *to* God's likeness; for the preposition *to* signifies a certain approach, as of something at a distance.

The *First-Born of creatures* [Jesus Christ] is the perfect Image of God, reflecting perfectly that of which He is the Image; and so He is said to be the *Image,* and never *to the image.* But man is said to be both *image* by reason of the likeness, and *to the image* by reason of the imperfect likeness. And since the perfect likeness to God cannot be except in an identical nature, the Image of God exists in His first-born Son as the image of the king is in his son, who is of the same nature as himself; whereas it exists in man as in an alien nature, as the image of the king is in a silver coin. . . .

We may speak of God's image in two ways. First, we may consider in it that in which the notion of image chiefly consists, that is, the intellectual nature. From this point of view, the image of God is more perfect in the angels than in man, because their intellectual nature is more perfect. . . . Secondly, we may consider the image of God in man as regards its accidental qualities, and from this point of view, we may observe in man a certain imitation of God, consisting in the fact that man proceeds from man, as God from God....[15]

Questions: What argument does Aquinas present to support his claim that human beings, unlike Jesus Christ, are not the perfect image of God? How do human beings bear God's image, according to Aquinas?

A criticism against the constitutive view revolves around the negative impact of sin upon human cognitive faculties. If reason (used broadly here as the capacity of rational thought, self-determination, and free will) was the most distinguishing mark of human beings, do human beings still retain this property in their sinfulness? Does sin have a negative effect on human beings' ability to reason? Some advocates of the constitutive view of the *imago Dei* may respond to these questions by distinguishing human *possession* of the divine image and human *resemblance* to God. Although human beings retain the image of God (in the sense of a "relic"), in their post-fall condition they no longer resemble or image God's holiness and moral rectitude because of sin.[16] Another criticism against the constitutive view focuses on the wedge it drives between the human body and human mind. As Paul Sands argues, "The substantialist view does . . . assume a rationalistic, mind-body dualism inconsistent with scripture. Nowhere does the Bible suggest that only the 'higher,' intellectual (or spiritual) part of human beings is made in the image of God. The whole person—body and mind—bears the *image* of God."[17] Many theologians now do theological anthropologies that "highlight the interplay of various faculties, the organic connection between humanity and the rest of the earth, and the complexity and interconnections of the 'mind' and 'body.'"[18]

Operative View

The *operative* view, also known as the "vocational" or "functional" view argues that the *imago Dei* consists in what human beings *do*. Human beings

15. Thomas Aquinas, *Summa Theologica* 1:93.1, 3, in *Basic Writings of Saint Thomas Aquinas*, 1:885–86, 89.

16. Sands, "*Imago Dei* as Vocation," 33.

17. Ibid., 33–34.

18. Kapic, "Anthropology," 122.

image God because they "represent God in a way analogous to kings representing deity and statues representing the kings."[19] For the advocates of this view, the author of Genesis provides helpful information on the meaning of image and likeness in Gen 1:28. After the author noted that God created Adam and Eve in God's image, the author moved on to state the assignment God gave to them. Adam and Eve were to "increase in number, fill the earth and subdue it. Rule over the fish of the sea and the birds of the air and over every living creature that moves on the ground" (Gen 1:28 NIV; see also Ps 8:5–8). For the theologians that hold the operative view, human beings truly image God when they exercise their divinely given authority over the rest of creation.[20] As J. Richard Middleton argues, the "symbolic world of Genesis 1 does indeed suggest that the *imago Dei* refers to human rule, that is, the exercise of power on God's behalf in creation."[21] Some supporters of the operative view, such as Paul Sands, prefer the term "vocational." Sands preference for "vocation" is due to the capacity of the term "vocation" to convey the ideas of divine summons and obligations. Like ambassadors, humans' failure to fulfill their God-given vocation "incurs guilt" but does "not remove the obligation. Nor does it blot out the dignity of the summoned individual."[22]

A major argument against the operative view of the *imago Dei* is that having dominion over other creatures is the *consequence* of being made in the God's image and not the *essence* of being God's image-bearer.[23] In other words, God calls human beings to rule over other creatures because they are already God's image-bearers and not because ruling over other creatures will make them God's image-bearers. Some other theologians have also warned that the operative view of the *imago Dei* can be misunderstood as empowering human beings to exploit creation for the benefit of human beings. Dominion in the creation narrative, however, should be governed by good stewardship of nature rather than exploitation. As Daniel Migliore has argued, "the dominion entrusted to humanity, like God's own exercise of dominion involves respect, protection, and care for others rather than . . . manipulation."[24]

19. Sands, "*Imago Dei* as Vocation," 37.

20. Mouw, "*Imago Dei* and Philosophical Anthropology," 256–57.

21. Middleton, *Liberating Image*, 88.

22. Sands, "*Imago Dei* as Vocation," 36.

23. Skinner, *Genesis*, 32.

24. Migliore, *Faith Seeking Understanding*, 141.

Relational View

In the *relational* view of the *imago Dei*, human beings image the Triune God because God made them to be social beings. "To be human," Daniel Migliore writes, "is to live freely and gladly in relationships of mutual respect and love."[25] Unlike the constitutive view, which sees the *imago Dei* as what human beings possess, the relational view sees the *imago Dei* as an act of being or existing in a relationship. As Timothy Phillips and Dennis Okholm argue, "Our relationality is also directed toward other humans. When God made us in the image of his trinitarian being, the text specifies that he made us male and female (Gen 1:27). That is to say, to be created in the image of God is to be created a social being; to be fully human the way God intended for us to be is to be a human-in-relationship."[26] Human beings' desire for relationship and act of being in relationships (with God, other human beings, and other creatures in the world) are indicative of God's relational life.

The relational view of the *imago Dei* is at home with Christians living in cultures where "being human" is primarily understood in relational terms. For example, some scholars of African traditional or indigenous cultures note that for the traditional African "an individual is an abstraction; Man [i.e., humanity] is a family."[27] The Cartesian slogan "I think, therefore I am" (the famous dictum of the French philosopher René Descartes, 1596–1650) is in opposition to the traditional African understandings of what it is to be human. As John Taylor observes, "The sense of the personal totality of all being, and of a humanity which embraces the living, the dead and the divinities" is expressed and experienced in one's solidarity with "the extended family, the clan, and the tribe. This is the context in which an African learns to say, I am because I participate."[28] An individual in the African traditional thought exists as *person-in-relation*. John Mbiti has noted that an individual does not and cannot exist alone; an individual, as a person, exists corporately.[29] The issue here is not whether an individual's personhood is contingent upon the individual's act of relating to others in his or her community. Rather, the individual exists, by definition as a person, in relation to others. The community of the individual is responsible for shaping the identity of the individual.[30]

25. Ibid.

26. Phillips and Okholm, *Family of Faith*, 74.

27. Taylor, *Primal Vision*, 85.

28. Ibid.

29. Mbiti, *African Religions and Philosophy*, 108.

30. Ezigbo, *Re-imagining African Christologies*, 264.

Theologians that hold the relational view of the *imago Dei* draw insights from the doctrine of the Trinity.[31] God, whose *perichoretical* (interdependent) life is manifest in the relationship God (the Father) shares with the Son and the Holy Spirit, calls human beings into a life relationship. For some theologians, the personal pronouns in Gen 1:26–27 (such as "we," "us," and "our") highlight the social dynamics and characteristics of human beings. Whether the personal plural pronouns in Gen 1:26–27 actually speak to the social traits of human beings or merely highlight the grammatical structure in the passage, taken as a whole, the author of Genesis presents humans—male and female—as beings whose existence is characterized by relationship. Women and men "need one another to participate fully in the image of God."[32]

Some theologians are critical of the view that presents God as "the powerful, solitary sovereign over the world."[33] Conceiving God as a solitary being, for these theologians, has fatal theological consequences both for the theology of God and for theological anthropology. On its effect on the theology of God, the concept of a solitary God undercuts the trinitarian view of God: that God is in God's being relational. On its impact on theological anthropology, conceiving God as a solitary being diminishes God's summons to human beings to live in relationship, a life characterized by mutuality and interdependence. In the social version of the trinitarian interpretation of the *imago Dei*, the term "person" occupies a central place. Representatives of the social understating of the Trinity argue that "person" is primarily about communion rather than substance. As Stanley Grenz notes, "'person' has more to do with relationality than with substantiality and . . . the term stands closer to the idea of communion or community than to the conception of the individual in isolation or abstracted from communal embeddedness."[34]

One of the criticisms against the relational view of the *imago Dei* is that human relationships are not normally governed by self-giving, which is characteristic of the Triune God. Human beings are prone to enter into relationships because of self-love and what they can benefit from the relationships. Is the natural tendency toward self-love and self-accumulation that are characteristic of human relationships a distortion of the ideal relationship God desires for human beings to enjoy? If one answers this question in the affirmative, as most theologians do, what then is responsible for such

31. For an extensive discussion on the doctrine of the Trinity, see Ezigbo, *Introducing Christian Theologies*, vol. 1, ch. 4.

32. Horowitz, "Image of God in Man," 204.

33. Grenz, "Theological Foundations for Male-Female Relationships," 616.

34. Grenz, *Social God and the Relational Self*, 4.

distortion of God's desirable forms of human relationships? Does not such distortion of the ideal relationship God desires for humanity indicate that human beings no longer adequately image God? Migliore seeks to resolve this theological dilemma by positing that human beings in their coexistence with others are created to *reflect* "the living, triune God made known to us in Jesus Christ and at work among us by the Holy Spirit."[35] In order for human beings to truly reflect God's self-giving life of relationship and communion, humans should live their lives in conformity to the life of Jesus who is the true image of God and also "the fullest expression of what God intends for humanity to be."[36]

Christological View

Many Christian theologians agree that the "fall" (Adam's sin) has a negative effect on the *imago Dei*. While some hold that sin has wiped out the image of God in human beings, others believe sin has greatly distorted the image of God in humans but has not eradicated it completely. Most Christian theologians are in agreement that Jesus Christ is the only hope for knowing what it means to be (and for how to become) God's image-bearer on the grounds that the New Testament presents him as the "image of God." I will focus on this christological interpretation of the *imago Dei*. Theologians that opt for a christological interpretation of the *imago Dei* concentrate on the New Testament usages of the phrase "image of God" for Jesus Christ (see 2 Cor 4:4; Col 1:15; cf. Heb 1:3). They argue that a person cannot successfully understand what the Bible teaches about human beings as God's image-bearers in isolation from the life of Jesus Christ. They, however, do not always agree on the exact ways Jesus can be used as a model for understanding the concept of the *imago Dei*. I will highlight three theologians that have adopted a christological view of the *imago Dei* but have moved in different directions in their theological anthropologies.

Karl Barth's christological interpretation of the *imago Dei* is noteworthy. For Barth, human beings are God's creatures whom God makes God's

> "Adam was at first created after the image of God, and reflected, as in a mirror, the Divine righteousness; but that image, having been defaced by sin, must now be restored in Christ. The regeneration of the godly is indeed . . . nothing else than the formation anew of the image of God in them."
>
> —Calvin, *Commentaries*, 21:296

---

35. Migliore, *Faith Seeking Understanding*, 142.
36. Ibid.

covenant-partners, and whom God enables to live in fellowship with God and with each other.[37] Barth goes out of his way to make the point that God, and not human beings, initiates the covenant relationship. Barth writes, "We do not ask concerning an ability on the part of man to take up relationship to God in covenant with Him, to be His covenant-partner. His creaturely essence has no power to do this. He can do it only as God makes him His partner, as He calls him to take up this relationship, as he exists as the one who is summoned to do so."[38] In typical christocentric (Christ-centered) fashion, Barth grounds the covenant relationship into which God summons humanity in the humanity of Jesus Christ. According to Barth, human beings "are not simply and directly the covenant-partners of God as His creatures; they are destined to become [God's covenant-partners]. And this means concretely that they are destined to participate in the benefits of the fellow-humanity of that One [Jesus Christ] to be delivered by him."[39] Just as it is in Jesus that human beings come to know God's being (who God really is), it is also in Jesus that human beings come to know what it means to be made in God's image. In other words, by participating in the life of Jesus Christ and by living a life that is governed by the life of Jesus, human beings can gradually discover what it is to be God's imager bearer.

The second theologian is Rosemary Radford Ruether. In *Sexism and God Talk: Towards a Feminist Theology*, Ruether argues that the *imago Dei* indicates what "humanity is potentially and authentically," which human beings historically have not always exhibited because "human nature is fallen, distorted, and sinful."[40] Ruether goes on to argue that the *imago Dei* (i.e., "authentic humanity united with God") has re-manifested "in history as [Jesus] Christ to reconnect us with our original humanity."[41] Most feminist theologians, like Ruether, use the concept of the *imago Dei* to reclaim the full humanity of women.[42] One of the primary goals of Ruether's theological anthropology is to answer the question: How does theological dualism of *imago Dei*/fallen Adam connect with sexual duality, or humanity as male and female? Ruether answers this question in a manner that (*a*) exposes the oppressive nature of patriarchal theological anthropology, and (*b*) reestablishes that men and women are image-bearers of God. Regarding the patriarchal theological anthropologies that judge women to be deficient

37. Barth, *CD* III/2, 224.
38. Ibid.
39. Ibid., 225.
40. Ruether, *Sexism and God-Talk*, 93.
41. Ibid.
42. Gonzalez, *Created in God's Image*, 125.

bearers of God's image, Ruether faults some theologians such as Augustine and Thomas Aquinas for perpetuating the idea "that woman, in her physical, sexual nature, not only symbolizes but incarnates lower human nature," which has led some to deny that a woman is God's image-bearer.[43] On the contrary, Ruether praises egalitarian theological anthropologies that uphold "woman's original equality with man, restored in Christ."[44] Ruether sees Jesus Christ as embodying a partial representation of what the fullness of the redeemed humanity will look like. For Ruether, we are to recognize that Jesus is one of several partial models for true redeemed humanity. Our task, she argues, is to "recognize that [Jesus' example of true redeemed humanity] is partial and needs to be joined by other models, other memories, particularly those that disclose the journey to redemptive personhood from women's experience."[45] Some Christian theologians may raise concerns about Ruether's representation of Jesus Christ, especially in the context of Jesus' unique identity as God incarnate vis-à-vis other human models of true humanity.

The third theologian whose christological interpretation of the *imago Dei* is noteworthy is David Kelsey. For Kelsey, the three New Testament texts (2 Cor 4:4; Col 1:15; Heb 1:3) that describe Jesus as "the image of God" do not present Jesus as one who images God ontologically—that is, one who in his nature images the incarnation of the divine. Kelsey, on the contrary, argues that these three New Testament texts present Jesus, in his personal human body, as the image of God in light of his "distinctive relationship to God, in God's unique relationship to him, and in his distinctive relationships with fellow living human personal bodies in their proximate contexts."[46] As the image of God, Jesus is the agent through and by whom God draws human beings into fellowship. Kelsey argues that Jesus' particularity—his historical background, what he did, and what he experienced (as presented in the Gospels, especially in the Synoptic Gospels)—informs the content of the New Testament writers' understanding of his identity as God's image-bearer.[47]

To say that Jesus is the image of God requires some clarifications. The ambiguity of Jesus' life, Kelsey contends, demands such clarifications. On the one hand, Jesus did things that drew attention to him as one with authority. On the other hand, Jesus' lack of material resources and special

43. Ruether, *Sexism and God-Talk*, 94–97.

44. Ibid., 99.

45. Ibid., 114–15.

46. Kelsey, *Eccentric Existence*, 2:906.

47. For more discussion, see ibid., 625–48.

training would make him an ordinary villager who was "executed, possibly for sedition, probably unjustly."[48] Kelsey is less concerned with how one could come to know that Jesus is the image of God. He is more interested in unpacking the anthropological and theological implications of the claim that Jesus definitively is the image of God. For Kelsey, a major anthropological-theological implication of the claim that Jesus is the image of God is a reciprocal life of relationship that God initiates and invites human beings to participate in and through Jesus Christ.[49] In Jesus Christ, God draws "all else to eschatological consummation and, when it is estranged from God, to reconcile it to God."[50]

Exercise 1.1

(*a*) Identify what Barth, Ruether, and Kelsey share in common. (*b*) Identify what each holds that the others do not hold.

Holistic and All-Inclusive View

Some theologians recognize each of the four preceding interpretations (constitutive, operative, relational, and christological) as legitimate ways of conceptualizing the *imago Dei* but insist that each only captures an aspect of what the Bible teaches about human beings. Representatives of the holistic and all-inclusive view argue that the *imago Dei* describes who human beings are (their constitution), what they are to do (their function), how they ought to live (relational), and what they ought to become in the light of Jesus Christ who is the true image of God (christological). Anthony Hoekema, for example, asked: "Must we think of the image of God in man as involving only what man is and not what he does, or only what he does and not what he is, or both what he is and what he does?" He answered the question in this way: "It is my conviction that we need to maintain both aspects. Since the image of God includes the whole person, it must include both man's structure [capacity of reason, morality, etc.] and man's functioning [capacity of love, to rule, to serve, etc.]."[51] In Hoekema's theological anthropology the fall has anthropological consequences. He writes, "Man's fall into sin . . . has done damage to the way he images God. Whereas before the fall we

48. Ibid., 906–7.

49. Ibid., 908–9.

50. Ibid., 912.

51. Hoekema, *Created in God's Image*, 69.

imaged God in the proper way, after the fall we are no longer able to do so in our strength, since we are now living in a state of rebellion against God."[52] For Hoekema, human beings continue to bear God's image after the fall but only in the constitutive or structural sense. Human beings, however, lost the capacity to bear God's image *adequately* in the operative or functional sense. In the fallen state, human beings use their God-given capacities and gifts in the manner that gratifies their selfish interests and not in the ways that glorify God. This human condition, for Hoekema, is redeemable, although the redeeming and renewing processes take a lifetime.[53] God's Spirit renews God's image "in fallen human beings," helping them "once again to use their God-reflecting gifts in such a way as to image God properly . . ."[54] Hoekema also highlights Jesus' role in the renewing of the *imago Dei* that has been distorted by the fall. He contends that human beings can only know and see what the *imago Dei* "is really like" in the life of Jesus who is the true image of God.[55] The proper functioning of the image involves being transformed by Jesus Christ to live in a manner that moves human beings toward love for God, toward love for neighbor, and toward appropriate ruling over nature.[56]

A major criticism against the holistic or all-inclusive view of *the imago Dei* is that some of the views it seeks it uphold concurrently are not always compatible. For example, some advocates of the relational view argue that Genesis 1 does not teach that having dominion over the earth (the functional view) is essential to being God's image-bearer. Some representatives of the constitutive view argue that there is no direct statement in Genesis 1 "correlating the image with the development of relationships, nor making it dependent upon the exercise of dominion."[57]

Concluding Reflections on the *Imago Dei*

Most of the interpretations of the *imago Dei* I have discussed focus on what human beings share in common with God. While the emphasis on human beings' resemblance to God has been the primary way of understanding the doctrine of the *imago Dei*, I suggest that it is misleading to discuss the *imago Dei* without exploring simultaneously *what human beings share in common with God* and *what they do not share in common with God*. This

52. Ibid., 72.

53. Ibid., 91–96.

54. Ibid., 72.

55. Ibid., 73.

56. Ibid., 75.

57. Erickson, *Christian Theology*, 532.

simultaneity allows us to hear two important messages the doctrine of the *imago Dei* proclaims. The first message is that human beings should live their lives in relation to and not in isolation from God. To live one's life in isolation from God is to reject God as the giver of life. Human beings are to live a life that is not governed by a mistrust of God but rather a life of obedience to God's purpose for humanity. Our understandings of human beings should be grounded in who they are and are to become when measured in the light of God's expectations for humanity represented in the life of Jesus Christ. Our doctrines of the *imago Dei* should learn from Jesus whose life exemplifies what it means to be a true image-bearer of God. We must learn to ask: What does it mean to be human in the light of the Christ-Event? In order to discover what God intends for humanity to be, we need to look to the person and work of Jesus Christ (2 Cor 3:18; Rom 8:24; John 3:2) for instruction and guidance. The second message the *imago Dei* proclaims is that biological sexes, social roles, human accomplishments, and human failures should not determine human dignity and worth. Human beings' dignity and worth are the consequence of being God's creatures. To put it differently, human beings derive their worth from God who made them. Human beings are to live a life that does not rob others of the protection of dignity and worth because of what they have become or will become, and what they accomplished or failed to accomplish.

Table 1.1

Summary of the Theological Interpretations of the *Imago Dei*

View	Description of the *Imago Dei*	Strengths of the View	Weakness of the View
Constitutive	*Imago Dei* refers to the properties human beings possess that are similar to God's properties.	Its linking of human dignity to universally shared properties is helpful for preserving the dignity and worth of all persons.	It elevates cognitive faculties above other components of human beings such as the body.
Operative	*Imago Dei* is related to what human beings are called to do—namely, to rule over God's creation.	Some versions of this view provide a forceful reminder that human beings are not called by God to abuse nature but to be its good stewards.	Having dominion over the earth appears to be the *consequence* of being God's image-bearer and not the *essence* of being God's image-bearer.
Relational	*Imago Dei* refers to humans' relational nature. They are beings-in-relationship.	This view calls to order a life of selfishness that is driven by individualism and narcissism.	There is no clear indication in the first creation story that *being made in God's image* correlates with *being in relationship*.
Christological	Jesus—his human life—embodies the image of God. Human beings can discover how to become God's image-bearers by living the life that is governed by the life of Jesus Christ.	It retains the Christian theological flavor by presenting Jesus as one whose life models for Christians how to relate to God's creatures, human beings in particular.	Some versions of the christological model do not show *how exactly* Jesus, as a human being, is God's image-bearer in the ways other human beings are not.
Holistic	*Imago Dei* is a robust theological term that describes the nature, function, and purpose of human beings as God intended them to be.	It recognizes the nuances of the *imago Dei* and shows that most interpretations of the *imago Dei* are not mutually exclusive.	This view fails to adequately account for and deal with the differences of the constitutive, operative, relational, and christological interpretations of the *imago Dei*.

Christian Theology and Anthropological Issues

Human Ontology

Theologians, like other experts in the field of studies that deal with human beings, are now aware that they cannot assume that the meaning of human nature is unequivocal. The concepts of "humanity" and "human" are becoming more obscure as scholars attempt to explain them in precise terms. Yet some theologians and philosophers have not shied away from discussing humans' *individual-essence* (a cluster of properties essential for an individual's existence as a particular being) and *kind-essence* (a cluster of properties essential for an individual's class or kind of being).[58] Traditionally, Christian theologians have thought of the ontological constitution of human beings either in a *tripartite* sense (body, soul, and spirit), or in a *bipartite* sense (body or material part and soul or the immaterial part), or in *monist* terms (a single complex entity or being).[59] Advocates of the bipartite and tripartite ontology acknowledge the unity of an individual person. Theologians who favor the tripartite view of human ontology usually cite 1 Thess 5:23 where Paul said: "May your whole spirit, soul and body be kept blameless at the coming of our Lord Jesus Christ" (NIV). These theologians distinguish "soul" from "spirit."[60] Representatives of a bipartite ontology allude to Gen 2:7 to support their claim that a human being is composed of a material component ("dust of the earth") and an immaterial component ("breath of life").[61] The monist ontology focuses on the unity of a human being. Some representatives of the monist view point out that the Bible does not describe human ontology in a biological and scientific manner. They agree that the overarching picture of a human being the Bible presents is that of "a totality, a whole, and a unitary being."[62] The word "soul" (*nephesh* in Hebrew and *psychē* in Greek), they argue, is used in the Bible to describe the whole person, a human being.[63] They also argue that the words used in the Bible in relation to human beings such as "spirit" (*rûaḥ* in Hebrew and *pneuma* in Greek) and "heart" (*lēbhābh* in Hebrew and *kardia* in Greek) are used to describe a whole human person from a particular perspective and not to describe the parts of a human being.

---

58. Morris, *Our Idea of God*, 163.

59. See Heard, *The Tripartite Nature of Man: Spirit, Soul, and Body*.

60. See also Heb 4:12.

61. See Berkhof, *Systematic Theology*, 191–92.

62. Hoekema, *Created in God's Image*, 210.

63. See Gen 2:7.

In recent years, theological conversations on human ontology have moved more in the direction of human *personhood*. While the question about what constitutes a human being has not been abandoned entirely, it has been recast in light of the idea of *being-in-relationship*. At the heart of this major shift in theological anthropology is the reluctance of many theologians to discuss human beings primarily in abstract metaphysical and substantialist terms. Some theologians have insisted, however, that the question about what it is to be human can only be successfully answered when approached from both the notion of *substance* and the notion of *relation*. W. Norris Clarke is an example of such a theologian. Clarke argues that the notion of substance and the notion of relation are to be understood as distinct and yet complementary aspects of what it means to *be* or to exist. For Clarke, to be a person is to "be substance-in-relation."[64] He argues that conceiving of a *being* merely as "a pattern of relations with no subjects grounding them" distorts what it means to be a *being*. Also, conceiving a *being* merely as consisting of a substance equally distorts what it is to be a *being*. Clarke proposes what he calls a "dyadic synthesis of substance and relation" as the solution to the unhealthy polarity between substance and relation. For Clarke, all beings (God, human beings, etc.) are to be perceived as substance-in-relation.[65]

Human Sexes and the Issue of Authority

The doctrine of the *imago Dei* implies the sacredness of the human body. This does not mean God has a human-body-like structure but rather human beings (including their bodies), as creatures of God, are by definition a sacred work of God. The author of Genesis went out of his way to state that God created human beings, in their bodily human existence, as God's image-bearers (Gen 1:27). The sacredness of human body has not always been emphasized by Christian theologians. Several reasons may be identified as the causes of the underrepresentation or even denial of the sacredness of human bodies. In early Christianity, particularly in the second century CE, some Christian theologians adopted a gnostic dualism that drove a wedge between spirit and body. They praised spirit as good and pure and denigrated the body as evil. Some ascetics who adopted such dualism subjected their bodies to severe torture in order to liberate their spirits, supposedly imprisoned in "body," so as to be able live in conformity to the life God desires for human beings.

64. Clarke, *Explorations in Metaphysics*, 102.
65. Ibid., 104.

Christian theologians have followed two disparate approaches in their discussions on the theological implications of human biological sexes. Some theologians see human biological sexes as having theological implications. They believe that women are created by God to complement and support men whereas men are divinely ordained to lead women. I will call this view of women and men as the *complementarian* approach. Other theologians see biological sexes as accidental and as such do not indicate any divinely assigned roles beyond reproductive purposes.[66] This understanding of males and females will be described as the *egalitarian* approach. Within these broad approaches, theologians have worked out various models. For example, within the complementarian model, there are two different approaches. One grounds the complementarity of males and females in the assumption that they possess unique characteristics, which when combined bring out the fullness of human personhood. This we will call the *additive complementarian* model. The other, the *integrative complementarian* model, grounds complementarity in the completeness or wholeness of both males and females. Theologians that hold the *integrative complementarian* model argue that God has not created men and women with characteristics that are incomplete in themselves, which must be merged together in order to attain full humanity. While they do not deny there is an enrichment (not limited to the reproductive purposes) that results from the coming together and sharing of life of males and females, they attribute such enrichment to the consequence of being interdependent beings.[67] Both the additive and integral complementarian models hold that men and women have different asymmetric social roles although they are ontologically equal.

Two trends can be discerned within the egalitarian approach: the *androgynous egalitarian* model and the *non-androgynous egalitarian* model. In both models, female and male biological sexes have only reproductive functions. Therefore, biological sexes should not be used as criteria for making judgments about the leadership roles of men and women in the church, in homes, and in society at large. However, unlike the non-androgynous egalitarian model, the androgynous egalitarian model holds that there is a common asexual human nature that men and women partially represent. In other words, males and females "possess the psychic capacities that have been traditionally separated as masculinity and femininity."[68] Supporters of the non-androgynous egalitarian model contend that the androgynous egalitarian model is susceptible to a form of complementarity because "it

66. Carr, *Transforming Grace*, 51.

67. See Allen, "Integral Sex Complementarity and the Theology of Communion."

68. Ruether, *Sexism and God-Talk*, 111.

suggests that males should integrate their androgynous identity around a 'masculine' core of psychic capacities and females should integrate their androgyny around a 'feminine' core."[69]

An extensive theological reflection on males and females in the context of the church will be taken up in the chapter on the church (see chapter 4). For now it suffices to say that whatever one thinks about the two predominant biological sexes (male and female) and the social, political, and economic significances attached to these sexes (as made known in gender studies), the author of Genesis claims that God has made men and women in God's image. This claim should govern our understandings of the issue of authority vis-à-vis the tasks males and females perform in the church and at home. Genesis 3 teaches the submission of wives to their husbands: "To the woman he said . . . 'Your desire shall be for your husband, and he shall rule over you'" (Gen 3:16 ESV). Two observations are noteworthy. First, the submission of wives to their husbands in the context of the Genesis narrative has no ontological value. To put it differently, wives are not to submit to their husbands because, as women, they are ontologically inferior to men. The submission of women to men in this context only has a functional value. Therefore, Genesis 3 should not be used in support of the subordination and subjugation of women. Second, the issue of submission of wives to husbands only arose as a result of sin. If God has embarked on redeeming God's creation from the bondage of sin (Gen 3:15), are women excluded from the effect of God's salvific work? Shouldn't women be liberated from the punishment of a one-sided submission to their husbands (and by extension to all men in the context of the church)? Is the continuing requirement of women to submit to men (both at homes and in the church) tantamount to refusing to embrace the redemptive work of God? Anne Carr has argued that the submission of women derived from Genesis chapters 2 and 3 "is given in the context of the Fall, of human sin."[70] In other words, the submission of women to men is the consequence (or punishment) of sin and not God's original intention for women. Carr goes on to contend that the Christian gospel message liberates humanity from all the consequences of the fall, which includes women's submission to men.[71] God's salvific work extends to all areas of human life and creation. If the submission of women mentioned in the Genesis fall story is a punishment of sin, we cannot exclude it from God's work of salvation.

69. Ibid.

70. Carr, *Transforming Grace*, 49–50.

71. Ibid., 50.

Human Dignity

In November 2011, during a conversation on a book project that will explore themes such as postcolonialism, colonial mentality, and mission, I was struck when a female theologian expressed in tears her internal struggles to please her male colleagues. She was responding to my earlier comment that some African theologians suffer from a colonial mentality when they are preoccupied with pleasing the Western theological guilds. I left the meeting wondering how Christian male theologians knowingly or unknowingly, through their attitudes and writings, are dehumanizing women. I also pondered different ways people act in order to deny the dignity of others, especially people with disabilities, people of other religious faiths, and people of other cultures and ethnic backgrounds.

Exercise 1.2: Theological Practice

A Case Study: Maria is the daughter of Mexican illegal immigrant parents who reside in the United States of America. For the majority of her teenage life, Maria has witnessed her parents' dignity being trampled upon by their employers, who are taking advantage of their illegal immigration status. Maria has also been on the receiving end of racial and derogatory slurs because of her parents' immigration status.

Student Task: Imagine that Maria has met you and in the course of conversation has pressed you for what Christianity teaches about human dignity. Write a short theological anthropology paper that (*a*) takes seriously the immigration debates and dynamics in your country, (*b*) upholds human dignity, and (*c*) confronts dehumanization.

Human dignity means different things to different people. To some, dignity is what a human being earns through personal achievements. More than ever, people's worth and dignity are assessed and classified not primarily by reason of their humanity but because of their social status, ethnic identity, national identity, and religious identity. To others, dignity is inherent in human nature. The doctrine of the *imago Dei* presupposes not only human equality but also human dignity. What determines human self-worth and dignity is not personal achievements but rather human beings' status as divine image-bearers. As Maryanne Horowitz has noted, "It would appear that whatever one's interpretation of the 'image' and 'likeness' of God, one would have to recognize that the biblical text makes explicit that in resemblance to the Divinity and in our dominion over the earth and animals, men and women share a common human dignity."[72]

Talks about human dignity in Christian theology have not always maintained and preserved the dignity of *all* persons. In some cases it has taken the work of feminist theologians to unearth the indignity of women that are sometimes buried in some classical and contemporary Christian theologies. Theologians from Africa, Asia, and Latin America have also helped theologians from Europe and North America acknowledge and critique some anthropological assumptions that derogate Africans, Asians, and Latin Americans. Within each of the continents mentioned above one can find sufficient evidence of stereotypes, non-dignifying attitudes, and dehumanizing assumptions that characterize human relations. For example, in many African societies, as the Cameroonian Theresa Souga has pointed out, women are frequently spoken to and related to in derogating ways by men. To her, women are "among those who are the most marginalized" in African societies. To highlight her claim, she cites three proverbs or sayings used in some Cameroonian societies that either demean women or stress their inequality with men. The sayings are as follows: "*Ye mining a kad kobo ai bod*? Does a woman speak in public? *Ye ba lain mining ai tañ bod*? Is the woman considered a person? *Wa yi bie mon abod afé (mon fam)*? When are you going to make me a baby (child)?"[73] Although Souga is writing from the context of Cameroon, the sayings she highlights capture the perception of women in many sub-Saharan African societies.

The Ghanaian-Nigerian Mercy Amaba Oduyoye has discussed human dignity theologically in a manner that highlights the dehumanization of women in Africa but at the same time argues for the preservation of the dignity of all persons. Oduyoye's major concerns are to unearth the sources of dehumanization in Africa and also to offer solutions to the outward manifestations of dehumanization both in the church the society. For her "African [traditional] culture has guaranteed the patriarchal takeover of even the most mother-centered structures." She makes this claim in order to show that it is "too easy to lay the blame solely at the feet of westernization." She insists Africans must recognize that "within the African religio-cultural heritage is to be found the seeds of the objectification and marginalization of women."[74] From the point of view of Oduyoye, Christian churches in Africa must share the blame for the continuing existence of dehumanization

---

72 Horowitz, "Image of God in Man," 175–76.

73. Theresa Souga, "The Christ-Event from the Viewpoint of African Women," in Fabella and Oduyoye, *With Passion and Compassion*, 27.

74. Oduyoye, "Feminist Theology in African Perspective," 173.

of women, and people of non-Christian religions. They must also seek to rediscover the scriptural teaching on the dignity of people. In the excerpt below, one can see Oduyoye's understanding of what an adequate Christian theology of human dignity should be.

In Africa, the very idea of a "free woman" conjures up negative images. We have been brought up to believe that a woman should always have a suzerain, that she should be "owned" by a man, be he father, uncle, or husband. A "free woman" spells disaster. An adult woman, if unmarried, is immediately reckoned to be available for the pleasure of all males and is treated as such. The single woman who manages her affairs successfully without a man is an affront to patriarchy and a direct challenge to the so-called masculinity of men who want to "possess" her. Some women are struggling to be free from this compulsory attachment to the male. Women want the right to be fully human, whether or not they choose to be attached to men.

Liberation for women must also happen in the church. It was a "church father" (Augustine of Hippo, a city in ancient Africa) who declared that a woman apart from a man is not made in the image of God, whereas a man apart from a woman is. Furthermore, it was a "protesting" monk, pastor, and theologian, Martin Luther, who declared that women were fit only to go to church, to work in kitchens, and to bear children. So, who defines the humanity of woman? Is it the male or is it God? If it is God, how do we get at the God-originated definition of womanness? Is family life a vocation, a demand of biology, or a convenient base for organizing human society? Patriarchal systems often forbid questions of this genre.

So, in the heightened debate surrounding the role of women, some Africans are puzzled when Christian women say that it is the will of Christ (if not of the church) that women should be free to respond to the fullness God expects of all human beings. What constitutes this fullness, and who determines its dimensions? Women want to join in the search for the truth about human life and how to live it; we want to decide for ourselves, for our day and situation, what constitutes a liberating and liberative life.

As a Christian African woman . . . I seek the quality of life that frees African women to respond to the fullness for which God created them. It is my experience that Christianity as manifested in the Western churches in Africa does little to challenge sexism, whether in church or in society. I believe that the experience of women in the church in Africa contradicts the Christian claim to promote the worth (equal value) of every person. Rather, it shows how

> Christianity reinforces the cultural conditioning of compliance and submission and leads to the depersonalization of women.[75]
>
> Question: What themes did Oduyoye use to underscore the dehumanization of women in Africa and in African churches?

Humanity and Sin

Concepts of Sin

Talk about "sin" is usually met with a severe resistance partly because sin does not only concern human beings but also implicitly or explicitly God. Many people, particularly in the Western world, despise the word "sin" because of its close association with the language of God. For some, the increasing disappearance

> **FOCUS QUESTION:**
> What does Christianity teach about *sin* and its impact upon humanity?

of God-talk in the public sphere should also mean relegating sin-talk to the private and personal spheres. Many Christian theologians in the Western world, however, doubt that evacuating sin of its theological meaning will lead to its broad acceptance in the public spheres as an effective word for describing human pathologies and evil acts.[76]

Christian theologies of sin must be ready to address three major concerns people raise about the idea of sin, particularly *original sin* (both in the sense of *originated* sin—the first sin committed by Adam and Eve—and in the sense of *originating* sin—an inherited tendency to sin).[77] First, a Christian theology of sin should demonstrate its distinctiveness from the sin-talk that is deployed merely as a rhetorical tool by some to convey their sociopolitical agendas.[78] Second, a Christian theology of sin should show that *original sin* is not an unfortunate concept used by the early theologians who knew nothing about DNA and natural selection. Christian de Duve has argued that the idea of original sin is a myth developed by people who knew about human hereditary traits but lacked the sophistication to explain the

75. Oduyoye, *Daughters of Anowa*, 4–5, 9.

76. See McFadyen, *Bound to Sin*, 5–6.

77. Blocher, *Original Sin*, 37.

78. Weaver, "Taking Sin Seriously," 45.

traits in appropriate biological terms.[79] Third, a Christian theology of sin should avoid a form of reductionism that focuses on original sin but fails to address people's own or actual sins. Some theologians, fearing that emphasizing actual sins may lead to the abandonment of the doctrine of original sin, have failed to devote adequate time to address sinful acts committed by people. To address the danger of undue focus on Adam's sin, some theologians use the term "original sin" to refer to structural sins identifiable with a particular community or nation. Elizabeth Johnson, for example, refers to slavery as the "original sin" of the United States of America in her discussions on the history of African Americans in the United States.[80] Delores Williams, writing specifically about the experience of African American women, argues that theologians engaged in the discussion of sin in the context of the United States of America should not ignore the devaluation of "Black women's womanhood."[81]

Our era has witnessed a tremendous rise and expansion of religions, immense developments in technology, knowledge about the world and humans, military prowess, and immense knowledge of people of other cultures. These developments have not resulted in a decrease in terrorism, murder, human trafficking, dehumanization, selfishness, greed, bullying, mistreatment of immigrants, robbery, adultery, and racially motivated acts. It could in fact be argued that in some cases the developments I have highlighted above have led to an increase in the acts that can be categorized as wrongdoings and moral evils. Does the increase in such acts indicate that something is wrong with human beings and/or the ways in which human beings negotiate their existence and survival in the world? People need not be religious to identify, resent, and confront such wrongdoings. But why are human beings prone to these wrongdoings in the first place? Why do people classify these acts as "wrongdoings," "evils," and sometimes "sins"? Christian theologians speak of the acts I have listed above as sinful or as the manifestations of *sin*. In the official Roman Catholic teaching, the human condition, since Adam's sin, "no longer manifests in itself friendship with God and participation in his life. For from the very beginning of humanity, sin entered the world, affecting every man and it has proliferated."[82] The proliferation of sin in the world can be seen in the sinful acts and wrongdoings carried out by individuals, groups, and institutions. I will now turn to discuss some concepts of sin in Christian theology.

79. De Duve and Patterson, *Genetics of Original Sin*, 149–50.

80. Johnson, *Quest for the Living God*, 130.

81. Williams, "Womanist Perspective on Sin," 143.

82. *Official Catholic Teachings, Update*, 11.

Sin as Rebellion against God

Seeing "sin" as a *rebellion against God* implies that neither an individual nor a community has ultimate power to determine what is or isn't sin. On the contrary, sin is measured by God's character and moral rectitude. The biblical ideas of sin (*chatta't* in Hebrew and *hamartia* in Greek) means "missing a target" or "transgression."[83] To paraphrase the words of the Apostle Paul, sin is falling short of the glory of God and God's intended purpose for humanity (Rom 3:23).

For many Christian theologians, wrongdoings (e.g., murder, human trafficking, and bullying) pose both socio-anthropological and theological problems for humanity. In Christian thought, human beings cannot fully explain the reasons for the continual existence of wrongful and evil acts by focusing only on the social and anthropological factors. They should also seek to understand the continuing existence of such acts theologically—that is, (*a*) in light of God's purpose and intentions for creating human beings, and (*b*) in light of God's judgment on sin—human beings' mistrust of God's intention and purpose for creating them. Many Christian theologians see sin as a powerful external force that lurks at human wills and impels human beings to mistrust God's will and purpose for humanity (Gen 4:7; Rom 7:7–20).

If sin, theologically speaking, is *mistrusting God*, it follows that sin and its manifestations (wrongdoing and evil acts) should be judged primarily in light of God's intentions for humanity. Many Christian theologians employ the word "fall" to express the idea that sin is the human act of revolting against and mistrusting God. Colin Gunton makes this point vividly when he writes: "The essence of sin consists in wanting to be like God otherwise than in the way he invites and enables us to be like him. Repeatedly in scripture idolatry, both of the kind which actually bows down before images and the modern variety which worships things other than God while pretending not to do so, is diagnosed as the ill of which the gospel sets out to heal us. When we seek to displace the loving God from our lives, we replace him with an idol which,

> "Sin is folly—that is, an inappropriate response to the triune God relating to us creatively. The opposite of living in 'the fear of the LORD' that leads to life, to sin is to live in distorted faith in God. To sin is not simply to live in the total absence of any trust in or loyalty to God and God's own cause, although that may be its limiting case, but to live in a trust and a loyalty that are distorted versions of an appropriate response to God's active creating."
>
> —Kelsey, *Eccentric Existence*, 1:408.

83. See Judg 20:16; cf. Gen 4:7 and 1 John 3:4.

though inanimate, yet devours us."[84] If we construe sin as a mistrust of God, it follows that the sin of humanity, which the author (and redactor) of Genesis describes in chapters 2 & 3, consisted in human beings' (represented by Adam and Eve) failure to acknowledge that God is the source of truth, the one who determined humanity dignity, and the one who defined what is a right action and a wrong action (see Gen 2:17; 3:4–5). The acts of disobedience, rape, and hate crimes that the author of Genesis discusses in some great lengths can be understood as the outward manifestations of human mistrust of God. Sin, as Serene Jones reminds us, is to be understood in light of the will of God against whom sin is committed.[85]

> "The Fall of man in God's creation is both inconceivable and unalterably inexcusable, and therefore the word 'disobedience' does not exhaust the facts of the case. It is revolt, it is the creature's departure from the attitude which is the only possible attitude for him, it is the creature's becoming Creator, it is the destruction of creatureliness. It is defection, it is the fall from being held in creatureliness."
>
> —Dietrich Bonhoeffer,
> *Creation and Fall*, 84

Personal and Social Dimensions of Sin

Sin has both personal and social dimensions. The personal dimension should not be confused with the understanding of sin as merely a *personal failure of self* or *one's inability to bring oneself to accomplish* what one perceives as being authentically human. In this context, being authentically human includes the idea of personal morality. By sin's personal dimension I mean sinful acts committed by individuals (whether or not such actions are compelled by external and social factors). An act is sinful if it transgresses God's commands and opposes God's rectitude. Sin pays a "wage," according to the Apostle Paul: "the wages of sin is death" (Rom 6:23 NIV). Death in this context should be understood as *living in opposition to* God and *apart from* God.[86]

The Puerto Rican theologian Orlando Costas has described three manifestations of sin. While each of these forms has social consequences, they are also rooted in individuals' acts. First, Costas describes sin as "disobedience to the lordship of God." To disobey God is to reject God's word, to refuse to follow God's instructions, and to willfully distort God's truth.[87]

---

84. Gunton, *Christian Faith*, 61.

85. Jones, "What's Wrong with Us?," 148.

86. Gunton, *Christian Faith*, 139.

87. Costas, *Christ Outside the Gate*, 22.

The second form of sin according to Costas is "injustice and alienation." He writes, "Sin represents a deliberately aggressive action against others. If disobedience implies rejection of the lordship of God, injustice signifies hatred and repudiation of the neighbor. Sin, then, is every unjust act—every lack of consideration for the well-being of one's neighbor, every insult to human dignity, every act of violence done to someone else."[88] The third form of sin is "unbelief and idolatry." By "unbelief" Costas means one's refusal to believe in God. Unbelief, for Costas, leads to idolatry—creating one's own god. He writes, "The absence of God leads to the invention of gods. Idols are thus projections of human vanity and its deifying presumptions."[89]

Sin also has a social dimension. The social dimension of sin should not be confused with the understanding of sin as a *social construct*—a view of sin that also rejects God as the ultimate point of reference for what sin is. In the social construct understanding of sin, to be human is to be cognizant of certain moral rules, which when broken cause personal injuries and by extension injuries to the community to which the individual (lawbreaker) belongs. The preservation of the identity, values, and interests of a community functions as an important factor in determining the meaning of sin. Sin is not a force inherent in human beings. The ideas of original righteousness, inherited sin, and inherited guilt have been increasingly perceived by many people since the Enlightenment to be morally and intellectually absurd.[90] The preservation of the identity of a community or society rather than the preservation of an individual's self-identity or self-interest is of paramount importance in the understanding of sin as rebellion against societal norms. For example, since the unspeakable horror of Auschwitz, some Jews such as Emil Fackenheim measure a Jew's "morality" by the action he takes to preserve the Jewish state and also to confront or defeat the forces of anti-Judaism.[91] While this understanding of sin does not necessarily view sin as a rebellion against God, it relegates the discussion on God and sin to the background. Sin is rarely considered a theological issue; it is primarily viewed as a social and institutional problem.

We need not reject God as the ultimate point of reference in order to truly talk about the social dimensions and implications of sin. Most Christian theologians recognize that sin does not affect only an individual sinner. Sin can also affect the community to which the sinner belongs. The policies of an unjust ruler can have severe consequences on the lives of his or her

88. Ibid., 23.

89. Ibid., 24.

90. Williams, "Sin and Evil," 195.

91. See Fackenheim, *Jewish Return into History*, 44–45, 97.

subjects, particularly those that are marginalized. Sin can become structural when the ruler builds and maintains structures that dehumanize and oppress people. The Bible teaches that the sin of an individual affects others to some degree (see Exod 34:6–7; Rom 5:12–21). Orlando Costas rightly notes that "just as personal sin affects the community, social sin also affects the individual."[92]

Sin as Weighty Load

In the Old Testament "sin" is presented metaphorically as a burdensome load a sinner carries (see Exod 10:17; Lev 5:1; 24:15; Num 11:11–14; Isa 1:2–4; Ezek 4:4–6).[93] The Hebrew idiom used by the biblical writers to express this concept of sin is "to bear the burden of sin" (*nāśā' 'āwōn* in Hebrew). The metaphor of a *weighty load* describes both the *act* of sin (a burden a sinner takes on himself or herself) and the *consequence* of the sin, a burden God lays upon the sinner and sometimes upon the community of the sinner). An example is Moses' dialogue with God about carrying the burden (sin) of the people of Israel. In Num 11:11, Moses asked God, "Why have you brought this trouble on your servant? What have I done to displease you that you put the burden of all these people on me?" (NIV). Sin, as Gary Anderson notes, has a "certain 'thing'-like quality" that is "manufactured ex nihilo [out of nothing] upon completion of the forbidden act."[94]

The force of a *weighty load* as a metaphor for sin is also highlighted in sin's solution. In the Jewish religious practices, the Day of the Atonement is marked by the symbolic laying of the burden of sin on a scapegoat. The High Priest, on the Day of Atonement, lays both hands on the "head of the goat, and confesses over it all the iniquities of the sons of Israel." After the ritual of laying on of hands on the heads of the goat and confessions of the sins of the people of Israel, the High Priest sends the goat away into the wilderness with the expectations that the goat will bear upon itself "all the iniquities" (Lev 16:20–22 NASB). Symbolically, the scapegoat relieves the community of the burden of sin. There are two related possible significances of the "wilderness" in the atonement ritual. First, the wilderness represents the domain of the demons, the sources of temptations and evil. The scapegoat that is sent to the wilderness carries sin to its nonhuman sources. Second, since the wilderness is the area of the demonic powers and not God's domain, there is an assumption that the scapegoat carries the sin to an area "beyond

92. Costas, *Christ Outside the Gate*, 26.

93. Anderson, *Sin: A History*, 16.

94. Ibid., 19.

God's supervisory powers," where God can no longer see the sins God has forgiven.[95] In Christian thought, Jesus is likened to a scapegoat used in the ritual of the atonement. He is construed as the lamb upon whom God lays the burden of the world's sin (1 Pet 1:19; Rev 5:6; 13:8). The Apostle John describes Jesus as "the Lamb of God, who takes away the sin of the world!" (John 1:29 NIV).

Sin as Debt

In the New Testament, sin is predominantly spoken of in terms of debt. While sin continued to be perceived as a weighty burden, there was a move toward the language of debt. Gary Anderson has argued that the move from burden as a way of speaking of sin to the language of debt began in the Second Temple period (ca. 530 BCE–70 CE). Anderson traces the shift to the influence of Aramaic on the Hebrew dialect spoken during the Second Temple period. Anderson notes that the Aramaic word *ḥôbâ* for a debt is the common word for denoting sin.[96] In the Targum (the Aramaic translations of the Hebrew Bible), the expression "to bear the weight of sin" (*nāśā' 'āwōn* in Hebrew) is almost in every instance translated "to assume a debt" (*qubbēl ḥôbâ* in Aramaic).[97] The influence of Aramaic can also been seen in Jesus' discussions on sin. Jesus used the metaphors of debts, debtors, and forgiveness to describe sin. In the prayer he taught his disciples, these metaphors figure prominently (Matt 6:9–15). The disciples are to ask God the Father to forgive their debts (sins) and should be ready to act in the same way toward those who sin against them. Anderson argues that the language of remitting or forgiving debts (sins) only makes sense when understood in its Semitic (Aramaic and Hebrew) contexts.[98]

Sin as Stain or Damage

Some of the Old Testament and New Testament writers viewed sin as a stain on a sinner's life. The author of the book of Isaiah uses a powerful image to describe sin: "'Come now, let us reason together,' says the LORD. 'Though your sins are like scarlet, they shall be as white as snow; though they are red as crimson, they shall be like wool'" (Isa 1:18 NIV). Here the author uses the

---

95. Anderson, *Sin: A History*, 22–23.
96. Ibid., 27.
97. Ibid., 27–28.
98. Ibid., 32.

imagery of contrasting colors—"scarlet and white," "crimson and wool"—to emphasize the stain or damage of sin on a sinner's life. The color red represents sin and its stain, whereas white represents the condition of the sinner after his or her sin has been cleansed. Rita Nakashima Brock has argued that the metaphor of damage or stain has some important theological values: it evokes in us a sense of responsibility and desire to restore the damage caused by sin rather than dwelling on blame and guilt. Brock's aim is to show that sin "is not something to be punished, but something to be healed."[99] Brock's claim, however, disregards scriptural teaching on sin's consequences, which includes God's punishment or discipline (see Gen 3:14–24; Rom 6:23). Also, healing and punishment are not mutually exclusive. Punishment may come in the form of pruning designed to correct, cleanse, and heal the effect of sin on the lives of a sinner.

Theological Interpretations of the Fall and Its Implications for Humanity

The theological ramifications of the story of the sin of Adam and Eve and its connection to the continuing presence of sinful acts in the world have been a matter of intense debate in Christianity. Christian theology of sin (harmatiology) largely rests on the identity and acts of Adam and Eve in the Genesis creation narratives. Theologians that connect the presence of sin in the world to Adam and Eve appeal to the Apostle Paul's words in Rom 5:12–13. Paul writes in this passage, "Therefore, just as sin entered the world through one man, and death through sin, and in this way death came to all men, because [*eph hō* in Greek] all have sinned—for before the law was given, sin was in the world. But sin is not taken into account when there is no law" (NIV).[100] Other relevant biblical passages are Ps 51:5 and Eph 2:3. The psalmist presents, with poetic force, the scope of sin and its power in people's lives: "Behold, I was brought forth in iniquity, and in sin did my mother conceive me" (Ps 51:5 ESV). The Apostle Paul, focusing more on the impact of sin on humanity, writes that we are "by nature children of wrath" (Eph 2:3). In his commentary on Eph 2:3, the English theologian John Wesley (1709–91) argues that human beings do not become children of God's wrath or displeasure by "education, or by imitation, or by custom in sinning." On the contrary, human beings were children of God's wrath "by nature," signifying they were born "fallen creatures." In other words, they

---

99. Brock, *Journeys by Heart*, 7.

100. See also 1 Cor 15:20–22.

"came into the world sinners, and as such liable to wrath, in consequence of the fall of our first father [Adam]."[101]

Throughout Christian history many theologians have developed theologies of sin that are grounded in the belief that Adam and Eve were historical figures who were God's first human creatures. Others have constructed their theologies of sin without accepting the historicity of Adam and Eve. They see Adam and Eve as the product of the literary ingenuity the author (or redactor) of Genesis employed to describe the prominent human sexes and genders. What the theologians who ground their theologies of sin in the identity and acts of Adam and Eve share is the belief that Adam's and Eve's acts of mistrust of God have both social-anthropological and theological consequences for humanity and God's creation. Theologians most often use the word "fall" to describe Adam's and Eve's sin and its consequences for them and the world. The *fall*, for many theologians, has negatively impacted the relationship between God and humanity (vertical consequence), human interrelationships (horizontal consequences), and how human beings misuse natural resources.

Prior to the fifth century CE, theologians tersely addressed the implications of Adam's and Eve's sin for humanity.[102] Some focused primarily on the individual responsibility of sin and emphasized God's gift of free will to human beings. For example, in his dialogue with Trypho the Jew, Justin Martyr argued that the human race, as the result of the sin of Adam, "had fallen under the power of death and the guile of the serpent" while maintaining that everyone is responsible for his or her "personal transgression." To justify his claim about the responsibility of each person for his or her transgression, Justin Martyr appealed to the free will God gave to angels and human beings.[103] Other theologians emphasized the corruption human beings have inherited from Adam and Eve. In his discussion on the importance of the baptism of infants, Cyprian of Carthage (died ca. 258 CE) highlighted the consequences of Adam's and Eve's sin for humanity. He argued that an infant who "has not sinned, except in that, being born after the flesh according to Adam . . . has contracted the contagion of the ancient death and at its earliest birth" should not be hindered from the sacrament of baptism. For Cyprian, water baptism is required for the remission of the effects of the sin of Adam and Eve on infants.[104]

---

101. Wesley, *Doctrine of Original Sin*, in *Works of John Wesley*, 12:430.

102. For discussions on the historical development of the doctrine of original sin, see Williams, *The Ideas of the Fall and of Original Sin: A Historical and Critical Study*.

103. Justin Martyr, *Dialogue with Trypho* 88 (*ANF* 1:243).

104. Cyprian, *Epistles* 58.5 (*ANF* 5:354).

In the remainder of this section I will discuss the theologies of sin of some key theologians, focusing on their understandings of the character and effect of the fall. These theologies have followed one of two major models: (*a*) the imitation model or (*b*) the biological model. I will also discuss the modifications of these two models by some theologians, highlighting their unique contributions to the discussions on Christian theological anthropology. While some of these models may share some common assumptions, each has a unique characteristic that distinguishes it from the others.

Imitation Model

Description: The imitation model explains the pervasiveness of sinful acts in the world as the result of copying morally bad examples. Human beings' sinful acts are not the result of the *sin-nature* they inherited from their parents, a transmission of a corrupt human nature that can be traced back to Adam and Eve. Rather, sin is a social condition that is deeply rooted in the imitation of the sinful behaviors of others.

Impact of Adam's and Eve's Sin on Humanity: Pelagius (ca. 354–420 CE), a monk and moral reformer, who was most probably of British origin, championed the imitation model. Many students of theology know Pelagius as a heretic whose theology Augustine of Hippo (354–430) and Jerome (ca. 345–420 CE) destroyed to its core. The condemnation of Pelagius's theologies of sin and salvation by both the Council of Carthage (418 CE) and the Council of Ephesus (431 CE) carved his name on the infamous wall of heretics whose theologies threatened Christianity's orthodoxy. Some Pelagius scholars, however, have questioned the justification for labeling Pelagius a heretic. Robert Evans, for example, has cautioned that many set Pelagius up "as a symbolic bad man" and "heap upon him accusations which often tell us more about the theological perspectives of the accuser than about Pelagius."[105] B. R. Rees declared Pelagius's theology to be "evangelical, salvationist and didactic."[106] William Phipps argues that if faithfulness to the apostolic teaching is the measure of orthodoxy and heresy, then Augustine's theologies of sin and salvation, and not Pelagius's theologies of sin and salvation, are heretical. For Phipps, while Augustine's theologies of sin and salvation are deeply shaped by Neo-Platonism, Pelagius's theologies are grounded in Paul's writings. He writes, "Augustine defended some doctrines that are traceable to the teachings of Plato and Mani rather than to Paul. Of course, every generation reinterprets the Scriptures with attention

105. Evans, *Pelagius*, 66.
106. Rees, *Pelagius: Life and Letters*, 2:12.

35

to its contemporary culture, so it would be absurd to claim that Pelagius expressed no new nuances of interpretation. Rather, it is contended that Pelagius's doctrine was a genuine outgrowth from apostolic roots."[107]

For Pelagius, the descendants of Adam are guilty of his sin because they re-enact his sin by their own volitional sinful acts. The relationship of the freedom of human will (*velle* in Latin) and God's grace occupy a central place in Pelagius's theological anthropology. God, for Pelagius, created human beings as rational creatures with the capacity of rational and volitional choices. Human choices are therefore neither the result of a corrupt nature nor the result of God's preordained plan for human beings. On the contrary, people sin because they choose to do so.[108]

How does Pelagius explain his understanding of the relationship between Adam's sin and the presence of sin in the world? For Pelagius, Adam was the first sinner whose sin provided a bad example for his descendants. Adam's sin has remained in the world by "example or by pattern."[109] As Robert Evans elaborates, "The injury which Adam worked upon his descendants was the injury of being both the first man and the first disobedient man, and this injury takes effect through man's fateful living by the model of that disobedience."[110] Pelagius did not undermine the *power of sin* over human beings. This does not mean that Pelagius perceived sin as a necessary force rooted in a corrupt human nature that infants inherit from their parents. Rather, the power of sin is rooted in sin's pervasiveness in the world, which is the consequence of human beings' habitual sinful acts. There is no room for the theology of a transmission of a corrupt human nature through procreation or any other means in Pelagius's theological anthropology. Pelagius maintained that Adam's descendants, like Adam, possessed the capacity of free will. The concept of an inherited or transmitted sin-nature contradicted the Christian teaching of God's gift of free will to human beings. Also, Pelagius feared that the concept of a sin-nature implied sin's independent ontological existence apart from human free choices and acts. Such understanding of sin, Pelagius reasoned, shared the theology of the Manicheans who held that sin was a *necessary* component of human existence.[111]

Remedies for Sin: As one who thought of himself as an orthodox (Catholic or creedal) theologian, Pelagius did not see infant baptism as an irrelevant sacrament of the church. However, he did not hold that baptism

---

107. Phipps, "The Heresiarch: Pelagius or Augustine?," 133.

108. Williams, *Ideas of the Fall*, 334.

109. Pelagius, *Commentary on St. Paul's Epistle to the Romans*, 92.

110. Evans, *Pelagius*, 97.

111. Ibid.

was necessary for the remission of original sin in infants. Baptism, for him, provided spiritual illumination in infants and marked their adoption into God's family.[112] Since sin is the consequence of human beings making volitional bad choices and the pervasiveness of sin in the world is the result of copying bad examples, sin's remedy is grounded in God's gracious act of providing alternative examples that can motivate human beings to make righteous choices. In Pelagius's theology of salvation, God's gift of free will enabled the people who chose to obey God and to live holy lives from the time of Adam to Moses (*period of nature*). In this era, the law of God implanted in all people and "written as it were on the tablet of the heart" assisted and guided people on the path of holy living.[113] Sin's pervasiveness in the world, however, moved God to give the world the gift of written laws on clay tablets to people from the time of Moses to Jesus Christ (*period of law*), to assist them in making moral choices. From the time of Jesus Christ onward (*period of grace*), God has graciously given the world Jesus as moral example. Jesus' life of obedience to God is a powerful example to human beings to subject their wills and choices to the will and desire of God. "Father, if you are willing," Jesus asked at the Garden of Gethsemane, "take this cup from me; yet not my will, but yours be done" (Luke 22:42 NIV). Jesus calls people to follow his example and decision to put God the Father's will above their own wills. Jesus' death is an expression of God's commitment to humanity to provide a way of out of sin and its consequences.

To Pelagius, it is possible for a person to work toward sinlessness and also to achieve sinlessness. Jesus Christ and Adam, for Pelagius, are two figures whose actions have affected the course of human history and human relationship with God. Both are two antithetical figures: Adam is the source of sin whose pattern of transgression leads his descendants to death. Jesus is the source of righteousness who offers "forgiveness of sins to those who believe, setting an example of righteousness to enable them to avoid transgression."[114] The possibility of sinlessness, it should be noted, is rooted first and foremost in God's gracious gift of *freedom* (endowed natural capacity of choice) to human beings to enable them to make choices. For Pelagius and his followers, God would not expect humans to be morally perfect if it were not a possible task.[115]

---

112. Williams, *Ideas of the Fall*, 344.

113. Pelagius, *To Demetrias* 2, in Rees, *Pelagius: Life and Letters*, 2:40.

114. Theodore de Bruyn, "Introduction," in Pelagius, *Commentary on St. Paul's Epistle to the Romans*, 41.

115. Caspari, *On the Possibility of Not Sinning* 2.3, in Rees, *Pelagius: Life and Letters*, 2:167.

The excerpt below is taken from Pelagius's letter to Demetrias, a rich young Roman woman who shortly before her marriage decided to take the vow of virginity.[116] This letter contains theological ideas and arguments that Pelagius used in defense of his view of the freedom of human will prior, during, and after Adam and Eve sinned.

It was because God wished to bestow on the rational creature the gift of doing good of his own free will and the capacity to exercise free choice, by implanting in man the possibility of choosing either alternative, that he made it his peculiar right to be what he wanted to be, so that with his capacity for good and evil he could do either quite naturally and then bend his will in the other direction too. He could not claim to possess the good of his own volition, unless he were the kind of creature that could also have possessed evil. Our most excellent creator wished us to be able to do either but actually to do only one, that is, good, which he also commanded, giving us the capacity to do evil only so that we might do his will by exercising our own. That being so, this very capacity to do evil is also good—good, I say, because it makes the good part better by making it voluntary and independent, not bound by necessity but free to decide for itself. We are certainly permitted to choose, oppose, approve, reject, and there is no ground for preferring the rational creature to the others except that, while all the others possess only the good derived from their own circumstances and necessity, it alone possesses the good of free will also....

Since we have said enough on these matters in my opinion, let us now begin our instruction of a perfect virgin who by the purity of her moral life bears witness at one and the same time to the good of nature and the good of grace, since she has always drawn her inspiration from both of these sources. A virgin's first concern and first desire ought therefore to be to get to know the will of her Lord and seek out diligently what pleases and what displeases him; in this way she may render to God, in the words of the apostle, her "spiritual obedience" (Rom 12:1), and may be enabled to direct the entire course of her life in accordance with his purpose....

Let us make an end of all sloth and useless complacency based on the success of our labors in the past. If we do not want to go back, we must run on; the blessed apostle, living for God day by day, always paying attention not to what he has done before but to what he ought to be doing now, says: Brethren, I do not consider that I have made it my own; but one thing I do, forgetting what lies behind and straining forward to what lies ahead, I press on towards the goal for the prize of the upward call of God (Phil 3:13, 14). If the blessed Paul, the vessel of election, who had been so clothed in Christ that he could

116. Rees, *Pelagius: Life and Letters*, 2:30.

say: It is no longer I who live but Christ who lives in me (Gal 2:20), yet still strains forward, still grows and progresses, what should we do whose only desire must be that at our end we may be compared with Paul at his beginning? Imitate therefore the one who said: Be imitators of me, as I too am of Christ (1 Cor 4:16). Forget all that is past and think that you are starting afresh each day, and not reckon the past to be the present day, since it is on the present day that you must serve God. You will guard your gains best if you are always searching for more; if you cease to acquire more, your present store of acquisitions will suffer loss.[117]

Questions: What theological arguments does Pelagius present in defense of his views of the freedom of human free will? What role does God's grace play in a Christian's morality and holy living?

Critique of the Imitation Model: The imitation model, both Pelagius's and Semi-Pelagian versions, has faced severe attacks since the days of Jerome and Augustine. While Jerome attacked Pelagius's theology of the possibility of sinlessness, Augustine devoted much of his effort to attacking Pelagius's views that human beings sin not because they are compelled to do so by a corrupt human nature and that sin's pervasiveness can be explained as the consequence of copying bad examples from others. Pelagius was accused of being theologically inconsistent in denying that infants (who have not committed actual sins) are not born with a corrupt human nature and original sin and at the same time holding that infant baptism is a necessary sacrament.[118] Augustine accused Pelagius of paying lip service to the doctrine of God's grace only to avoid condemnation at the Synod of Jerusalem (415). He wrote, "Pelagius feared the episcopal judgment of Palestine; and when it was objected to him that he said that the grace of God is given according to our merits, he denied that he said so, and condemned those who said this with an anathema. And yet nothing else is found to be defended in the books which he afterwards wrote, thinking that he had made a fraud upon men who were his judges, by lying or by hiding his meaning, I know not how, in ambiguous words."[119] For Augustine, Pelagius and Pelagians who described divine laws (those written on both hearts and tablets) as God's grace that enables people to avoid sinning are gravely mistaken. Citing the

117. Pelagius, *To Demetrias* 3.2; 9.1; 27.4, in ibid., 38, 45, 67.

118. Note that for Pelagius, infant baptism produces spiritual illumination in infants and also marks their spiritual adoption in God's family.

119. Augustine, *Against Two Letters of the Pelagians* 8.4 (NPNF[1] 5:379–80).

Apostle Paul (see 2 Cor 3:6), Augustine argued that the law "kills" rather than "gives life." Augustine insisted that people are able to do good works by the power of the Holy Spirit and not by the power of their own will.[120]

SEMI-PELAGIANISM

Some theologians have faulted both Pelagius and Augustine for going to dangerous extremes in their theological anthropologies and theologies of salvation. I will describe briefly a position that has come to be known as *Semi-Pelagianism*. A cautionary comment is noteworthy about the term. Some of those accused of holding this view could also technically be described as "Semi-Augustinians," because while they rejected Pelagius's radical view of the freedom of human will, they also rejected Augustine's view of the bondage of human free will.[121]

John Cassian (ca. 365–435), a monk and scholar, is credited with the earliest form of Semi-Pelagianism. He was a contemporary of St. Augustine. His two major works on monastic life are the *Institutes* and *Conferences*. To Cassian, human beings have the natural capacity to do good works without an antecedent divine help or enlightenment. However, when God sees the human initiative or will to do good works, God immediately responds by strengthening the human will and "urges it on toward salvation, increasing that which He Himself implanted or which He sees to have arisen from our own efforts."[122] Cassian's aim was to reconcile the Bible passages that teach that God desires for us to seek God's will and the passages that emphasize God's grace toward humans, which enables them to do good. Cassian upheld simultaneously the *freedom* of the human will to do good or evil and the *weakness* of the human will. He wrote, "For Holy Scripture supports the freedom of the will where it says: 'Keep thy heart with all diligence' [Prov 4:23], but the Apostle indicates its weakness by saying 'The Lord keep your hearts and minds in Christ Jesus' [Phil 4:7]."[123]

Cassian was well aware of the tension between God's grace and the freedom of the human will, particularly if one asked: which preceded the other, God's grace or the freedom of human will? Unlike Pelagius, he accepted that human beings are born with sin-nature. Unlike Augustine, he rejected that human will after the fall had no capacity to do good without a prior divine help. He resolved the tension by arguing that the natural (and

---

120. Augustine, *On Grace and Free Will* 23.11 (NPNF[1] 5:453).

121. Kyle, "Semi-Pelagianism."

122. John Cassian, *Third Conference of Abbot Chaeremon* 8 (NPNF[2] 11:426).

123. Ibid., 427.

God-intended) way was for humans to, on their own, will to do good works or seek God's help. He argued that humans are "unwilling or have grown cold"; however God stirs in their "hearts with salutary exhortations, by which a good will is either renewed or formed" in them.[124] Although Cassian had hoped his view did not break "the rule of the Church's faith,"[125] his view was condemned in 529 CE by the Council of Orange, most probably because the Council feared Cassian's view was unduly sympathetic to the teaching of Pelagius.

Biological Model

Description: In the biological model, Adam and Eve were historical figures. They became both guilty and morally corrupt after they sinned against God (see Gen 3). Sin affected their human nature. Adam passed on the "sinful gene" or "sinful nature" through semen to his posterity. To put it differently, since the fall of Adam, all human beings (with the exception of Jesus Christ) are conceived in sin. The psalmist's words may be cited in support of the biological model: "Behold, I was brought forth in iniquity, and in sin did my mother conceive me" (Ps 51:5 ESV). The Apostle Paul could also be used as an ally. In Eph 2:3, Paul wrote, "We all once lived in the passions of our flesh, carrying out the desires of the body and the mind, and were by nature children of wrath, like the rest of mankind" (ESV).

Impact of Adam's and Eve's Sin on Humanity: Theologians that hold the biological model recognize the difference between "original sin" (the sinful condition into which human beings are born as a result of the fall of Adam and Eve) and "actual sins" (personal sins). Representatives of the biological model, however, argue that original sin is the cause of actual sins. Human beings sin because they are sinners. Sin, for these theologians, is an external force that exerts influence on people's will.

The North African theologian Augustine of Hippo is the classical representative of the biological model. Augustine is credited as the theologian who formally articulated the doctrine of original sin. Augustine's theology of original sin should be understood against the backdrop of his understanding of Pelagius's imitation model. From around 412 CE until his death in 430 CE, Augustine devoted enormous energy to attacking Pelagius's theologies of sin and grace. In Augustine's judgment, Pelagius's theology was "hostile to salvation by Christ" and also a "poisonous perversion of the

124. Ibid., 428.
125. Ibid.

truth."[126] Augustine argued that even infants who have not committed personal sins (or actual sins) are not free from sin.[127]

For Augustine, Adam would not have experienced physical death if he had not sinned. He understood Gen 2:17–19 literally and argued that Adam "would have passed into the incorruptible state, which is promised to the faithful and the saints, without the peril of death."[128]

Augustine argued that prior to the fall Adam (in his original state) was created with the capacity to use his free will to do what is right (glorify God) or to sin (glorify self). In this original state, Adam was created to be "able not to sin" (*posse non peccare* in Latin) and to be "able not to die" (*posse non mori* in Latin).[129] When Adam *mis*used his free will and chose to sin, he lost the capacity to use his free will to satisfactorily glorify God. Adam, for Augustine, plunged all of humanity into a sinful condition, a condition in which human beings are "not able not to sin" (*non posse non peccare* in Latin). In other words, human beings since the fall lack the capacity, without God's grace, to overcome the power of sin. In this dire condition, infants, who have not committed their own sin, are both guilty and condemned before God on the account of Adam's sin. While Augustine conceded Adam was a bad moral example and also that his immediate descendants imitated his sinful acts, he insisted that Adam was the "progenitor of all who are born with sin."[130]

Remedies for Sin: For Augustine, since in the post-fall state human beings are "not able not to sin," they are bereft of the capacity to redeem themselves. The remedy for sin is God's grace, which is grounded in the work of Jesus Christ and communicated to infants through water baptism. The sacrament of baptism functions as the spiritual "medicine" God uses to cure infants of the sickness of original sin and its consequences (namely, enmity with God, depravity, concupiscence or lust, and death). The elect, the people whom God has predestined to salvation, at the consummation of time will be re-created *non posse peccare* (inability to sin) and *non posse mori* (inability to die).[131] Augustine's theologies of sin and evil, it should be noted, were influenced by his reaction to Manichaeism—the movement that

126. Augustine, *On the Proceedings of Pelagius* 47 (*NPNF*[1] 5:203).

127. Augustine, *Treatise on the Merits and Forgiveness of Sins, and on the Baptism of Infants* 1.2 (*NPNF*[1] 5:16).

128. Augustine, *Treatise on the Merits and Forgiveness of Sins, and on the Baptism of Infants* 9 (*NPNF*[1] 5:18).

129. Augustine, *On Rebuke and Grace* 33 (*NPNF*[1] 5:485).

130. Augustine, *Treatise on the Merits and Forgiveness of Sins, and on the Baptism of Infants* I.10 (*NPNF*[1] 5:18).

131. Augustine, *On Rebuke and Grace* 33 (*NPNF*[1] 5:485).

held that evil was the result of a cosmic conflict between two eternal forces, namely, Light and Darkness. Augustine, with the help of Neo-Platonism, argued that evil is a lack, a privation, and an absence of good that is the consequence of misusing God's gift of free will.

The short passage below contains some of the arguments Augustine presented in support of his view of original sin, its transmission, its consequences for humanity, and its remedy.

They [the Pelagians] refuse to believe that in infants original sin is remitted through baptism, for they contend that no such original sin exists at all in people by their birth. But if the apostle [Paul] had wished to assert that sin entered into the world, not by natural descent, but by imitation, he would have mentioned as the first offender, not Adam indeed, but the devil, of whom it is written, that 'he sinneth from the beginning'; of whom also we read in the Book of Wisdom: 'Nevertheless through the devil's envy death entered into the world' [Wis 2:24].... Accordingly, the apostle, when mentioning sin and death together, which had passed by natural descent [biologically] from one upon all men, set him down as the introducer thereof from whom the propagation of the human race took its beginning.

No doubt all they imitate Adam who by disobedience transgress the commandment of God; but he is one thing as an example to those who sin because they choose; and another thing as the progenitor of all who are born with sin. All His saints, also, imitate Christ in the pursuit of righteousness; whence the same apostle . . . says: "Be ye imitators of me, as I am also of Christ" [1 Cor 11:1 KJV]. But besides this imitation, His grace works within us our illumination and justification, by that operation concerning which the same [apostle] says: "Neither is he that planteth anything nor he that watereth, but God who giveth the increase" [1 Cor 3:7]. For by this grace He engrafts into His body even baptized infants, who certainly have not yet become able to imitate any one....

"The Father loveth the Son, and hath given all things into His hand. He that believeth on the Son hath everlasting life; while he that believeth not the Son shall not see life, but the wrath of God abideth on him" [John 3:35–36 KJV]. Now in which of these classes must we place infants—amongst those who believe on the Son, or amongst those who believe not on the Son? In neither, say some, because, as they are not yet able to believe, so must they not be deemed unbelievers. This, however, the rule of the Church does not indicate, for it joins baptized infants to the number of the faithful. Now if they who are baptized are, by virtue of the excellence and administration of so great a sacrament, nevertheless reckoned in the number of the faithful, although by

43

their own heart and mouth they do not literally perform what appertains to the action of faith and confession; surely they who have lacked the sacrament must be classed amongst those who do not believe on the Son, and therefore, if they shall depart this life without this grace, they will have to encounter what is written concerning such—they shall not have life, but the wrath of God abideth on them. Whence could this result to those who clearly have no sins of their own, if they are not held to be obnoxious to original sin?[132]

Question: What are the theological warrants Augustine provided to support his understanding of original sin, its transmission, and its remedy?

Criticism against Augustine's Biological Model: Three criticisms can be made against the biological model. First, the Latin translation (Vulgate) of the Greek words *eph hō* in Rom 5:12 as *in quo* ("in whom") misled Augustine to think Paul taught that Adam's sin and its consequences were passed on to his descendants biologically (through semen). Many biblical scholars today see "in whom" as a faulty translation of *eph hō*. The Greek expression *eph hō* should be understood in a causal sense (as "inasmuch as" or "seeing that" or "because").[133] When taken in a casual sense, *eph hō* is a conjunction that Paul uses to express humanity's solidarity with Adam. Paul's argument is, as the descendants of Adam, human beings *collectively*, in a covenantal sense, participated in Adam's primal transgression.[134] Augustine's view of the transmission of Adam's sin through procreation or seminally has no biblical basis.[135] Second, if one holds the theological conclusion of the biological model—that all people, including those who have not committed personal sins are guilty of Adam's sin—then, logically one is expected to conclude that the righteousness of Jesus Christ will extend to all people, including those who have not explicitly placed their faith in his salvific work (Rom 5:12–21). Maximos Aghiorgoussis faults Augustine for arguing that the human race inherited Adam's guilt. On the contrary, Aghiorgoussis argues that human beings only inherited a "sinful condition, the corruption of human nature, and the consequence of death." Also he argues that human beings are sinners not because they have *sinned in Adam* but rather because

132. Augustine, *Treatise on the Merits and Forgiveness of Sins, and on the Baptism of Infants* I.9, 10, 28 (*NPNF*[1] 5:18–19, 25).

133. See Cranfield, *Commentary on the Epistle to the Romans*, 1:274–81.

134. Ibid., 277.

135. Blocher, *Original Sin*, 28.

they personally sin.[136] Third, if truly, as Augustine taught, baptism washed away the effect of original sin or rendered it ineffective, it is reasonable to expect that infants whose parents were baptized would not inherit an original sin.[137]

Modifications of Augustine's Biological Model

I will discuss three major modifications of Augustine's theology of original sin in the works of John Calvin, James Arminius, and Millard Erickson. Their views represent three variants of the *covenantal* view (also known as the headship or federal view). The covenantal view argues in favor of a legal and an organic solidarity of humanity in Adam's sin, who acted in the capacity of humanity's representative.

COVENANTAL AND INSTANT IMPUTATION VIEW

Like the biological model, the *covenantal and instant imputation* view argues that Adam's sin and its consequences extend to their descendants. Like the imitation and biological model, the covenantal model treats Adam and Eve as historical figures. Unlike the biological model, the covenantal model rejects that Adam and Eve have transferred their sinfulness to their descendants through procreation. On the contrary, the covenantal–instant imputation model argues that God entered into a covenant relationship with humanity in which Adam served as humanity's representative. Therefore, when Adam sinned, God held him, and also those represented by him, accountable. I will use the concept of a country's ambassador to illustrate this view. An ambassador of a nation is the legal representative of his or her nation in a foreign country. An American ambassador to Nigeria, for example, is the representative of the United States of America in Nigeria. The official property where the ambassador resides is legally the property of the United States of America. Nigerian government and all Nigerians are expected to treat the property as they would treat any official American government property located in the United States of America. If the ambassador breaks any official treaty with the Nigerian government, Nigerians are legally justified to treat the United States and all of its citizens, like the ambassador, as those who have broken the treaty. Adam acted in the capacity

136. Aghiorgoussis, *Together in Christ*, 58.
137. Evans, *Pelagius*, 73.

of the "ambassador" of humanity. God, therefore, in the covenant model, is justified in treating humanity as having sinned against God when Adam sinned.

The *covenantal and instant imputation* view argues that God's judgment on Adam and Eve was immediately imputed to his descendants—all human beings (with the exception of Jesus). John Calvin (1509–64) is a major exponent of this view. Calvin argues that God "ordained . . . that the first man [Adam] should at one and the same time have and lose both for himself and for his descendants, the gifts that God had bestowed upon him."[138] To Calvin, Adam's sin resulted in the "depravation" of his nature, which was originally created "good and pure."[139] Adam's descendants, for Calvin, inherited both guilt and corruption from him. He writes, "Therefore, after the heavenly image was obliterated in him [Adam], he was not the only one to suffer this punishment—that, in place of wisdom, virtue, holiness, truth, and justice, with which adornments he had been clad, there came forth the most filthy plagues, blindness, impotence, impurity, vanity, and injustice— but he also entangled and immersed his offspring in the same miseries."[140] Like Augustine, Calvin faults Pelagius for contending that "Adam sinned only to his own loss without harming his posterity."[141] Also, like Augustine, Calvin believes that Adam's sin is "transmitted" to his descendants, implying that "all without exception are defiled at their begetting."[142] Adam's descendants have been inflected with his corruption. But *how exactly* were Adam's descendants infected with his corruption? Calvin differs with Augustine in his answer to this question. Calvin answered the question in two related ways. First, Adam's corruption is transmitted to his descendants through *imputation*. God is the one who "conferred upon human nature" the corruption of Adam.[143] In other words, God imputed Adam's corruption to his descendants. Human beings bear the penalty that is not theirs by nature but by divine judicial decision.[144] Second, Adam's corruption is transmitted to his descendants through *inheritance*. In Calvin's words, "Original sin . . . seems to be a hereditary depravity and corruption of our nature, diffused into all parts of the soul, which makes us liable to God's wrath, then also

---

138. Calvin, *Institutes of the Christian Religion*, 2.1.7.

139. Ibid., 2.1.5.

140. Ibid.

141. Ibid.

142. Ibid., 2.1.6.

143. Ibid., 2.1.7.

144. Jones, *Feminist Theory and Christian Theology*, 101.

brings forth in us those works which Scripture calls 'works of the flesh.'"[145] Original sin is likened to a corrupt "root" (that is, *human nature* in its post-fall condition) that grows into sinful branches (Adam's descendants).[146]

The Swiss theologian Karl Barth also held the *covenantal* view but developed it in a slightly different way from Calvin's theology. For Barth, sin is nontemporal (timeless), but *its first actual manifestation in the life of humans* can be traced to Adam. He writes that the "sin which entered the world through Adam is, like the righteousness manifested to the world in Christ, timeless and transcendental. . . . In the first man [Adam], in his life in the world, and in the world in which he lived, this disposition is seen in actual operation. The nontemporal Fall of all men from their union with God is manifested in that they imprison the truth in ungodliness and unrighteousness. . . . The Fall is not occasioned by the transgression of Adam; but the transgression was presumably its first operation."[147] Barth sees Adam as one who represented the whole of humanity and whose sin implicated the whole of humanity.[148] Barth recognizes the actual sins of all human beings but views such sins as the "repetition and variation" of Adam's life, "of his beginning and his end, of his sin and his death."[149] Although Barth uses expressions such as "Adam in us" and "ourselves in Adam" he does not intend for such expressions to be understood biologically but metaphorically.[150] Adam, for Barth, was the covenant head and representative of humanity. Therefore, being "in Adam" means to be in a condition governed by the power of sin and to be "under the wrath of God."[151] But Adam is only relevant to the discussion of humanity in the context of Jesus Christ. This is because, for Barth, the "essential and original nature" of human beings is not to be found in Adam but in Christ. Adam, Barth insists, can "be interpreted only in the light of Christ and not the other way round."[152] In his commentary on Barth's interpretation of Romans 5, Kenneth Oakes argues, "Barth's interpretation is that we cannot understand Adam and his Fall without understanding Christ and his righteousness. It is not the historical relationship of Adam

---

145. Calvin, *Institutes of the Christian Religion*, 2.1.8.

146. Ibid., 2.1.7.

147. Barth, *Epistle to the Romans*, 171–72.

148. Barth, *Christ and Adam*, 40.

149. Ibid., 34.

150. Ibid.

151. Barth, *Epistle to the Romans*, 165.

152. Barth, *Christ and Adam*, 40.

to Christ that interests us, but the non-historical, invisible relationship of Adam to Christ (just as with Abraham and Christ)."[153]

Advocates of the representative model are not in agreement on the solutions to humanity's sinful condition. Barth in his reflections on Romans chapter 5 focuses primarily on God's act in and through Jesus Christ.[154] To Barth, the remedy for being "in Adam" is to be "in Christ." He writes, "If a man be *in Adam*, he is an old, fallen, imprisoned, creature: if he be *in Christ*, he is a creature, new, reconciled and redeemed (2 Cor 5:17)."[155] Barth's understandings of being *in Christ* and being *in Adam* imply a movement or transfer of condition: humanity, which was previously *in Adam*, was transferred by God into the new condition enacted by Christ. Barth describes this "moment" in this way: "But only in the light of the critical whole, from the old to the new, from 'here' to 'there,' from the present to the coming age, does the distinction between the two become apparent."[156] When does such movement occur? Is it after Adam and Eve sinned? Is it when an individual consciously enters into a relationship with Christ through faith? Posing these questions can in fact be misleading, for Barth thinks of "moment" as a series of moments. For him, God united humanity with God's Word in the incarnation.

> "This person [Jesus Christ] is appointed and stands before God for the person of all other men. We all have to recognize in the commission and work of this person the accomplishment of the will of God in our own stead. Root and branch, we all belong to this person and not to ourselves."
>
> —Barth, *CD* II/1, 606.

NEUTRALIZED (ORIGINAL SIN'S) GUILT

The Dutch reformed minister and professor of theology James Arminius (1560–1609) championed the *neutralized original sin's guilt* view. Arminius understood Adam's sin as an act of disobedience and transgression of God's law.[157] God entered into a covenant with Adam, a contract in which God required Adam's obedience to God's law. When Adam, in his own free will, sinned against God, he incurred God's displeasure and wrath. Adam also became subject to death and was "deprived of the primeval righteousness and holiness in which a great part of the image of God consisted (Gen 2:17;

---

153. Oakes, *Reading Karl Barth*, 74.

154. Barth, *Christ and Adam*, 40–41.

155. Barth, *Epistle to the Romans*, 165.

156. Ibid.

157. Arminius, *Public Disputations* 7.2, 3, in *The Writings of James Arminius*, 1:480.

Rom 5:19; Gen 3:3–6, 23, 24; Rom 5:12, 16; Luke 19:26)."[158] Unlike Calvin who construed the moral consequence of the original sin in terms of *depravity*, Arminius understood original sin's moral consequence in terms of *privation* or God's withdrawing of original righteousness from Adam.[159]

On the manner in which Adam's sin and its consequences affected Adam's descendants, Arminius writes: "The whole of this sin . . . is not peculiar to our first parents, but is common to the entire race and to all their posterity, who, at the time when this sin was committed, were in their loins, and who have since descended from them by the natural mode of propagation, according to the primitive benediction. For in Adam 'all have sinned' (Rom 5:12, 18, 19)."[160] Like Augustine, Arminius believes Adam's sin corrupted human nature, which is passed on to his posterity through "the natural mode of propagation."[161] Also, like Augustine and Calvin, Arminius contends it is the corrupt human nature that compels human beings to sin. However, unlike them, he argues that human beings have retained the capacity to freely choose to yield or not to yield to the cravings of their corrupt human nature. He writes, "The efficient cause of actual sins is, man through his own free will. The inwardly working cause is the original propensity of our nature toward that which is contrary to the divine law, which propensity we have contracted from our first parents, through carnal generation."[162]

SUSPENDED AND CONDITIONAL IMPUTATION OF ORIGINAL SIN'S GUILT

This view claims that Adam's descendants (including infants) are responsible for his sin and its consequences (corrupt nature, death, and moral culpability). However, people activate the effect of the original sin when they consent and approve of the corrupt human nature through *actual* sins. According to Millard Erickson, "We become responsible and guilty when we accept or approve of our corrupt nature. There is a time in the life of each one of us when we become aware of our own tendency toward sin. At that point we may abhor the sinful nature that has been there all the time."[163]

---

158. Ibid., 7.3.
159. Ibid., 4.15.
160. Ibid., 4.16.
161. Ibid.
162. Ibid., 8.13.
163. Erickson, *Christian Theology*, 656.

Erickson understands union between Adam and his descendants primarily in terms of *natural headship*.[164] For Erickson, human beings were present within Adam and therefore inherited his corrupt human nature when he sinned. To him, "the entirety of our human nature, physical and spiritual, material and immaterial, has been received from our parents and more distant ancestors by way of descent from the first pair of humans. On that basis we were actually present within Adam, so that we all sinned in his act. There is no injustice, then, to our condemnation and death as a result of original sin."[165] Erickson, however, goes on to argue that God only holds people responsible for the guilt and condemnation associated with the original sin only when and if they commit personal sins. Erickson's context is the fate of infants (who have not yet attained the "age of accountability") and individuals who cognitively could not make moral choices (for example, some cases of people with mental disability). Although Erickson recognizes the difficulty with making a conclusive judgment on the condition of these two categories of people, he argues there is sufficient indication in the Bible that God would not hold them responsible for Adam's sin because they had "no awareness of right and wrong."[166] The suspended guilt and condemnation becomes active, however, when we commit personal sin. By committing sin we acquiesce in our inherited sinful nature, which in effect implies we approve of Adam's sin.[167]

Concluding Reflections on Original Sin and Actual Sins

Two major theological values of the Christian doctrine of original sin are noteworthy. First, whether or not original sin (a primordial sin and its consequences on humanity) truly exists, it offers a rationally plausible explanation for the rifeness of sin in the world. Sin is pervasive in the world. It is almost impossible to imagine a world in which children have not been born into sinful structures, institutions, and behaviors. As Joy Ann McDougall notes, "sin is an all-encompassing condition; none of us are immune to its deceptions or escape its destructive power."[168] Human sins (actual sins) are greatly influenced by the antecedent sinful behaviors of others, institutions, and societies. It is not unimaginable that children inherit certain behavioral traits from their parents. At an astonishingly early period in their lives,

164. Ibid., 654.
165. Ibid.
166. Ibid., 655.
167. Ibid., 656.
168. McDougall, "Feminist Theology," 679.

children can do things (such as lie) without having observed their parents or anyone else doing the same. Such behavior can be traced back to the power of sin over humans. Sin can be construed both as an internal force (within humans) and external force. Mark Biddle has argued that the "idea of 'bondage of sin' must mean, among other things, that the sin of the world is already standing there to greet each and every human being who comes to full moral consciousness."[169] Second, the doctrines of original sin and actual sins can help Christians to appreciate more fully both the reality of human struggles with sin and God's gracious work of remolding them through God's agents, particularly through the life of Jesus Christ and the church (community of Christ's followers). The doctrine of original sin should not serve as an escapist mindset to justify a Christian's failure to address sin and to confront its outward manifestations, such as dehumanization, racism, sexism, terrorism, human trafficking, and climate abuse. Christians are to actively work to prevent and curb the perverseness of sinful and evils acts, institutions, and structures within and beyond their societies.

Glossary

Actual Sins: refer to the personal sins of people, which some theologians argue are rooted in the sin-nature inherited from original sin.

The Fall: theological term employed by many theologians to describe the sin of Adam and Eve and the impact of their sin upon humanity.

Imago Dei: Latin term meaning "image of God," used by Christian theologians to express the belief that (*a*) human beings are God's creatures, (*b*) human beings are created with godlike characteristics such as capacity of thought and relationality, and (*c*) God has commissioned humans to be co–caretakers of God's creation.

Non posse non peccare: Latin phrase meaning "not able not to sin," used by Augustine to describe the condition of the human will after the fall.

Non posse peccare: Latin phrase meaning "not able to sin," used by Augustine to describe the condition of the human will in a glorified state when God renews all things.

Original Sin: term used by some theologians to describe both the *first* sin committed by the first humans and the *root* of sinful acts in the world.

169. Biddle, *Missing the Mark*, 134.

Posse non peccare: Latin expression meaning "able not to sin," used by Augustine to describe the human condition before the fall.

Soteriology: term for the discourse about God's salvific work.

Total Depravity: term used mostly in the Reformed Christian tradition to describe the inability of humans (due to the effect of original sin) to do any good work that is sufficient to earn them God's salvation.

Review Questions

1. What role does the *imago Dei* play in developing a Christian theological anthropology?

2. In what ways have Christian theologians construed "original sin" and "actual sins"? Explain the strengths and weaknesses of each of the major views of original sin.

3. What are the implications of constructing a Christian theological anthropology that is attentive to the issues of human dignity, human ontology, and the place of humans in creation?

Suggestions for Further Reading

Alison, James. *The Joy of Being Wrong: Original Sin through Easter Eyes*. New York: Crossroad, 1998.

Anderson, Gary A. *Sin: A History*. New Haven: Yale University Press, 2009.

Carr, Anne E. *Transforming Grace: Christian Tradition and Women's Experience*. New York: Continuum, 1996.

Hall, Douglas John. *Imaging God: Dominion as Stewardship*. Grand Rapids: Eerdmans, 1986.

Wesley, John. *The Doctrine of Original Sin: According to Scripture, Reason, and Experience*. In *The Works of John Wesley*, vol. 12, *The Doctrinal and Controversial Treatises I*, edited by Randy L. Maddox, 117–481. Nashville: Abingdon, 2012.

2

Salvation

This chapter takes up some of the issues I highlighted in the preceding chapter. Christian *soteriology* (discourse about God's salvation) is intrinsically connected to Christian theological anthropology, particularly Christianity's teaching about humanity's sin. Most Christians see God's salvation as an "antidote" to a "spiritual virus" (sin and its consequences—death, depravity, and alienation from God). Many theologians also ground their theologies of salvation in God's response to the human sinful condition and acts. In the words of Orlando Costas, "Sin and salvation are two fundamental themes in the communication of the gospel. On the one hand, the gospel is a saving message; on the other, it is a message addressed to a sinful world."[1] In the preceding chapter, I explored the effects of sin on God's creation. In this chapter, I will discuss Christian theologians' answers to the question, What is God doing about the fallen creation, and human beings in particular? In answering this question, I will focus on the

---

1. Costas, *Christ Outside the Gate*, 21.

Christian ideas of salvation, the Triune God's role in salvation, human being's responsibility in God's salvation, and the outcomes of salvation.

Christian Ideas of Salvation

No other Christian doctrine has received more attention and criticisms than the doctrine of salvation. Criticisms of the Christian doctrine of salvation come from within Christian communities, from people of other religions, and from people with no religious affiliations. Christian theologians disagree on the nature of salvation. For some, salvation is God's gift of eternal life to some people whom God has pre-chosen to save before creating the world and before the fall (*supralapsarian* view) or after the fall (*infralapsarian* view). Some see salvation as God's act of working cooperatively with willing sinful humans to restore them to divine fellowship. Yet to others, salvation is God's act of restoring the whole creation from its fallen state and also moving it to its originally intended goal. Some non-Christian theologians accuse Christianity of promoting religious exclusion for teaching there is no salvation outside of Jesus of Nazareth, the Christ. These issues make studying Christian doctrine of salvation both intriguing and challenging.

The Bible uses different words and metaphors to describe God's salvation. Among the many terms used for God's salvation, "justification," "forgiveness," "sanctification," "atonement," "redemption," and "reconciliation" are well known. Each of these terms provides a unique, albeit, limited picture of God's salvific acts. These soteriological terms have history: they emerged from religious, socioeconomic, and political contexts. Some biblical writers drew insights from the arenas of trading, commerce, the slave market, military, peace treaties, and Jewish religious rituals. Theologians have developed their soteriologies with some of these terms in mind. For example, Origen of Alexandria (ca. 185–254 CE) construed salvation as consisting in God's act of redemption, which God accomplished by *paying* Jesus Christ as a ransom to Satan in order to free humanity from Satan's enslavement.[2]

Three broad paths can be discerned in the Christian discourses on God's salvation. The differences of the paths lie in their emphases. The first path is *anthropocentric* and future-oriented. Theologians whose discussions on salvation have followed this path focus on the future redemption of sinful *humanity* (anthropocentric) at the *consummation* or *end* of the present world (futuristic). While the social order of this world and the condition of nature (including the climate and ecosystem) are not totally ignored,

---

2. Origen, *Commentary on Matthew* 13.8–9 (ANF 10:479–81).

they are rarely a focal point of discussion in the works of such theologians. Their emphasis is primarily on the salvation of human beings and not the whole creation.[3] For the theologians who follow the anthropocentric and futuristic oriented path, nature does not sin against God; human beings sin against God. Human beings, therefore, are the object of God's salvation. The anthropocentric-futuristic understanding of salvation has provided the impetus for missionary work throughout Christian history. Many missionaries have given their resources and in some cases their lives to the cause of bringing Christianity's gospel message to the people they feared could die without encountering God's salvific work in Jesus Christ.

The second path may be termed *cosmological*-oriented. God's salvation is imagined as God's gradual remaking of the whole creation (or cosmos), which "waits with eager longing the revealing of the sons of God" and also waits to be "set free from its bondage to decay and obtain the freedom of the glory of the children of God" (Rom 8:19–20 ESV). Paul Fiddes has argued that salvation "assumes that the life of human beings, and that of the wider natural world is distorted, self-destructive, or failing to reach its true potential. Against this background, 'salvation' denotes the healing or making whole of individuals and social groups, and the conserving of a natural environment which is ravaged and polluted by human greed."[4] Theologians who follow the cosmological-oriented path are concerned with the liberation of the whole creation, especially *nature* (ecology). They propose that creation (a term that presupposes a creator—God) is under its creator's watchful eyes. While some see God primarily as an "artist" who makes certain aesthetic judgments about creation with the goal of making it better, others see God as a "monarch" who makes moral judgments about creation, holding it accountable.[5]

The third path is *social* and *praxis*-oriented. Some theologians focus on the social conditions and problems of this present world in their discussions on salvation. A "social problem" is the condition that threatens the quality of life of a society. When poverty, lack of medical care, and violence threaten the security, property, and the lives of people in a society, they constitute a social problem.[6] For many theologians that follow the social and praxis-oriented track, salvation refers to God's work (which God accomplishes most times through God's people) of healing the world of its social problems. This, of course, does not mean that such theologians are

3. Pappas, *Are You Saved?*, 27–31.

4. Fiddes, "Salvation," 176.

5. Williams, *On Christian Theology*, 69.

6. Kornblum and Julian, *Social Problems*, 4–5.

not concerned with the ultimate destiny of humans. However, they oppose the use of the idea of a future salvation of humans as an excuse for not exposing the causes of social problems and also for failing to tackle them with solutions that are grounded in the Christian message. The theme of human liberation reigns supremely in the social and praxis-oriented path. The works of contextual, political, and liberation theologians have highlighted the social implications of the Christian doctrine of salvation for human contexts. The Peruvian theologian Gustavo Gutiérrez, for instance, has argued that God's salvific work includes "transforming this world." This transformation requires "struggle against misery and exploitation" with the intent to "build a just society" and to move human beings toward the fulfillment God desires for them.[7]

Although the three paths I have described above highlight three areas of emphases in Christian discourses on salvation, they all share the idea of God's salvation as *healing*. The anthropocentric and future-oriented path focuses on God's healing of humanity from the effects of sin and also restoring humans back to divine fellowship. The cosmological-oriented path focuses on God's healing of God's creation, which has been groaning for redemption. The social and praxis-oriented path concentrates on God's healing of human societies of social problems (such as terrorism, poverty, racism, human trafficking, and so on) through human agents. Salvation should therefore be imagined as the Triune God's gracious act of redeeming all spheres of creation and particularly human beings, bringing them into fellowship for the purposes of healing, communion, pruning, and restoration. This salvific work of the Triune God involves human cooperation: human beings are to carry out God's commission to them to be good stewards of God's creation, which entails being emissaries of God's *salvific healing* in the world. I will now turn to discuss the roles of Triune God in salvation.

The Triune God's Roles in Salvation

Salvation is like a wellspring flowing from the Triune God (Father, Son, and Holy Spirit). Each of the persons of the Trinity plays a vital role in the economy of salvation. In chapter four of *Introducing Christian Theologies*, volume one, I discussed the concept of "economic Trinity"—the activities of the persons of the Trinity in creation and salvation of the world. In this chapter I will discuss their roles in salvation in more detail. Although I have chosen to discuss the roles of the divine persons in salvation separately, it should be borne in mind that their roles are not mutually exclusive. They

7. Gutiérrez, *Theology of Liberation*, 91.

share the same goal—to restore creation, human beings in particular, to the divine life of fellowship. Also, there is continuity in their salvific work. For example, the sanctifying work of the Holy Spirit would have no value had God the Father not chosen to extend salvation to humanity (2 Thess 2:13). Yet it is important to distinguish the roles of the divine persons because often the roles of the Father and the Holy Spirit are rarely discussed in Christian theology of salvation. Attention is usually given to Jesus Christ, especially his death on the cross.

God the Father's Role

The Christian doctrine of salvation cannot be understood in isolation from God's *election* to salvation. I am using the word "election" broadly here to refer to God's choice not to abandon human beings in their sinful condition and also God's choice and desire to restore human beings into divine fellowship. There is no salvation outside of God's election. God's choice to extend salvation to humans rather than abandon them in their sin is the ground for God's gracious giving of God's son in order to bring humans back to fellowship (John 3:16). Christian theologians do not deny that the Bible teaches "election"—God's *acts of choosing* for the purpose of salvation (Matt 22:14; 24:22–24, 31; Mark 13:20; Rom 9:11–15; 2 Thess 2:13; Eph 1:4–6; Jas 2:5; 1 Pet 1:1; 2:9; Rev 17:14). They differ on three crucial points, however: (*a*) the *nature* of election, (*b*) the *basis* of election, and (*c*) the *scope* of election. For some, the doctrine of election is a testimony to God's graciousness toward some people. Others contend that the doctrine of election can lead people to live immorally since the doctrine may imply that the elect will not lose their salvation. Augustine of Hippo wrote, "If any one of these [i.e., the elect] perishes, God is mistaken; but none of them perishes, because God is not mistaken. If any one of these perishes, God is overcome by human sin; but none of them perishes, because God is overcome by nothing."[8] Yet to other Christians, the doctrine of election (or more accu-

> FOCUS QUESTION:
> What role does God the Father play in salvation?

> "Blessed be the God and Father of our Lord Jesus Christ, who has blessed us in Christ with every spiritual blessing in the heavenly places, even as he chose us in him before the foundation of the world, that we should be holy and blameless before him."
>
> (Eph 1:3–4, ESV)

8. Augustine, *On Rebuke and Grace* 14 (*NPNF*[1] 5:477).

rately, some versions of the doctrine of election) is bad news to those whom God has not unconditionally chosen to save. Most of my theology students who have prior knowledge of the doctrine of election before the topic is introduced in class assume there are only two views on election—Calvin's and Arminius' views. Those who agree with John Calvin's view of election most times timidly share with other students their reasons for agreeing with him that God has elected some to salvation and sentenced others to eternal damnation. The students who disagree with Calvin are usually ready to share with other students that Calvin's view of election makes God an unjust Creator.

Theological Notes on Romans 9:14–16

Does the Hebrew idiom "I will have mercy on whom I have mercy, and I will have compassion on whom I have compassion" (Rom 9:15; cf. Exod 33:19) indicate a *restriction* of God's power and freedom to be merciful and gracious? Or is the idiom intended to express the *bounty* of God's power and freedom to be merciful and gracious? The issue here is whether Paul is asserting (*a*) that God has the freedom to arbitrarily show mercy on those whom God favors unconditionally and to deny others such act of mercy, or rather (*b*) that God's mercy knows no bounds and is ultimately determined by God. Note that option (*a*) requires taking the idiom literally, while option (*b*) retains the idiomatic and metaphorical nature of the expression. Another question that is relevant to the meaning of the idiom: Does the implied divine choice relate to "election to service" or "election to salvation"? While some have understood the text to refer to "election to salvation,"[9] others argue that Paul is here referring to God's election to service.[10]

I will discuss the views of three theologians whose writings continue to shape contemporary discourses on God's election to salvation, namely, James Arminius, John Calvin, and Karl Barth. I will discuss their understandings of the nature, basis, and scope of God's election. Finally, I will assess their views, highlighting their strengths and weaknesses.

---

9. Ware, "Divine Election to Salvation," 9.

10. Cottrell, "Responses to Bruce Ware," 60.

James Arminius (1560–1609)

In 1593, the Dutch theologian James Arminius wrote to Gellius Snecanus, a pastor, expressing his gratitude for Snecanus' commentary on Romans chapter 9. Arminius was struck by the similarities of their ideas and understandings of the chapter. As Arminius wrote, "For when I saw that your idea of the scope of the Apostle, and of the use of his principle argument, was the same, as I had recently presented to my congregation . . . I was greatly confirmed in that opinion, both because I have great confidence in your judgment, and because I found proofs in the arguments, which you advanced."[11] In his commentary on Romans 9, Arminius outlined some biblical and theological warrants for his understanding of God's election to salvation. He vehemently opposed theologians who argued that Paul in Rom 9 taught that God had unconditionally elected some (the elect) and condemned others (the reprobate) without considering their choices.[12] On the contrary, Arminius argued that Paul discussed two classes of people: "children of the flesh"—those who seek salvation through the *works of law*— and "children of promise"—those who *respond in faith* to God's call.[13] Paul used the terms "Esau" and "Jacob" typologically to describe these two classes of people; Jacob representing the children of promise and Esau representing the children of flesh.[14] For Arminius, the children of the flesh are deprived of salvation in accordance with God's pre-temporal (or eternal) election. On the contrary, God bestows salvation upon the children of promise in accordance with God's pre-temporal election.[15] Arminius perceived God's election and God's justification of sinners as two inseparable acts of God. For him, God, from eternity, chose individuals (divine election) whom God foreknew would freely believe in Christ.[16]

Nature and Basis of God's Election

To Arminius, election refers to God's pre-temporal decision to bestow upon people whom God foreknew would believe in God's promise as made manifest in Jesus Christ. God's election is grounded in God's *mercy*. God could

---

11. Arminius, *Analysis of the Ninth Chapter of the Epistle to the Romans*, in *The Writings of James Arminius*, 3:527.

12. Ibid., 539.

13. Ibid., 536.

14. Ibid., 532–33.

15. Ibid., 536.

16. Ibid., 538.

have abandoned fallen humanity in their sin and punished them "without hope of pardon." However, in an act of mercy, God chose to extend an offer of salvation to humanity and to make "a covenant of grace" with humans.[17] God's election is also grounded in God's *will*. Arminius concedes that God's *will* governs all things.[18] But rather than discussing God's will abstractly, Arminius locates his discussion within *God's law*, which God wills "should be obeyed by all."[19] He dismisses the notion of God's "two wills": *revealed will* (relates to what pleases or displeases God, both of which human beings can choose to do) and *secret will* (relates to the things God wills should be done or not done, which humans cannot resist or change).

To Arminius, the concept of God's two wills implies that God has two contradictory wills. He also argues that the idea of two divine wills is foreign to the Bible. He writes, "To those who rightly consider the subject, the will of God will appear to be *one and the same thing in itself*—distinct in its objects."[20] God operates with a single will, which God does not always reveal to humans. God's character is at stake if God, on the one hand, wills for all people to obey God's law and, on the other hand, wills that only some can accomplish such task. For example, if God willed for the Egyptian Pharaoh not to obey God's command to let the people of Israel to leave (and consequently hardened his heart) and at the same punished Pharaoh for not allowing the people of Israel to leave, then, God was unjust. According to Arminius, God only hardens the hearts of individuals who are "preserving in their sins against the long suffering of God, who invites them to repentance. . . ."[21]

> "For 'God can not compel, nor can the will be compelled,' but it is sufficient to excuse the man, and to exempt him from the just wrath of God, if there exist any force of divine impulse, which is followed by the inevitable necessity of doing that to which he is moved."
>
> —Arminius, *Analysis of the Ninth Chapter of Romans*, 550

Arminius contends that people do not believe because they are the elect but rather people become members of the community of the elect because God has chosen them on the condition of their faith in Christ. While locating election within God's eternal choice, he insists that God's choice of people who will benefit from God's offer of salvation is contingent upon their act of belief or faith in Christ. He writes, "God determined, after the

17. Ibid., 544.

18. Ibid., 548.

19. Ibid.

20. Ibid., 549; emphasis mine.

21. Ibid., 550.

former condition added to the legal covenant had not been performed, and man had by the fall been made unable to perform it, to enter into a covenant of grace with us through Christ; and of grace to change the condition of the former covenant into faith in Christ, by which we, believing in Christ, might obtain the same thing as we should have previously obtained by plenary obedience to the law, rendered by ourselves."[22]

Jesus' Role in God's Election

In Arminius' thought, Jesus Christ is the foundation of God's election and predestination with respect to human salvation. God elects, predestines, and carries out God's purpose for these divine acts in and through Jesus Christ. He writes, "Predestination is the decree of the good pleasure of God, in Christ, by which he determined, within himself, from all eternity, to justify believers, to adopt them, and to endow them with eternal life, 'to the praise of the glory of his grace,' and even for the declaration of his justice."[23] Jesus is the channel through which believers access God's salvation. Jesus is also the one who mediates between God and humanity. There is no election outside of the work of Jesus Christ, who "solicits, merits, obtains, brings back, and dispenses God's salvation" to believers.[24]

Objects of God's Election

Since God's election is partly contingent upon people's faith, it follows that God elects partly on the basis of a *foreseen faith*. To put it differently, God elects on the basis of God's *foreknowledge* (here used in the sense of *seeing in advance* or *seeing ahead of time*) of those whom God foreknew would believe when and if presented with the gospel. A similar idea of election and predestination was present in the writing of Justin Martyr, the second century CE Christian apologist. According to Justin Martyr, God "foreknows that some are to be saved by repentance, some even that are perhaps not yet born. In the beginning He made the human race with the power of thought and of choosing the truth and doing right, so that all men are without excuse before God; for they have been born rational and contemplative."[25]

22. Ibid., 540.

23. Arminius, *Private Disputations* 40.2, in *The Writings of James Arminius*, 2:99–100.

24. Clarke, *Ground of Election*, 90.

25. Justin Martyr, *First Apology* 28 (*ANF* 1:172).

Arminius' views may be summarized as follows: (*a*) God's election is conditional—it is based on the faith of the believer, which God has foreseen. (*b*) God's election is grounded in God's "prevenient grace"—the grace that restores in all sinners, through the Holy Spirit's enablement, the ability to choose or reject God. (*c*) God's election is founded on the mediatory work of Jesus Christ. (*d*) God's salvation is synergistic—it is actualized by the co-operative work of God and human beings. Below is an excerpt from James Arminius' review of William Perkins' (a Cambridge theologian's) views of the fall, predestination, and election. In this review, Arminius expresses his own understanding of the role of God and of human beings in the "drama" of salvation.

It is certain that God can by the act of His own absolute power prevent all things whatever, which can be done by the creature, and it is equally certain that He is not absolutely under obligation to anyone to hinder him from evil. But He cannot, in His justice, do all that He can in His absolute power. He cannot, in His justice (or righteousness), forget the "work and labor of love" of the pious (Heb 6:10). The absolute power of God is limited by the decree of God, by which He determined to do anything in a particular direction. And though God is not absolutely under obligation to anyone, He can yet obligate Himself by His own act, as, for instance, by a promise, or by requiring some act from man....

Christ according to the Apostle is not only the means by which the salvation, already prepared by election, but, so to speak, the meritorious cause, in respect to which the election was made, and on whose account that grace was prepared. For the Apostle says that we are chosen in Christ (Eph 1:4), as in a mediator, in whose blood salvation and life is obtained for us, and as in our "head," (Eph 1:22) from whom those blessings flow to us. For God chooses no one unto eternal life except in Christ, who prepared it by his own blood for them who should believe on his name. From this it seems to follow that, since God regards no one in Christ unless they are engrafted in him by faith, election is peculiar to believers.... For Christ is a means of salvation to no one unless he is apprehended by faith. Therefore, that phrase "in Christ" [in Eph 1:4] marks the meritorious cause by which grace and glory are prepared, and the existence of the elect in him, without which they could not be elected in him.[26]

26. Arminius, *Examination of the Treatise of William Perkins*, in *The Writings of James Arminius*, 3:300, 311.

Criticisms of Arminius' View of God's Election

Arminius' theology of election has been criticized by some theologians for its tendency to make God's election dependent on human merits. If God elected people on the basis of their belief and faith in Jesus Christ, albeit which God foreknew in eternity, it implied that the elect merited their salvation. The Scripture clearly teaches that salvation is dependent on God's grace and not on human merits. Paul in Eph 2:8 writes, "For by grace you have been saved through faith; and that not of yourselves, it is the gift of God; not as a result of works, so that no one may boast" (NASB). Some critics of Arminius have also argued that his view diminishes the severe impact of original sin on humanity. For these theologians, the original sin incapacitates human beings from doing any good work that can bring about salvation. Therefore, "saving faith" is God's gift and not the result of human works of righteousness. Michael Horton has argued that the gift of salvation will be received by only those who God chose to save before the creation of the world and who are in history *efficaciously* called to believe by the Holy Spirit of God.[27]

John Calvin (1509–64)

Many undergraduate theology students, especially those in colleges and universities with Protestant ties, associate the French theologian John Calvin with the soteriology represented by the acronym TULIP (T: total depravity; U: unconditional election; L: limited atonement; I: irresistible grace; P: perseverance of the saints). Many of such students, however, are unaware that it was the Synod of Dort (Netherlands) of 1618–19, and not John Calvin himself, that constructed these five points of Calvinism in response to the soteriology of some followers of James Arminius. This section focuses on the "U" in TULIP. I will examine John Calvin's view of election as God's choice of some individuals to benefit from God's salvation.

27. Horton, *Christian Faith*, 566.

Nature and Basis of God's Election

In John Calvin's theology, election is God's pre-temporal (i.e., before time) choice of some individuals as the objects (or recipients) of God's salvation. God decreed in eternity to save some individuals and to sentence some to condemnation. To understand Calvin's view on God's election, we should be attentive to two assumptions that governed his thought. First, Calvin prioritizes the importance and usefulness of a doctrine of election to Christian living in his discussions. He highlights four values of the doctrine of election: (*a*) it reminds Christians of God's glory because God pays no rewards and owes no one, (*b*) it reminds Christians of God's mercy, (*c*) it serves as a reminder to Christians to be humble and to recognize they are saved because of God's mercy and not because of their own work, and (*d*) it gives Christians the assurance that their salvation is secure.[28] Second, Calvin locates his discussions on election in *God's eternal decree*, which is hidden from humans. God has not given human beings, Calvin insists, the capacity "to search out things that the Lord has willed to be hid in himself."[29] For Calvin, the doctrine of election and predestination should be grounded in what the Scriptures say about them. On the one hand, the Scriptures attest to some things which God has not revealed to humans. Therefore, theologians should confine themselves to the scriptural testimony about God's election and predestination.[30] On the other hand, since the Scriptures attest to God's election and predestination, theologians should not be silent on the subjects or disregard them in their teaching because of the difficulties associated with these theological topics.[31]

Jesus' Role in God's Election

In Calvin's doctrine of election, Jesus performs dual roles, namely, an authorial role (the author of Election) and mediatory role (the executor of God's election). As member of the Trinity, Jesus (God Incarnate), like the Father and the Holy Spirit, elects people to salvation. In his commentary on John 13:18, which describes Judas' betrayal of Jesus, Calvin argued that Judas was able to do so because Jesus, as member of the Trinity, has predetermined Judas' course of life and action. To Calvin, Jesus' words in John 6:70—"Have I not chosen you, the Twelve? Yet one of you is a devil!"—testify to his

28. Calvin, *Institutes of the Christian Religion*, 3.21.1.
29. Ibid.
30. Ibid., 3.21.2.
31. Ibid., 3.21.3.

divinity. Calvin writes, "Christ gives here a clear poof of his Divinity; first when he declares that he does not judge after the manner of men; and, secondly, when he pronounces himself to be the Author of *election*. For when he says, I *know*, the *knowledge*, of which he speaks, belongs peculiarly to God; but the second proof—contained in the words, *whom I have chosen*—is far more powerful, for he testifies that they who were *elected* before the creation of the world were *elected* by himself."[32]

Jesus performs a mediatory role in God's election. He is the executor of God's election. For Calvin, Jesus is the instrument or means through which God actualizes God's eternal decree to unconditionally bestow salvation upon some people. Calvin distinguishes the role of the Second Person of the Trinity (the eternal Son of God in his pre-incarnate state) from the role of Jesus Christ, God incarnate. This distinction is vital for understanding the place of Christology in Calvin's theology of election. As the Second Person of the Trinity, the pre-incarnate Word or Son of God was part of the decision of the Triune God's decree to save some and to condemn others. As the Incarnate Word of God, Jesus Christ is God's mediator who executes the Triune God's decree to save some and to condemn others. Also, as the "Mediator" between God and humanity, Jesus Christ performs two interrelated roles. First, Jesus Christ is the "locus" of God's election—the one in whom the elect find their salvation. Second, Jesus Christ is the "executor"—the one who brings about or actualizes the salvation of those whom God has decreed to save.[33] God the Father in eternity had chosen some "in Christ" (Eph 1:4). Those whom God decreed to save God also adopted through Jesus Christ. Calvin writes, "It is not from a perception of anything that we deserve [God's election], but because our heavenly Father has introduced us, through the privilege of adoption, into the body of Jesus Christ. In short the name of Christ excludes all merit . . . for when he [Paul] says that we are chosen in Christ, it follows that in ourselves we are unworthy."[34]

Objects of God's Election

Individual persons, in Calvin's thought, are the objects of God's salvation. The elect, according to Calvin, are not the people whom God foreknew would believe. On the contrary, the elect are the individuals God freely and unconditionally chose to save even before they were born. Those that God has elected in eternity, God gave them "the spirit of regeneration" to

32. Calvin, *Commentaries*, 18:64–65; emphasis in the original.
33. Gibson, *Reading the Decree*, 4.
34. Calvin, *Commentaries*, 21:198.

respond to the gospel and to persevere in a covenant relationship with God to the end.[35] To Calvin, those who receive the gospel and blessing of God's salvation are able to do so because of God's election.[36] John Piper, an ardent admirer of John Calvin's view of election, has argued: "who it is that believes and is saved, and who it is that rebels and is not saved, is ultimately decided by God. This is mysterious, and I do not claim to have all the answers to the questions it raises."[37] In his commentary on Romans 9, Calvin argues that the Apostle Paul makes it clear that God does not elect on the basis of human works but rather on God's mercy. Calvin argues that God "can see nothing" worthy of God's salvation "in the corrupt nature of man."[38] All persons, Calvin reasons, are implicated in Adam's sin. Adam's descendants, like Adam, after he sinned, are "with no particle of righteousness" in them.[39]

If God has decreed to save some and not all, are there people who, through no fault of their own, are excluded from God's salvation? Calvin would propose "yes" and "no" as the answer to the question. On the one hand, Calvin would answer "yes" because God decreed to save some in eternity and on the basis of his *good pleasure* (the remote cause of election and reprobation). Therefore, "God has a sufficient just reason for electing and for reprobating, in his own good will."[40] Calvin's view of election and reprobation is similar to Augustine's. In *On the Soul and Its Origin*, Augustine argued that there are two classes of people: those whom God has "appointed . . . to be regenerated [and] predestined to everlasting life" and those whom God "has predestined to eternal death"[41] For Augustine, God does not elect on the basis of a foreseen faith, a view he attributed to Pelagius. On the contrary, Augustine argues that God elects solely on God's "good pleasure" and not on a human merit.[42] Augustine, however, conceded two points. First, God's purpose in predestining some to eternal life and some to eternal death is a mystery, a truth which God has not revealed to humans. Second, human beings do not have the cognitive capacity to unequivocally identify the elect, some of whom may not be part of a visible church. Augustine believed that the identity of the two classes of people is only known by God.[43]

35. Calvin, *Institutes of the Christian Religion*, 3.21.7.

36. Calvin, *Commentaries*, 21:198.

37. Piper, *Bloodlines*, 143.

38. Calvin, *Commentaries*, 19:349.

39. Ibid., 349

40. Ibid., 350.

41. Augustine, *On the Soul and Its Origin* 16 (*NPNF*[1] 5:361).

42. Augustine, *On the Predestination of the Saints* 36 (*NPNF*[1] 5:15–16).

43. Augustine, *On Rebuke and Grace* 12 (*NPNF*[1] 5:476).

On the other hand, Calvin would answer "no" to the question, If God has decreed to save some and not all , are there people who, through no fault of their own, are excluded from God's salvation? No, because all human beings were implicated in *original sin*—Adam's sin and its consequences (the proximate cause of election and reprobation).[44] Therefore, God has not sentenced to destruction those who technically had no fault. However, we need to recognize that in Calvin's thought God's *good pleasure* (the remote cause of election and reprobation) is primary whereas *original sin* (the proximate cause of election and reprobation) is secondary. Calvin makes this point in his commentary on Romans 9:12. He writes, "Since the purpose of God according to election is established in this way—that before the brothers were born, and had done either good or evil, one was rejected and the other chosen; it hence follows, that when any one ascribes the cause of the difference to their works [good or evil], he thereby subverts the purpose of God."[45]

The excerpts below highlight some of Calvin's assumptions and arguments in his discussion on the doctrine of election.

We shall never be clearly persuaded, as we ought to be, that our salvation flows from the wellspring of God's free mercy until we come to know his eternal election, which illumines God's grace by this contrast: that he does not indiscriminately adopt all into the hope of salvation but gives to some what he denies to others.

No one who wishes to be thought religious dares simply deny predestination, by which God adopts some to hope of life, and sentences others to eternal death. But our opponents, especially those who make foreknowledge its cause, envelop it in numerous petty objections. We, indeed, place both doctrines in God, but we say that subjecting one to the other is absurd.

When we attribute foreknowledge to God, we mean that all things always were, and perpetually remain, under his eyes, so that to his knowledge there is nothing future or past, but all things are present. And they are present in such a way that he not only conceives them through ideas, as we have before us those things which our minds remember, but he truly looks upon them and discerns them as things placed before him. And this foreknowledge is extended throughout the universe to every creature.

We call predestination God's eternal decree, by which he compacted with himself what he willed to become of each man. For all are not created in equal

---

44. Calvin, *Commentaries*, 19:350; see also Calvin, *Commentaries*, 21:198.

45. Calvin, *Commentaries*, 19:351; see also Calvin, *Institutes of the Christian Religion*, 3.22.1–6.

condition; rather, eternal life is foreordained for some, eternal damnation for others. Therefore, as any man has been created to one or the other of these ends, we speak of him as predestined to life or to death.

God has attested this not only in individual persons but has given us an example of it in the whole offspring of Abraham, to make it clear that in his choice rests the future condition of each nation.

As Scripture, then, clearly shows, we say that God once established by his eternal and unchangeable plan those whom he long before determined once for all to receive into salvation, and those whom, on the other hand, he could devote to destruction. We assert that, with respect to the elect, this plan was founded upon his freely given mercy, without regard to human worth; but by his just and irreprehensible but incomprehensible judgment he has barred the door of life to those whom he has given over to damnation.[46]

Questions: How does John Calvin understand God's foreknowledge? How does Calvin understand the relationship between God's election and predestination in his soteriology?

Criticisms of Calvin's View of God's Election

Four criticisms can been put forward to counter Calvin's view of election. First, some theologians and biblical scholars fault Calvin for construing election as God's choice of individuals. They propose that individual predestination contradicts dozens of other scriptures. God chooses corporately and not individually (Deut 4:37; 7:6–8; Rom 9–11; Gal 3–4).[47] Some theologians see God's election to salvation as a corporate reality and some construe it as individually focused. Stanley Grenz, a representative of the "corporate" position argues that when viewed "from the perspective of the divine intention, election is fundamentally corporate."[48] People are the elect because they belong to the community that God calls and unites to Jesus Christ through the Holy Spirit. To Grenz, being an "elect" means being "in Christ," and hence participating in a corporate reality."[49] Second, some argue that when scriptural teaching on salvation is taken as a whole, it is most compelling to conclude that God saves people on the basis of their free choices. They follow Arminius' claim that God's election is based on God's foreseen

46. Calvin, *Institutes of the Christian Religion*, 3.21.1, 5, 7.
47. See Abasciano, "Corporate Election in Romans 9."
48. Grenz, *Theology for the Community of God*, 453.
49. Ibid.

faith of individuals who will freely come to accept the gospel. Third, some have argued that if God bestows salvation upon some without factoring in their freedom to choose or not to choose God, the doctrine of election will become an impetus for unholy living. Calvin responded to the criticism by stating that election should be no ground for licentiousness because God elects in order to make the "elect" holy.[50] He, however, maintained that holiness of the elect originated from God's election.[51] Fourth, Calvin's view of election can discourage people from genuinely preaching the gospel to the un-evangelized. If God has already determined those whom God will save, and God's eternal decree cannot be altered, then, it is needless to genuinely attempt to evangelize those who have not heard the gospel and those who have not yet responded positively to gospel. The English theologian John Wesley (1703–91) contended that the election spoken of in Romans 9 is God's choice to save those who believe and to damn those who do not. For Wesley, the doctrine of reprobation entails that those whom God has not unconditionally elected to salvation are not the "objects of God's love." Wesley concluded that the doctrine of unconditional election implies unconditional reprobation, which he argued are both unbiblical.[52] To Wesley, both unconditional election and unconditional reprobation undermine God's justice and morality.[53]

Karl Barth

Election implies *choice* and *rejection*. For Barth, Jesus embodies these two classes of people—the elect and the rejected. In Barth's words, "The election of grace is the eternal beginning of all the ways and works of God in Jesus Christ. In Jesus Christ God in His free grace determines Himself for sinful man and sinful man for Himself. He therefore takes upon Himself the rejection of man with all its consequences, and elects man to participation in His glory."[54] God accomplished this work in the *Incarnation*, God's identification with humanity and also God's self-disclosure in Jesus of Nazareth. In the Incarnation, God confronts and deals with humanity's rejection of God. Barth's dialectical mindset is clearly seen when he argues that the *rejected*

---

50. Calvin, *Commentaries*, 21:199.

51. Calvin, *Institutes of the Christian Religion*, 3.22.3.

52. Wesley, "Predestination Calmly Considered," in *Works*, 10:210–11.

53. Ibid., 10:216.

54. Barth, *CD* II/2, 94.

(those who live in opposition to God) are precisely those whom God, in Christ, has elected to live in covenant relationship with God.[55]

If God has dealt with humanity's rejection and resistance of God in Jesus Christ, as Barth contends, does it imply that God will save all people? Barth's response to this question can be summarized in this way: Given that God has taken upon God's self the sin of humanity in God's Son (Jesus Christ), it follows that through a divine decision God has annulled human rejection of God. Therefore, we can be *hopeful* that God will ultimately bring all people into covenant relationship.[56] Individuals can be called the "elect" only in relation to Jesus, who is God's elect—the one in whom God has partnered, redeemed, and reclaimed humanity.

Nature and Basis of God's Election

Karl Barth sees the doctrine of election as God's decree to confront and also to undo *sin*—that is, human rejection of and disobedience to God. This divine confrontation of sin is grounded in Jesus Christ in whom we encounter God's self-revelation. For Barth, then, election is God's choice (or will) to be God (self-determination) in God's movement toward humanity in Jesus Christ (God's self-disclosure). Therefore, Barth sees election as the sum of the Christian gospel. Christians cannot speak of the "gospel" in isolation from Jesus Christ. Barth also insists that the doctrine of election cannot be understood in isolation from Jesus Christ, whom he construes as both "the electing God" and the "elected man."[57] Barth is careful to locate his understanding of election in the Scriptures because of his conviction that all Christian doctrines should be constructed in a manner that upholds "the self-revelation [i.e., Jesus Christ] of God attested in Holy Scripture."[58] Barth praises John Calvin for taking the Scriptures seriously in his discussion on election, noting that theologians should not begin their theological discussions from already established theological systems. On the contrary, theologians should recognize that "it is to Scripture alone" they "must ultimately be responsible."[59]

55. Sharp, *Hermeneutics of Election*, 86–87.
56. Barth, *CD* II/2, 295, 306.
57. Ibid., 3.
58. Ibid., 35.
59. Ibid., 36.

Jesus' Role in God's Election

To Barth, Jesus performs dual roles in election: he is both the "subject" (electing God—*erwählende Gott* in German) and the "object" (elected man—*erwählte Mensch* in German) of God's election.[60] By describing Jesus Christ as both the "subject" and "object" of election, Barth hopes to rescue the doctrine of election from the speculation that is characteristic of Calvin's reflection on God's eternal (hidden) decrees. In proposing that Jesus Christ is the one and the same *Logos asarkos* ("Word without flesh" of John 1:1), Bruce McCormack argues, Barth shows that the electing God is determined and defined "by what God reveals himself to be in Jesus Christ, namely, a God of love and mercy toward the whole human race."[61]

Barth's interpretation and use of Eph 1:4 to demonstrate his claim that Jesus is both the subject and object of God's election are noteworthy. He differs from theologians who use the text to support the claim that Jesus is merely the *executor* of God's election. Barth also argues that beyond Eph 1:4, the biblical references to God's election point us in the direction of one central figure, namely, Jesus Christ. He writes, "Who and what is the God who rules and feeds His people, creating and maintaining the whole world for its benefit, and guiding it according to His own good-pleasure—according to the good-pleasure of His will as it is directed toward this people? If in this way we ask further concerning the one point upon which, according to Scripture, our attention and thoughts should and must be concentrated, then from first to last the Bible directs us to the name of Jesus Christ."[62]

In the following excerpts taken from Karl Barth's *Church Dogmatics*, I have highlighted some of the major claims in his theology of God's election.

The election of Jesus Christ is the eternal choice and decision of God. And our first assertion tells us that Jesus Christ is the electing God. We must not ask concerning any other but Him. In no depth of the Godhead shall we encounter any other but Him. There is no such thing as Godhead in itself. Godhead is always the Godhead of the Father, the Son, and the Holy Spirit. But the Father is the Father of Jesus Christ and the Holy Spirit is the Spirit of the Father and the Spirit of Jesus Christ. There is no such thing as a *decretum absolutum* [absolute decree]. There is no such thing as a will of God apart from the will of Jesus Christ. . . . And He is this not simply in the sense that our election can be known to us and contemplated by us only through His election, as an election

60. Ibid., 145.

61. McCormack, *Orthodoxy and Modern*, 183.

62. Barth, *CD* II/2, 53.

which, like His and with His, is made (or not made) by a secret and hidden will of God. On the contrary, Jesus Christ reveals to us our election as an election which is made by Him, by His will which is the will of God. He tells us that He Himself is the One who elects us.

Starting from Jn. 1:1ff., we have laid down and developed two statements concerning the election of Jesus Christ. The first is that Jesus Christ is the electing God. This statement answers the question of the Subject of the eternal election of grace. And the second is that Jesus Christ is elected man. This statement answers the question of the object of the eternal election of grace.

The man who is isolated over against God is as such rejected by God. But to be this man can only be by the godless man's own choice. The witness of the community of God to every individual consists in this: that this choice of the godless man is void; that he belongs eternally to Jesus Christ and therefore is not rejected, but elected by God in Jesus Christ; that the rejection which he deserves on account of his perverse choice is borne and cancelled by Jesus Christ; and that he is appointed to eternal life with God on the basis of the righteous, divine decision.

Certainly the election of Jesus Christ relativises the election of individuals, but it also establishes their election alongside and apart from Him. Their election is not void because it can be real or significant only when included in the election of Jesus Christ. It is, indeed, their election which is at issue in the election of Jesus Christ. It is in order that every man may understand that he has been elected in his authentic individuality that the election of Jesus Christ must be attested and proclaimed to him. The individual who as the original object of divine election is for all the rest Another does not deprive them by that in which He precedes them, but preceding them in everything—He is indeed the original object of election—He is everything for them and gives them all things.[63]

Questions: How does Barth explain the relationship between the *elect* and God's election of Jesus Christ? What does the passage tell us about Barth's view of God ?

Criticisms of Barth's View of God's Election

Two main arguments have been made against Barth's theology of election. First, some accuse Barth of teaching universal election and universal salvation (i.e., universalism). For them, Barth's theology of election does not

63. Ibid., 115, 145, 306, 310.

account for the biblical passages that speak of God's judgment of those who reject God's work in Jesus Christ. Second, some accuse Barth of misunderstanding the expression "in him" (*en autō* in Greek) in Eph 1:4, which refers to Jesus Christ. Some argue that the object of election according to Eph 1:4 is "us" (*hēmas* in Greek) and not Jesus Christ. While Barth's critics disagree on the identity of "us" (for the Arminians, "us" refers to those whom God has chosen on the basis of their faith, and for the Calvinists, "us" refers to those whom God has unconditionally chosen to save), they agree that Eph 1:4 does not present Jesus as the "object" of God's election but rather as the "executor" of God's election.[64] Barth is aware that when taken on its own (and also on an exegetical ground), Eph 1:4 does not present Jesus as the *elected man* or both the *electing God* and the *elected man*. To resolve this exegetical problem, Barth appeals to John 1 to show that God's Word (*Logos* in Greek) who became Jesus of Nazareth (John 1:14) has been with God from the beginning and as such God's election is not grounded in an abstract divine decree but rather in the person of Jesus Christ.[65] People become God's "elect" because they are "in Christ."

Table 2.1

Summary of Arminius', Calvin's, and Barth's Views of the Doctrine of Election

Theologian	Nature and Basis of Election	Jesus' Role in Election	Object of God's Election
Arminius	• Election is God's gracious choice to save people whom God foreknew would freely (with the help of God's *prevenient grace*) believe in Christ.	• Jesus is the executor of God's election.	• Some individuals whom God *conditionally* (on the basis of their faith) elected in eternity.
Calvin	• Election is God's gracious and *unconditional* choice to save some people.	• Jesus is both the *author* and *executor* of election.	• Some individuals whom God *unconditionally* elected in eternity.
Barth	• Election is the Triune God's choice to save sinful humanity in and through Jesus Christ.	• Jesus is both the *electing God* and the *elected man*.	• Jesus Christ—the one who represents fallen humanity and in whom humanity is redeemed.

64. See Brown, *Karl Barth and the Christian Message*, 106.

65. Cunningham, *What Is Theological Exegesis?*, 22.

Concluding Reflections on the Doctrine of Election

In the context of salvation, the doctrine of election should be understood in terms of the series of choices that the Triune God (although particularly God the Father) has made for the purpose of having a loving relationship with God's creation, particularly human beings. These choices include (*a*) God's choice to be in a loving relationship with human beings; (*b*) God's choice to give human beings freedom to accept or reject God's relationship; (*c*) God's choice of God's Son to embody obedience in a loving relationship and also to be the agent of salvation; (*d*) God's choice of the Holy Spirit to prepare people for Christ and to nurture their faith in Christ; (*e*) God's choice to graciously bestow well-being and eternal life to those who are in a loving relationship with God; and (*f*) God's choice of the church (the community of Christ-followers) as the proclaimer of God's salvific work. This series of choices must be held together in our doctrine of election. Therefore, any doctrine of election that focuses on only some of these divine providential choices is doomed to distort the scriptural teaching on God's election to salvation. We should not take these divine choices piecemeal but rather cohesively, as interconnected constants in the drama of salvation.

The Holy Spirit's Role in Salvation

As in many other areas of Christian doctrine, the Holy Spirit's role in humanity's salvation is usually hidden in the discussions of the roles of God (the Father) and Jesus Christ. Such marginalization has done a disservice to both pnuematology (discourse about the person and work of the Holy Spirit) and soteriology. The Greek Orthodox theologian Kallistos Ware has noted that a major reason for the marginalization of the Holy Spirit and the difficulty in identifying the specific work of the Holy Spirit is that "the Holy Spirit . . . points, not to himself, but to the risen Christ."[66] The Christian Scriptures (particularly the New Testament), however, assign numerous soteriological roles to the Holy Spirit. I will focus on one of these roles in this section.

Holy Spirit as Regenerator

The word "regenerator" is used here in the sense of "one who brings back to life" or "one who gives new life" to people who are dead in sin.

66. Ware, *Orthodox Way*, 94.

"Regeneration" (*palingenesia* in Greek) means "new birth," or to be "born again" (John 3:16). In his letter to the Christians of Rome, the Apostle Paul reminds them that God (the Father) has given them new life *through* the Holy Spirit (Rom 8:9–11). In this passage, the Holy Spirit is presented as the executor of the regenerating work of God. Paul in some of his letters also assigns the "author" of the work of regeneration to God the Father (Eph 2:5; Col 2:13). But is the Holy Spirit merely the "executor" of regeneration or is the Holy Spirit also, theologically speaking, the "regenerator"? Two arguments can be made in support of the position that the Holy Spirit is equally the author of regeneration. First, on a Trinitarian ground, God the Father can be presented as the source of life and work of the Triune God. The Father, in eternity, begot the Son and breathed out the Holy Spirit. Also, in the economy of salvation, the Father, in eternity, commissioned the Son and the Holy Spirit to accomplish specific tasks. While God the Father may be construed as the remote author of regeneration (because God the Father commissioned the Holy Spirit to do the work of regeneration), the Holy Spirit is the *immediate* author of regeneration because the Holy Spirit is the one that quickens a sinner (who is dead in sin) and gives the sinner a new life.

Second, being the *author* of regeneration does not disqualify the Holy Spirit as the *executor* of regeneration. The Holy Spirit has these dual roles. In John 6:63, Jesus described the Holy Spirit as the one who "gives life." Earlier, in John 3, Jesus told Nicodemus, a Jewish religious leader, "unless one is born again he cannot see the kingdom of God" (John 3:3 ESV).[67] The strangeness of Jesus' language of one being "born again" prompted Nicodemus to pose the question, "How can a man be born when he is old? Can he enter a second time into his mother's womb and be born?" (John 3:4). On realizing that Nicodemus misunderstood him, Jesus responded by making a direct connection between being *born again* and being *born of the Spirit* (John 3:5–8). Here the Greek word *anothen* is better translated as "anew" rather than "again," or "from above." Nicodemus needed to experience a new birth or a new life that is given and governed by the transformative power of the Holy Spirit in order to understand the nature of God's kingdom proclaimed by Jesus Christ.

Regeneration is the Holy Spirit's work of (metaphorically speaking) *forming Jesus Christ in the life of people*, to use the words of the Apostle Paul (Gal 4:19). The regenerative work of the Holy Spirit involves illuminating one's intellect, liberating one's will from bondage to sin, and cleansing one's

---

67. The Greek word *anothen* can mean "again," "anew," or "above." Jesus' words may be translated as "born from above," "born anew," or "born again."

life in order for the person to conform to the image of Jesus Christ.[68] Theologians have disagreed on the scope of the regenerative work of the Holy Spirit. Also, they have disagreed on the relationship between the Holy Spirit's work of regeneration and human actions such as the sacrament of baptism and faith.

Some theologians equate regeneration with *sanctification*—the Holy Spirit's lifelong work of transforming believers to live in conformity with the life of Jesus Christ (Rom 12:1–2). Some theologians have linked regeneration to *conversion*—in this context, regeneration is a one-time experience in which the Holy Spirit renews the life of an unbeliever, making her or him a believer. To John Wesley, for example, regeneration entails "being inwardly changed by the almighty operation of the Spirit of God—changed from sin to holiness, renewed in the image of him that created us."[69] Being born again (i.e., regeneration), for Wesley, is required for sinners to be able to please God. Wesley also argues that regeneration "is not the *progress* . . . or the whole of *sanctification*, but the *beginning* of it—as the natural birth is not the whole of life, but only the entrance upon it."[70]

> "In short, regeneration occurs as the Spirit applies Christ's work of reconciliation to us in order thereby to transform our hostility toward God into fellowship with him."
>
> —Stanley Grenz,
> *Theology for the Community of God*, 434

Other theologians associate regeneration with the *sacrament of water baptism*. In the theologies of some early theologians such as Augustine, water baptism is necessary for the new life or new birth of an infant. Some theologians within the Reformed tradition, particularly those who hold the Calvinistic view of election, understand regeneration somewhat synonymously with *effectual calling*—that is, the Holy Spirit's act of granting to an unbeliever a new life by illuminating his or her heart and mind to see God's salvific work (internal call) through the hearing of the gospel (external call).[71] Yet other theologians imagine the regenerative work of the Holy Spirit in the context of the universality of the salvific work of God. A major concern of such theologians is that placing too much "emphasis on the uniqueness of Jesus Christ" creates the impression that those who do not hear about Jesus Christ are excluded from God's work of salvation.[72] In

---

68. Ferguson, *Holy Spirit*, 121–22.

69. Wesley, *Doctrine of Original Sin*, in Wesley, *Works*, 12:298.

70. Ibid., 300.

71. Horton, *Christian Faith*, 573–74.

72. Pinnock, *Flame of Love*, 186.

what follows, I will discuss the doctrine of regeneration within the context of water baptism and the universality of God's salvation.

HOLY SPIRIT'S REGENERATION AND INFANT BAPTISM

I will use the Roman Catholic teaching on infant baptism as an example of the theological position that connects the regenerative work of the Holy Spirit to the sacrament of baptism. Although the term regeneration or the more common parlance "born again" is not popular in Roman Catholicism, the concept is discussed in Roman Catholic soteriology. Arthur Canales has noted that the expression "born again" is in fact appalling to most Roman Catholics because it conjures up negative feelings that are rooted in the term's association with the Evangelical fundamentalists "who do not have an authentic spirit of ecumenism, but rather a spirit of division, strife and anti-Catholicism."[73] Canales notes that Roman Catholics prefer the expression "born from above" to "born again."

For most Roman Catholic theologians, however, regeneration, faith, and the sacrament of baptism are important aspects of the process of a conversion experience.[74] In the official teaching (*ecclesiastical magisterium*) of Roman Catholicism, the faith (not necessarily the *faithfulness*) of the church is an important factor in the sacrament of baptism's conveyance of God's gracious work of salvation to an infant who lacks the cognitive capacity to make a personal profession of faith.[75] This means that a personal faith is not a necessary precondition for the reception of the sacrament of baptism. While the Roman Catholic Church recognizes that sometimes the New Testament seems to present a sequence in which faith precedes the sacrament of baptism, it insists that a deeper reflection on the New Testament, as shown by the Council of Trent (1545–63), indicates that "baptism is not simply a sign of faith, it also is a cause of faith."[76] The short passage below highlights some of the arguments made by the Roman Catholic Church in support of the necessity of infant baptism and its relation to God's work of salvation.

73. Canales, "Rebirth of Being 'Born Again,'" 99.

74. Duffy, "Baptism and Confirmation," 213–14.

75. "Traditional Teaching on Infant Baptism," in *Official Catholic Teachings, Update,* 358.

76. Ibid., 359.

> For baptism shows forth the Father's prevenient love; it gives human beings a share in the paschal mystery of the Son; it bestows on them a new life in the Spirit; it leads them to a divine heritage; and it makes them members of Christ's body, which is the Church.
>
> For all these reasons, the warning Christ addresses to us in the Gospel according to John: "No one can enter into God's kingdom without being begotten of water and spirit," is to be taken as an invitation that is inspired by a universal and infinite love. The words are those of a Father who calls all of His children and desires that they attain to the greatest possible good.
>
> The transmission of the faith and the administration of baptism, which are closely connected in this mandate [the Great Commission; see Matt 28:19], play a necessary role in the Church's mission, which is universal and can never cease to be universal.
>
> The fact that infants are not yet able to make a personal profession of faith does not prevent the Church from conferring the sacrament [of baptism] on them since she [the Church] baptizes them in virtue of her own faith. This point of doctrine was clearly set forth by St. Augustine, who wrote: "Infants are brought forward in order to receive spiritual grace, not so much from those whose hands they are carried . . . as from the entire society of holy believers. Mother Church, which exists in the saints, does this in her entirety because in her entirety she brings forth all and each."[77]

Holy Spirit's Regeneration and Universal accessibility of Salvation

An extensive discussion on the work of the Holy Spirit outside the church will be taken up in the next chapter. In this section, I will highlight the viewpoints that argue the Holy Spirit is operating both within and outside of the Christian community. Theologians that associate the regenerative work of the Holy Spirit with the universal accessibility of salvation understand regeneration as part of the larger work of the Holy Spirit in the world from creation to redemption. The African theologian Kä Mana has argued that the Holy Spirit "is the guarantee and the permanent force behind what the Son reveals, by firmly rooting God again into the fabric of the world."[78] Some who hold the position that the Holy Spirit is an agent of God's salvific work contend that the Holy Spirit's work in the world is "geographically"

77. Ibid., 356–58.

78. Mana, *Christians and Churches in Africa*, 72.

larger than the work of Jesus of Nazareth, the Christ. The Spirit of God has been operating in the world before the Incarnation. In the words of Clark Pinnock, "The mystery of God was uniquely and unsurpassably revealed in Jesus (particularity), but this happened with the aid of the Holy Spirit, who had always been working in creation and in history before that time (universality). God sent his Son in the 'fullness of time' to a work being prepared by the Spirit (Gal 4:4)."[79] Pinnock goes on to note that the Holy Spirit precedes Christian missionaries in mission fields. The Holy Spirit is "already present," he writes, "in all places where" the missionaries go.[80]

In recent years, some theologians have become interested in exploring *pneumatico-centric* (Spirit-centered) and *pneumatico-trinitarian* (Spirit-Trinity) soteriologies as a way of underscoring that a *Christo-centric* (Christ-centered) soteriology is not the only viable way of exploring the universal accessibility of God's salvation.[81] Pentecostal theologians such as Amos Yong, focusing on Christian theology of religions, argue the Bible presents the Holy Spirit as God's universal agent that mediates knowledge of God in the world.[82] Some, like Pinnock, aim to show in their soteriologies that the Holy Spirit may accomplish the salvific preparatory work of salvation in all people through religions. Other theologians such as Najeeb George Awad aim to show that people of other religions can "experience God's salvation by means of the particular work of the Holy Spirit" even if they have not known about Jesus Christ.[83] To Awad, the particularity of God's mediation of salvation (through Jesus Christ) should not exclude or eclipse God's universal mediation of salvation (through the Holy Spirit).[84] Whether or not an appeal to a Spirit-centered soteriology moves the discussion on Christian understandings of God's salvation beyond the depth or width of a Christ-centered soteriology remains to be seen. I will take up this issue in chapter 3 ("Christian Theologies of Religions").

Jesus' Role in Salvation

In volume 1 of *Introducing Christian Theologies*, I discussed the identity of Jesus Christ, focusing on his humanity and divinity as construed in Christianity. In this section, I will concentrate on theological interpretations of his

79. Pinnock, *Flame of Love*, 197–98.

80. Ibid., 199.

81. See Awad, "Theology of Religions, Universal Salvation, and the Holy Spirit."

82. Yong, *Beyond the Impasse*, 37.

83. Awad, "Theology of Religions," 253.

84. Ibid.

death, particularly how it relates to Christian soteriology. Jesus is proclaimed to be the savior of the world by the majority of Christians. The Apostle Peter,

FOCUS QUESTION:
What does it mean to say that Jesus of Nazareth, the Christ, is the savior of the world?

before the Jewish religious and political leaders, declared: "Salvation is found in no one else, for there is no other name under heaven given to men by which we must be saved" (Acts 4:12 NIV). The force of Peter's declaration about Jesus may elude contemporary hearers who are unaware that for Peter's Jewish audience the gift of salvation is Yahweh's prerogative (Ps 53:6). For them, Peter was not merely guilty of religious naiveté but also of blasphemy.

The centrality of the death of Jesus Christ in Christianity is evident even to the most casual observer of Christian worship and rituals. It is not unusual to find crosses inside church buildings and in the homes of Christians. It has become a common practice in certain Christian denominations for Christians to make the sign of the cross on themselves or on other people. Some Christians today wear necklaces and wristbands with a sign of the cross. Many Christians today proudly and openly sing songs with lyrics that revolve around the cross of Jesus Christ. But the freedom and openness with which Christians today speak of the cross of Jesus Christ was missing in the earliest Christian practice and worship. The Apostle Paul speaks of the scandal of the cross of Jesus Christ when he writes: "we preach Christ crucified, a stumbling block to Jews and folly to Gentiles, but to those who are called, both Jews and Greeks, Christ the power of God and wisdom of God" (1 Cor 1:23–24 ESV). The cross was not a popularly used symbol in the earliest Christian communities. The reasons for this were, first, the fear of its direct association with Jesus Christ that exposed Christians to Roman persecution. Second, there was a quest to steer away from the scandal of the cross because of "its association with the execution of common criminals."[85] Third, the cross was associated with the ideas of exclusion, curse, and disgust.[86]

Why should a form of death, which was considered inappropriate for Roman citizens except in extreme cases of treason, become a universal symbol for a religion? Jürgen Moltmann has argued that the cross of Jesus Christ is the foundation of Christianity. Many Christians will agree with him with little hesitation. Moltmann also contends that the task of Christian theology is that of "committing itself radically to the event which is the origin of faith

85. Stott, *Cross of Christ*, 20.
86. Moltmann, *Crucified God*, 33.

in the cross; that is, of becoming a theology of the cross."[87] But how and why did a shameful death, which signified alienation from God, death of the one accursed by God, and exclusion from God's community, become a central event that defined the identity of Christianity? In order to do justice to this question, I will explore the following: (*a*) Jesus' understanding of his death, and also the post-Easter understandings of the meaning and significance of his death in some earliest Christian communities; and (*b*) major theological interpretations of the meaning and significance of Jesus' death from the second century CE to the present.

Jesus' Self-Understanding of His Anticipated Death and the Post-Easter Understandings of His Death

Theologians who want to know what Jesus believed about his life, experience, and work will need to depend on the *reconstructed information* preserved in the writings of the New Testament, particularly in the Gospels. To put it differently, we can only hear Jesus through the writings and theological lenses of his earliest followers.[88] It will be helpful to approach Jesus' understanding of his death by highlighting his prediction of his death and his understanding of the purpose or significance of his death. That Jesus anticipated his death was clearly indicated in his passion predictions. In fact, he spoke about it in a way that made some of his disciples (if not all of them) doubt if he was really the expected Messiah (see Matt 16:16–23).

The disciples must have wondered: the Messiah is expected to bring political freedom to God's people by crushing his enemies; if our master really believes he will be killed by the enemies of God and the people of Israel, then it is possible he is not the Messiah. Such an assumption would explain Peter's stern rebuke of Jesus: "Never, Lord! This shall never happen to you." For Peter, it was not possible for the Messiah to die a kind of death that was reserved for people who are under God's curse and excluded from God's community (Deut 21:23; cf. Gal 3:13). It was this Jewish understanding of the Messiah that made Cleopas (or perhaps his

> "Jesus answered them, 'Destroy this temple, and I will raise it again in three days.' But the temple he had spoken of was his body. After he was raised from the dead, his disciples recalled what he had said. Then they believed the Scripture and the words that Jesus had spoken."
>
> John 2:19, 21–22 NIV

87. Ibid., 37.

88. Morris, *Cross in the New Testament*, 14.

unnamed companion) say, with great frustration and disappointment, "we had hoped that he was the one who was going to redeem Israel" (Luke 24:21 NIV).

It is not striking that Jesus predicted or expected his death; after all he was deeply disliked by some Jewish religious leaders and the Roman political leaders. The Jewish leaders considered his teaching a distortion of the established Jewish tradition and theologies. The Romans feared his teaching could incite rebellion that would disrupt the *pax Romana* (Roman peace). So, for many Romans, the death of Jesus was nothing more than the death of a common criminal or a political traitor. What is, however, striking is Jesus' belief that his death was not the end of his story even though his disciples could not immediately see any hope for their master beyond the cruelty of the Roman crucifixion. John reminded his readers that it was only after Jesus' resurrection that his disciples "believed the Scripture and the words that Jesus had spoken" about his death and resurrection (John 2:22 NIV).

In Mark's gospel account, Jesus described his function as the Son of God in a way that overturned the Jewish messianic expectations. The "Son of Man," he said "did not come to be served, but to serve, and to give his life as a ransom for many" (Mark 10:45). In parabolic and metaphoric ways he conveyed similar predictions. "I am the good shepherd. The good shepherd lays down his life for the sheep. . . . The reason my Father loves me is that I lay down my life—only to take it up again. No one takes it from me, but I lay it down of my own accord. I have authority to lay it down and authority to take it up again. This command I received from my Father" (John 10:11, 17–18 NIV). Again he said, "This is my blood of the covenant, which is poured out for many for the forgiveness of sins. I tell you, I will not drink of this fruit of the vine from now on until that day when I drink it anew with you in my Father's kingdom" (Matt 26:28–29 NIV). The writers of the Gospels incorporated Jesus' prediction of his death and resurrection in their materials, although (in most cases) in paraphrased forms. For example, Mark wrote, "He [Jesus] began to teach them that the Son of Man must suffer many things and be rejected by the elders, chief priests and teachers of the law, and that he must be killed and after three days rise again" (Mark 8:31 NIV). Most probably the earliest extant recorded account of the first Christians' knowledge of and belief in the purpose of Jesus' death and resurrection is 1 Thess 1:10. Here, the Apostle Paul wrote, ". . . and to wait for his Son from heaven, whom he raised from the dead—Jesus, who rescues us from the coming wrath" (NIV).

What is special about the death of Jesus? If the Jewish religious leaders of Jesus' time demanded his crucifixion because they deemed his teaching and self-estimation blasphemous (John 5:16–30), why did his followers understand his death as the event used by Yahweh to accomplish something positive for humanity? How was the death of Jesus different from the deaths of false prophets, thieves, and religious martyrs of his day? How on earth did the death of Jesus on the cross become the ground for God's salvation—forgiveness for human sins and restoration of human beings to divine fellowship? Christian theologians have answered these questions in different ways. Their answers can be subsumed into the *constitutive* and *illustrative* perceptions of the meaning of the death of Jesus.[89] Those who hold the constitutive view of the death of Jesus Christ argue that in the death of Jesus Christ God accomplished something necessary for the salvation of God's creation. Conversely, those who see the death of Jesus Christ merely as illustrative insist it is intended to teach a spiritual lesson, perhaps God's love for humanity. In this sense, then, the death of Jesus Christ is not a precondition for human salvation. But there is no need to treat the constitutive and illustrative views as mutually exclusive. The death of Jesus Christ on the cross simultaneously conveys God's critique of humanity's quest for ontological freedom—the desire to become independent of God and to be human in a way God does not desire for human beings (Mark 12:1–11)—and also God's identification with and restoration of human beings to what God intends for them. In the cross of Jesus Christ God both suffers and undoes human pain and injuries. As Rowan Williams observes,

> Without [the cross of Jesus], we cannot begin to understand forgiveness of sins. Jesus crucified is God crucified, so we believe. Jesus is the total and final embodiment in history of God's loving mercy; and so this cross is a unique, terrible, extreme act of violence—a summary of all sin. It represents the human rejection of love. And not even that can destroy God: with the wounds of the cross still disfiguring his body, he returns out of hell to his disciples and wishes them peace. Because Jesus as preacher and teacher had proclaimed and enacted God's identification with the world of human beings, Jesus the condemned criminal speaks of God's presence in the extremity of suffering, in abandonment and death—God as victim. And thus he proclaims God as the one who, above all others, has the right to forgive.[90]

Christians, however, face another crucial question, namely, what is the warrant for believing that God has actually acted in and through the death of Jesus Christ? For Williams, the answer to this question is "faith." He

89. McGrath, *Christian Theology*, 407.
90. Williams, "Forgiveness of Sin," 80.

writes, "To see God in Christ crucified is a matter of faith; to believe in the unyielding and inexhaustible love of God is a matter of faith; and to believe there is a future for us despite the reality of our sins is a matter of faith."[91] This faith—a complete trust—must include a belief in God's existence, God's ability to raise Jesus from the dead, and God's decision to localize God's presence in Jesus of Nazareth. Was Jesus willing to die because he hoped his death would move people's heart to follow his teaching and his understandings of God and the world? Was Jesus a martyr and one who died for what he believed? Perhaps we should narrow our questions to: What did Jesus expect his death on the cross to accomplish?

Jesus' prediction of his death has several theological implications. I will highlight only two here. First, it appears that *Jesus believed his death was what God [the Father] willed for him and therefore was central to his life and ministry*. His prayer and request to God at Gethsemane shows he construed his death in this manner. "'Abba, Father,' he said, 'everything is possible for you. Take this cup from me. Yet not what I will, but what you will'" (Mark 14:36 NIV). Bernard Ramm argues that for the Apostle John, Jesus' crucifixion is "a date kept by the Son with the Father." To Ramm, John used the Greek words *hora* (hour) in 1:39, 2:4, 11:9, *kairos* (season) in 7:6–8, and *entole* (commandment) in 10:18 to express Jesus' death as a "date" with God the Father.[92]

Second, *by predicting his death (because he was convinced it was what God had willed for him), and resisting the temptation to reject this will of God for him, Jesus exemplified a profound act of obedience to God*. Although God willed—or to put it in another way, God allowed Jesus to suffer—the horror of the cross, it is important to note that God did not force Jesus to accep death. Jesus submitted to the Roman crucifixion out of his own volition as an act of obedience to God the Father. The willingness of Isaac to die at the hands of his father, Abraham, is echoed here (Gen 22:69–19). Just as Isaac left his life and death in the hands of Abraham, Jesus also left his life and death in the hands of God, whom he fondly called *Abba*, "father." Of course, the difference between the obedience of Isaac and Jesus is that while Abraham hoped that God would provide a lamb for the sacrifice, Jesus did not expect God to provide another sacrificial lamb for he believed he was the "lamb" (Mark 10:45; John 1:29). Citing an old christological ode, the Apostle Paul poetically described Jesus' act of obedience to God in the following way: "And being found in appearance as a man, he humbled himself and became obedient to death—even death on a cross" (Phil 2:8). Jesus'

91. Ibid., 81.

92. Ramm, *Evangelical Christology*, 87.

obedience, even to the point of dying a shameful death, was for Paul, an indication that Jesus Christ rejected self-ambitions and vain conceit.

Christians typically interpret the death of Jesus Christ soteriologically. They believe that God achieved something constructively and/or illustratively in the cross-event. Some of the earliest followers of Jesus stunned the Romans, Greeks, and Jews when they began to proclaim that the death of their master on the cross was an "event of glory and not an event of shame."[93] But for early Christians, God intentionally chose to use a shameful event to "shame the wise." In the words of Paul, "Jews demand miraculous signs and Greeks look for wisdom, but we preach Christ crucified: a stumbling block to Jews and foolishness to Gentiles, but to those whom God has called, both Jews and Greeks, Christ the power of God and the wisdom of God" (1 Cor 1:22–27 NIV). I turn now to discuss some of the major Christian soteriological interpretations of Jesus' death.

Major Soteriological Interpretations of Jesus' Death

Given that Jesus' earliest followers believed he was the Messiah (Mark 8:30), his death was bewildering to them. It was the hope of the Jewish people that the Messiah would conquer his enemies and also establish the reign of God. They did not expect the Messiah to die shamefully, such as by crucifixion.[94] Jesus' death on the cross, therefore, was either an indication that he was not the expected Messiah or God's critique of the traditional Jewish understanding of the function and life of the Messiah. Christians believe that Jesus is in fact the Messiah, albeit the one who is also God incarnate (see *Introducing Christian Theologies*, vol. 1, ch. 5). Christian theologians have understood Jesus' death on the cross and its soteriological implications in a manner that has followed three broad pathways, namely, the *substitutionary violent-atonement* pathway, the *nonviolent-atonement* pathway, and the *non-atonement* pathway.

> FOCUS QUESTION:
> What is the soteriological significance of Jesus' death as imagined by Christians?

93. Ibid., 88.

94. This is perhaps one of the reasons why Peter rebuked Jesus when he spoke about his death.

The Substitutionary Violent-Atonement Pathway

Theologians whose interpretations of Jesus' death follow this pathway see it as the penalty for humanity's sin, which is paid *on behalf of* (substitutionary) human beings in order to *compensate* (atone) for their sins. Second Corinthians 5:21 is a common biblical passage employed by theologians to support this interpretation of the cross-event. Paul in this passage wrote, "For our sake he [God the Father] made him [Jesus Christ] to be sin who knew no sin, so that in him we might become the righteousness of God" (ESV). In the *substitutionary violent-atonement* path, the death of Jesus Christ, a violent event, is understood to be necessary in order (*a*) to appease God's wrath or compensate for the insult on God's honor caused by human sin, (*b*) to demonstrate God's love for humanity, (*c*) to show that human beings broke God's law, and (*d*) to reconcile sinful humanity to God (for some, God imputes humanity's sin and its consequences to Jesus Christ).[95] All the understandings of Jesus' death that have followed the *substitutionary violent-atonement* path share the assumption that God willed and endorsed the death of Jesus Christ. Four theories of the soteriological significance of Jesus' death can be classified under the substitutionary violent-atonement pathway.

Satisfaction Theory: Jesus as God's Honor-bearer

Description: In the satisfaction theory, sin is an affront to God's honor. Sin implies disobedience and disloyalty. The satisfaction theory should be understood in its medieval feudalistic context. Disloyalty to a king in the medieval world required compensation in order to amend the honor of the king. For example, a knight who is disloyal to a king dishonors the king. In order to amend (and also preserve) his honor and pacify his anger, the king normally would require the knight to pay restitution. Such compensation is required in order to maintain harmony, dignity, and stability of the kingdom. In the satisfaction theory, the death of Jesus, which is grounded in his obedience to God the Father, brings harmony to the world and also brings honor to God the Father.

Proponent: Anselm of Canterbury (ca. 1033–1109 CE) is credited with the articulation of the satisfaction theory. Like in the medieval world, the death of Jesus Christ, for Anselm, is a compensation required to amend the

95. John Wesley wrote, "God imputes our *sins* or the *guilt* of them to Christ. He consented to be responsible for them, to suffer the punishment due for them" (*Doctrine of Original Sin*, in Wesley, *Works*, 12:420).

injury to God's honor caused by sin. The difference between the death of Jesus Christ and the compensation that a knight who is disloyal to a king is required to pay is that human beings are unable to provide an adequate compensation for God's honor. On the one hand, since sin has caused injury to God's (i.e., God the Father's) honor, compensation is required. One who is human is required to pay the compensation (which requires both complete obedience and death—*death* because the wages of sin is death; see Rom 6:23). On the other hand, since human beings are finite and therefore unable to provide an adequate compensation for an infinite God, one who is merely human cannot provide a satisfactory compensation. Anselm reasoned that only a person who is both divine and human can provide an adequate compensation for human insult to God's honor. Since human beings cannot provide the required compensation, God takes it upon God's self to provide the compensation through God's eternal son who became Jesus of Nazareth. As Kathryn Tanner notes, in Anselm' soteriology, Jesus "offers up to death his own sinless life in honor to God, thereby rendering the satisfaction that human beings owe God but in a divine way that their dishonoring of God demands and merely human lives are incapable of providing."[96] For Anselm, the primary reason for the Incarnation is to provide a satisfactory compensation demanded by God for the injury to God's honor caused by the sins of human beings.

The excerpt below highlights Anselm's interpretation of the Incarnation of Jesus Christ and crucifixion.

Do you not understand that if any other person redeemed man from eternal death, man would rightly be reckoned as his servant? But in that case man would in no sense have been restored to the dignity he would have had if he had not sinned. For he who was to be the servant of God alone, and equal in everything to the good angels, would be the servant of a being who was not God, and whom the angels did not serve.

God did not compel Christ to die, when there was no sin in him, but Christ himself freely underwent death, not by yielding up his life as an act of obedience, but on account of his obedience in maintaining justice, because he so steadfastly persevered in it that he brought death on himself.

It can be said that the Father commanded him to die, when he gave him the commandment through which he met death. In this sense, therefore, he did "as the Father gave" him "commandment," and drank the "chalice" which his "Father gave him," and became "obedient" to the Father "unto death," and

96. Tanner, "Incarnation, Cross, and Sacrifice," 36.

so "learned obedience by the things which he suffered"—that is, how far obedience should be maintained.

It is true that he speaks of the Father's will, but not because the Father preferred the death of his Son to his life—rather, because the Father was unwilling for the human race to be restored unless man performed a great act, equal to the Son's death. Since reason did not demand what another could not do, the Son says that the Father wills his death, while he himself prefers to suffer the death rather than leave the human race unsaved.[97]

Questions: Why does Anselm believe that the death of Jesus Christ is necessary for human salvation? Why did God the Father require the death of Jesus Christ?

Criticism: The satisfaction theory has been criticized by some theologians for presenting God as an unforgiving being whose mercy toward humanity is contingent upon satisfying personal honor and dignity. Why does God not simply will to forgive humans? Why does God require a violent act as a means for redeeming humanity? Whether God *willed* the violent act (Acts 2:23) or merely *allowed* it, does not resolve the question regarding God's use of violence as a means to forgive, redeem, and reconcile sinful humanity.[98] Some feminist theologians have argued that the traditional understanding of Jesus' death as the penalty for the sin of humankind suggests divine child abuse. It presents God as an abusive father who inflicts enormous pain and suffering on an innocent child. Joanne Carlson Brown has questioned the Christian belief that a child "who suffers without even raising a voice" is "the hope of the world."[99] Some theologians also fault Anselm for reducing God's soteriological work vis-à-vis the death of Jesus Christ to a mere "commercial transaction" between God the Father and Jesus Christ.[100]

97. Anselm, *Why God Became Man*, in Fairweather, *Scholastic Miscellany*, 106, 113, 115.

98. Weaver, "Narrative *Christus Victor*," 1.

99. Brown, "Divine Child Abuse?," 24. For more discussions of this criticism of the traditional understanding of the atonement, see Schüssler Fiorenza, *Jesus: Miriam's Child, Sophia's Prophet*; Peacore, *The Role of Women's Experience in Feminist Theologies of Atonement*.

100. Horton, *Christian Faith*, 504.

MORAL INFLUENCE THEORY: JESUS AS MORAL EXEMPLAR

Description: In Rom 3:25–26, the Apostle Paul wrote that God put forward Jesus Christ "as a propitiation by his blood, to be received by faith. This was to show God's righteousness, because in his divine forbearance he has passed over former sins. It was to show his righteousness at the present time, so that he might be just and justifier of the one who has faith in Jesus" (ESV). The moral influence theory construes Jesus' crucifixion as God's exemplary action for humanity. In this horrific event, God demonstrates God's commitment to pursue a relationship with humans even in their sinfulness. Jesus' death shows God's love for humanity. Also, his death is designed to kindle the love of God in humans and to move them to voluntarily submit to God's will for them as exemplified in the life of obedience of Jesus Christ. The moral influence theory emphasizes the ethical implications of Jesus' death, especially its implication for the Christian life.

Proponent: Peter Abelard (1079–1142 CE), whose interpretation is partly a critique of Anselm's satisfaction theory, developed the moral influence theory. Abelard also rejected the *ransom theory* (the theory that argues Jesus' death is the ransom God paid to Satan in order to secure the freedom of humans from Satan's enslavement). In his critique of the ransom theory, Abelard argued that human beings sinned against God and not against Satan. God has only employed Satan to punish sinners, albeit with God's permission and within the scope God allows. Satan, for Abelard, is like a jailor who punishes an offender on behalf of the state. As such, God cannot pay a ransom to Satan.[101] To Abelard, God intends Jesus's death to be a powerful moral example that is designed to awaken in sinners the desire to love and seek God's relationship. Sin, in Abelard's soteriology, promotes ignorance. Sin also hurts God but God does not need to be appeased. No propitiation is really needed. It is divine knowledge of love that is needed and required to deal with sin. Jesus' mission was to teach and to illuminate the hearts of people. His work from the beginning to the end is the manifestation of God's love. The death of Jesus demonstrates God's love. This can be understood as a "sacrificial death" only in the sense that God allowed Jesus to die in order to illuminate the world by God's wisdom and to compel or excite human beings to love God.

The short passage below is taken from Abelard's commentary and theological reflection on Rom 3:20–26.

---

101. Peter Abelard, *Commentary on the Epistle to the Romans*, 165.

How does the Apostle say that we are justified or reconciled to God through the death of his Son, who should have been all the more angry with man because men forsook him so much more in crucifying his Son, than in transgressing his first commandment in paradise with the taste of one apple?

Nevertheless it seems to us that in this we are justified in the blood of Christ and reconciled to God, that it was through this matchless grace shown to us that his Son received our nature, and in that nature, teaching us both by word and by example, persevered to the death and bound us to himself even more through love, so that when we have been kindled by so great a benefit of divine grace, true charity might fear to endure nothing for his sake. We do not doubt that the benefit kindled the ancient fathers, expecting this through faith, in the supreme love of God just as it kindled the men of the time of grace, since it is written, "And they who went before him and they who followed him cried out, saying, 'Hosanna to the son of David,'" etc. Each one is also made more righteous after the Passion of Christ than before; that is, he loves God more, because the completed benefit kindles him in love more than a hoped-for benefit.

Therefore, our redemption is that supreme love in us through the Passion of Christ, which not only frees us from slavery to sin, but gains for us the true liberty of the sons of God, so that we may complete all things by his love rather than by fear.[102]

Questions: What does Abelard's understanding of the death of Jesus Christ say about God's character and God's way of salvation? How does Abelard's interpretation of Jesus' death indicate an emphasis on ethics?

Criticism: A major criticism of the moral influence theory is that it fails to take evil and its destructive power seriously and consequently neither holds human beings responsible for their evil actions nor empowers humans to confront evil. The death of Jesus Christ was a violent human evil action. The cross exposes the evil of violence that destroys lives. The moral influence theory reduces *nonviolence* to "human moral effort guided by an inspiring example."[103]

102. Ibid., 166–68.

103. Finger, "*Christus Victor* as Nonviolence Atonement," 104.

Governmental Theory: Jesus as "Evidence" of God's Breached and Restored Law

Description: In the governmental theory, the world is seen as a form of "government" comprised of a leader of the government and people living within the parameter of the government. God is the head or leader of the government and human beings are God's subjects. As with all governments, law is important for maintaining order. Sin is construed as the transgression of God's law. As the head of the government, God passed an important law: the "soul that sins will die" (Gen 3:3; Ezek 18:20). Since unenforced laws are an incentive for lawlessness, God was determined to enforce the law regarding sin. God accomplished two interrelated things in the death of Jesus Christ. First, Jesus' death demonstrated that God's law has been broken. Second, Jesus' death showed that the penalty for sin has been paid although God did not "*require* such an act of atonement for the purposes of satisfying divine justice."[104] In other words, Jesus' death is designed to satisfy God's "rectoral justice" (the type of justice that relates to God's governance of the world in accordance with God's moral law) and not "retributive justice" (the type of justice that concerns rightful punishment for those who have broken God's law).[105]

Proponent: The Dutch political theorist and theologian Hugo Grotius (1583–1645) was a key proponent of the governmental theory. Grotius' knowledge of medieval law influenced his interpretation of the death of Jesus Christ and how it relates to God's salvific work in the world. For Grotius, an all-powerful God need not (and in fact did not) require any payment for human sin. Jesus' death on the cross, therefore, was not a payment for human sin. Yet he argued that God willed the death of Jesus Christ. But for what purpose did God will the death of Jesus? God, for Grotius, is like a ruler who can relax or alter a "positive law" for the general good of people.[106] A ruler, however, cannot always completely abrogate a law. Failure to enforce a law can endanger the unity and peace of society. For Grotius, God willed the death of Jesus Christ to show that God's law was broken and also to attest to God's forgiveness or willingness to forgive sinners. As Gregg Allison notes, Jesus' "death underscored the terrible nature of sin and emphasized that the law must be respected."[107] Grotius also argued that Jesus' death is the basis of humanity's redemption "because God is induced by it to liberate us from

104. Crisp, "Penal Non-Substitution," 143.

105. Ibid., 148.

106. Grotius, *Defense of the Catholic Faith*, 75.

107. Allison, *Historical Theology*, 403.

punishment." For Grotius, understanding Jesus' death in this way helps one explain the biblical passages that show "Christ died for our sins, that he bore our punishment, and so obtained remission of sins for us, because God was placated by his death."[108]

The following excerpts from *A Defense of the Catholic Faith Concerning the Satisfaction of Christ against Faustus Socinus* capture some of the major themes in Grotius' interpretation of Jesus' death.

And . . . since God, as we have proved, is to be considered here as a ruler, it follows that his act is an act of the administration of justice, generally so called. . . . If we take our stand here, the act of God of which we treat will be the punishment of one to obtain the impunity of another. . . . But if further we have regard to the sanction, or penal law, the act will be a method of relaxing or moderating the same law, which relaxation we call, in these days, dispensation. It may be defined: The act of a superior by which the obligation of an unabrogated law upon certain persons or things is removed. This is the sanction: the man that eateth of the forbidden tree shall surely die [Gen 2:17]. In this passage by one species of sin every class of sin is indicated, as is expressed by the same law more clearly brought out, "Cursed is every one that continueth not in all the precepts of the law" [Deut 27:26]. By the words *death* and *curse*, in these passages, we understand especially eternal death. For this reason it is as if the law had been expressed in the manner: Every man that sinneth shall bear the punishment of eternal death.

But all positive laws are absolutely relaxable; and we are not compelled to resort to hypothetical necessity, of a definite decree, where no mark of such decree exists.

It is a great error to be afraid, as some are, lest in making such concession [that God relaxes positive laws] we do injury to God, as if we made him mutable. The law is not something internal within God, or the will of God itself, but only an effect of that will. It is perfectly certain that the effects of the divine will are mutable. By promulgating a positive law which at some time he may wish to relax God does not signify that he wills anything but what he really does will. God shows that he seriously wills that the law should be valid and obligatory, yet with the reserved right of relaxing it.

To begin, therefore, with the question of justice or injustice, we must first make a distinction between the two following inquiries: whether it were just that Christ should be punished on account of our sins; and whether this could effect anything in obtaining pardon for us.

108. Grotius, *Defense of the Catholic Faith*, 161.

God teaches not what he must do of necessity, but what he has freely decreed to do. It no more follows from this that it is unjust for a son to bear any punishment of his father's crime than it is unjust that the sinner should not die. The passage [Ezek 18:20] itself proves that God is not speaking here of perpetual and immutable right, but of the ordinary course of his providence, which he declares he will hereafter so conduct toward the Jews as to take away all occasion of false accusation.

The act of conferring a reward or benefit is a beneficial act, which by its own nature is possible for all. The act of punishing is an injurious act, which is not granted to all nor for all. That the punishment may be just, it is therefore required that the infliction of penalty be within the power of the punisher. This may occur in three ways—either by the previous right of the punisher, or by the valid consent of the one to be punished, or by the crime of the same. When an act is made lawful in these ways, nothing prevents that it should be ordained as punishment for another's sin, provided there is a certain connection between the one who has sinned and the one who is to be punished. Such a connection must be either natural, as between father and son; or mystic, as between king and people; or voluntary, as between the guilty person and the surety.[109]

Questions: How does Grotius justify God's action for punishing Jesus Christ on behalf of sinful humanity? How does he show that God is within God's rights to relax the law?

Criticism: Some critics of the governmental theory complain that the violent death of Jesus on the cross is too much of a price to pay merely to demonstrate God's law has been broken or God's willingness to forgive sinners. The issue here is, if the death of Jesus Christ is not *absolutely necessary* for human salvation, why should God require it? Holders of the penal substitution theory (see below) argue that there are a host of scriptural passages that teach that Jesus died for humanity's sin. For them, the death of Jesus is constitutive—it made human salvation possible.

109. Ibid., 72–73, 75–76, 81–82, 84, 89.

PENAL SUBSTITUTION THEORY: JESUS AS BEARER OF THE PENALTY OF HUMANITY'S SIN

Description: The penal substitution theory is prominent among Evangelicals. This theory argues that God punished (penal) Jesus Christ in the place (substitution) of sinful humanity. The Nigerian Evangelical theologian Yusufu Turaki contends: "It is at the cross that the full penalty of our SIN [original sin] and sins were paid. [The] Apostle John pointed to Jesus the Messiah and said, 'Behold the Lamb of God [who takes away the sin of the world]' (John 1:36)."[110] In the penal substitution theory, Jesus is the legal substitute, whose death on the cross appeased the wrath of God provoked by humanity's sin. Jesus paid the penalty of death that is due to fallen humanity. Theologians who hold the penal substitution theory of the atonement cite Isaiah 53, Mark 10:45 Heb 2:17, 9:23–24, and Gal 3:13 among other biblical passages, in support of their theory. They sometimes cite the Jewish ritual of sin offering, in which the offender lays his hand on the animal offered (Lev 4:4). They also cite the Jewish celebration of the *Day of the Atonement*—the day when the high priest would lay his hands on a goat (before it was sent into the desert) as he confessed the sins of the nation to God (Lev 16:21–22). For theologians who hold the penal substitution theory, the laying of hands on the animal signifies that the offender is identifying with the animal as a penal substitute. In the words of the British Evangelical theologian John Stott, "When we review . . . the Old Testament material (the shedding and sprinkling of blood, the sin offering, the Passover, the meaning of 'sin-bearing,' the scapegoat and Isaiah 53), and consider its New Testament application to the death of Christ, we are obliged to conclude that the cross was a substitutionary sacrifice. Christ died for us. Christ died instead of us."[111]

Proponent: The American theologian Charles Hodge (1797–1878) was one of the prominent proponents of the penal substitution theory in the nineteenth century. Many Evangelicals today continue to defend the penal substitution theory, although with some modifications. Central to Hodge's version of the penal substitution theory is God's justice. For Hodge, God, as a good judge, cannot pardon sin in a manner that fails to satisfy the necessity of justice. Sin brings both divine wrath and alienation. Hodge admits that the death of Jesus Christ can kindle divine love, exert moral influence on people, and demonstrate God's victory over evil powers (as in the *Christus Victor* theory). But for him, the primary purpose of Jesus' death is to

---

110. Turaki, *Unique Christ for Salvation*, 191.

111. Stott, *Cross of Christ*, 149.

bear, on humanity's behalf, the penalty of sin. The excerpt below is taken from his *Systematic Theology*.

> The first and most obvious consequence of sin is subjection to the penalty of the law. The wages of sin is death. Every sin of necessity subjects the sinner to the wrath and curse of God. The first step, therefore, in the salvation of sinners, is their redemption from that curse. Until this is done they are of necessity separated from God. . . . In effecting the salvation of his people, Christ "redeemed them from the curse of the law," not by a mere act of sovereignty, or power; not by moral influence restoring them to virtue, but by being "made a curse for them." No language can be plainer than this. The curse is the penalty of the law. We were subject to that penalty. Christ has redeemed us from that subjection by being made a curse for us (Gal 3:13). That the infinitely exalted and holy Son of God should be "accursed" . . . is so awful an idea, that the Apostle Paul justifies the use of such language by quoting the declaration of Scripture, "Cursed is every one that hangeth on a tree." Suffering, and especially the suffering of death, judicially inflicted on account of sin, is penal. . . . The sufferings of Christ, and especially his death upon the cross, were neither calamities, nor chastisements designed for his own good, nor symbolical or didactic exhibitions, designed to illustrate and enforce truth, and exert a moral influence on others; these are all subordinate and collateral ends. Nor were they the mere natural consequences of his becoming a man and subjecting Himself to the common lot of humanity. They were divine inflictions. It pleased the Lord to bruise Him. He was smitten of God and afflicted. These sufferings were declared to be on account of sin, not his own, but ours. He bore our sins.[112]
>
> **Question:** What does Hodge's text tell us about his association of Jesus' death on the cross with God's punishment for humanity's sin?

Criticism: Critics of the penal substitution theory argue that it presents God as unnecessarily rigid and preoccupied with keeping the penal code. Also, it presents God as a violent "father" who orders the death of his son in order to save others. The main question here is *why* an omnibenevolent God would require a violent act—the crucifixion of Jesus—for the salvation of others. God seems to derive "pleasure or satisfaction from death and

112. Hodge, *Systematic Theology*, 2:516–17.

suffering."[113] Some theologians have responded to the charge by noting that the Bible teaches Jesus' death is the last and ultimate atonement, which puts an end to the shedding of blood as a means of atonement.[114] But Darrin Belousek has called into question the biblical warrant for the penal substitution theory. According to Belousek, the Bible does not teach that sacrificial atonement is the propitiation of God's wrath or the payment of a penalty to God. On the contrary, sacrificial atonement is the means God provides in which God acts to "remove sin, guilt, and impurity and so cleanse pollution from the holy place, things, and people that are consecrated to God's service."[115]

Nonviolent-Atonement Pathway

The second broad direction some Christian theologians have followed in their interpretations of Jesus' death may be described as the "Nonviolent-Atonement" pathway. The goals of the theologians that follow this pathway are threefold. First, they seek to show that the death of Jesus on the cross is neither divinely ordained nor necessary for salvation. Second, they present Jesus' death as an example of human rejection of God and the human propensity to do evil. Third, they seek to demonstrate that God has abrogated the evil human intention of dethroning God by raising Jesus from the dead. I will give two examples below to illustrate the interpretations of Jesus' death that follow the *nonviolent-atonement* pathway.

CHRISTUS VICTOR THEORY: JESUS AS GOD'S VICTORIOUS "WARRIOR"

Description: Spiritual warfare is central to the *Christus Victor* (Latin expression that means "Christ is victorious") theory of the atonement. Jesus' death is understood in the context of a cosmic battle between God and evil powers that are spearheaded by Satan. The death of Jesus Christ appeared to signal God's defeat until God raised him from the dead. By raising Jesus from the dead, God sealed God's victory over the evil powers (Heb 2:14–18). Some proponents of the *Christus Victor* theory, like Gregory Boyd, highlight its cosmic significance and implications for Christians' battle against demonic

---

113. Tanner, "Incarnation, Cross, and Sacrifice," 37.

114. Kärkkäinen, *Christ and Reconciliation*, 321.

115. Belousek, *Atonement, Justice, and Peace*, 189.

forces. To Boyd, "our personal and social victories participate in Christ's cosmic victory. Everything the New Testament says about the soteriological significance of Christ's work is predicated on the cosmic significance of his work."[116]

Proponent: Some versions of the *Christus Victor* theory can be traced back to the works of some early church theologians, especially in the *recapitulation* theory of Irenaeus of Lyons (ca. 130–202 CE)[117] and the *ransom* theory of Origen of Alexandria (ca. 185–254 CE).[118]

In the twentieth century, Gustaf Aulén gave a clearer formulation of the *Christus Victor* theory. He argued that Jesus' death was God's main tactic in drawing the evil forces (including Satan, demons, and the power of sin) closer, and also that the resurrection was God's decisive blow that defeated those forces.[119] More recently, J. Denny Weaver has presented a version of the *Christus Victor* theory that he calls the "Narrative *Christus Victor*." To Weaver, "Jesus' rejection of the sword" should be central to Christians' theological reflections, especially their reflection on the significance of the work of Jesus Christ.[120] He argues that God did not order the death of Jesus Christ. Also, the God incarnate did not come to the world primarily to die but rather to live and to proclaim God's reign in the world. The excerpt below highlights some of the main arguments of Weaver's "Narrative *Christus Victor*" view.

> "He [God's eternal Word that became Jesus Christ] summed up in Himself the ancient formation of Adam."
> —Irenaeus, *Against Heresies* 5.1.1
> (*ANF*, 1:527)

---

116. Boyd, "Christus Victor View," 34.

117. To Irenaeus, God's work of creation is summed up in Jesus Christ. Also, as the "second Adam," Jesus Christ reverses the consequences of humanity's disobedience to God that was embodied by the "first Adam." He writes that when the Son of God "became incarnate, and was made man, He commenced afresh the long line of human beings, and furnished us . . . with salvation; so that what we had lost in Adam—namely, to be according to the image and likeness of God—that we might recover in Christ Jesus" (*Against Heresies* 3.18.1 [*ANF* 1:446]).

118. Origen writes, "And there is nothing absurd in a man [Jesus] having died, and in His death being made not only an example of death endured for the sake of piety, but also the first blow in the conflict which is to overthrow the power of that evil spirit the devil, who had obtained dominion over the whole world" (*Against Celsus* 7.17 [*ANF* 4:617]).

119. Aulén, *Christus Victor: An Historical Study of the Three Main Types of the Idea of the Atonement.*

120. Weaver, *Nonviolent Atonement*, 14.

Narrative Christus Victor restores to the equation the devil that Anselm removed. However, the form taken by the "devil" or "Satan" in narrative Christus Victor differs greatly from the devil envisioned by Anselm.

I follow Walter Wink in understanding the devil or Satan as the accumulation of earthly structures which are not ruled by the reign of God. This devil is real, but it is not a personified being who may or may not have rights in the divine order of things. Wink argued that the principalities and powers, demons, and so on of the Bible are not independent entities that inhabit a place. Instead, they are the "spiritual" dimension of material structures.... It was the total accumulation of evil, the reign of Satan, which killed Jesus—and the blame for his execution should not be limited to specific persons or institutions.... But Jesus is victorious over the rule of Satan only when all dimensions of evil perceive Jesus as a threat and then collectively attempt to eliminate him. The subsequent resurrection of Jesus then reveals the reign of God as the ultimate shaper of reality, and the ultimate power of the universe. The devil or Satan is the name for the locus of all power that does not recognize the rule of God.

In narrative Christus Victor, the cause of Jesus' death is obviously not God.... There is no need to play a sleight-of-hand language game concerning whether Jesus willed himself to die or whether God willed the death of Jesus. In either case, the answer is profoundly "No." Rather, in narrative Christus Victor the Son is carrying out the Father's will by making the reign of God visible in the world—and that mission is so threatening to the world that sinful human beings and the accumulation of evil they represent conspire to kill Jesus. Jesus came not to die but to live, to witness to the reign of God in human history.

When Jesus confronts the rule of evil, as he does in narrative Christus Victor, there is no longer the difficulty of a problematic image for victims of abuse. Jesus depicted in narrative Christus Victor is no passive victim. He is an active participant in confronting evil. Salvation happens when or because Jesus carried out his mission to make the reign of God visible. His saving life shows how the reign of God confronts evil, and is thus our model for confronting evil.[121]

Questions: How does Weaver imagine the identity of Satan and also Satan's role in the death of Jesus Christ? How does he understand the salvific significance of Jesus' life?

121. Weaver, *Nonviolent Atonement*, 306–8.

Criticism: Some versions of the *Christus Victor* theory are criticized for not taking the violent death of Jesus seriously and for presenting suffering as a divine gift. "By denying the reality of suffering and death," writes Joanne Carlson Brown, "the 'Christus Victor' theory of the atonement trivializes tragedy and defames all those who suffer."[122] Also, the *Christus Victor* theory may lead to the Gnostic and Manichean dualisms that assume the world is locked in a cosmic war between two powers (Light and Darkness). Some theologians are also critical of the triumphalist tendency of *Christus Victor*. It may lead people to deny the continuing force and power of evil in the world.[123]

DIVINE SUFFERING THEORY: JESUS AS SELF-SACRIFICING GOD

Description: This theory aims to show that God (the Father) through the cross of the incarnate Son of God (Jesus) suffers the pain inflicted on him by human beings.[124] God did not order the death of Jesus Christ. Jürgen Moltmann contends that to present God as the one who ordered "judges and executioners" to kill Jesus is to make God a monster.[125] God's power and love are hidden in the suffering of Jesus Christ on the cross. God (the Father) suffered when Jesus suffered on the cross.[126] For Moltmann, theologians should not approach the cross as an attempt to understand "what God means for us humans in the cross of Christ." Rather, they are to seek to understand what the *"human cross of Christ means for God."*[127]

Proponent: Theologians whose understandings of the death of Jesus on the cross fit the *divine suffering* theory are indebted to the German Protestant reformer Martin Luther. In the 1518 *Heidelberg Disputation*, Luther proposed that a theologian is one "who comprehends the visible and manifest things of God seen through suffering and the cross. A theologian of glory calls evil good and good evil. A theologian of the cross calls the thing what it actually is."[128] To Luther, we cannot truly see God in God's glory unless we see God in the "humility and shame of the cross."[129] God is hidden in the suffering of Jesus Christ on the cross. God's submission to the

---

122. Brown, "Divine Child Abuse?," 26.

123. Migliore, *Faith Seeking Understanding*, 183.

124. Moltmann, *Way of Jesus Christ*, 177.

125. Ibid.

126. Ibid., 172–74.

127. Moltmann, *Crucified God*, x.

128. Luther, *Heidelberg Disputation*, 31.

129. Ibid., 43–44.

suffering caused by human beings, however, is bewildering. Why did God have to suffer? Jürgen Moltmann answers the question by stating, "What is manifested in the cross is God's suffering of a passionate love for his lost creatures, prepared for sacrifice."[130]

An important scholar whose work on divine suffering is largely ignored in many Christian theological circles is the Japanese theologian Kazoh Kitamori (1916–98). In *Theology of the Pain of God*, Kitamori, whose work is deeply shaped by Luther's theology of the cross, argued that the heart of the Christian gospel is the pain of God.[131] For Kitamori, the Christian Scriptures present God's pain as a way of understanding the God who is hidden or obscured in the cross of Jesus Christ. Kitamori employed both Jeremiah and Paul as his signposts to guide his search into the depth of the pain of God, which is the heart of the Christian gospel. Kitamori contended that God experiences pain when God's love penetrates God's wrath. God's wrath reveals God's love, both of which are expressed in the death of Jesus on the cross.[132] The following short passage will highlight some of Kitamori's theological insights.

God in pain is the God who resolves our human pain by his own. Jesus Christ is the Lord who heals our human wounds by his own (1 Pet 2:24).

First of all, we must proclaim that the gospel is indeed "glad tidings." God in the gospel is the One who resolves our pain and the Lord who heals our wounds. This means that he is our "Savior." What is salvation? Salvation is the message that our God enfolds our broken reality. A God who embraces us completely—this is God our Savior. . . . Accordingly the pain of God which resolves our pain is "love" rooted in his pain. There is reason to believe that the same Hebrew word used in Jeremiah 31:20 and Isaiah 63:15 is translated as "my heart yearns" and "compassion" respectively.

Just as Paul implies "the word of the cross and the resurrection" by his phrases "the word of the cross" (1 Cor 1:18), so I imply "theology of love rooted in God's pain" by the phrase "theology of the pain of God." Luther calls the death of Christ "death against death" (*mors contra mortem*), I call the pain of God "pain against pain" (*dolor contra dolorem*). Just as "death against death" is the resurrection, so "pain against pain" is God's love which resolves our pain. For this reason, the message of the pain of God is called *glad* tidings.

130. Moltmann, *Crucified God*, x.

131. Kitamori, *Theology of the Pain of God*, 19.

132. Ibid., 111.

Why are the glad tidings bound up with the "pain" of God? Why does the Lord who heals our wounds suffer wounds himself? Our reality is such that God ought not to forgive or to enfold it.... The living and true God must sentence us sinners to death. This is the manifestation of "his wrath." "Thus shall my anger spend itself, and I will vent my fury upon them and satisfy myself ..." (Ezek 5:13). This wrath of God is absolute and firm. We may say that the recognition of God's wrath is the beginning of wisdom.

The "pain" of God reflects his will to love the object of his wrath.... God who must sentence sinners to death fought with God who wishes to love them. The fact that this fighting is not two different gods but the same God causes his pain. Here heart is opposed to heart within God.

Sinners are won to complete obedience to God by his love—that is, his pain—which reaches those turning their backs on God's love. If one is obedient, he cannot be separated from the love of God, and one can no longer be separated from the pain of God who captures sinners. What is happening here is the victory of God over sinners. The victory is that of a love which completely penetrates and goes through the pain, a love rooted in the pain of God.[133]

Question: How does God's pain, as explicated by Kazoh Kitamori, bring salvation to humanity?

Criticism: Critics of the divine suffering theory contend that it neither empowers the victims of violence to fight against their oppressors nor offers them liberation from violent, oppressive powers and structures. The theory may also encourage the victims of violence to internalize their victimization or accept their experience simply as God's will for them. JoAnne Marie Terrell argues that the belief Jesus died *sacrificially* on humanity's behalf conjures up the notion of "surrogacy." Writing from the experience of African Americans (especially women) in the United States, Terrell contends that the concept of surrogacy—bearing other people's burdens and suffering—encourages violence and victimization.[134] Terrell asserts, "God did not condone the violence of the cross or black women's surrogacy." On the contrary, "God indeed sent Christ, but for more honorable purposes"—for example, to proclaim God's love for the world.[135] The divine suffering theory also fails

133. Ibid., 20–22, 37.
134. Terrell, *Power in the Blood?*, 107.
135. Ibid., 121–22.

to take seriously the need to bring to justice the culprits in the death and sufferings of Jesus Christ.

Non-atonement Pathway

The third direction some theologians follow in their explication of the death of Jesus Christ can be described as the "Non-atonement" pathway. Theologians that follow this track aim to show that the death of Jesus Christ does not atone for human sins (non-atonement).

DIVINE JUSTICE AND NON-ATONEMENT THEORY:
JESUS AS GOD'S OPPOSITION TO VIOLENCE

Description: The theory I describe as the *Divine Justice and Non-atonement theory* contends that the salvific work of Jesus Christ is not grounded in his violent death on the cross. On the contrary, Jesus' salvific work can be seen in his teaching, proclamation of good news about God, and confrontation of unjust structures and powers. The theory repositions Jesus' public ministry at the center of his message of God's salvation. Although it was Jesus' obedience and dedication to his mission that brought about his death on the cross, it should be borne in mind that his death itself was "an impediment to the mission and not its positive culmination."[136] The *Divine Justice and Non-atonement* theory questions the traditional views of the atonement that assumes Jesus' death on the cross is necessary for the salvation of human beings from the original sin. It rejects the traditional view of the atonement for condoning divine child abuse. As Rita Nakashima Brock argues, the classical doctrines of the atonement reflect by analogy "images of the neglect of children or, even worse, child abuse, making it acceptable as divine behavior—cosmic child abuse, as it were. The father allows, or even inflicts, the death of his only perfect son. The emphasis is on the goodness and power of the father and the unworthiness and powerlessness of his children, so that the father's punishment is just, and children are to blame."[137] The *Divine Justice and Non-atonement* theory also criticizes the view of Jesus' death that holds on to the concept of atonement but describes his death as a voluntary and personal sacrifice made for the liberation of humanity from the bondage of sin. For example, they accuse the theologians that hold the *Christus*

---

136. Tanner, "Incarnation, Cross, and Sacrifice," 39.

137. Brock, *Journeys by Heart*, 56.

Victor theory for perpetuating the sentiment of self-sacrifice that promotes self-pity and violence, especially among the victims of violence.

Proponent: The American theologian Joanne Carlson Brown has been one of the champions of what I am describing as the *Divine Justice and Non-atonement* theory. Brown argues that Jesus' death is not redemptive: it does not bring salvation to sinful humanity. For her, the proclamation that God demands the death of Jesus Christ in order to save humanity "encourages victimization" of people, women in particular.[138] Brown argues for the rejection of the idea that Jesus' death saves humanity from sin as one of the effective ways to liberate Christianity from its involvement in the victimization of women in churches. For Brown, Jesus is one of the manifestations of God in the world that reveal God's justice. The excerpt below underscores Brown's understanding of Jesus' death.

I believe Christianity has been a—sometimes *the*—primary force in shaping our acceptance of abuse. The image of Christ on the cross as savior of the world communicates the message that suffering is redemptive. If the best person who ever lived gave his life for others, then we should likewise sacrifice ourselves. Any sense that we have a right to care for our own needs conflicts with being a faithful follower of Jesus.

I still maintain that Christianity is an abusive theology that glorifies suffering. If Christianity is to be liberating for the oppressed, it must itself be liberated from this theology. We must do away with the atonement, this idea of a blood sin upon the whole human race which can be washed away only by the blood of the lamb. This bloodthirsty God is the God of patriarchy who at the moment controls the whole Christian tradition.

If we throw out the atonement, do we still have Christianity? I believe we do, if it can affirm that:

- Christianity is at heart and essence justice, radical love, and liberation.

- Jesus is one manifestation of Immanuel but not uniquely so, whose life exemplified justice, radical love, and liberation.

- Jesus did not choose the cross but chose integrity and opposition to injustice, refusing to change course because of threat to his life.

- Jesus' death was an unjust act. The travesty of it is not redeemed by the resurrection.

- Jesus was not an acceptable sacrifice for the sins of the whole world, because God demands not sacrifice but justice. No one was saved by the death of Jesus.

138. Brown, "Divine Child Abuse?," 25.

- To be a Christian means keeping faith with those who live God's call for justice, radical love, and liberation.[139]

Question: How does Brown's understanding of Jesus' death on the cross teach God's justice?

Criticism: The *Divine Justice and Non-atonement* theory rejects or disregards the traditional Christian teaching about original sin and its consequences on humanity (Rom 5:12–21; 6:23). Also, the theory sees the cross purely in a negative light and therefore fails to see any positive or salvific value of the cross. Some biblical passage teach that Jesus' death on the cross has salvific value (Mark 10:45; Rom 5:9; Eph 1:7). Kathryn Tanner believes that one way of addressing the problem of seeing the cross of Jesus as a meaningless sacrifice with no salvific value is to locate Jesus' death within the broader divine act of partnering with humanity in the Incarnation. She writes, "Understood as an act of redemption that follows from God's decision to be incarnate—understood indeed as a continuation of God's decision to make humanity its own in Christ—God's action on the cross to save takes center stage. The sacrifice of the cross is then viewed accordingly—as a rite performed by God and not human beings."[140] Tanner, here, places emphasis on what God does for humanity's sake (through Jesus' violent death). To her, God is the *performer* rather than the *recipient* of the sacrificial death of Jesus Christ.[141]

Concluding Reflections on the Death of Jesus Christ and Its Salvific Import

Christian theology of the cross should interpret Jesus' death in a manner that does not oppose the "gospel", which is concretized in Jesus' teaching, miraculous works, obedience to God, and resurrection. Christian theology of the cross should avoid three major theological pitfalls.

First, it should avoid the trap of presenting God as an angry being who does not will to forgive sinners without a violent retributive death of God's Son. The scriptural teaching that *Jesus died for us* (Gal 1:4; Heb 9:28) should be understood in two interrelated senses: (*a*) his death on the cross was an

139. Ibid., 24, 28.
140. Tanner, "Incarnation, Cross, and Sacrifice," 52–53.
141. Ibid., 53.

Table 2.2
Summary of Christian Interpretations of
the Death of Jesus Christ

Theory	Pathway	Major Claims
Satisfaction	Substitution-ary violent-atonement	• Jesus' death satisfies God's honor, which is necessary for restoring sinful humanity to divine fellowship.
Moral Influence	Substitution-ary violent-atonement	• Jesus' death is intended by God primarily to inspire human beings (*a*) to recognize the severity of sin and (*b*) to seek to love God in a self-sacrificial manner.
Governmental	Substitution-ary violent-atonement	• Jesus' death demonstrates that (*a*) human beings have broken God's law and that (*b*) God has taken the initiative to amend the breached divine law.
Penal Substitution	Substitution-ary violent-atonement	• Jesus' death is the penalty for humanity's sin.
Christus Victor	Nonviolent-atonement	• Jesus' death demonstrates (*a*) humans' evil act against God and creation and (*b*) God's victory over evil forces.
Divine Suffering	Nonviolent-atonement	• Jesus' death demonstrates God willingness to suffer for the sake of partnering with humanity and also for the purpose of re-deeming humanity.
Divine Justice and Non-atonement	Non-atonement	• Jesus' death has no salvific value and it does not atone for humanity's sin.

expression of the sinful act of human rejection of God's reign and humans' quest for ontological freedom—their determination to live and be human in a manner contrary to God's desire (Mark 12:1–12), and (*b*) God turned his death into a wellspring of hope, reconciliation, forgiveness, and restoration for sinful humanity (1 Pet 3:18). Second, Christian theology of the cross should avoid the pitfall of presenting Jesus' death as an excuse for violence or for failure to expose and confront gratuitous violence, particularly the violence that maims or takes human life. For instance, Jesus' death on the cross should not motivate hatred directed against the Jews or promote anti-Semitic sentiments. Third, Christian theology of the cross should avoid the temptation to discuss Jesus' death in isolation from the totality of his life—from the incarnation to the resurrection. The incarnation is God's movement toward sinful humanity. The death of Jesus on the cross unveils humanity's flight from God and also represents human beings' rejection of God's lordship over God's creation. His miraculous works testify that God's kingdom or reign is already present in this world. By raising Jesus from the dead, God confronted humans' rejection of God. This divine confrontation of human rejection of God implies (*a*) God's lordship over God's creation, (*b*) God's willingness to pursue human beings for relationship, and (*c*) God's invitation to human beings to join in the disarmament of evil acts that are represented in the crucifixion of Jesus.

Human Beings' Responsibility in Salvation

Many Christian theologians cautiously speak about "human responsibility" or "humans' role" in their theologies of salvation because of the fear of suggesting that human beings can *merit* God's salvation. But Christians should recognize that some "components" of God's salvation require human action or activity. I will discuss two of these actions, namely, *faith* and *repentance*.

Faith

As we have seen in earlier discussions, some theologians contend that regeneration precedes faith, implying that every necessary component of salvation is supplied by God. Ephesians 2:8–10 is one of the prominent biblical passages that are cited in the discussions on salvation. Paul in this passage states, "For by grace you have been saved through faith. And this is not your own doing; it is the gift of God, not a result of works, so that no one may boast. For we are his workmanship created in Christ Jesus for good works, which God prepared beforehand, that we should walk in them" (ESV). What exactly does it mean to say that humans are "saved *through* faith"? What is the *nature* of this faith? What is the *source* of this faith? Many theologians frame their answers to these questions along the lines of "faith–work" relations. The main issue here is the function of faith and its relation to other components of God's salvation (such as Christ's faithfulness and obedience). Paul in Romans 3:22 says that salvation is grounded in "the righteousness of God through faith in Jesus Christ for all who believe" (ESV). How may we understand the expression "through faith in Jesus"? Linguistically (in the Greek context), if we understand the expression as *genitive possessive*, it can be rephrased as "through the faith of Jesus Christ." If we see the expression as *subjective genitive*, it can be rendered "through the faithfulness of Jesus Christ." In both senses, people benefit from God's salvation not because they have placed their faith in the work Christ but rather because of the (faithful) work of Jesus Christ. Many theologians continue to interpret the expression as an *objective genitive*, that is, "through faith in Christ." In this sense, Jesus is the object of people's faith.[142] Faith is construed as an "act of believing." Faith, like repentance, is also seen as an important aspect of conversion experience.

If faith is understood as an "act of believing" (a person's response to God's work in Christ), does this imply that faith is the product of human work? Earlier, I noted that many Christian theologians are wary of the danger of crediting any aspect of salvation to human beings. Therefore, speaking of "works" in the context of human faith can be deeply concerning to such theologians. But if it is humans that exercise the act of faith, is faith not a human effort? In Christianity, faith in the context of salvation is normally understood as a gift from God. As such, faith should not be understood as the product of human work. Proposing that faith is God's gift, however, does not take us very far. The real issue is not *whether faith is a gift from God*, but rather *whether this divine gift is given to all people* and *if they have the freedom to accept or reject it.*

In the Roman Catholic Church's official teaching, water baptism is believed to be the cause of one's faith in God's salvific work. Since infants do not have the cognitive capacity to consent, the issue of acceptance or rejection of God's gift of faith is of no consequence. In Protestantism, theologians whose allegiance lies with James Arminius see faith as the action human beings freely exercise that is followed by the Spirit's regenerative work. Theologians who accept the Calvinistic soteriology argue that regeneration logically precedes faith. The issue underlying the disagreement between Calvinists and Arminians is whether salvation is God's work alone (*monergism*), or both the work of God and humans (*synergism*).

First John 5:1 is one oft-quoted biblical text in the discussions on the relationship between faith and regeneration in God's salvific work. John writes, "Everyone who believes that Jesus is the Christ has been born of God, and everyone who loves the Father loves whoever has been born of him" (ESV). Some theologians see this text as the clearest example in the New Testament that regeneration precedes faith. They contend that the text teaches that a person who *believes* (an act of faith) does so because he or she *has been born* of God (regeneration).[143] These theologians focus on the Greek tenses of the words "believes" (present tense) and "has been born" (perfect tense). Others, however, are less persuaded by such simplistic readings of 1

---

142. Carson, "Atonement in Romans 3:21–26," 125–27.

143. Stott, *Letters of John*, 175.

John 5:1.[144] For example, some argue that in the Greek language tense forms do not always indicate time (except in future tenses). Some who concede that the Greek tense most often indicates time argue that the expression "Everyone who believes" (which is the present active substantival participle in the Greek tense) is better understood as a noun and therefore translated "the believer."[145] In this case, the nature of the action (and not the time of the action) is of paramount importance. John's primary interest is the character and attitude of the one who has been born of God toward others: "Everyone who loves the Father loves whoever has been born of him" (1 John 5:1; see 1 John 3:9). Those who argue that faith precedes regeneration may cite John 1:12, in which John states that to those "who believed in his name, he gave the right to become the children of God." John goes out of his way to note that "becoming children of God" is God's work, that is, what God does (John 1:13).

Should we derive from these biblical texts that people only have the capacity to accept God's work in Christ in faith because the Holy Spirit has raised them to life from the condition of spiritual death? Answering this question in the affirmative only has an important theological consequence when it is understood in the contexts of (a) the scope of the work of the Holy Spirit and (b) humans' capacity, after they have been spiritually revived by the Holy Spirit, to freely choose to either accept or reject God's salvific work in Christ. For many Calvinists, God gives "the gift of faith through the proclamation of the gospel" only to the elect.[146] To them, those whom the Holy Spirit has regenerated would accept God's salvific work. As Michael Horton puts it, "Election makes salvation certain, and Christ's redeeming work secures it. Nevertheless, when the [Holy] Spirit grants the gift of faith in Christ through the proclamation of the gospel, all of Christ's riches are actually bestowed. Whether or not one is conscious of this moment, it is the effectual calling of God the Spirit, and it brings justification and renewal of the whole person in its wake."[147] Conversely, Arminians and Wesleyans contend that regeneration is the work of the Holy Spirit within humans in which the Holy Spirit enlightens their hearts and minds with the intention that they will come to know of and freely accept the salvation offer of the Triune God. For these theologians, only those who freely choose to accept God's work in faith (1 Tim 4:10) will experience the new birth. Faith, for them, is a gift from God. Yet faith is what human beings freely exercise without divine coercion.

144. See also 1 John 2:29; 3:9; 4:7.

145. Abasciano, "Does Regeneration Precede Faith?," 307–9.

146. Horton, *Christian Faith*, 572.

147. Ibid. See also Ware, "Divine Election to Salvation," 19.

Repentance

The nature of repentance and its necessity in God's salvation is debated in Christianity. In the late 1980s, North American Evangelicals debated the role of faith, repentance, and the lordship of Jesus Christ in their soteriologies.[148] Theologians that believe *exercising faith in Christ* is necessary for salvation usually also believe that *repentance* (in this context referring to a change of mind) is also required for salvation (Mark 1:15). Fearing that if repentance is seen as an essential component of a *conversion* experience (understood as "a moment in which God bestows salvation upon a person as a result of the person's faith") will lead to the doctrine of "salvation by work," these theologians insist that repentance is not a necessary requirement for salvation.[149] On the contrary, for theologians who contend that *exercising faith in Christ* is not necessary for salvation, repentance (here meaning a "change of mind," which results in a gradual change of behavior) is not necessary for salvation. These theologians, however, contend that repentance is essential for experiencing the spiritual blessings that come with God's salvation.[150] Irrespective of their stances on the relationship between faith and regeneration, Christian theologians agree that "repentance" is a requirement for living in conformity to the life of Christ.

Theologians sometimes raise the issue of the relationship between a *change of mind* and a *change of behavior* in their discussion on repentance. The issue here is whether what is required in order to benefit from God's salvation is merely a *change of mind* or both a *change of mind* and a *change of behavior*. For many Christians, however, a person who has genuinely repented of his or her sin will *change his or her mind* (i.e., from running away from God to running toward God for salvation) and also will *change his or her lifestyle* (i.e., from living to please self to living to please God). Kallistos Ware has noted that repentance is the "starting point" of the Christian "journey." Repentance entails a "change of mind" and re-centering of one's life upon the life of the Triune God.[151] Ware notes also that repentance should be a lifelong habit of Christians. Repentance requires an initial step. But Christians should also form a habit of repentance, "an attitude of heart . . . that needs to be ceaselessly renewed up to the end of life."[152]

148. For more on this debate, see MacArthur, *The Gospel According to Jesus*; Hodges, *Absolutely Free*; and Ryrie, *So Great Salvation*.

149. Grudem, *Systematic Theology*, 714.

150. Croteau, "Repentance Found? The Concept of Repentance in the Fourth Gospel."

151. Ware, *Orthodox Way*, 113.

152. Ibid., 114.

Repentance entails a *change of direction* (from living in opposition to God to living in obedience to God). Repentance requires turning back from the direction that moves away from God to the direction that points toward God's gracious salvific work. There is no consensus among Christian theologians on what is involved in the process of salvific repentance. However, many will agree the act of turning toward God involves sorrowing about sin, forsaking sin, sincerely asking God for forgiveness, and living a life that conforms to the life of Jesus Christ.[153] The Apostle Paul makes it clear in his Epistle to the Romans that Christ's followers should not go on sinning so that God's grace may increase (Rom 6:1–2). On the contrary, Paul instructs Christians to live in a manner that pleases God rather than self (Rom 12:1–2).

Exercise 2.1

Answer the question below in ways that demonstrate consistency in your understanding of God's love for God's creatures, God's just character, and the biblical teaching on sin and its consequences.

Does the salvation Jesus achieved through his life and work (from the incarnation to his resurrection) become effective only when people, without divine coercion, freely choose to accept it in faith?

Outcomes of Salvation

Theologians speak variously of the *ends* (or ultimate goals) of salvation. Two prominent goals or outcomes of salvation that appear in theological discussions will be discussed in this section. The first of these goals (deification) is emphasized by theologians of Orthodox Churches. The second goal (justification) appears, albeit with modifications, in the works of Protestant and Roman Catholic theologians. Of course, I am not suggesting that theologians of Orthodox Churches do not talk about *justification* in the context of salvation or that Protestant and Roman Catholic theologians do not discuss *deification* in their soteriologies.

Salvation as *Theosis* (Deification)

The Orthodox Christian traditions are known for their emphasis on *theosis* (a Greek term that means "deification" or "partaking of God's life"). Theologians from other Christian traditions also speak of *theosis*, although

153. Grudem, *Systematic Theology*, 713.

largely in dialogue with either early church theologians (such as Irenaeus of Lyons)[154] or Orthodox Church theologians. Some Lutheran theologians argue that the concept of *theosis* is present in Luther's theology. For example, the Finnish theologian Tuomo Mannermaa has argued that Luther sometimes discussed the idea of deification under topics such as "the real presence of Christ in the believer, the union of Christ and the Christian, joyous exchange."[155]

The doctrine of deification in Orthodox Churches accentuates God's grace toward sinful humanity, God's transformation of the corrupt human nature, and God's restoration of estranged humanity back to divine life of fellowship. While Orthodox theologians do not disregard the idea that sin is an offense against God, they emphasize the corruption of human nature caused by sin and how such corruption impacts human beings' relationship with God. As such, they see salvation as primarily "deification": *the Triune God's gracious work of transforming corrupt human beings, creating them anew, in order for them to share in God's life*. One of the biblical passages that speaks about human beings' partaking in God's life is 2 Pet 1:4. Peter writes that God calls us so that we "may participate in divine nature and escape the corruption in the world caused by evil powers" (NIV). In the Orthodox theological tradition, *theosis* is the ultimate purpose for which God created human beings. In the words of the Greek theologian Christoforos Stavropoulos, "Humanity was created in the image of God, and each and every human being is called to become like God. We are called to become divine, not only before our fall into sin, but afterwards as well."[156]

The *incarnation* of the Word of God and the transformative work of the Triune God make deification possible.[157] Orthodox theologians locate deification of human beings within God's gracious salvific work that begins with the incarnation of God's eternal Word (John 1:1–14). As Vladimir Lossky writes, "The redeeming work of Christ—or rather, more generally speaking, the Incarnation of the Word of God—is seen to be directly related to the ultimate goal of creatures: to know union with God." Lossky goes

154. Irenaeus wrote that "the Word of God, our Lord Jesus Christ . . . did, through His transcendent love, become what we are, that He might bring us to be even what He is Himself." He also argued that "the Lord thus has redeemed us through His blood, giving His soul for our souls, and His flesh for our flesh, and has also poured out the Spirit of the Father for the union and communion of God and man, imparting indeed God to men by means of the Spirit, and, on the other hand, attaching man to God by His own incarnation, and bestowing upon us at His coming immortality durably and truly, by means of communion with God" (Against Heresies 5.1.1 [*ANF* 1:526–27]).

155. Mannermaa, "Theosis as a Subject," 37.

156. Stavropoulos, "Partakers of Divine Nature," 185.

157. Louth, "Place of Theosis in Orthodox Theology," 34–41.

on to posit: "If this union has been accomplished in the divine person of the Son, who is God become man, it is necessary that each human person, in turn, should become god by grace, or 'a partaker of the divine nature,' according to St. Peter's expression (II Peter 1:4)."[158] God's Word (*Logos* in Greek) in the incarnation became human in order for humans to become divine. There is a sort of mysterious exchange (or union) of natures: God's eternal Word in the incarnation "shared our life, to the point of death, that he might be redeemed from death and come to share the divine life."[159]

Transformation of corrupt human nature into an incorrupt nature is the goal of deification. The incarnation has made deification possible: by becoming human, God's Word assumed humanity with the intention to transform human beings into people who share in divine life. Human deification is grounded in divine-human union, a mystery which in Orthodox Churches is better expressed in liturgical poetry during worship.[160] Human beings are required to cooperate with God's transforming power by engaging in "a genuine and costly commitment to ascetic struggle" in the lifelong process of deification—continuous partaking in God's life.[161] What is intended here is not merely an outward change of behavior but the recovery of what it is to be human as originally intended by God. To use the words of Andrew Louth, it is the transformation that "restores human nature to its true purpose, to be companions of God."[162] This transformation may be construed as divine healing of human beings' corrupt nature by which God restores humans to what God originally intended them to be.[163]

Salvation as Divine Acquittal (Being Justified by God)

In many Christian traditions, sin is primarily viewed as an offense against God, which gravely affects human beings' legal and moral standings before God. Salvation in these traditions is construed as God's granting of a "new" standing to believing sinners. John 3:18 is one among several biblical passages that are alluded to in support of this understanding of salvation. In this passage, we read: "Whoever believes in him is not condemned, but whoever does not believe stands condemned already because he has not believed in the name of God's one and only Son" (NIV). Two

158. Lossky, *In the Image and Likeness of God*, 98.

159. Louth, "Place of Theosis in Orthodox Theology," 34.

160. Ibid., 41.

161. Ibid., 39.

162. Ibid., 40.

163. Thomas, *Deification in the Eastern Orthodox Tradition*, 19.

primary theological terms used by theologians to describe the new standing of sinners before God are "justification" and "sanctification." The meanings and relationship of "justification" (to be *declared* righteous) and "sanctification" (to be *made* righteous), however, have been understood differently in Christianity. These terms took on important status in the history of Christian theology in the sixteenth century with Martin Luther's conviction that one's legal and moral standings before God are gained through God's "grace alone" (*sola gratia* in Latin) and through "faith alone" (*sola fide* in Latin). How Luther intended these soteriological terms to be understood is

> "In him we are given a new humanity and a new righteousness in the very righteousness of God. The work of justification is no empty word but deed of flesh and blood. As the Word was made flesh in Jesus Christ, so in justification the Word is made flesh in the new humanity which we have in Jesus Christ who was raised for our justification."
>
> —Thomas F. Torrance, "Atonement in the Teaching of St. Paul," 104

hotly debated among Reformed theologians and Luther scholars. The traditional interpretation of Luther is that salvation in its entirety is God's work alone (the "monergistic" interpretation of Luther). Although Luther taught that God's salvation precedes human work, he encouraged Christians to live righteously as an act of "obedience, thanksgiving, and praise" to God.[164] Also, some theologians have argued that Luther intended "justification" and "sanctification" to be two distinct concepts. Others, on the contrary, argue that seeing justification and sanctification as two distinct concepts is foreign to Luther's soteriology.[165]

The meaning of *justification* has troubled Protestants and Roman Catholics for decades. The debate is usually framed along the lines of the *forensic* (legal) aspect of justification and the *operative* aspect of justification. "Forensic justification" refers to God's *declaration* of a sinner to be "righteous" or "not guilty" on the account of Christ's righteousness. To put it differently, a sinner's legal and moral standings are changed (from an enemy of God to an object of God's love and salvation) by God's gracious act of crediting to the sinner Christ's righteousness or faithfulness. This is the traditional Lutheran understanding of Luther's theology of justification. "Operative justification" (also called "effective justification") refers to God's gracious work of *making* a sinner righteous. Some Lutherans associate "operative justification" with Roman Catholic soteriology, which for them is

---

164. Raunio, "Natural Law and Faith," 111.

165. For more discussion on the debate over Martin Luther's soteriology, see Braaten and Jenson, *Union with Christ: The New Finnish Interpretation of Luther.*

foreign to Luther's theology of justification. Some Lutherans prefer to describe "operative justification" with the term "sanctification."

After several decades of disagreement (and sometimes hatred toward each other) some Roman Catholic and Lutheran theologians, in the spirit of ecumenical dialogue, reached an accord on the doctrine of justification. The *Joint Declaration on the Doctrine of Justification*, signed by the chief officers of the Lutheran World Federation and the Roman Catholic Church in October 1999, is an artifact of such common ground reached by Lutherans and Roman Catholics on the doctrine of justification. In articles 15 and 16, the declaration states,

> In faith we together hold the conviction that justification is the work of the Triune God. The Father sent his Son into the world to save sinners. The foundation and presupposition of justification is the incarnation, death, and resurrection of Jesus Christ. Justification thus means that Christ himself is our righteousness, in which we share through the Holy Spirit in accord with the will of the Father. Together we confess: By grace alone, in faith in Christ's saving work and not because of any merit on our part, we are accepted by God and receive the Holy Spirit, who renews our hearts while equipping and calling us to good works.
>
> All people are called by God to salvation in Christ. Through Christ alone we are justified, when we receive this salvation in faith. Faith is itself God's gift through the Holy Spirit, who works through the Word and Sacrament in the community of believers and who, at the same time, leads believers into that renewal of life which God will bring to completion in eternal life.[166]

The theological consensus on the doctrine of Justification reached by the Lutheran World Federation and the Roman Catholic Church is an attempt to deal with the theological tension between "God's role" and "humans' role" in the process of salvation, without denying that salvation is God's gift to humanity. The tension continues to trouble many theologians today. But justification is not the sum total of God's salvation. Rather, it should be taken as one among many essential components of God's salvation (Rom 8:28–30). Therefore, justification, in the context of salvation, should not be explored in isolation from other components such as sanctification. As the Chinese theologian K. K. Yeo has noted, "Justification is not just a restoration, it is also the giving of new life. It calls for constant renewal

166. Lutheran World Federation and the Roman Catholic Church, *Joint Declaration*, 15–16.

and transformation."[167] To be justified is to be set on a new course of life in which the person whom God justifies receives God's gift. People who are justified are also summoned to live righteously (Eph 2:10).

Glossary

Atonement: The belief that the death of Jesus Christ compensates for humanity's sin (both original sin and actual sins).

Election: Broadly, this term refers to God's eternal choice to extend salvation to fallen humanity. Some theologians, however, use the term "election" to describe the *class of people* (the elect) whom God has pre-temporally and unconditionally chosen to save. Others use it to describe the class of people whom God has chosen to save on the merit of a *foreseen faith*.

Imputed Sin: Term used to describe God's act of crediting or ascribing Adam's sin and its consequences to humanity.

Imputed Righteousness: Term referring to God's act of crediting or ascribing Jesus' righteousness to sinners in order to draw them back into divine fellowship.

Infralapsarian: Term meaning "after the fall"; used by some theologians to show, *logically* in God's thought, that God first decided to permit or decree the fall (sin) and then to save some sinners.

Justification: Term used forensically to describe God's gracious act of *declaring* a sinner to be "righteous" on account of Jesus' righteousness.

Monergism: The theological position that salvation is God's work alone. God does not need humans' cooperation to bring about their salvation.

Ordo Salutis: Latin expression that means "order of salvation."

Predestination: Term employed by theologians to describe God's eternal decrees concerning God's creation.

Predestination: Broadly refers to the doctrine that God has in eternity decreed the destiny of all human beings.

Regeneration: The Holy Spirit's work of resurrecting (or giving a new life to) people who are dead in sin.

167. Yeo, *Musing with Confucius and Paul*, 259.

Reprobation: Term employed by some theologians to described the belief that God has chosen to deny salvation to some people and also to hold them accountable for both original sin and actual sins.

Supralapsarian: Term meaning "before the fall"; used by some theologians to show, *logically* in God's thought, that God first decided to save some from sin and then permitted or allowed the fall.

Synergism: The theological position that holds that God requires human beings' cooperation in order to bestow salvation upon them.

Review Questions

1. How does Augustine's view of divine grace differ from Pelagius' view of divine grace?

2. What are the differences between Arminius', Calvin's, and Barth's views of election?

3. In what ways have Christian theologians interpreted the saving significance of Jesus' death? Summarize what you consider to be the strengths and weaknesses of each theory.

4. What are the major outcomes or ends of salvation?

5. How does Karl Barth understand election? Examine and critique his understanding of election.

6. What are the roles of the Holy Spirit in human salvation?

7. What is the place and nature of "faith" in God's salvific work?

Suggestions for Further Reading

Belousek, Darrin W. Snyder. *Atonement, Justice, and Peace: The Message of the Cross and the Mission of the Church*. Grand Rapids: Eerdmans, 2012.

Gibson, David. *Reading the Decree: Exegesis, Election and Christology in Calvin and Barth*. London: T. & T. Clark, 2009.

Kitamori, Kazoh. *Theology of the Pain God*. Richmond: John Knox, 1965.

Martin, Ralph. *Will Many Be Saved? What Vatican II Actually Teaches and Its Implications for the New Evangelization*. Grand Rapids: Eerdmans, 2012.

Terrell, JoAnne Marie. *Power in the Blood? The Cross in the African American Experience*. Maryknoll, NY: Orbis, 1998.

Thomas, Stephen. *Deification in the Eastern Orthodox Tradition: A Biblical Perspective*. Piscataway, NJ: Gorgias, 2007.

3

Christian Theologies of Religions

In January 2013, I co-led a Bethel University and Jerusalem University College cross-listed course titled "Israel Study Tour." As a theologian, my task was to engage the theological issues that would arise from students' encounter with archeological findings in the Holy Land, the implications of the findings for the Christian Scriptures, and also their import for contemporary religious tension in Israel. Mine was an ambitious task. Although I have been fascinated by interreligious exchanges since my undergraduate days, I have not studied religious conflicts in contemporary Israel. I made it clear to some of my colleagues that I was going to Israel to learn, and I am glad I did. As one trained in contextual theology, I listened to the complex stories and experiences that condition interreligious conflicts and exchanges in Israel. I recall the answer of a bus driver, a Palestinian who lives in the Israeli territory, to my question regarding the experience of Palestinians residing in Israel. After a long pause (as if he were discerning my motive for asking the question), he said, "I don't live in Israel. I live in an occupied territory." A day later, at the Temple Mount, I experienced the magnitude of the task of negotiating one's religious identity, one's national identity, and one's existence in the multireligious context of the city of Jerusalem. The division of the Old City into religious quarters, the armed military personnel who walked closely with groups of visitors, and the ban on the use of the Christian Scriptures on the Temple Mount all informed my experience. When we returned to the United States, I wrote the following words on my Facebook page: "In Jerusalem, the Old City in particular, I experienced the complexity of interreligious and intra-religious tensions. Amazingly, many adherents of [competing] religions are still able to negotiate their coexistence, hopes, and aspirations." These words continue to serve as a reminder to me of the necessity and complexity of interreligious conversations in the world today.

The Roman Catholic theologian James Frederickson notes that "Christians now live in a time when looking on the plurality of faiths as a subsidiary problem for their theology and practice is no longer possible."[1] Frederickson's observation is particularly true for many Christians living in Western Europe and North America. The attacks on the World Trade Center (the symbol of American wealth and economic ingenuity) and the Pentagon (the symbol of American military prowess) on September 11, 2001, awakened many Christians living in America and outside of America from their religious slumber; they now had to face the nagging new challenge of religious exchanges and tensions. I was one such person. I had been in the United States barely three months when the towers collapsed. This catastrophic event opened new wounds, reopened old wounds, and moved people from around the world to rethink their perceptions of religiously motivated violence and acts of terrorism. It also opened new vistas for engaging in interreligious dialogues in many religious circles. In the political arena, many governments of the world's nations learned the hard way that the battle against terrorism and measures for counterterrorism cannot be successfully waged in isolation from insights emerging from religious communities. They learned that religion is implicated in terrorism. The world would no longer be the same; neither would religious discourses, nor the ways the large majority of Americans treat people from the "non-Western world."

1. Fredericks, "Introduction," ix.

Prior to the time that terrorist attacks and wars became present in most North Americans' and Europeans' consciousness, many Christians from the continents of Europe and North America deferred discussions on interreligious conversation to "experts," especially to the missionaries who operated overseas. The events of September 11, 2001, however, reconfigured and remapped the geographical boundaries of Christian mission. American and European Christians would no longer need to travel to Africa, Asia, Latin America, the Middle East, and Native American reservations before they could engage in interreligious conversations. But people who live in societies in which some religions preceded the arrival of Christianity or in societies in which Christianity is a minority religion know firsthand the complexity of religious exchanges. In such societies, engaging in interreligious dialogues is not an act of leisure; it is a way of living, and also a way of surviving. In Asia, for example, Christians negotiate their existence in the midst of Confucianism, Hinduism, Buddhism, and Islam, among other religions. Christians in tropical Africa continue to answer the question, Can we be simultaneously Africans and Christians in the contexts of Christianity-indigenous religions or Christianity-Islam relations? In the Middle East, Christians experience the difficulty of living in their communities as people with the minority religion. The contemporary landscape on which Christian theologians must construct their theologies of religions is very treacherous. The landscape is saturated with incredulity toward absolute truth claims, religiously motivated mistrust, hatred, violence, and people who have become increasingly impatient with Christians' views of other religions. Christian theologians cannot successfully steer away from this landscape nor should they attempt to do so. They must press this landscape for theological materials and also use such materials to construct their theologies of religions.

"Christian theologies of religions" is used in this chapter to describe Christians' attitudes toward, reflections on, and interpretation of *other religions* (i.e., non-Christian religions). The chapter answers three paramount questions. First, how should Christians, whose understandings of God's salvation are grounded in the triune God's work, relate to people of other religions? Second, how should a Christian be a faithful *adherent* of Christianity and at the same time a responsible *citizen* of a world characterized by a plurality of religions most of which teach competing truth claims and ethics? Third, are people who explicitly reject Christianity's view of salvation excluded from God's salvation? A Christian's answers to these interrelated questions will have a significant impact on her or his estimation of the people of other religions. To answer these questions, I will discuss three topics: (*a*) approaches in Christian theologies of religions, (*b*) major objectives of

119

Christian theologies of religions, and (c) Christian theologies of religions and the doctrine of salvation.

Approaches in Christian Theologies of Religions

Two important documents appeared in the 1960s and 1970s that have to a large extent conditioned Christians' attitudes toward people of other religions. The documents have equally shaped many Christians' forms of interreligious engagement and also their goals in interreligious conversations. The first document, titled *Nostra Aetate*, was produced by the

> FOCUS QUESTION:
> What forms of engagement do Christian theologians employ in their theologies of religions?

Second Vatican Council (1962–65) and marked Roman Catholics' openness to engaging non-Christian religions and to viewing them favorably in some substantive ways. In this document, the Council summoned Christians to enter into dialogue and collaboration with people of other religions. Also, Christians were to recognize the spiritual and moral values found in other religions. For example, the document states,

> Buddhism, in its various forms, realizes the radical insufficiency of this changeable world; it teaches a way by which men, in a devout and confident spirit, may be able either to acquire the state of perfect liberation, or attain, by their own efforts or through higher help, supreme illumination. Likewise, other religions found everywhere try to counter the restlessness of the human heart, each in its own manner, by proposing "ways," comprising teachings, rules of life, and sacred rites. The Catholic Church rejects nothing that is true and holy in these religions. She regards with sincere reverence those ways of conduct and of life, those precepts and teachings which, though differing in many aspects from the ones she holds and sets forth, nonetheless often reflect a ray of that Truth which enlightens all men. Indeed, she proclaims, and ever must proclaim Christ "the way, the truth, and the life" (John 14:6), in whom men may find the fullness of religious life, in whom God has reconciled all things to Himself.
>
> The Church, therefore, exhorts her sons, that through dialogue and collaboration with the followers of other religions, carried out with prudence and love and in witness to the Christian faith and life, they recognize, preserve and promote the

good things, spiritual and moral, as well as the socio-cultural values found among these men.[2]

The second document, which was originally drafted in 1977, was adopted in 1979 by the World Council of Churches (WCC) during its meeting in Jamaica. Although circumspect of the dangers of syncretism (such as compromising the integrity of Christianity's teaching), the members of the Central Committee of the WCC deemed it fitting to accept people of other religions as "fellow pilgrims" in the spiritual journeys of knowing and experiencing God.

> In dialogue Christians seek "to speak the truth in a spirit of love," not naively "to be tossed to and fro, and be carried about with every wind of doctrine" (Eph 4.14–15). In giving their witness they recognize that in most circumstances today the spirit of dialogue is necessary. For this reason we do not see dialogue and the giving of witness as standing in any contradiction to one another. Indeed, as Christians enter dialogue with their commitment to Jesus Christ, time and again the relationship of dialogue gives opportunity for authentic witness. Thus, to the member churches of the WCC we feel able with integrity to commend the way of dialogue as one in which Jesus Christ can be confessed in the world today; at the same time we feel able with integrity to assure our partners in dialogue that we come not as manipulators but as genuine fellow-pilgrims, to speak with them of what we believe God to have done in Jesus Christ who has gone before us, but whom we seek to meet anew in dialogue.[3]

The preceding two documents share a commitment to witness to people of other religions. This commitment can be traced back to Christian beginnings. The earliest followers of Jesus witnessed to people about Jesus Christ in Jerusalem and beyond in obedience to his command to them (Acts 1:7–8). From the earliest beginnings in Palestine, Christians have had to live in a world of difference—a world characterized by different religions and cultures (see Acts 15). Historically, Christians have answered the question about how best to engage in interreligious conversations in ways that are conditioned by their sociocultural, religious, economic, and political situations. For example, theologians in Christian communities persecuted by governments that charge them with the crime of unpatriotic behaviors may opt to *defend* (apologia approach) the Christian manner of living and also

2. Vatican II, *Nostra Aetate*, 2.

3. WCC, *Guidelines on Dialogue with People of Living Faiths and Ideologies*.

to show that Christians are good citizens. Christian theologians living in societies characterized by religious conflicts and tensions may undertake the task of *dialoguing* (dialogical approach) with theologians of other religions with the intent to achieve peaceful coexistence. In some cases, Christian theologians engage in conversation with people of other religions for the purpose of *comparing* Christianity with other religions (comparative approach). I will describe these three approaches further, highlighting their agendas, strengths, weaknesses, and proponents. Although these three approaches are not mutually exclusive, they merit distinguishing because of the differences in their focus and agendas. In practice, theologians combine elements from each of these three approaches even though one of them may stand out as the primary mode of engagement.

Apologia Approach

Description: All religions, however similar they may appear to be, have some competing truth claims. Adherents of major (or popular) religions are expected by their leaders to share their religious beliefs and practices with people of other religions, sometimes to convert them, and, upon request, to provide supporting evidence for holding their religious truth claims. Christian theologians who adopt the apologia approach aim to defend Christianity's truth claims against attacks from external (or non-Christian) challengers and also against internal (or Christian) detractors. They provide proofs to support Christian truth claims, such as the claim that Christianity is the only true (or the most reliable) religion and that Jesus Christ is the only savior of the world.

For theologians who use the apologia form of interreligious engagement, compromising Christian truth claims, especially the christocentric understanding of salvation, is detrimental to Christian witness and identity. The theologians' aims are (*a*) to show that the Christian religion provides universal and objective answers to people's perennial religious questions, and (*b*) to persuade non-Christians to accept Christianity's answers to such questions.[4] Advocates of the apologia approach, depending on their training, borrow ideas from other fields of study such as philosophy and cosmology to strengthen their arguments.

Strengths: A major strength of the apologia approach is its ability to make a Christian an intellectually responsible believer. In our religiously pluralistic world, Christians should be intellectually ready to explain and demonstrate the justification for their religious beliefs. The Apostle Peter

4. Netland, *Encountering Religious Pluralism*, 250.

encourages Christians to be "prepared to give an answer to everyone who asks" about their hope that is grounded in Christ Jesus (1 Pet 3:15 NIV). Origen of Alexandria (ca. 185–ca. 251 CE) expressed the necessity of the apologia motif in his refutation of Celsus' charges against Christians. Origen wrote that there "are some who are capable of receiving more than an exhortation to believe, and to these we address them alone; while we approach others, again, as far as possible, in the way of demonstration, by means of question and answer."[5] Origen's point is that in some situations Christians may only need to preach the gospel, but in other situations they need to demonstrate the reasonableness of the gospel before non-Christians. Another strength of the apologia approach is that an apologist can prepare other Christians, who otherwise would have shunned contact with people of other religions for fear of being contaminated by non-Christian religious ideas, to become willing to interact with non-Christians.

Weaknesses: The apologia approach has two major weaknesses. First, very rarely do people convert to Christianity because they are convinced by an apologist that Christianity's truth claims are true or the most reliable when compared to other competing religious truth claims. Most people convert to Christianity because they grew up in Christian homes and with Christian ideas. Others may convert to Christianity because they find it *pragmatically* appealing (that is, it works for them) and not because they believe that all of Christianity's truth claims can be shown to be true or logically consistent. For example, many people, including Christians, may continue to doubt that the claim "Jesus of Nazareth is God incarnate" can be proven. Also, even if people of other religions accept this belief to be plausible, it may never be sufficient for them to abandon their own religions since they may hold a similar exalted view of the central figures of their religions. Second, when the apologia approach is armed with a conversion mindset, it may be useless in engaging in dialogical conversations that aim to achieve a peaceful coexistence with people of competing religions. Apologists usually arrive at conversations fully convinced that the truth claims of their religions are true and that the truth claims of other religions are false or seriously wanting. Such a mindset often does more harm than good in interreligious conversations and dialogues. In true dialogues, as David Bohm rightly argues, a person "does not attempt to *make common* certain ideas or items of information that are already known to him." On the contrary, the person must strive together with other people to make "something *in common*, i.e., creating something together."[6] Apologists arrive

---

5. Origen, *Against Celsus* 5.10 (*ANF* 4:577).

6. Bohm, *On Dialogue*, 3.

at the table usually with the goal to convince people to accept their beliefs rather than to discover along with others a new way of understanding God and the world. Christian apologists desire to show people of other religions "that it is unreasonable or irrational for them not to" accept the Christian religion or truth claims.[7]

Proponents of the Apologia Approach: I will discuss two figures who are rarely encountered in Christian theology but whose works remain relevant to the apologia approach. The first is the eighth-century Syrian Patriarch, Timothy I of Baghdad, and the second is the twentieth-century Nigerian Evangelical theologian, Byang Kato. Both theologians employed the apologia approach in their conversations with non-Christian religions: Timothy focused on Islam and Kato interacted with African indigenous (or traditional) religions.

Timothy I of Baghdad

Timothy I of Baghdad (d. 823 CE) of the East Syrian Church was an early Christian leader who defended Christianity before al-Mahdi, an Abbasid caliph (Islamic ruler) in the city of Baghdad (modern-day Iraq). His apology remains an example of a Christian theologian who was ready, when called upon, to present a defense for Christianity's truth claims and also to proclaim Christianity's gospel in a non-Christian environment. In 781 CE, al-Mahdi invited Timothy I of Baghdad to the palace to discuss his religious ideas and beliefs. Baghdad at this time was a center of learning and the residence of many great intellectuals. Al-Mahdi's goal was to learn more about the Christian faith, which Timothy I of Baghdad had shared with him on a previous occasion.[8] Timothy I of Baghdad saw the invitation by al-Mahdi as an opportunity to freely share his faith since he would be protected by the *majlis*—a legislature "that encouraged those invited to the palace to talk freely about whatever they knew of their religion and Islam without any threat of death."[9] In the two-day interreligious conversations, Timothy I of Baghdad and al-Mahdi discussed a range of theological issues including the scriptures, the doctrine of the Trinity, the Muslim teaching about Prophet Muhammad, and Christians' and Muslims' understandings of the Jews. The excerpt below highlights Timothy I of Baghdad's approach and arguments for the Christian doctrine of the Trinity.[10]

7. Netland, *Encountering Religious Pluralism*, 260.

8. Norris, "Timothy I of Baghdad," 135.

9. Ibid., 135.

10. See *Apology of Patriarch Timothy of Baghdad before the Caliph Mahdi*, in Coakley and Sterk, *Readings in World Christian History*, 1:231–42.

AL-MAHDI: You should . . . accept the words of the Prophet [Muhammad].

TIMOTHY I OF BAGHDAD: Which words of his our victorious King believes that I must accept?

AL-MAHDI: That God is one and that there is no other one besides Him.

TIMOTHY I OF BAGHDAD: This belief in one God, O my Sovereign, I have learned from the Torah, from the Prophets and from the Gospel. I stand by it and shall die in it.

AL-MAHDI: You believe in one God, as you said, but one in three.

TIMOTHY I OF BAGHDAD: I do not deny that I believe in one God in three, and three in one, but not in three different Godheads, however, but in the persons of God's Word and His Spirit. I believe that these three constitute one God, not in their person but in their nature. . .

AL-MAHDI: How is it that these three persons whom you mention do not constitute three Gods?

TIMOTHY I OF BAGHDAD: Because the three of them constitute one God, O our victorious King, and the fact that He is only one God precludes the hypothesis that there are three Gods.

AL-MAHDI: The mind of rational beings will not agree to speak of God who is eternally one in Himself in terms of Trinity.

TIMOTHY I OF BAGHDAD: Since the mind of the rational beings is created, and no created being can comprehend God, you have rightly affirmed, O King of Kings, that the mind of the rational beings will not agree to speak of one God in terms of Trinity. The mind, however, of the rational beings can only extend to the acts of God, and even then in an imperfect and partial manner; as to the nature of God we learn things that belong to it not so much from our rational minds as from the Books of Revelation, i.e., from what God Himself has revealed and taught about Himself through His Word and Spirit.

AL-MAHDI: O Catholicos [Primate], if this is your religion and that of the Christians, I will say this, that the Word and the Spirit are also creatures, and there is no one who is uncreated except one God.

TIMOTHY I OF BAGHDAD: The Books teach us that He created the world by means of His Word and His Spirit—by means of whom did He then create this Word and Spirit? If He created them by means of another word and another spirit, the same conclusion would also be applied to them: will they be created or uncreated? If uncreated, the religion of the Catholicos and of the Christians is vindicated; if created, by means of whom did God create them? And this process of gibberish argumentation will go on indefinitely until we stop at that Word and that Spirit hidden eternally in God, by means of whom we assert the worlds were created.

AL-MAHDI: You are right in what you said before and say now on the subject that God is above all the thoughts and minds of created beings, and that all the thoughts and minds of created beings are lower not only than God Himself but also His work. The fact, however, that you put the servant and the Lord on the same footing you make the creator equal with the created, and in this you fall into error and falsehood.[11]

Questions: In what areas do Timothy I of Baghdad and al-Mahdi agree in their conversations on God's identity? In what areas do they disagree? How do both employ the apologia approach in their interreligious conversations? What are al-Mahdi's concerns about the Christian doctrine of the Trinity?

Byang Kato

Before his death in 1975, the Nigerian theologian Byang Kato (1936–75) of the Evangelical Church of West Africa (now Evangelical Church Winning All), served as the General Secretary of the Association of Evangelicals in Africa. He was a visiting scholar at Dallas Theological Seminary (where he obtained his doctorate degree in theology) and a theology lecturer at ECWA Theological Seminary Igbaja (Nigeria), and he spoke at prestigious conferences such as at the Lausanne Congress of 1975. Kato is representative of some African Evangelicals who contend that the destruction of African indigenous religions is required in order for Christianity to take deep roots in Africa. The selections below are from *Theological Pitfalls in Africa*, the only major theological work of Kato.

The second purpose of [*Theological Pitfalls in Africa*] is to bring to attention of the proponents of "African Theology," ecumenists, and all others with universalistic tendencies, the fact that there is another way of looking at the relationship between Christianity and African [traditional or indigenous] religions. It is not neo-colonialism to plead the uniqueness and finality of Jesus

11. Ibid., 1:232–33, 237–39.

Christ. It is not arrogance to herald the fact that all who are not "in Christ" are lost. It is merely articulating what the Scriptures say.

African religions, as traditionally known, are breaking at the seams, and yet they are far from vanishing. Since they have been part and parcel of African culture, hence the name traditional African religions, they are not likely to be eliminated wholesale. Yet Christianity cannot incorporate any man-made religion. But some theologians are seeking recognition of the so-called "common ground" between Christianity and African traditional religions. This is where the battle is raging.

Non-Christians can and do conceive of God and prove it by the name they give the Supreme Being and their use of this name in songs and proverbs. Animistic worship is no proof that man is trying to worship God. It, however, shows man's awareness of the existence of God. It also shows the deep search for the Reality in spite of the unconscious flight from Him. Only Jesus Christ can meet this thirst, not by filling up the measure of idolatry but by transformation.

The Evangelical also rejects the veneration of African traditional religions. This is not due to lack of patriotism. It is only to safeguard the unique gospel of Christ, which alone provides the way to salvation. African culture as such is not all bad. But like any other culture it is tainted with sin. It needs to be redeemed. The redemption is a surgical process which hurts. Practices incompatible with the Bible will have to give way. This is not a lack of respect for one's culture. The good part of African culture which meets the Biblical standard will be preserved and promoted. [For example,] Christians encourage the use of local languages through Bible translation.

The test for loyalty and patriotism should not lie in ecumenical cooperation, [or] in the area where the ruler has overstepped his human ordained position. In this area obedience to God and defense of the faith is the necessary prerogative of the Bible-believing Christian. The plea of the early apologists is the same plea by their spiritual descendants in twentieth-century Africa.[12]

Questions: What are the underlying goals of Kato in his apologia? What does Kato believe is the appropriate Christian attitude toward African indigenous religions? What does the text say about Kato's view of Christianity's origins?

12. Kato, *Theological Pitfalls in Africa*, 16–17, 114, 177–78.

Dialogical Approach

Description: The *dialogical* approach is rooted in a form of communication between disparate groups or individuals whose overarching aim is to create *something in common*—to collaboratively attain a common understanding on an issue under discussion.[13] What is achieved in common in this context may not be a doctrinal consensus but a common and clearer way to understand a religion's doctrine. In the dialogical approach people freely listen to each other, abstain from superimposing their views on others, are interested in truth and coherence, are willingly to drop their old ideas and intentions, and are ready to arrive at a new decision if necessary.[14] The dialogical approach does not encourage uncritical compromises and does not promote incredulity toward absolute truths. While theologians that favor the apologia approach present Christianity's truth claims as proven presuppositions and use them as the basis for argumentation, theologians with the dialogical approach consider Christianity's truth claims (like the truth claims of other religions) as mere hypotheses, which are open to interrogation and even rejection. Christian theologians that use the dialogical approach enter the public religious space for conversation with the goal of arriving at a *common* understanding of religiously motivated conflicts and strife. They neither aim to *convert* people of other religious traditions to Christianity nor attempt to persuade them to accept Christianity's beliefs and practices. They also abstain from seeking to prove that the beliefs and practices of other religions are false and, therefore, should be abandoned. They amplify *what is common* among religions, which has the capacity to unite people of competing religions.[15]

Strengths: The dialogical approach exemplifies a genuine spirit of toleration that is often absent in the apologia approach. In the dialogical approach, people encounter opposing views that have on many occasions instigated dehumanization, hegemony, violence, hatred, and terrorism. The dialogical approach has pushed some Christians to develop the skills required to live in harmony with people whom otherwise they will avoid or refuse a hand of fellowship. The dialogical approach also fosters an environment that is conducive for people with opposing religious views to talk honestly about their differences and to mutually enrich their knowledge about their own religions and other religions. In the words of Charlotte Klein, an "essential component in dialogue is the willingness to reexamine one's

13. Bohm, *On Dialogue*, 3.

14. Ibid.

15. Cox, *Many Mansions*, 3.

faith in the light of how others relate to their tradition and the ability to strengthen or adjust one's own engagement and interaction with the sacred based on the experiences of the other. Understanding the faith of others should strengthen rather than weaken a person's commitment to his or her tradition."[16] The dialogical approach's main goal to collaboratively achieve a common understanding opens new opportunities to discuss religious issues other than doctrines. For example, people engaged in interreligious dialogue may find fresh ways of imagining social justice, human dignity, human flourishing, and peaceful coexistence.

Weaknesses: A major weakness of the dialogical approach is its ability to hide destructive undercurrents that meet the eyes. One such undercurrent is the *superiority complex* that most times goes unnoticed during dialogues. It is not "natural" for people engaged in religious dialogue to see others as *equal holders of truth*. Although seeing religious competitors as equal holders of truth is not a precondition for a meaningful dialogue, failing to see theologians as equal holders of truth will condition the dialogue and can move discussion in a non-dialogical direction. There is a tendency for a theologian of a religion to assume his or her view of God, for example, is superior to the views held by theologians of other religions. A Christian theologian that is governed by such self-estimation may neither truly listen to others nor genuinely seek to learn from others. Consequently, what may appear to be a dialogical discourse may turn out to be mere *conversation* or exchange of information about different religions. There is also the issue of *class inequality*. While it is not impossible, it is highly improbable for those commissioned to engage in religious dialogues to share the same social location, ethnicity, education, and economic status. If unchecked, class inequality can become a dangerous virus that destroys interreligious dialogues. Class inequality discourages full participation. People who see themselves as individuals of a "superior" class may unknowingly intimidate others and also force their views on others. Such people may be unaware of the coercive influence of their tones, appearance, body language, personal accomplishments, prestige, and power on other participants with lesser accomplishments.

Proponents of the Dialogical Approach: Two theologians whose works I discuss below are representative of Christian intellectuals who advocate for the dialogical form of engagement in today's treacherous climate of religious conflicts and disagreements.

16. Takim, "From Conversion to Conversation," 346.

Rowan Williams

Former archbishop of Canterbury Rowan Williams provides an example of the dialogical approach. In his July 14, 2008, response to the invitation by some Muslim leaders to Christian leaders for a religious dialogue (which came through an open letter sent on October 13, 2007), Williams bravely took on the issue of the doctrine of the Trinity, a doctrine that is appalling to most Muslims. This excerpt is taken from *A Common Word Between Us and You.* While honoring the irenic spirit of the invitation, Williams underscored that the invitation should not be understood as an attempt to merely "affirm an agreed and shared understanding of God."[17]

There are many things between us [Christians and Muslims] that offer the promise of deeper insights through future discussions. Thus for us your letter makes a highly significant contribution to the divinely initiated journey into which we are called, the journey in which Christians and Muslims alike are taken further into mutual understanding and appreciation. The confession that "God knows best" reminds us of the limits of our understanding and knowledge.

Muslims see the belief that God could have a son as suggesting that God is somehow limited as we are limited, bound to physical processes and needing the co-operation of others. How can such a God be truly free and sovereign—qualities both Christianity and Islam claim to affirm, for we know that God is able to bring the world into being by his word alone?

Here it is important to state unequivocally that the association of any other being with God is expressly rejected by the Christian theological tradition. Since the earliest Councils of the Church, Christian thinkers sought to clarify how, when we speak of the Father "begetting" the Son, we must put out of our minds any suggestion that this is a physical thing, a process or event like the process and events that happen in the world. They insisted that the name "God" is not the name of a person like a human person, a limited being with a father and mother and a place that they inhabit within the world. "God" is the name of a kind of life, a "nature" or essence—eternal and self-sufficient life, always active, needing nothing. But that life is lived, so Christians have always held, eternally and simultaneously as three interrelated agencies are made known to us in the history of God's revelation to the Hebrew people and in the life of Jesus and what flows from it. God is at once the source of divine life, the expression of that life and the active power that communicates that life. This takes us at once into consideration of the Trinitarian language used

17. Williams, "Common Word for the Common God," 188.

by Christians to speak of God. We recognize that this is difficult, sometimes offensive, to Muslims; but it is all the more important for the sake of open and careful dialogue that we try to clarify what we do and do not mean by it. . . .[18]

Question: How does this text highlight the dialogical approach?

Naim Stifan Ateek

Naim Ateek is one of the leading Palestinian theologians whose theologies of religions weave together theology and politics. Ateek's theological reflection on Jerusalem, the Holy Land, raises important theological questions about how to imagine the sacredness of Jerusalem and the need for a shared governance of Jerusalem by Jews, Christians, and Muslims. Ateek's position offers a perspective on how to engage in interreligious conversations in the contemporary Israeli-Palestinian context. The excerpts that follow underscore some of Ateek's major proposals on how to deal with religious conflicts in Israel.

We cannot deny that the adherents of Judaism, Islam, and Christianity firmly believe that God has in the past and continues in the present to hear them, speak and relate to them actively and authentically in this city [Jerusalem]. Pilgrims from the three religious traditions come or want to come (political climate permitting) to offer their worship and devotion to their Holy Places.

Jerusalem itself, I believe, will ultimately withstand and defy any attempts to exclusivity. Jerusalem cannot be only Jewish. The sooner Israel recognizes that this holy space called Jerusalem must be shared equally, the better it would be for the peace and security of all. In other words, although the religious significance is not totally dependent on the political, the political cannot ignore the religious. Therefore, the best requirement for a just peace would be the sharing of political sovereignty. The political must bow down to the demands of the religious.

The political sharing of sovereignty must be our human response to the holiness of this space. The arrogance of an exclusive sovereign claim must be resisted vehemently. The world community must approach the issue of Jerusalem from its religious significance rather than from its political significance. It is essential to comprehend deeply that what makes Jerusalem great is not

18. Ibid., 189, 192–93.

its political character but its religious character, which is equally important to Jews, Muslims, and Christians. This is why it is mandatory for the political sovereignty to be shared. An exclusive Israeli political claim will drastically diminish the equal religious significance of the city for the three religions, therefore giving an unjust edge to one.

Christians should not think of Jerusalem without thinking of plurality and inclusiveness. Over the centuries, Jerusalem has evolved as a city for Muslims, Christians and Jews, both foreign and local. It is, indeed, a mosaic. At their best, plurality and inclusiveness imply acceptance, normal relationships, and life together as good neighbors.[19]

Questions: What does this text reveal about Ateek's approach to theology of religions? In what way does Ateek understand the relationship between religion and politics in his theology of the Holy Land, Jerusalem?

Comparative Approach

Description: Three major assumptions condition the *comparative* approach. First, people who are serious adherents of a religion are usually unwillingly to give up the essential truth claims of their religion. Second, no religion is immune to the impact of the clash of religions that is the result of a close proximity and contact of different religions. Third, all religions can benefit from interreligious conversations.[20] On the basis of these assumptions, theologians that adopt the comparative approach focus on "interreligious learning" with the intent to enrich their understanding of both their own religion and other religions.[21] Unlike the apologia approach, the comparative approach is noncombative. The comparative and the dialogical approaches have similar characteristics. The difference between the dialogical approach and the comparative approach lies in their primary agendas and not so much in the forms of engagement. In both approaches, people must arrive at the table of interreligious conversations with an open mind, a willingness to learn from others, a commitment to check at the door *a priori* judgments on other religions. Unlike the dialogical approach, however, the comparative approach does not aim to collaboratively attain a common understanding or decision on an issue.

19. Ateek, "Palestinian Theology of Jerusalem," 89, 92–93.
20. For more discussion, see Clooney, *Comparative Theology*, 3–5.
21. Ibid., 5.

Christian theologians operating with the comparative approach seek to gain new insights into other religions, which may in turn push them to rethink their preconceived notions of those religions (and sometimes their views of Christianity). This approach requires a Christian theologian to leave his or her Christian comfort zone and to proceed into the religious space of another religion. For example, the theologian may not rely on the writings of Christian theologians about another religion. The prejudice of many such writings (some of which describe other religions pejoratively as "cults") inhibit a serious inquirer from seeing other religions on their own terms and forms of expression. The more adventurous theologians may attend religious meetings and sacred places of worship of people of other religions. They read also the sacred texts of other religions. As the Orthodox Church theologian Gavin Flood has argued, reading the sacred texts of people of other religions "can serve to highlight the neglected, yet important, aspects of the reader's tradition." The reader, Flood insists, must be "genuinely open to another tradition, and to let that tradition enrich the reader's own."[22]

Strengths: The comparative approach is perhaps the most nonintrusive of all the three approaches I have discussed. In the comparative approach, theologians remain committed to their own religious truth claims and at the same time respect the truth claims of other religions. Since the theologians neither aim to convert people of other religions nor desire to reach an inter-religious theological consensus, the comparative approach avoids confrontations. Also, theologians that use this approach see themselves as "seekers" who are open to gain insights into different religions rather than "custodians" whose task is to clean up the mess of other religions. Some religious conflicts are the result of misunderstanding the teaching of other religions. The comparative approach provides theologians with the opportunity to learn from experts who are committed adherents of other religions.[23] Learning from such experts will prevent distortions, generalizations, and wrong understandings of the truth claims, values, precepts, and practices of other religions.

Weaknesses: A major weakness of the comparative approach is that it forces Christian theologians to ignore Christian teaching on evangelism (Matt 28:16–20). The work of "making disciples," which Jesus commanded his disciples to do, involves a conscious attempt to preach to non-Christians with the intent to convert them to the way of Christ. Another criticism of the comparative approach is that adopting it requires abstaining from making judgment on the theological claims of other religions. Certainly,

22. Flood, "Orthodox Christianity and World Religions," 575.
23. Fredericks, *Faith among Faiths*, 164.

all religions do not make the same truth claims. Since most of the essential truth claims of religions compete, it follows that some of them are false or are at least misleading. As Gavin D'Costa argues, "What is perplexing is the interesting phenomenon that none of the comparativists seem willing to make these types of judgment concerning questions of truth."[24]

Proponents: Two theologians below provide a good example of the comparative approach. While Francis Clooney interacts with Hinduism, K. K. Yeo focuses on Confucianism.

Francis X. Clooney

The Jesuit Roman Catholic theologian Francis Clooney is an example of comparative theologians who emphasize the need for an attentive and respectful reading of sacred texts. In his comparative approach, Clooney, whose study focuses on Christian-Hindu relations, argues that having a close contact with the people and sacred texts of other religions is essential for engaging in interreligious conversations. Learning the sacred texts of other religions, Clooney argues, results in the self-transformation of the learner. He writes, "We see ourselves differently, intuitively uncovering dimensions of ourselves that would not otherwise, by a non-comparative logic, come to the fore."[25] The passage below underscores Clooney's usage of the comparative approach in his engagement with Hinduism. It shows also Clooney's conception of "comparative theology."

Comparative theology is therefore *comparative* because it is interreligious and complex in its appropriation of one's own and another religion in relation to one another. In some instances this comparison may involve evaluation, but ordinarily the priority is more simply the dynamics of a back-and-forth learning. It is a theological discipline confident about the possibility of being intelligently faithful to tradition even while seeking fresh understanding outside that tradition.

Commenting on the text of another religious tradition as a comparative practice will normally involve continued loyalty to our home community, even if now that loyalty is accompanied by the cultivation of empathy for a new tradition. For example, it is as a Roman Catholic that I read Srivaisnava Hindu texts and commentaries. Admitting that I am a Christian commentator rules out a guise of entirely neutural scholarship—objectivity remains

24. D'Costa, *Christianity and World Religions*, 42.
25. Clooney, *Comparative Theology*, 11.

important, but more is at stake. Bias is hard to eradicate but, good or bad, it gives us a direction. If we see our biases and watch them in operation, we can become freer, more vulnerable in our reading.

Let me illustrate all this with an example. . . . I wrote *The Truth, the Way, the Life: Christian Commentary on the Three Holy Mantras of the Srivaisnava Hindus* (2008) for a new series of Christian commentaries on the sacred texts of non-Christian traditions. . . . In writing it, I decided from the start not to read alone. I am therefore heavily indebted to the commentary of Vedanta Desika, the great fourteenth-century Srivaisnava Hindu theologian. The project was therefore a somewhat lavish act of attention to three brief mantras, and yet, by the obligations arising in that project, a plunge into the much broader world of a particular faith community. . . . I wanted to learn in such a way as to make myself able to take to heart words such as those of the Tiru Mantra:

Aum, obeisance to Narayana [God] with *Sri* [reverence].

I wanted to read the tradition of the mantras in such a way as to enable me to pray differently when I returned to words familiar to my own tradition, now with a double mindfulness crossing spiritual borders:

Abba, Father

Aum, obeisance to *Narayana* with *Sri*.[26]

Questions: What does the passage say about the importance of reading other religions' sacred texts in interreligious conversation? How does the passage suggest we approach the reading of the sacred texts of other religions?

K. K. Yeo

I turn now to the Chinese Christian theologian K. K. Yeo, whose theological and intercultural works engage both Christianity and Confucianism. Yeo adopts a model of comparative approach that grounds both Christianity and Confucianism (Confucian ethics in particular) in their specific historical milieus with the intent to reimagine how Chinese Christians can negotiate their identities in a diverse religious context. In *Musing with Confucius and Paul: Toward a Chinese Christian Theology*, Yeo focuses on Confucius' *Analects* (a collection of ethical and social teaching of Confucius and his disciples) and Paul's Epistle to the Galatian Christians. Yeo uses these two religious texts as guides as he wrestles with the complex problem of negating

26. Ibid., 11, 64–65.

one's identity "in a world of violence, fear, and difference" with the hope that it is possible to "coexist peacefully" in our diverse world.[27]

The cross-cultural lens through which Paul critically views his own sacred cultural tradition, transforming it through Christ for the benefit of the Gentiles, is a critical tool applicable to my own reading of the Confucianist culture in which I was raised. The task of appropriating traditional texts, such as the *Analects* and Galatians, in our contemporary era poses a challenging question: How can a cross-cultural and global interpretation of such texts not be trapped by ethnocentrism? I am aware that how I reappropriate these texts for the establishment and clarification of my own identity does not mean it is the only way of being a Chinese Christian. I understand that many Chinese Christians will find John, or James, or Buddhist, or Daoist—or other cultural and religious—texts more prominent for and meaningful in their lives.

The criteria of inclusivity and plurality cannot alone determine the correctness of a point of view; otherwise, polytheism becomes a valid religion, and racism becomes a valid way of social interaction. While the *Analects* contains discourses on human flourishing, it does not have a totalizing theory of a global culture. Also, while it presents an ethic of virtue and attempts to argue for it persuasively, it does not seek to conquer other, non-Chinese nations by its supposedly superior Zhou-*li* (propriety of the Zhou dynasty). The rhetoric of the *Analects* seeks to invite readers to participate in the pursuit of virtue, and it uses the rhetoric of consent rather than of domination.

Paul consistently uses the criterion of Christ's salvation for all humanity to define the gospel truth, and Confucius consistently uses the ideal of the virtuous life to define the *telos* (purpose and goal) of ethics. Any thought or action adverse to such a criterion or ideal is rejected. As a Chinese Christian, my work in cross-cultural hermeneutics supports inclusivity and plurality *only in ways* that fit the criteria of Christ's work of salvation and Confucius' ideal of ethics of virtue. Thus, I do not believe that hatred saves a person, [and] I do not accept that violence or war can form virtue in a community.[28]

Question: Why does Yeo find Confucius' *Analects* and Paul's Epistle to the Galatians non-mutually exclusive?

27. Yeo, *Musing with Confucius and Paul*, xvii–xviii.
28. Ibid., 84–85.

Concluding Reflections

A Christian theology of religions should make relevant contributions to the discussions that are aimed at (*a*) preventing religious conflicts, (*b*) rediscovering the place of religions in shaping human society, (*c*) and preserving the integrity of religion as a viable path to follow in seeking satisfying answers to human beings' search for the ultimate meaning of existence. No single religion on its own can successfully meet these three requirements. Christians must collaborate with people of other religions if Christianity is to remain relevant in contemporary discourse on interreligious conversations. But what in-house principles should govern Christians as they enter into interreligious conversations? This is an extremely difficult question to answer because the answer must not disregard the nonnegotiable truth claims of Christianity (such as Jesus Christ is *the* Savior of the world). I suggest the following three broad principles.

Principle I: *Preserving God's prerogatives.* Christians must steer clear of making universal religious claims on issues of which no human being has an exclusive knowledge. For instance, Christians cannot claim beyond the shadow of doubt that they have an exclusive access to the knowledge of all that God desires for the world. That God's words cannot be reduced to human words and that God remains a *mystery* even after revealing God's self to humanity are consistently taught in the Christian Scriptures. To cite a few examples from the writing of the Apostle Paul, no mere human beings have an access to God's mind. In a doxological section of his Epistle to the Christians living in Rome, Paul writes, "Oh, the depth of the riches of the wisdom and knowledge of God! How unsearchable his judgments, and his paths beyond tracing out. Who has known the mind of the Lord? Or who has been his counselor? Who has ever given to God, that God should repay him? For from him and through him and to him are all things" (Rom 11:33–36 NIV; see also 1 Cor 2:11–13). In his letter to the Christians in Corinth, Paul writes, "For we know in part and we prophesy in part, but when perfection comes, the imperfect disappears. . . . Now we see but a poor reflection as in a mirror; then we shall see face to face. Now I know in part; then I shall know fully, even as I am fully known" (1 Cor 13:9–12 NIV). Scriptural teaching about God's *mystery* should be a stark reminder to Christians of the danger of making absolute claims regarding matters that clearly are God's prerogatives. As such, Christians must enter the religious public arena with the openness to allow God to be God to all people of all nations. By insisting that Christianity is *the* arbiter of true religions and true statements about God, some Christians may have unknowingly "colonized" God in interreligious conversations.

Principle II: *Retaining the Christian evangelistic motif.* Christians cannot freely preach the gospel in a world saturated with religious conflicts and antagonism. Many Christians blame the ills of their societies on non-Christian religious values and beliefs. People of other religions or no religious affiliations also blame Christians for some religious conflicts in the world. There is certainly enough blame to go around. The issue, however, is how Christians can continue to carry out the mission mandate in the world that has become increasingly antagonistic to Christians' claim about the superiority of Christianity to other religions. Many people are increasingly turned off by what they consider Christianity's arrogant and belligerent truth claims. Some Christians may respond to this attitude of non-Christians toward Christianity by insisting, as Harold Netland contends, that Christians "must embrace with confidence what the Scriptures clearly affirm, even when doing so puts [them] at odds with the reigning ethos of [their] time."[29] Netland, however, gives a helpful caution: "But we must treat with greater tentativeness those matters on which the Bible is less clear and over which there can be responsible disagreement."[30]

A Christian theology of religions should allow the Christian "gospel" (good news) to be the gospel in the public sphere. The greatest challenge facing Christians' proclamation of the gospel in the secular and multireligious world may no longer be securing the freedom to preach the gospel. It is rather the unwillingness of many Christians to give God's gospel (embodied by Jesus of Nazareth, the Christ) the freedom to be the gospel in the world. Similarly, a Christian theology of religions should not reduce the Christian gospel to a *set of propositions* (such as "explicit faith in Jesus Christ in this present life is necessary for salvation"). On the contrary, a Christian theology of religions should be centered on the life (teaching, experience, and good deeds) of Jesus Christ. In the conversation on interreligious conversations in the public sphere, Christians' preeminent aim should not be to bring to the table their doctrinal statements about Jesus Christ and salvation. Rather, Christians must aim to point people in the direction of Jesus and also invite them to rethink their ways of being human in light of Jesus' vision as witnessed by the Christian Scriptures. Our Christologies (including our christological propositions) only help us to speak about the person and significance of Jesus. They do not exhaust the vistas of Jesus' person and significance and, therefore, should not take his place in interreligious discourses.

29. Netland, *Encountering Religious Pluralism*, 314.
30. Ibid.

Principle III: *Focusing on social problems.* Frequently, interreligious discussions are hijacked by people interested in making doctrinal claims and solving doctrinal problems. While doctrines are important to religious communities' beliefs and practices, it should be noted that people who are not members of a religious community will most likely be uninterested in adopting it as a way of life. Living in multiple religious communities requires tolerating disparate and competing religious doctrines. Given that religion is implicated in many lingering social problems (such as terrorism and racism), Christians should be ready to show that Christianity has substantive contributions to make on how to deal with existing social problems and also how to prevent social problems in their societies and in the world at large. Jürgen Moltmann rightly argues that "Jesus did not found a new religion; he brings life into the world." Christians' responsibility is to preserve the dignity of human life. Christians should work collaboratively with adherents of other religions, and people without a religion, to engage in a "common struggle for life, for loved and loving life, for life that communicates itself and is shared, life that is human and natural—in short, life that is worth living in the fruitful living space of this earth."[31]

31. Moltmann, *Sun of Righteousness, Arise!*, 77.

Table 3.1

Summary of Approaches in Christian Theologies of Religions

Approach	Agenda	Strengths	Weaknesses	Proponents
Apologia	• To make a case for the truthfulness of Christian beliefs and practices.	• Inspires Christians to defend their beliefs and practices boldly in the presence of competing religions.	• Rarely leads to the conversion of non-Christians to Christianity. • Its combativeness most times leads to unhelpful confrontations.	• Timothy I of Baghdad • Byang Kato
Dialogical	• To arrive at an agreeable parameter within which adherents of competing religions can address religious issues and problems.	• Promotes religious toleration. • Its emphasis on collaboration builds bridges between competing religions.	• Has the capacity to hide destructive mindsets (e.g., superiority mindset) that obstruct meaningful dialogue.	• Rowan Williams • Naim Ateek
Comparative	• To converse with people of other religions with the intent to gain insights into both Christianity and non-Christian religions.	• Gives Christians the opportunity to learn about other religions, which can eliminate wrong perceptions of other religions.	• Does not empower Christians to witness the gospel of Jesus Christ to people of other religions and to seek to convert them. • Shies away from making theological judgments on other religions' truth claims.	• Francis Clooney • K. K. Yeo

Exercise 3.1

Critique the theologians discussed above. Discuss the strengths of their arguments and forms of interreligious engagement. Also, discuss the weaknesses of their arguments and why their forms of interreligious engagement may not be sustainable in the context of your community.

Major Objectives in Christian Theologies of Religions

Christians do not usually engage in interreligious conversation without agendas or goals. Several goals can be discerned in Christian theologies of religions. I have already hinted at some of these goals in the preceding section. I will explore them further in this section, drawing out their import for engaging in meaningful interreligious conversations and activities. The vast majority of Christians aim to convert people of other religions to Christianity whenever they engage in interreligious conversations. The *conversion* objective remains prominent in Christian theologies of religions. However, an increasing number of Christian theologians have begun steering away from making conversion the preeminent purpose of their theologies of religions. Some of these theologians are concerned that the conversion motif blocks meaningful conversations with people of other religions. For them, when the claim to superiority and the concern for the eternal salvation of humanity are combined, people tend to engage in polemics instead of dialoguing with people of other religions.[32] Many such theologians now focus more on Christian responsibility: how Christians should act as citizens of the world in the manner that is responsible both in the eyes of the people of other religions and as well as in the eyes of their fellow Christians. I will focus my discussion on the *conversion object* and *irenic object*.

> FOCUS QUESTION:
> What goals drive Christian theologians' interreligious conversations?

Conversion Object

Many Christians enter into interreligious conversations with the intent to convert non-Christians to Christianity. For these Christians, converting non-Christians is central to Christianity's theology of evangelism. The Great Commission, which Jesus gave to his followers—"go and make disciples

32. Lindbeck, *Nature of Doctrine*, 55–56.

of all nations" (Matt 28:16–20, see also Acts 1:1–9)—has been the major impetus for Christian witness and missionary work. But what exactly does "conversion" mean? In the New Testament, the Greek words *epistrophē* ("conversion") and *epistrephō* ("to change," "to convert") are used to convey the idea of turning from idols and turning to God (see Acts 14:15). I have discussed elsewhere three principal presuppositions underlying Christians' mission to "convert" people of other religions. First, some Christians believe that destroying the core beliefs of other religions is required in order for Christianity's gospel to take firm root in people's lives (destructionist presupposition). Second, other Christians see Christianity as the only religion that can satisfy and fulfill the deep religious aspirations found in other religions (gap and fulfillment presupposition). Third, for some Christians, other religions are to be reconstructed in the light of Christianity's truth claims (deconstructionist presupposition).[33]

The history of the usage of the term "conversion" in Christian circles is shrouded in linguistic complexities. Theologically, "conversion" may involve both internal (inward) and external (outward) changes. The inward change is the turning of one's will and heart from a godless life to a life of obedience to God. In the Christian sense, an inward change entails turning to a life of obedience to God as governed by the life of Christ and empowered by the Holy Spirit. Protestants have traditionally understood the internal or inward aspect of conversion to mean "an early stage of the pilgrimage of the soul awakened to God."[34] In other Christian denominations, such as the Eastern Orthodox Churches, conversion is used in a more robust sense to emphasize the lifelong process of partaking in the life of God (*theosis* in Greek). Regarding the external aspect (outward change), some Christians expect that an inward change should be followed by a movement from a different religion to Christianity.[35] For most Christians, "conversion" entails abandoning one's non-Christian religious beliefs and accepting Christianity's teachings. Christians who see "conversion" in this way will contend that it is not sufficient for a Christian convert to remain an adherent of another religion. It is not sufficient to merely adopt some aspects of Christianity's teachings but remaining loyal to a non-Christian religion. For such

33. For detailed discussion of these presuppositions, see Ezigbo, *Re-imagining African Christologies*, 25–46.

34. Walls, "Converts and Proselytes?," 2.

35. Within Christianity, some Christians expect people of other denominations to leave their church to join a new church when they experience a true inward conversion. For example, many Evangelicals around the world preach to Roman Catholics with the expectation that when they become born again they will leave Roman Catholic churches to join Evangelical churches.

Christians, turning back on one's former religion is viewed as a necessary precondition for a true conversion.

Some Christians understand "conversion" as a process involving regeneration, exercise of faith, and repentance in which a sinner is gradually transformed into a follower of Jesus Christ. It involves a change in behavior, and of worldview. The sinner comes to accept Jesus as savior and allows Jesus' life and teaching to redirect and govern his or her life.[36] Sometimes Christian converts use the expression "old ways" to describe their pre-Christian religious beliefs and the expression "new way" to indicate they have now abandoned their old religions for a new one. Stanley Grenz shares this understanding of conversion. He writes, "Conversion is that life-changing encounter with the triune God which inaugurates the process of forsaking our old ways as fallen creatures and living in accordance with God's design for human existence."[37]

The ideas of conversion described above have been met with severe criticisms. Some theologians argue that such views of conversion are utterly naïve. It assumes religion can always be neatly separated from the cultures of a society. In many societies, religious beliefs inform the cultures and vice versa. For example, the earliest Christians were Jewish in terms of birth, inheritance, culture, and religion.[38] Becoming followers of Jesus Christ did not mean they had to abandon their religion. On the contrary, they rethought and reimagined their religious teachings, expectations, and beliefs in the light of Jesus, the Messiah. In the words of Andrew Walls, it was "Jewish life and thought turned toward Messiah Jesus."[39] Some African theologians have argued for an idea of conversion in which the indigenous religious beliefs and practices are turned toward Jesus Christ rather than requiring African Christian converts to abandon all aspects of indigenous religious thoughts and practices. For these theologians, the task of removing the layers of indigenous religions and cultures from Africans with the intent to replace them with Christian cultures is bound to be unsuccessful. The issue here is not whether the task can be accomplished per se but rather the end product. The earliest Western missionaries who worked in sub-Saharan Africa between the 1700s and mid-1900s eventually learned, albeit painfully, the difficulty of such a task. Most of them, for the sake of preserving what they believed to be "biblical Christianity" required the abandonment of many African cultures (such as African names, dance steps, forms of

36. See ch. 2 for more discussion on the Christian doctrine of conversion.

37. Grenz, *Theology for the Community of God*, 433.

38. Walls, "Converts and Proselytes?," 3.

39. Ibid., 4.

preaching, forms of worship, and so on) as a prerequisite for becoming a member of a church. The consequence, of course, was making Africans "Western Christians" (that is, Africans who behave and act like Western-ers) rather than "African Christians." The missionaries, however, underes-timated the power of the indigenous cultures and religions. Many African Christians, at difficult times, revert to the indigenous religions' solutions to their existential needs. Some, for example, visit native doctors and oracles of local deities to seek knowledge of the causes of and solutions to their health problems, poor harvest, and dying businesses.[40]

Some African Christian scholars have been very critical of the "old" missionary ways. They propose alternative approaches that can enable African converts to Christianity to avoid the error of construing African indigenous religions as "evil and irrelevant once one becomes a Christian."[41] African Christians and theologians, Lovemore Togarasei argues, must stop "preaching a 'Europeanized' gospel" and start preaching "an 'African-ized gospel.'" Togarasei's goal is to legitimatize the use of some concepts, thoughts, and precepts of African indigenous religions in constructing Christian theology.[42] Writing from the Native American (or First Nations) context, the Lakota/Sioux theologian Richard Twiss makes a similar argu-ment. Twiss scolds Christians who see all of Native American cultures as idolatrous and counter to Christian cultures. Twiss contends that human cultures are tainted by sin. Consequently, he concludes, "When we come to Christ as First Nations people, Jesus does not ask us to abandon our sin-stained culture in order to embrace someone else's sin-stained culture."[43] To Twiss, all Christians are to judge their *own* cultures "by the light of God's Word" and not by a foreign culture.[44]

To be a "Christian" (that is, a person who has converted to Christian-ity) is to commit to the *way* of Jesus: his redirection, critiquing, and remold-ing of one's life according to his vision of the world. In this context, the term "Christ's follower" is very helpful in capturing what Christians ought to be and how they ought to behave. Followers of Christ must experience *conversion*: a lifelong act of turning their former ways of life and beliefs that have been conditioned by their cultures and religious or nonreligious values toward Christ. Andrew Walls highlights this understanding of Christian

---

40. For extensive discussions on this issue, see Ezigbo, *Re-imagining African Chris-tologies*, ch. 3.

41. Togarasei, "Conversion of Paul," 118.

42. Ibid., 121.

43. Twiss, *One Church, Many Tribes*, 79.

44. Ibid., 77.

conversion. He writes, "Converts face a much riskier life. Converts have to be constantly, relentlessly turning their ways of thinking, their education and training, their ways of working and doing things toward Christ. They must think Christ into the patterns of thought they inherited, into their network of relationships and their process of making decision."[45] Conversion stands in sharp contrast with proselyting. Proselytes, Walls contends, play safe: "They give up their old customs and beliefs and take up those of someone else."[46] On the contrary, in conversion, emphasis is placed on redirecting what is *already there* and turning it toward Christ.

Irenic Object

Some atheists charge religion with the crime of obstruction: as a phenomenon that prevents human beings from developing scientifically and socially. To cite one example, Richard Dawkins in *The God Delusion* justifies his hostility toward what he calls "fundamentalist religion" on the grounds that religion in general inhibits people from developing intellectually and scientifically. He writes, "As a scientist, I am hostile to fundamentalist religion because it actively debauches the scientific enterprise. It teaches us not to change our minds, and not to want to know exciting things that are available to be known. It subverts science and saps the intellect."[47] Dakwins also blames religion for many violent acts that destroy world peace.[48] Critics of Dawkins' antagonism toward religion have pointed out his failure to recognize that there are many religious people (not in the sense of Dawkins' "Einsteinian religion" but in the sense of what he calls "supernatural religion") who are great scientists.[49] Dawkins is doubtful that a true scientist can genuinely believe in an "interventionist, miracle-wreaking, thought-reading, sin-punishing, [and] prayer-answering God of the Bible, of priests, mullahs and rabbis, and of ordinary language."[50] For Dawkins, people who believe in such God are deranged or delusional.

---

45. Walls, "Converts and Proselytes?," 6.

46. Ibid.

47. Dawkins, *God Delusion*, 321.

48. Ibid., 46–50.

49. Dawkins defines "Einsteinian religion" (from Albert Einstein) as a naturalistic form of "religion," which uses the term "God" metaphorically for nature. In contrast, "supernatural religion" is the form of "religion" that teaches the existence of a personal God who created the world and is actively involved in its governance.

50. Dawkins, *God Delusion*, 41.

I suspect that religious people (as some atheists) may not share most of Dawkins' negative assessments of religion. Dawkins' diehard atheistic propensity prevents him from acknowledging the intellectual integrity of both religious and nonreligious people who are convinced that questions about the universe cannot be answered from the perspective of science alone. Many people disagree with what Dawkins perceives as an irreconcilable chasm between "science" and "religion."[51] But religious people must take seriously Dawkins' critique of religion, particularly his critique of religiously motivated violence that threatens the world's peace. And one must not let Dawkins' denial of violence perpetrated by atheists against religious people lessen the seriousness of religiously incited violence.[52] That religions have sometimes been disruptive is also evident. Religious conflicts are more rampant in the world today.[53] These issues raise questions about the peaceful coexistence of religions and the continuing relevance of religion *as a public phenomenon* (and not merely a private matter) in the world. But is strife a necessary consequence of coming together of diverse religions and cultures? While this may appear to be the case, it is not necessarily the case. The coming together of disparate religions (which has become more prevalent through cross-immigration of adherents of competing religions) need not produce destructive conflicts and evils. The Orthodox Church theologian John McGuckin has noted that a person may not support the views of people who do not share his or her religious beliefs and yet can refrain from making "judgments about their respective claims" and at the same time show sincere respect for them. For McGuckin, religious people must respect the otherness of competing religions and desist from "advocating violence in the name of the God of peace."[54]

Students of religion know too well that religion is implicated in violence. On many occasions, religious people have perpetrated violent acts. As I write this chapter, I pause to reflect on the sufferings of Nigerian parents whose daughters were abducted in April 2014 by an Islamic militia group (led by Abubakar Shekau) that claims to be doing the work of God or Allah. Similar religiously motivated conflicts, evils acts, and wars historically

51. For an accessible critique of Dawkins' *God Delusion*, see McGrath and McGrath, *The Dawkins Delusion? Atheist Fundamentalism and the Denial of the Divine.*

52. For a recent indictment of religion's involvement in violence, see de Kadt, *Assertive Religion: Religious Intolerance in an Multicultural World.*

53. Some Christian theologians argue that religion is implicated in violence not because it is the causative factor (what causes violence) but rather because it is an instrumental factor (the means through which violence is executed and justified). See Samartha, "Cross and the Rainbow," 108.

54. McGuckin, *Orthodox Church*, 427.

have happened and continue to occur in many parts of the world. When examined in light of the life and teaching of Jesus Christ, Christianity is to remain a religion that proclaims peace to the world and also opposes violence. Christians betray Jesus Christ's mission of healing, liberation, and peace (Luke 4:16–21) when they are complicit in social strife and fail to act as agents of peace in the world.[55] The words of the French sociologist and theologian Jacques Ellul (1912–94) regarding what ought to be Christians' attitude toward violence are informative. Ellul writes that a Christian "must struggle against violence precisely *because*, apart from Christ, violence is the form that human relations normally and necessarily take. In other words, the more completely violence seems to be of the order of necessity, the greater is the obligation of the believers in Christ's lordship to overcome it by challenging necessity."[56]

The religion that does not inspire its adherents to be agents of peace and reconciliation is irrelevant and unhelpful to the world. Adherents of Christianity have the responsibility to show that their religion has the capacity to produce people who are agents of peace in *this* world. One may begin by asking: Is Christianity in itself violent? Or is the violence associated with Christianity to be attributed only to some Christians' distortion of their religion? Students of religious conflicts and resolutions know that answering these questions requires exercising caution. Religion cannot be successfully discussed in the abstract. People make "religion" present in the public sphere. In other words, as soon as a religion leaves a private sphere to enter into the public realm, it uses humans as its mode of being (presence) and operation. Therefore, the noble goal to discuss a given religion from a neutral standpoint and also in insolation from its adherents is doomed to failure.

How can Christian theologies of religions inspire actions that promote the peaceful coexistence of people with different religions in a world in which religion has become one of the principal causes of (or mode of executing) conflicts and wars? The public religious space has become somewhat like unchartered waters filled with dehumanizing assumptions, acrimonious attitudes, and increasing intolerance of people with opposing religions. Christian theologians have not shied away from negotiating their religious identity in these difficult waters. For some people, talks about interreligious relationships and the peaceful coexistence of competing religions must be grounded in justice. Writing in the context of the Middle East— the Israeli-Palestinian religious and political contexts in particular—Naim

---

55. Volf, "Social Meaning of Reconciliation," 159.
56. Ellul, *Violence*, 127–28.

Ateek boldly asserts, "Where peace is, a meal is prepared; it is the feast of reconciliation ready to be celebrated. There is, however, no entrance except through the door of justice."[57] Justice as Ateek imagines it must be holistic: it must extend to the people of Israel and to the Palestinians. For him, those who achieve their own justice on unjust grounds live unjustly.[58] Curtiss DeYoung, after reflecting on the works of African American Brenda Salter McNeil, the Native American Richard Twiss, the Palestinian Jean Zaru, and the South African Allan Boesak, argues that "reconciliation cannot proceed without liberation, and in particular restitution or reparation."[59]

Is it *Christian* to say "no justice, no peace"? Put differently, must Christians insist on prioritizing justice and making it the prerequisite for peaceful coexistence with adherents of other religions that persecute Christians? The questions about justice, the means to attain it, and the possibility of attaining it without injuring others, open up complex issues that have hindered talks about peaceful coexistence. For example, can justice be done without, to some reasonable measures, *punishing* (which sometimes is driven by retaliation as its remote motive) perpetrators of unjust actions? Sunday Agang has argued that some Nigerian Christians believe it is only through violent retaliation that they can redress the religious wars and conflicts between Christians and Muslims in Nigeria. This belief has driven some Christians to burn down mosques and to murder some Muslims in retaliation for the terrorist attacks against Christians in Northern Nigeria by Muslim militants.[60] Also, can justice be attained without violence? Some people seeking justice engage in violent acts to bring attention to the people and structures that preserve injustices. The problem with achieving justice through violence (which may result in indiscriminate mass killings), of course, is that it stains the conscience of the religion whose adherents have committed the violent acts. Also, violence breeds future violent behaviors and acts. Violence breeds a long-lasting hatred, which becomes a fertile ground for nurturing future (retaliatory) hate crimes.

Given the problems associated with the quest for justice as the primary goal in redressing conflicts and strife, some theologians have proposed replacing justice with reconciliation. The Croatia-born theologian Miroslav Volf is one such theologian. Volf has argued that making liberation and justice, instead of reconciliation, the primary categories of Christian social responsibility "divorces the character of social engagement from the very center of the

---

57. Ateek, *Justice, and Only Justice*, 177.

58. Ibid.

59. DeYoung, *Coming Together in the 21st Century*, 148.

60. Agang, "Breaking Nigeria's Fatal Deadlock," 48.

Christian faith—from the narrative of the cross of Christ which reveals the character of the triune God."[61] Volf goes on to contend that another problem with making liberation or justice the primary categories is that they can lead Christians to reduce "the moral complexity of the situation [. . .] feeding into the self-righteousness of each party by assuring them that God is on their side."[62] To Volf, the advantage of making reconciliation the primary category in conflict situations is that it highlights justice's relationship to grace and forgiveness. He argues that justice is subordinate both to grace and recon-ciliation. Volf is not undermining the need for justice but is rather contend-ing for Christian-talk about justice to be located within the framework of reconciliation. Drawing insights from the experience of Saul on the road to Damascus, Volf argues that Saul (who became Paul) was able to change from a persecutor to an outstanding missionary because God's response to Paul's appalling violent acts was governed by reconciliation rather than justice. He writes, "On the road to Damascus, Paul encountered the God who, though clearly opposed to Paul's intentions, did not let the demands of justice govern God's actions toward him but instead showed love by offering reconciliation to Paul, the enemy."[63] As a result, Paul returned God's gifts of forgiveness and reconciliation by giving his resources and his life to the community he had previously sought to destroy through violent means.[64] God's offering of recon-ciliation to Paul, Volf contends, deeply informed Paul's language of reconcilia-tion in his letters (see Rom 15:7; 2 Cor 5:17–21; Eph 2:14; Col 1:20). For Volf, "exclusion" is a powerful force that stands in opposition to "reconciliation." While "exclusion" leads to elimination of the other, reconciliation requires embracing the (violent) other.[65] Volf's proposal that we make "reconciliation" (or the embrace of the unjust other) the central focus may detract from the importance of seeking justice in *this* life. Embracing unjust people who are implicated in unjust structures, beliefs, and actions without exposing their injustices and reclaiming justice for those deprived of it, may be counterpro-ductive. Should people who are systematically deprived of justice continue to embrace the unjust structure and people that oppress them without "fighting" for justice? The danger of giving either reconciliation or justice the focal place, instead of viewing them in a symbiotic relation, is that when one of them is overemphasized the other is diminished.

61. Volf, "Social Meaning of Reconciliation," 163.

62. Ibid.

63. Ibid., 163–64.

64. Ibid., 164.

65. Volf, *Exclusion and Embrace*, 74–75.

Other theologians propose that interfaith dialogue should focus on concrete human experiences and shared human concerns. Paul F. Knitter is convinced that theology of religions should not be made an intellectual affair discussed in abstract scenarios. Theologies of religions, on the contrary, should be situated in real human situations. Writing specifically about Indian and Sri Lankan contexts, Knitter proposes that a true interreligious dialogue happens when people experience "'worldly' conversion," that is, "devoting oneself unrestrictedly to the well-being of our suffering relatives and planet."[66] The dialogue should be committed to "eco-human justice and well-being."[67] When the well-being of humans and ecology, and not religious truth claims, occupy the center stage in interreligious dialogues, people will learn to enter into interreligious dialogues expecting that their truth claims may be "relativized in the wider conversation with other strong claims and with even the stronger demand to remove human and ecological suffering."[68] Knitter's theology of religions is deeply informed by liberation theologies of Latin American theologians such as Gustavo Gutierrez and Leonardo Boff, whose works are grounded in the quest for the liberation of the poor and oppressed. Knitter contends that the requisites for globally responsible theology of religions and interreligious dialogues are the pre-reflective and pre-theological commitment to the liberation of the eco-human suffering. He writes, without limiting the "priority of praxis to simplistic chronological interpretations, this method urges that all our efforts at dialoguing or understanding each other be preceded or accompanied or pervaded by some form of shared practical efforts to remove eco-human suffering."[69]

Some theologians see human development or flourishing as what ought to occupy the privileged position in interreligious conversations. For some of these theologians, the primary task of interreligious exchange should not be to covert people of other religions. On the contrary, the task should be to help people of other religions reach their full potential and to become better citizens. George Lindbeck, for example, has argued that the "missionary task of Christians may at times be to encourage Marxists to become better Marxists, Jews and Muslims to become better Jews and Muslims, and Buddhists to become better Buddhists." Christians, however, must undertake this task only with the full cooperation of the people of

---

66. Knitter, One Earth, Many Religions, 133.

67. Ibid., 134.

68. Ibid., 134–35.

69. Ibid., 138.

other religions.[70] They must not superimpose Christian values on their ways of thinking and their manner of living.

What is striking about the issues I have discussed under the *irenic object* in Christian theologies of religions is the quest to underline the social consequences of Christianity's teaching about peace, justice, and human flourishing. Christians have the social responsibility to embody Jesus' teaching about the kingdom of God—the divine reign in which (*a*) God confronts God's creatures' attempt to enthrone themselves as lords of the universe and (*b*) God redirects the world to God's intended purpose. Christians must shoulder the responsibility to show how Jesus' message about the kingdom of God bears on their perceptions of the people of other religions. When their perceptions and treatment of people of other religions conflict with Jesus' life of self-giving as represented in the Scriptures, Christians must rethink their theologies of religions.

Christian Theologies of Religions and the Doctrine of Salvation

Luke in Acts narrates a story about two early Christian missionaries (Paul and Silas) whose experience in a jail in Philippi led to a jailor's conversion to Christianity. Prior to the jailor's conversion, Luke tells us about a young slave girl possessed by an evil spirit who followed Paul and Silas around and was saying these words: "These men are servants of

> FOCUS QUESTION:
> What are the implications of Christianity's soteriology for interreligious conversations?

the Most High God, who are telling you the way to be saved" (Acts 16:17). When Paul could no longer endure the slave girl's disturbance, he delivered her (through the power of the risen Christ) from demon possession. The owners of the slave girl, fearing the loss of their means of revenue, which they generated from the slave girl's ability to predict the future, brought Paul and Silas to the magistrates (Acts 16:19–24). The magistrates ruled against Paul and Silas and sent them to jail. An earthquake, however, was about to shorten their stay in the jail. Luke appears to attribute the earthquake to God's work, which he also associates with Paul' and Silas' singing of songs of praises to God (Acts 16:25). Fearing that Paul and Silas had escaped—an earthquake had shattered the jail's door—the jailor wanted to take his own life. Paul intervened, announcing their presence. The jailor's reaction was

70. Lindbeck, *Nature of Doctrine*, 54.

rather unusual—instead of expressing appreciation to Paul and Silas, he posed a soteriological question: "Sirs," he said, "what must I do to be saved?" (Acts 16:29 NIV). They said to him, "Believe in the Lord Jesus Christ, and you will be saved—you and your household" (Acts 16:31 NIV).

Are people whose theologies of salvation contradict Christianity's teaching about Jesus' role as *the* savior of the world excluded from God's salvation? Since the appearance of Allan Race's *Christians and Religious Pluralism,*[71] many theologians have classified the theological answers to the question I raised above into three categories: *exclusivism* ("yes": Jesus' salvific work and also people's knowledge of and response to Jesus' salvific work are necessary for salvation); *inclusivism* ("no but cautious": his salvific work makes salvation possible, and people need not hear about him and exercise faith in him before they can be saved); and *pluralism* ("no": all religions have valid salvific paths and people need not go through the Christian path to be saved by God). Some theologians have judged these three classifications unsatisfactory because of their narrowness that truncates the important nuances and contours of the theological positions that are typically associated with them.[72] Carl Braaten rather unhelpfully subsumes theologians into two classes based on their positions on the issues of interreligious dialogue and salvation: "those who stick somehow to the classical focus on the uniqueness of Christ Jesus and those who surrender his centrality so that his place becomes one among many in the pantheon of the religions."[73] I prefer to classify the theological viewpoints discussed in the remainder of this chapter into three broad categories, namely, "Christian-centric" positions (theological viewpoints that give special privilege to Christianity's soteriology), "Non-Christian-centric" positions (theological viewpoints that *do not* give special privilege to Christianity's soteriology), and "Indeterminate" positions (theological viewpoints that defer final decision about human destiny to God). Given the the similarity of some of these

71. Race, *Christians and Religious Pluralism.*

72. Terrance L. Tiessen has proposed five categories as a replacement for exclusivism, inclusivism, and pluralism. (1) Ecclesiocentrism: only those who hear the gospel through the church's witness can be saved. (2) Accessibilism: God does save some of the unevangelized, but he has not raised up the world's religions as instruments for achieving this. (3) Religious instrumentalism: the various religions of the world are instruments of God's saving work through Christ among the various peoples of the world. (4) Agnosticism: we don't know whether the unevangelized can be saved or not. (5) Relativism: all religions have salvific potential in and of themselves, apart from the specific saving work God does through Christ within the Christian church. See Tiessen, *Who Can Be Saved?*, 31–47.

73. Braaten, *Apostolic Imperative,* 33.

theological viewpoints, I have provided the chart below (chart 3.1) to help the reader track the discussions.

Chart 3.1 Mapping the Theological Viewpoints

Christian-centric Position

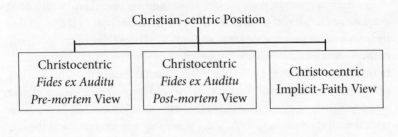

| Christocentric *Fides ex Auditu* *Pre-mortem* View | Christocentric *Fides ex Auditu* *Post-mortem* View | Christocentric Implicit-Faith View |

Non-Christian-centric Position

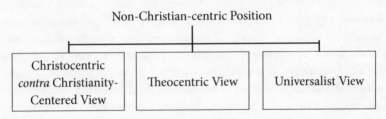

| Christocentric *contra* Christianity-Centered View | Theocentric View | Universalist View |

Description: The term "Christian-centric" (or Christianity-centered) is used here to describe the views that claim *there is no salvation outside of Christianity*: that is, Christianity is the only true religion that teaches the truth about God's salvation. This argument implies that non-Christian religions lead people away from God's salvation. The views that fit into the *Christian-centric position* argue that Christianity's teaching about Jesus Christ as the only savior of the world is true. Therefore, anyone who rejects Jesus as God's savior of the world will not be saved. As William Craig argues, "It is through him and through him alone . . . that God's forgiveness is available (Rom 5:12–21). To reject Jesus Christ is therefore to reject God's grace and forgiveness, to refuse the one means of salvation which God has provided. It is to remain under His condemnation and wrath, to forfeit eternally salvation."[74] The views I have grouped under the *Christian-centric position* have been variously labeled "restrictivism," "exclusivism," "particularism," and "inclusivism." While these labels are helpful in some cases, they are nevertheless too vague and fail to capture the nuances in the views they represent.

Biblical foundation/theological arguments: Several biblical passages can be cited in support of the *Christian-centric* position. In Acts 4:12,

74. Craig, "No Other Name," 39.

Luke recounts Apostle Peter's response to the Jewish religious leaders who warned him and John against "teaching people and proclaiming in Jesus the resurrection of the dead" (Acts 4:2 NIV). In response, Peter said, "Salvation is found in no one else, for there is *no other name* [i.e., no other authority] under heaven given to men by which we must be saved" (Acts 4:12 NIV; emphasis mine). Jesus himself can also be cited in support of the belief that he is both the author and executor of God's salvation. John 14 records Jesus' conversation with his disciples in which he told them, "You know the way to the place I am going" (John 14:4 NIV). Thomas, one of the disciples, was greatly perplexed by Jesus' assumption. He told Jesus, "Lord, we don't know where you are going, so how can we know the way?" (John 14:5 NIV). Jesus replied with the following words: "I am the way and the truth and the life. No one comes to the Father except through me" (John 14:6 NIV). This text has been interpreted by some theologians as saying no one can access God's salvation in isolation from Jesus Christ. Since Jesus is *the* access to God, they conclude that having knowledge of Jesus Christ and also exercising explicit faith in him are essential requirements for salvation. These theologians can also appeal to Rom 10:14–15 to substantiate this conclusion. Paul writes in this passage, "How, then, can they call on the one they have not believed in? And how can they believe in the one of whom they have not heard? And how can they hear without someone preaching to them? And how can they preach unless they are sent? As it is written, 'How beautiful are the feet of those who bring good news!'" (NIV) Theologians who contend that both *knowledge about Jesus Christ* and *explicit faith* in him are necessary for salvation usually interpret this passage as teaching the urgency of evangelism. For these theologians, preaching the gospel is closely tied to salvation.[75] In other words, salvific "faith comes by hearing" (*fides ex auditu* in Latin) the gospel of Jesus Christ.

Some theological viewpoints that fit into the Christian-centric position contend that the church is the *means* through which God communicates salvation to sinful humanity. In other words, there is no salvation outside of the church's sacraments, preaching, and nourishment. Other theological viewpoints contend that the church's role in God's plan of salvation is merely to preach the gospel to the unevangelized. What the theologians who hold either of these viewpoints share in common is the belief that Jesus is *ontologically necessary* for salvation. This means that the Triune God saves people on the ground of Jesus' *being* (ontological necessity): in the person and work of God incarnate (Jesus of Nazareth, the Christ), God has addressed sin and its consequences. They also hold that Jesus is *epistemologically necessary* for

75. Clark, "Is Special Revelation Necessary for Salvation?," 43.

salvation. This means that people must *hear* (have knowledge or conscious awareness) of Jesus' work of salvation and *accept in faith* (which involves personal relationship with and commitment to Jesus) in order for them to be saved. They disagree, however, on the timeframe of people's opportunity to hear the gospel.

Some theologians whose theological viewpoints fit into the *Christian-centric* position argue that God decides people's final destiny on the basis of "middle knowledge" (that is, God's knowledge of what *would* happen in all possible worlds and in all circumstances).[76] According to this view, on the basis of God's middle knowledge (*scientia media* in Latin), God has predestined the salvation of those whom God knew would freely choose "to respond to and persevere in God's grace." Similarly, the people whom God did not predestine to salvation "have no one to blame but themselves" because they would freely reject the divine grace that prompts people to respond to the offer of salvation.[77] A logical implication of this view, as William Craig, one of its advocates, has argued, is that for those whom God knew would accept Christ, God made it possible to live in a time and place where they would hear the gospel in their lifetime. Conversely, those who died without hearing the gospel are those whom God knew would not have accepted the gospel anyways. In Craig's words, "God in His providence has so arranged the world that anyone who would receive Christ has the opportunity to do so. Since God loves all persons and desires the salvation of all, He supplies sufficient grace for salvation to every individual, and nobody who would receive Christ if he were to hear the gospel will be denied that opportunity."[78]

Some theologians who believe people must hear about Jesus Christ in their lifetime and also exercise faith in him before they can be saved (christocentric *fides ex auditu* pre-mortem view), however, do not share the view espoused by William Craig. Other theologians claim that the people who through no fault of their own did not hear the gospel in this life would be given an opportunity to hear the gospel after death (christocentric *fides ex auditu* post-mortem view). Yet some theologians argue that people whose knowledge of God is limited to general revelation and who responded to such divine knowledge in faith will be saved on the basis of God's mercy, which is embodied by Jesus Christ (christocentric implicit-faith view). These three viewpoints are discussed in the following section.

---

76. For more discussions on the theological concept of "Middle Knowledge" (or Molinism), see Ezigbo, *Introducing Christian Theologies*, 1:241–42.

77. Craig, "No Other Name," 45.

78. Ibid., 51–52.

Christocentric Fides ex Auditu Pre-mortem View

Assumptions: Two primary assumptions govern the christocentric *fides ex auditu* pre-mortem view. First, Christianity is the only true saving religion and other religions lack salvific power. Therefore, any religion with truth claims competing with Christianity is false. Second, although God desires for all to be saved, God has not ordained that all will be saved.

Theological claims: The christocentric *fides ex auditu* pre-mortem view is highly nuanced. However, theologians whose theological positions fall within this view make the following claims. First, *special revelation* is neces- sary for salvation. Usually, God's special revelation is here reduced to divine propositional statements that are written in the Scriptures. Other theolo- gians define special revelation broadly to include God's supernatural acts, which may include visions, unusual events, and the Incarnation. Second, *general revelation* is non-salvific. Yet it is sufficient to erase ignorance of God's knowledge in human beings, rendering them inexcusable from God's judgment (Rom 1:18–23; see also Acts 17:22–31). Third, no one can be saved in isolation from *Jesus' objective work*: his death on the cross atones for and repairs the enmity between God and humans (John 14:6). Jesus is the only savior not merely because of his death on the cross, but also because of his *person*—he is the God incarnate. Fourth, hearing about Jesus and also explicitly exercising faith in him (in this life) as the only savior is neces- sary for salvation. This claim implies that conscious faith in Jesus Christ, which comes by hearing the gospel about Jesus Christ, is a prerequisite for salvation (Matt 28:19–20; John 3:16–18; Rom 3:21–26; 10:9–15). Fifth, hu- man destiny is permanently fixed "at the moment of physical death"[79] (Heb 9:27–28). This claim rules out the possibility of people hearing the gospel after they die.

Proponent: The American Evangelical philosophical theologian Ron- ald Nash defends the christocentric *fides ex auditu* pre-mortem view. The excerpt below is taken from Nash's *Is Jesus the Only Savior?* One of Nash's central aims in this book is to provide a reasoned argument for believing that people who do not exercise faith in Christ in this life will not be saved. Nash exercises caution by excluding infants and people with severe mental disabilities from this category. Note that Nash uses the broad term "exclu- sivism" for the view I have labeled the "christocentric *fides ex auditu* pre- mortem view."

---

79. Nash, *Is Jesus the Only Savior?*, 19–20.

A full account of Christian exclusivism should take note of several convictions. One of these is the belief that unevangelized mature persons will not only experience God's judgment, but deserve such. Yet it is important to remember that Christian exclusivists often disagree greatly about the nature of hell and the condition of the lost.

Another aspect of exclusivism . . . is the belief held by almost all exclusivists that human destiny is fixed at the moment of physical death. The attainment of Christ's redemption requires that people trust in Christ before death.

Physical death marks the boundary of human opportunity. Anyone who wishes to argue that Jesus and the authors of the New Testament believed otherwise must shoulder the burden of proof. Given the serious implications of a belief in post-mortem salvation for evangelism and missions, the total silence of Scripture regarding opportunities after death should trouble advocates of P. M. E. [post-mortem evangelism]

I have sought to say nothing in this book that implies that exclusivists lack concern for all the unevangelized who have died without Christ or for all the others for whom this fate is still future. When asked if there will be people in heaven who never had a chance to hear the gospel during their lifetime, the first thing a wise exclusivist will say is that he does not know. As Deuteronomy 29:29 states, "The secret things belong to the LORD our God, but things revealed belong to us and to our children forever." Although we know about the Lamb's Book of Life (Rev 20:12–15), we do not know whose names appear in it. But much that we do know suggests that men and women who have not confessed Christ as Savior will not be there.[80]

Questions: What does this text reveal about the central claims and agendas of the christocentric *fides ex auditu* pre-mortem view? How does Nash deal with the issue of those who through no fault of their own did not hear the gospel in their lifetime?

Assessment: The christocentric *fides ex auditu* pre-mortem view upholds the uniqueness of Christianity vis-à-vis other religions. While theologians who hold this view concede that some aspects of God's revelation can be found in other religions, they insist Christianity alone is founded on the revealed knowledge of God. For them, if what the Bible says about God's relationship with human beings is true, it follows that the truth claims of other religions are false or at least inadequate. The christocentric *fides ex auditu*

80. Ibid., 19–20, 157–58, 164.

pre-mortem view also brings to Christians' consciousness the *urgency* to evangelize people who have not heard the gospel.

The christocentric *fides ex auditu* pre-mortem view, however, has come under several criticisms. Three such criticisms are noteworthy. First, some theologians have argued that it does not explain adequately God's desire to save sinners as taught in the Scriptures. If knowledge of Jesus and explicit faith in him are necessary for salvation, and we know that numerous people have lived and died in *this* present world without having access to both requirements, it is unjust for God to deny them salvation on the basis of what is nonexistent in *their* "world." How can we be sure that such people would not have believed if they had the opportunity to hear the gospel? Second, the christocentric *fides ex auditu* pre-mortem view also makes God to be an untruthful or a hypocritical being at best. If God "desires for all people to be saved and to come to the knowledge of the truth" and also for them to know "there is only one mediator between God and men" (1 Tim 2:4–5 ESV), but decides on some people's salvation without giving them the opportunity to hear and respond to the gospel, then God is unjust. Third, the christocentric *fides ex auditu* pre-mortem view makes God's salvation dependent on human missionary efforts, that is, Christians' preaching of the gospel. This view places humans (Christians) in a position of great responsibility as those who to a large extent determine whether or not a person is saved.[81]

Christocentric Fides ex Auditu *Post-mortem View*

Assumptions: The christocentric *fides ex auditu* post-mortem view holds these two assumptions: first, Christianity's teaching about salvation through Jesus Christ alone is true; second, an explicit personal confession of faith in Jesus as the savior is necessary for salvation. Therefore, people who through no fault of their own did not hear the gospel in *this* life would be given an opportunity to hear and respond to the gospel before facing God's judgment.

Theological claims: Advocates of the christocentric *fides ex auditu* post-mortem view differ in their understandings of *when* and *where* people who did not have the opportunity in this life would be given the opportunity to hear and respond to the gospel. Some argue that people will be given the opportunity *at the point of death*. Others argue that an opportunity will be given to people *after death*. In Roman Catholic teaching, the doctrine of Christ's "descent into hell" (1 Pet 3:8–4:6) is used to justify the existence of purgatory (a place where those who are already saved are purged of their unconfessed sins before they proceed to enter into heaven). The doctrine

81. McGrath, "Response to R. Douglas Geivett and W. Gary Phillips," 258.

of the "descent into hell" is also used by some Roman Catholic theologians to justify the claim that God will provide opportunity to certain people in a post-mortem state to hear and respond to the gospel before making a decision on their final destiny.[82] Some early Christian theologians held a similar view. The second-century CE theologian Clement of Alexandria (ca. 150–215 CE) understood the "prisoners" to whom Jesus preached in Hades (1 Pet 3:19) to include the righteous Jews and those who "were righteous according to philosophy" who lived before the time of Christ. Clement of Alexandria also contended, "Straightway, on the revelation of truth [which came by way of Jesus' preaching], they also repented of their previous conduct."[83]

Advocates of the christocentric *fides ex auditu* post-mortem view contend that God has not intended general revelation to be salvific. For them, God will judge people on the basis of their response to the gospel. (John 3:16–21; 2 Thess 1:8). They also argue that there is no clear scriptural support for believing God passes judgment on the destinies of all humans at physical death.[84] Regarding the biblical warrant for the christocentric *fides ex auditu* post-mortem view, its advocates normally cite 1 Pet 4:6 as a text that points in the direction of God's willingness to give all people the opportunity to hear and respond to the gospel. "For this is why the gospel was preached even to those who are dead," Peter writes, "that though judged in the flesh the way people are, they might live in the spirit the way God does" (ESV). This text has been interpreted in various ways since the second century CE. Gavin D'Costa, as shown below, has provided a helpful summary of these interpretations.

Proponent: The Kenyan-Indian and Roman Catholic theologian Gavin D'Costa is one of the best-known advocates of the christocentric *fides ex auditu* post-mortem view. Drawing insights from the Apostles' Creed ("he descended into hell") and also from some biblical passages, D'Costa argues there is sufficient theological justification for the belief that people who died without hearing the gospel would be given an opportunity to hear and respond to the gospel. These are the class of people who are in the "limbo of the just" (the righteous people who lived before the time of Christ) and the unevangelized. D'Costa maintains, however, that non-Christian religions do not have a salvific status. The excerpts below are taken from D'Costa's *Christianity and World Religions*.

82. See D'Costa, *Christianity and World Religions*, 165–211.

83. Clement of Alexandria, *Stromata* 6.6 (*ANF* 2:490).

84. Sanders, *No Other Name*, 190.

The early church faced a very familiar problem to that faced by people today: what happened to their non-Christian relatives, their Jewish ancestors who had followed God, and those remarkable, wise, and upright figures such as Plato and Virgil? Could all these unevangelized be lost? The modern question can be analogically transposed by a Hindu convert, without suggesting Judaism and Hinduism are alike in revelatory features: what happens to all my Hindu relatives whom I know, in the light of Christ, to have led good and sometimes holy lives and sought to follow their conscience?

From the second century it was held by some that Christ's "descent into hell" was to the limbo of the just, to preach the gospel to those who had died before the incarnation and to guide them into heaven. . . . This teaching is grounded on a number of biblical texts, the most important being Luke 16:22—the parable of Dives and Lazarus at "Abraham's bosom"; Luke 23:43—where Jesus on the cross tells the penitent thief that "today you shall be with me in paradise"; Ephesians 4:9—where Paul says that before Jesus ascended he "also descended first into the lower parts of the earth;" and 1 Peter 3:18—4:6. . . .

There are different strands of interpretation [of 1 Peter 3:18—4:6]. First, some of the earliest commentaries on this text saw it as implying that Christ preaches to the dead in the underworld, to all those who came before him and had not heard the gospel. . . . Second, some of the commentaries saw this as referring only to the just who had died before the time of Christ. Third, some of the commentaries importantly included among the just both Jews and pagans. Fourth, some of the commentaries also indicate that, insomuch as Christ descends to the just, so does the church, thereby making sense of the requirement for inclusion into the church as a condition for salvation.

Just as the early church sought to address [the problem of the unevangelized] by positing the limbo of the just and preaching the descent into hell, so, I suggest, can Christians today confess this same descent, as they do in the Apostles' Creed in the liturgy. . . . [This] doctrine provides a sound solution to the problem we have been investigating: it does not require "conversion," but a coming to maturation or completion, or, in exceptional cases, the immediate enjoyment of the just. It does not require unconscious desire, but a response to the good news preached by Christ and his church, thereby explaining the epistemological, Christological, and ecclesiological elements that were problematic until this solution is employed. It does not negate or downplay the historical lives lived by people and communities as building God's kingdom in "inchoate" ways, in seeking goodness, truth, and beauty, as best they can. It is precisely in these ways that such peoples already begin to participate in the life of the triune God.[85]

Questions: What does D'Costa see as the theological benefits of the doctrine of the "descent into hell" for Christians' interreligious conversation? How have theologians used 1 Peter 3:18—4:6 to support the christocentric *fides ex auditu* post-mortem view?

Assessment: The christocentric *fides ex auditu* post-mortem view to a large extent addresses the question about the salvation of the people who through no fault of their own died without hearing and responding to the gospel. Here, it should be noted that the emphasis is on God's willingness to give all people the *opportunity* to hear and respond to the gospel. God is justified in denying salvation to those who wilfully turned down God's gift and offer of salvation. Also, it should be noted that the christocentric *fides ex auditu* post-mortem view does not teach the doctrine of "second chance" (that God will give people who already rejected the gospel in their lifetime another opportunity to hear the gospel after death). The christocentric *fides ex auditu* post-mortem view also preserves the centrality of Jesus Christ to God's salvific work. Also, the view upholds an understanding of the universal accessibility of the gospel that preserves the scriptural teaching on God's desire to save all people. As Clement of Alexandria (ca. 150–215 CE) argues, "For it is not right that these should be condemned without trial, and that those alone who lived after the advent [of the Lord] should have the advantage of the divine righteousness. But to all rational souls it was said from above, 'Whatever one of you has done in ignorance, without clearly knowing God, if, on becoming conscious, he repent, all his sins will be forgiven him' [see Acts 17:30]."[86]

The christocentric *fides ex auditu* post-mortem view has suffered several criticisms both in the hands of Christians and non-Christian theologians. Many non-Christian theologians (as well as some Christian theologians) reject this view because it gives an undue privilege to Christianity that it denies other religions. Even the attempts of some proponents of the christocentric *fides ex auditu* post-mortem view to divert this criticism by assigning to other religions a *preparatio evangelica* (Latin for "preparation for the gospel") status does not fully address the indictment. Some theologians have argued the Bible does not explicitly teach that people who did

---

85. D'Costa, *Christianity and World Religions*, 167–69, 179.

86. Clement of Alexandria, *Stromata* 6.6 (*ANF* 2:491).

not hear and respond the gospel of Jesus in their lifetime will be given the opportunity to do so. Some of these theologians question the use of the doctrine of the "descent into hell" (1 Pet 4:6) by the advocates of the christocentric *fides ex auditu* post-mortem view to justify their theological position. As Ronald Nash contends, "First Peter 4:6 may well be a reference to the common biblical practice of describing Christians as people who are now 'dead' to—that is, oblivious to—certain things in their past. . . . In Romans 6:2, Paul states that Christians have died to sin. Peter may well be saying something similar in 1 Peter 4:6."[87]

Christocentric Implicit-Faith View

Assumptions: The "christocentric implicit-faith" view is governed by the following assumptions. First, it is God, and not religion, that saves. Second, Jesus is the embodiment of divine grace: his life of self-giving, which he demonstrated in his life, teaching, and death on the cross, makes salvation possible. Third, God saves people on the basis of their faith in God and not on the basis of the content or extent of their knowledge of God's salvific work.

Theological claims: The *christocentric implicit-faith* view claims that God saves some people who do not have access to the knowledge of Jesus Christ or have heard about Jesus Christ without rejecting him as the savior. While not denying that explicit faith in Christ is the *standard* means to obtain salvation, advocates of the *christocentric implicit-faith* view contend that people who place their faith in God and live in obedience to God have unknowingly or implicitly placed their faith in the God incarnate, Jesus Christ. This view implies, as David Clark notes, that "information sufficient for salvation can be found outside of special revelation."[88] The expression "implicit faith" may be understood as inward trust in God and the desire to love and obey God—the *trust* and *desire* that are prompted by the knowledge of God gained through either general revelation or non-Christian religions.[89]

For the advocates of the *christocentric implicit-faith* view, saving faith can be "theocentric" (God-centered) or "christocentric" (Christ-centered) depending on the circumstances. These two types of saving faith are, however, not mutually exclusive. The Bible speaks about these two types of saving faith. In 1 Tim 4:10, Paul describes saving faith as being theocentric: "For to this end we toil and strive, because we have our hope set

87. Nash, *Is Jesus the Only Savior?*, 153.

88. Clark, "Is Special Revelation Necessary for Salvation?," 41.

89. Moffitt, "Interreligious Encounter," 1003.

on the living God, who is the Savior of all people, especially of those who believe" (ESV). The writer of the Epistle to the Hebrews also speaks of a theocentric saving faith (Heb 11:6). The Bible equally presents faith in Jesus Christ as necessary for salvation (Acts 4:12; Rom 10:14–15). What, then, is the relationship between "Theocentric saving faith" and "christocentric saving faith"? In the *christocentric implicit-faith* view, the knowledge of God gained through general revelation (through human conscience and reflection on nature) is made efficacious for salvation only on the grounds of the salvific work of Jesus Christ. Therefore, while people may be saved without being consciously aware of Jesus' identity, they are not saved apart from his work.[90] Jesus Christ remains essential to people's salvation in the *christocentric implicit-faith* view. This means that anyone who knowingly rejects Jesus Christ as the savior and also as one in whom God has atoned for the sin of the world will not be saved irrespective of the person's religion.

Proponent: Clark Pinnock's theology fits the *christocentric implicit-faith* view. He grounds his theology of religions and soteriology in the belief that God's salvation, which God provides through Jesus' objective redemptive work, is intended for the whole world.[91] Also, he argues that God saves people because of their *faith* in God and not because of the content of their theology. For Pinnock, Christians must not sacrifice their "high Christology" (the belief that Jesus of Nazareth is God incarnate, the one in whom God has dealt with humanity's sin) for the purpose of safeguarding an "optimism of salvation" (the belief that God's salvation is extended to some people who do not hear the gospel in their lifetime). Pinnock believes that high Christology and optimism of salvation are not mutually exclusive.[92] In *Flame of Love*, Pinnock argues that the Holy Spirit operates within and through non-Christian religions to point non-Christians to God.[93] Other theologians that have developed a Holy Spirit–centered (or pneumatological) theology of religions make similar arguments.[94]

To Pinnock, the Holy Spirit sometimes brings God's salvific blessings to people of other religions who have not heard the gospel. He writes, "Though Jesus is not named in other faiths, Spirit is present and may be experienced. God speaks to people's heart through the Spirit."[95] While he is open to God's operation in other religions and is optimistic that God will save people who

90. Clark, "Is Special Revelation Necessary for Salvation?," 42.

91. Pinnock, *Wideness in God's Mercy*, 17.

92. Ibid., 74.

93. Pinnock, *Flame of Love*, 200–208.

94. See Yong, *Beyond the Impasse*, 175.

95. Pinnock, *Flame of Love*, 204.

did not hear the gospel on the basis of their faith in God, Pinnock rules out the possibility of salvation for people who heard the gospel, had a clear understanding of the gospel, and rejected it.[96] This is the primary reason I have classified his view under the Christian-centric position. The excerpts below, taken from *A Wideness in God's Mercy*, show Pinnock's argument for optimism of salvation for those who did not hear the gospel on the grounds of implicit faith, or as he prefers to call it, "the faith principle."

God is present everywhere in his graciousness, not only where Jesus of Nazareth is named. God is present and at work in every sphere of human life, secular as well as sacred. He is free to act outside as well as inside ecclesiastical structures. We live in one world, which is the creation of the one God. There is no other source from which anyone draws life, and the mystery which surrounds us is the God who loves us in Jesus Christ. God has the whole world in his hands. He sees the sparrow fall. He sustains our life in the world. God is love.

Our primary desire ought to be to see people become followers of Jesus, whether or not they become baptized members of our churches. For in the kingdom of God there will be no Islam or Buddhism or Christianity, but only the triune God and the redeemed community. What God wants to do with religions in history is his business.

How is salvation within the reach of the unevangelized? How can anyone be saved without knowing Christ? The idea of universal accessibility, though not a novel theory, needs to be proven. It is far from self-evident, at least biblically speaking. How can it best be defended?

In my judgment, the *faith principle* is the basis of universal accessibility. According to the Bible, people *are saved by faith*, not *by content of their theology*. Since God has not left anyone without a witness, people are judged on the basis of the light they have received and how they have responded to that light. Faith in God is what saves, not possessing certain minimum information. Hebrews is clear: "And without faith it is impossible to please God, because anyone who comes to him must believe that he exists and that he rewards those who earnestly seek him" (Heb 11:6).

People cannot respond to light that did not reach them. They can only respond to revelation that did. Scripture and reason both imply that no one can be held responsible for truth of which they were inculpably ignorant; they are judged on the basis of the truth they know. A person is saved by faith, even if the content of belief is deficient (and whose is not?). The Bible does not

96. Ibid., 211–14.

teach that one must confess the name of Jesus to be saved. Job did not know it. David did not know it. Babies dying in infancy do not know it. It is not so much a question whether the unevangelized know Jesus as whether Jesus knows them (Matt 7:23). One does not need to be conscious of the work of Christ done on one's behalf in order to benefit from that work. The issue God cares about is the direction of the heart, not the content of theology. Paul says that faith makes the difference. God is the "Savior of all men (potentially), and especially of those who believe (actually)" (1 Tim 4:10).[97]

Questions: What does this text tell us about the theological reasoning behind the christocentric implicit-faith view?

Assessment: While not compromising the traditional Christian teaching about the centrality of Jesus Christ in human salvation, the *christocentric implicit-faith* view emphasizes the universal will of God to save people that live by faith in God's existence and providence. David Clark dismisses the charge against the *christocentric implicit-faith* view that it may "dilute the urgency of the missionary call to service." Clark contends that such a charge is based on a false assumption: that Christians are only to engage in missionary service in places where people have no other means of gaining knowledge of God's salvation. Clark argues that Christians must be willing to preach the gospel in societies where people have access to the gospel as well as in societies where people may not have access to the gospel.[98] The *christocentric implicit-faith* view addresses the problem associated with the views that suggest people's salvation depends largely on Christians' proclamation of the gospel. Theologians who reject the *christocentric implicit-faith* view, however, accuse its proponents of limiting God's salvific work to Christianity's teaching about salvation in so far at it holds that people who knowingly reject Jesus as the savior will not be saved. In reality, people of other religions will most likely reject this Christian teaching because their religions have different understandings of God's salvation and the means to obtain it.

Non-Christian-centric Positions

Description: The term "non-Christian-centric" (or non-Christianity-centered) is used here to describe the theological viewpoints that argue *there*

97. Pinnock, *Wideness in God's Mercy*, 76, 146–47, 157–58.
98. Clark, "Is Special Revelation Necessary for Salvation?," 43–44.

is salvation outside of Christianity. Theologians whose views fit the non-Christian-centric framework claim that people need not share Christianity's soteriology or explicitly commit to Christianity's understanding of the person of Jesus Christ before they can benefit from God's salvation. Such theologians will answer "no," albeit with some variations, to the question: "Are people whose theologies of salvation contradict Christianity's teaching about Jesus' role as *the* savior of the world excluded from God's salvation?"

Biblical foundation/theological arguments: Through her encounter with a Muslim student named Mohammed at the School of Oriental and African Studies (SOAS) in London, Jennifer Howe Peace writes that in retrospect she has learned to say, "My personal experiences did not give me full knowledge or exclusive rights to God. God is greater than my experience."[99] After sharing her (Christian) conversion experience with Mohammed, he told her, "I have a very good friend who described almost the exact same experience. He cried for three days and now he is devoted to Allah."[100] Her paradigmatic Christian conversion experience had been shattered; she had thought that only Christians have such religious experiences. Her friendship with Mohammed ended because his words diminished the "deepest moment" in her faith journey. She summed up the theological lessons she learned from her encounter with Mohammed in the following words:

> Christianity continues to be my spiritual home. But I cannot follow a one-track theology. For me, witnessing to my faith means sharing my experiences as honestly as possible while being equally open to listening deeply to the witness of others. The insights differ. I don't believe that all religions are fundamentally the same. People live with many different gods and with no gods at all. But the refrain for me as a Christian is simply this—God is greater than my experience. God is greater than any of our experiences. In Arabic, as Mohammed might have expressed it, this insight is recorded in the words, *Allahu Akbar*. Recited repeatedly during each of the five daily Muslim prayer times, it is alternatively translated as God is great, God is the greatest, or, as I prefer, God is greater.[101]

The Christian teaching about God as the creator of the world (Gen 1–2; Ps 148:1–5; Acts 4:24; Rom 11:36) and the one who calls human beings into relationship (1 Tim 2:4; 2 Pet 3:9) has profound theological implications. First, God is the author of salvation (Ps 37:39–40). In the words of a New

99. Peace, "Encountering the Neighbor," 28.
100. Ibid.
101. Ibid., 29.

Testament writer, "Salvation belongs to our God who sits on the throne, and to the Lamb" (Rev 7:10 ESV; see also Rev 22:2). Second, God's salvation is not contingent upon human righteousness but rather upon God's mercy and generosity (Rom 11:28–32). The Apostle Paul was unequivocal about his understanding of the vastness of God's salvation and the depth of God's mercy on humanity. In his letter to Christians in Ephesus, Paul wrote, "For it is by grace that you have been saved, through faith—and this not from yourselves, it is the gift of God—not by works, so that no one can boast" (Eph 2:8–9 NIV; see also Rom 11:32). Third, God's generosity and salvific work extend beyond religious, geographical, and ethnic boundaries. Jesus told an inquisitive inquirer: "people will come from east and west and from north and south, and recline at table in the kingdom of God" (Luke 13:29 ESV).

Jesus also resisted any attempt to localize God's presence in a particular religion or to make a religion the arbiter of God's salvific work in the world. To the surprise of a certain woman of Samaria (an adherent of a religion of Samaria), Jesus announced, "Believe me, woman, a time is coming when you will worship the Father neither on this mountain nor in Jerusalem. . . . Yet a time is coming and has now come when true worshipers will worship the Father in spirit and truth, for they are the kind of worshippers the Father seeks. God is spirit, and his worshippers must worship in spirit and in truth" (John 4:21–24 NIV). These words of Jesus were shocking to the woman because she most probably had anticipated that Jesus would defend Judaism against a religion of Samaria.

Some theologians whose viewpoints fit into the *non-Christian-centric* position argue that the *Christian-centric* position gives an unwarranted privilege to Christianity. For them, giving such privilege to Christianity is theologically dangerous because it forces God to act only within the confines of a single religion. Since God saves, and religion does not save, no single religion can speak universally on God's behalf or serve as the only divinely authorized "agent" of God's salvation. There is a vast range of views that fit the *non-Christian-centric* position. As shown below, some of the views are more sympathetic to Christianity's teaching than others.

Christocentric contra Christianity-Centered View

Assumptions: The *christocentric contra Christianity-centered* view operates with the following theological assumptions. God saves people on the basis of Jesus' work (christocentric) whether or not they heard Christianity's teaching about him. People may reject Jesus Christ after *hearing* the gospel and still be saved (contra Christianity-centered). God saves people who are adherents of non-Christian religions.

Theological claims: The central claim of the *christocentric contra Christianity-centered* view is that adherents of other religions can still benefit from God's salvation, which is embodied by Christ, without abandoning their own religions. However, no one can be saved in isolation from Jesus' *objective* work of salvation (his bearing of humanity's sin and its consequences). For these theologians, religion does not save; God saves on account of what God has accomplished in and through the God incarnate—Jesus Christ. They also teach that "saving faith" does not always require Jesus as its object. In some cases, God is the object of the "saving faith." As the author of the Epistle to the Hebrews writes, "And without faith it is impossible to please him, for whoever would draw near to God must believe that he exists and that he rewards those who seek him" (Heb 11:6 ESV). If the "saving faith" is theocentric (God-centered), it follows that having conscious *knowledge* (intellectual assent) of Jesus or exercising *faith* in him are not necessary preconditions for benefiting from God's salvation.

Proponent: Karl Rahner (1904–84), a Roman Catholic theologian, is one of the best known advocates of the *christocentric contra Christianity-centered* view. Rahner' theology of religion is partly driven by what he perceived as the threat of religious pluralism to Christians' exclusivist view of Christianity as the "one and only valid revelation of the living God."[102] Rahner was also convinced that non-Christian religions "will not disappear in the foreseeable future."[103] Although Rahner allowed for the salvation of people of other religions, he insisted that Christianity is normative and therefore remains the standard for measuring the teaching of other religions regarding God's salvation.[104] Given that Christianity has a beginning in history—its starting point began with Jesus of Nazareth—Christians must be ready to acknowledge that Christianity has not always existed as "the way of salvation" for people.[105] This implies that non-Christian religions (even with their distorted beliefs about God's saving activity) remain "lawful religions" for their adherents who have not encountered Christianity—*the* only true and lawful religion.[106] Rahner notes that this understanding of non-Christian religions in this particular context (i.e., before their adherents come into real and clear contact with Christianity) has two major theological

102. Rahner, "Christianity and the Non-Christian Religions," 116.
103. Ibid., 135.
104. Ibid., 118.
105. Ibid., 119.
106. Ibid., 121.

implications. First, it is reasonable to believe that "there are supernatural, grace-filled elements in non-Christian religions."[107] Second, other religions have a "lawful" status: that is, they are "positive means of gaining the right relationship to God and thus for the attaining of salvation, a means which is therefore positively included in God's plan of salvation."[108] Given that God's saving grace is operative in non-Christian religions, Christians need not continue to think of themselves as "the exclusive community of those who have a claim to salvation" but rather as the people whose task is to make explicit the hidden Christian hopes that are present in non-Christian religions.[109] The selections below highlight Rahner's understanding of the transcendence of God's grace over human sin, the role of non-Christian religions in God's salvation plan, and the centrality of Jesus Christ to God's salvific work.

> God desires the salvation of everyone. And this salvation willed by God is the salvation won by Christ, the salvation of supernatural grace which divinizes man, the salvation of the beatific vision. It is a salvation really intended for all those millions upon millions of men who lived perhaps a million years before Christ—and also for those who have lived after Christ—in nations, cultures and epochs of a very wide range which were still completely shut off from the viewpoint of those living in the light of the New Testament. If, on the one hand, we conceive salvation as something *Christian*, if there is no salvation apart from Christ, if according to Catholic teaching the supernatural divinization of man can never be replaced merely by good will on the part of man but is necessary as something itself given in this earthly life; and if, on the other hand, God has really, truly and seriously intended this salvation for all men— then these two aspects cannot be reconciled in any other way than by stating that every human being is really and truly exposed to the influence of divine, supernatural grace which offers an interior union with God and by means of which God communicates himself whether the individual takes up an attitude of acceptance or of refusal towards this grace. It is senseless to suppose cruelly—and without any hope of acceptance by the man of today, in view of the enormous extent of the extra-Christian history of salvation and damnation—that nearly all men living outside the official and public Christianity are so evil and stubborn that the offer of supernatural grace ought not even to be made in fact in most cases, since these individuals have already rendered

107. Ibid.
108. Ibid., 125.
109. Ibid., 135.

themselves unworthy of such an offer by previous, subjectively grave offences against the natural law.... It is furthermore impossible to think that this offer of supernatural, divinizing grace made to all men on account of the universal salvific purpose of God, should in general ... remain ineffective in most cases on account of the personal guilt of the individual. For, as far as the gospel is concerned, we have no really conclusive reason for thinking so pessimistically of men. However little we can say with certitude about the final lot of an individual inside or outside the officially constituted Christian religion, we have every reason to think optimistically—i.e. truly hopefully and confidently in a Christian sense—of God who has certainly the last word and who has revealed to us that he has spoken his powerful word of reconciliation and forgiveness into the world.

If [the claim that non-Christian religions have a "lawful" status] is correct, then Christianity does not simply confront the member of an extra-Christian religion as a mere non-Christian but as someone who can and must already be regarded in this ... respect as an anonymous Christian. It would be wrong to regard the pagan as someone who has not yet been touched in any way by God's grace and truth. If, however, he has experienced the grace of God—if, in certain circumstances, he has already accepted this grace as the ultimate, unfathomable entelechy of his existence by accepting the immeasurableness of his dying existence as opening out into infinity—then he has already been given revelation in a true sense even before he has been affected by missionary preaching from without.[110]

Questions: What does this text reveal about the scope of God's saving activity in the world? On what grounds does Rahner refer to a non-Christian as an "anonymous Christian"?

Assessment: This view, especially Rahner's version, forces Christians to rethink their understandings of the scope and means of salvation in the light of God's freedom to encounter God's creation outside of human structures. This view also corrects the negative view of non-Christian religions, an important correction that has the capacity to move Christians a long way in developing sympathetic attitudes toward other religions and favorable relationship with people of other religions.

Critics of Rahner argue that his understanding of saving grace and how it is communicated to non-Christians diminishes the role of Jesus Christ as the executor of God's grace. Also, people have questioned Rahner's

110. Ibid., 122–24, 131.

theological reasoning for granting non-Christian religions a salvific status.[111] If other religions can convey God's salvation, why is it still necessary for Christians to evangelize non-Christians? Ralph Martin points out that Rahner's view weakens the impetus for evangelization.[112] Other critics have argued that the characterization of non-Christians as "anonymous Christians" may be offensive to both Christians and adherents of other religions.[113]

Theocentric View

Assumptions: First, Christianity is not the only true religion. All religions are flawed, albeit redeemable. Second, Christian theologies of religions should focus on God rather than on Jesus Christ.

Theological claims: The *theocentric view* focuses on the universality of God's salvific work rather than on the universal significance of Christ's work. In other words, God, and not Jesus, is the point of departure and focal point of the *theocentric view*. Representatives of this view argue that the Christian Scriptures teach God is the God of all (Rom 3:29–30). Although the theological viewpoints that I describe under this section differ in their answers to the questions of a universal access to God's salvation, they agree that salvation is God's prerogative and also that God's salvation extends beyond Christianity's parameters. Having this robust understanding of God and refocusing salvation on God rather than on Christ requires that Christians recognize other religions as valid paths to salvation. Hans Küng, a notable Swiss Roman Catholic theologian and priest, is one of several theologians that have vigorously pursued interreligious dialogue between Christians, Muslims, and adherents to Judaism. In *Christianity and World Religions*, Küng argues that in order for Christians to engage meaningfully with Muslims in theological dialogue, they should not be merely tolerant of Muslims and Islam but should have a "whole new attitude toward Islam."[114] Küng demands that Christians acknowledge "Islam as a way of salvation," recognize "Muhammad as a prophet," and treat "the Qur'an as God's word."[115] Küng's theology of religion is informed by the Second Vatican Council's call for Christians to be open to God's activity in and through non-Christian religions. For Küng, however, serious dialogue demands

111. D'Costa, *Christianity and World Religions*, 21–22.

112. Martin, *Will Many Be Saved?*, 126.

113. Kärkkäinen, *Introduction to Theology of Religions*, 196.

114. Küng et al., *Christianity and World Religions*, 109.

115. Ibid.

that all parties rethink their attitude toward people who do not share their religious beliefs. Also, all parties should be ready to make necessary adjustments required to facilitate meaningful interactions with people of other religions. He calls Muslims to the task of "a universal tolerance and freedom of religion, including full civil rights (even for those who are not 'people of the Book' and for Islamic 'heretics,' such as the Ahmadiyya and the cruelly persecuted Bahá'is)."[116] The *theocentric view* has led some theologians to conclude that Jesus must take his place alongside other religious leaders of the world. Some of these theologians (such as John Hick) propose replacing the term "God" with other terms like the "Real" in an attempt to distance God's revelation and saving activity from any one religion's vantage point.

Proponent: John Hick's theology of religions was a watershed in contemporary theocentric understandings of God's salvation. Hick described his discovery of the need to move away from christocentric and ecclesiocentric (church-centered) approaches to a theocentric approach as being somewhat like a "Copernican revolution."[117] Hick was dissatisfied with the views that explicitly teach or imply that "God condemns the majority of the human race, who have never encountered or who have not accepted the Christian gospel, to eternal damnation."[118] To Hick, the God who would act in such manner is a "Devil." He contended that what is needed (a necessary implication of a theocentric view) is a redefinition of the concept of salvation in terms of observable change in people's lives rather than abstract and non-observable terms. This understanding of salvation, for Hick, requires abandoning the use of the Christian claim "Jesus is God incarnate" as a justification for failing to accept that non-Christian religions are valid paths to God or to God's salvation. For him, the doctrine of the Incarnation should not be taken as a "literal truth" but rather as a "metaphorical or mythical truth."[119] Therefore, this doctrine cannot be used to discredit other religions' truth claims. The selections below underscore Hick's concept of salvation, his view of Jesus Christ, and his understanding of religion's role in God's salvific plans.

116. Ibid.

117. Hick likens his discovery to that of the Polish mathematician and astronomer Nicolaus Copernicus (1473–1543), who demonstrated that the heliocentric (sun-centered) view offered a better of understanding of the solar system than the Ptolemaic, geocentric veiw.

118. Hick, *Christian Theology of Religions*, 19.

119. Ibid., 101.

Suppose, then, we define salvation in a very concrete way, as an actual change in human beings, a change which can be identified—when it can be identified—by its moral fruits. We then find that we are talking about something that is of central concern to each of the great world faiths. Each in its different ways calls us to transcend the ego point of view, which is the source of all selfishness, greed, exploitation, cruelty, and injustice, and to become re-centered in the ultimate mystery for which we, in our Christian language, use the term God.

The analogy that I am suggesting here is with the religious experience component of religion. And the possibility that I want to point to is that the ultimate ineffable Reality is capable of being authentically experienced in terms of different sets of human concepts, *as* Jahweh, *as* the Holy Trinity, *as* Allah, *as* Shiva, *as* Vishnu, and again *as* Brahman, *as* the Dharmakaya, *as* the Tao, and so on, these different personae and impersonae occurring at the interface between the Real and our differing religious mentalities and cultures.

It could be that representations of the infinite divine reality in our finite human terms must be much more radically inadequate than a two-dimensional representation of the three-dimensional earth. And it could be that the conceptual maps drawn by the great traditions, although finite picturings of the Infinite, are all more or less equally useful for guiding us on our journey through life. For our pilgrim's progress is our life-response to the Real. The great world faiths orient us in this journey, and in so far as they are, as we may say, in soteriological alignment with the Real, to follow their path will relate us rightly to the Real, opening us to what, in different conceptualities, we will call divine grace or supernatural enlightenment that will in turn bear visible fruit in our lives.

. . . if, as a Christian, you restrict your attention within your own tradition, then Christ will be your only clue to the nature of the divine. But if you look more widely you see that it's not the case that, to quote another critic, "The God of universal love at the center cannot be spoken of or recognized without Jesus." The other major theistic faiths have their own independent grounds for this belief. The idea of the universal divine goodness/love/compassion is common to Judaism, Islam, theistic Hinduism, Sikhism, Jainism, as well as Christianity.[120]

Questions: How does Hick resolve the tension of competing religious truth claims? How does Hick's view of the Real relocate the center of theology of religions to a theocentric focus?

---

120. Ibid., 17, 25, 27, 104–5.

Assessment: Hick's view attacks religious hegemony or any attempt by adherents of a particular religion to claim exclusive access to God or demand that their religion be seen as the only true religion. Also, Hick's view broadens one's perspective on the different forms of religions and the circumstances that condition the behavior, beliefs, and practices of their adherents. When a person's knowledge of other religions is broadened, the person will become more tolerant of adherents of those religions. Hick's view, therefore, has the capacity to help Christians overcome triumphalist and imperialistic mindsets.[121]

Critics of Hick's view (and other forms of unitive religious pluralism), however, argue that his views of religion fail to take seriously the distinctive and competing claims of different religions.[122] For example, not all religions that operate with the assumption of God as a personal being agree on the nature, mode of being, and mode of operation of God.[123] Other critics argue that Hick has failed to provide a doctrinal criterion for judging the truthfulness of a religion and by so doing reduces religion to mere ethics.[124] Also, how does Hick know that each religion teaches a partial truth about God or "the Real," to use his own term? He seems to be suggesting that he has the right to decide for all religions what they ought to believe and how they ought to express their beliefs.

Universalist View

Assumptions: The *universalist view* is founded on three major assumptions. First, God ultimately never shuts out anyone: God will save all people on the grounds that Christ's atoning work is efficacious for all. Second, God's infinite *love* will ultimately supersede humans' *sin*—the mistrust and rejection of God. Third, God's justice is restorative: God punishes sinners in order to purify them so that they may enter into fellowship with God and the community of the righteous.

Theological claims: If we accept Scriptures' teaching that God is *love* (1 John 4:7–12), it is reasonable to believe God is by nature self-giving—an attribute that moves God to embrace and extend a hand of fellowship to the evil "other" of sinful humanity. Paul appears to be making this point in his letter to Christians in Rome. "You see, at just the right time, when we were

---

121. D'Costa, *Christianity and World Religions*, 10.

122. Eddy, "Religious Pluralism and the Divine," 126. See also Eddy, "John Hick's Monotheistic Shadow," 117–37.

123. Fredericks, *Faith among Faiths*, 106–7.

124. D'Costa, *Christianity and World Religions*, 10.

still powerless, Christ died for the ungodly. Very rarely will anyone die for a righteous man, though for a good man someone might possibly dare to die. But God demonstrates his own love for us in this: While we were yet sinners, Christ died for us" (Rom 5:6–8 NIV). Other passages from Paul's letters may be cited in support of the *universalist view* (see Rom 5:12–19; 8:19–21; 11:28–32; Eph 1:3–14; Col 1:15–21). Of course, some theologians question the legitimacy of the use of these passages to support the universalist understanding of the final destiny of all human beings.

But if God will ultimately save all people, why preach the gospel or even preach about God's judgment of sinners? The early Christian theologian, Origen of Alexandria, answered this question by highlighting the "utility" or purpose of the Christian message about God's judgment. For him, preaching about God's judgment arouses and exhorts the wicked "to refrain from those actions which are followed by punishments" and also moves them to adopt the Christian vision of the world and lifestyle.[125] For the advocates of the *universalist view*, God's judgment in the context of the final destiny of humans should be understood primarily in terms of "restoration." The Greek term *apokátastasis* ("restoration"), which is used in Acts 3:20–21, is employed by the advocates of the *universalist view* to substantiate their claim that God will ultimately restore all things in Jesus Christ. In Acts 3:19–21, Luke records Peter's preaching to the audience that was baffled by his ability to heal a crippled man: "Therefore repent and return, so that your sins may be wiped away, in order that times of refreshing may come from the presence of the Lord; and that He may send Jesus, the Christ appointed for you, whom heaven must receive until the period of restoration of all things about which God spoke by the mouth of His holy prophets from ancient time" (NASB). For the proponents of the *universalist view*, God's justice is ultimately restorative rather retributive or punitive.

Proponent: John A. T. Robinson is one of the premier defenders of the *universalist view*. One of the distinguishing marks of his version of the *universalist view* is its christological focus. To Robison, locating the view that God will ultimately restore all people into divine fellowship within the universal efficacy of Jesus' atonement shows that the *universalist view* is not a wishful thinking.[126] Robinson also contends that the *universalist view* does not (and should not) diminish the scriptural teachings about human capacity of choice and the seriousness of hell.[127] Regarding human freedom, Robinson argues that God's demonstrative act of love shatters humans' "citadel

---

125. Origen, *Against Celsus* 3.78 (*ANF* 4:495); see also ibid., 4.13 (*ANF* 4:502).

126. Robinson, *In the End, God,* 119.

127. Ibid., 120.

of will" and moves them to willingly surrender to God's will.[128] In other words, in the end, the love of God will be too strong for disobedient people to resist.[129] On the implication of the doctrine of a universal salvation for the doctrine of hell, Robinson argues that hell must not be construed as a "bluff" required for keeping people moral.[130] However, hell is "eternal" only from the perspective of humans and not from God's perspective because it is not beyond God's infinite love. Also, when the term "eternal" is associated with hell, it communicates two related realities: hell's *endless seriousness* (for the person who lives in the "moment" of the rejection of the gospel) and its *limited consequences* (because God's infinite love will overcome it).[131] The excerpts below highlight Robinson's christological focus in his view of the universal salvation or restoration of all humans.

The remaining answer to the question concerning the ultimate issue of things is that of Universalism—the answer that God will be all in all because the whole world will be restored sinless to that relationship with him in which and for which he made it.

The universalist position has often been defended in ways and forms which do it little credit. It has been grounded in the doctrine of man, in the requirements of human reason or the demands of human longings. But the sole basis for such a doctrine, as more than wishful thinking, is the work of God in Christ. It is this and this alone which transfers it from the realm of daring speculation or moral postulate into the field of faithful assurance. There is no ground whatever in the Bible for supposing that all men, simply because they are men, are "going the same way"—except to hell. Once again, it is solely the divine "nevertheless," intervening beyond any expectation and merit, on which the Christian hope rests. If universalism is asserted on *this* ground, it can certainly lay claim to biblical support.

Under the constraint of the love of God in Christ this sense of self-fulfillment [that is, a person's capacity to freely surrender his or her will to God's will] is at its maximum. The testimony of generations is that here, as nowhere else, service is perfect freedom. . . . May we not imagine a love so strong that ultimately no one will be able to restrain himself from free and grateful surrender? If the miracle of the forcing of pride's intransigence, which is no forcing but a gentle leading, can be achieved in one case (St. Paul would say, in my

128. Ibid., 121.
129. Ibid., 122–23.
130. Ibid., 129.
131. Ibid., 132.

case), who are we to say that God cannot repeat it in all? One by one, may not each come to the point at which he finds himself constrained to confess the words of Charles Wesley:

I yield, I yield,

I can hold out no more;

I sink, by dying love compelled,

And own thee conqueror!

The knowledge that one is the object of another human's love, who, whatever one may do, will continue to love and to cherish, is not the signal to seize the opportunity for careless and thoughtless living. Rather, the knowledge brings with it an overwhelming constraint to pursue precisely the opposite course. It is only the man who does not really love, who looks at the matter "objectively," to whom the "logical" course of action could possibly suggest or commend itself. So it is in our dealing with God. It is only those who do not know grace, in the sole way in which it can be known, i.e., "subjectively," to whom the exhortation to "sin that grace may abound" can have the least plausibility.

As far as the final issue of God's purpose is concerned, there can be only one outcome. All things must be summed up in Christ, because in principle all things already are. Hell is an ultimate impossibility, because *already* there *is* no one outside of Christ. When the New Testament speaks from this point of view, this is its message.[132]

Question: How does Robinson construe God's infinite love and Christ's role in the final restoration or salvation of all people?

Assessment: The *universalist view* heightens the power of God's love over humans' non-love for God. This view also helps to resolve the question about the final destiny of many people who have already died and many more that will die without hearing the gospel. However, four primary objections have been raised against the *universalist view*. First, it contradicts scriptural teaching about God's judgment and punishment for those who reject God. Paul tells us that sin pays a wage, namely death—separation from God (Rom 6:23). Jesus pronounced harsh warning about the condition of those who refuse to accept the way of God's kingdom (John 3:15, 18; 6:22–59). Second, the universalist view deprives human beings of their freedom to choose or reject God. As Pinnock argues, "God does not purpose to

132. Ibid., 119–23, 127, 130

condemn anyone, but anyone can choose rejection."[133] Third, the universalist view equates the *universal accessibility of salvation* with the *salvation of all people*. For example, to say that Jesus' death makes salvation possible for all does not necessarily imply that all people will accept the gift of salvation.[134] Fourth, some theologians argue that the Bible teaches the eternal duration of hell as a place for people who rejected the gospel or God's offer of salvation. For them, passages such as Matt 25:46 and 2 Thess 1:8–9 indicate that "God's final judgment" does not include "restoration of those who ultimately reject God's grace."[135] John Stott also notes that the Bible records Jesus' warnings that God's final judgment "will involve a separation into two opposite but equally eternal destines." However, Stott holds the *annihilation* position, which states that God will destroy the wicked rather than punish them eternally in hell.[136]

Indeterminate Position

Description: I have labeled the third category of Christians' theological answers to the question about God's salvation for those who have not heard the gospel or have rejected the gospel due to their commitment to other religions the "Indeterminate position," which is sometimes described as "reverent agnosticism."[137] For the advocates of the *indeterminate position*, human beings have no access to God's decision on the final destiny of people who have not pursued God's salvation through the Christian way. Consequently, they contend that the best answer regarding the destiny of such people should be, "We don't know."

Biblical foundation/theological arguments: Many Christian theologians believe that people who have heard the gospel, fully understood it, and consciously rejected it will not be saved.[138] But what about the destiny of those who through no fault of their own did not hear the gospel, or those who heard it but did not understand it? John Stott argues that Christians should remain agnostic in their stance on the destiny of this class of people. He writes, "When somebody asked Jesus, 'Lord, are only a few people going to be saved?,' he refused to answer and instead urged them to 'enter through the narrow door' (Luke 13:23–24). The fact is that God, alongside the most

133. Pinnock, *Wideness in God's Mercy*, 156.

134. Sanders, *No Other Name*, 107–8.

135. Ibid., 109.

136. Edwards and Stott, *Evangelical Essentials*, 317–18.

137. Pinnock, *Wideness in God's Mercy*, 150.

138. Edwards and Stott, *Evangelical Essentials*, 320.

solemn warnings about our responsibility to respond to the gospel, has not revealed how he will deal with those who have never heard it. We have to leave them in the hands of the God of infinite mercy and justice, who manifested these qualities most fully on the cross."[139]

How does one define the scope of the commonly used expression "through no fault of their own"? To what class of people does this expression refer? Typically, theologians use this expression to describe dead infants, people with severe mental disorders who lack cognitive capacity to understand the gospel or make informed judgments, people who lived and died without actually hearing the gospel message, and people who lived before the time of Jesus Christ. But can we broaden the category to include people who heard and understood the gospel but rejected it because it competed with their understandings of God's salvific work as taught in their own religions? Some theologians, as indicated below, have chosen the indeterminate option, insisting that God alone knows the answer.

Proponent: The Orthodox Church theologian John McGuckin draws insights from several early church theologians, such as Justin Martyr and Clement of Alexandria, who used the theological concept "seed of Divine Word or Wisdom" (*Logos Spermatikos* in Latin) to make a case for God's "universal presence in the souls of the righteous pagans" who lived before the time of Jesus Christ. McGuckin also appeals to St. John Chrysostom, who argued that God's salvific law exists outside of the church in the forms of the natural law of conscience and the Torah (for the Jews). While remaining optimistic that God's salvation is extended to people who are outside the church, McGuckin warns that no human being has the "right" to make a decision about the destiny of other humans. The selections below are from his *Orthodox Church*.

In the domain of modern inter-faith dialogue some Western Christian theorist have adopted a syncretic pluralist approach based around the premise (or cliché) that all religions are the same and that they are all equally valid paths to the same God. Orthodoxy [that is, the Orthodox Church] rejects both statements. It sees the revelation of the ineffable Father, in Christ the Word incarnate, through the efficacy of the Holy Spirit, as the perfection and consummation of all truth, and thus the fulfillment of all the religious aspirations of the human race. But it is also aware that the plan of God for the salvation of the entire world in Christ does not proceed mechanically. The message of the Gospel has been heard across the globe; but it is an invitation that has to be freely accepted, and can never be forced on another.

139. Ibid., 327.

The church believes that it has a duty to witness to the message of Christ to a world deeply loved by God, in ways that are characterized by an open heart and a charitable rhetoric, but also in a way that never dilutes its proclamation of Christ as the center of all the religious aspirations of humankind: "The Way the Truth and the Life" [John 14:6]. The apostolic injunction is treated seriously: "Guard the truth that has been entrusted to you by the Holy Spirit who dwells within us" [2 Tim 1:14]. But the same Apostle also set out the command that inter-religious dialogue has to be undertaken with sensitivity, discretion, and respect [2 Tim 2:24–25]. It is not in accordance with that instruction to designate all those who are non-Christians as "under a curse of damnation" as parts of Protestant fundamentalism often do. Orthodoxy adheres to the dogmatic position that the church is the great ark of salvation. But those who are outside that ark are not *de facto* the damned (no creature on earth has the right to conclude that about another living soul); they are, rather, in the hands of the God of salvation and, strictly speaking, Orthodoxy does not know what their standings is: God alone knows it. Yet the church certainly has a deep and ancient sense that men and women who have tried to live justly, honestly, and mercifully will be recognized by God as having kept the vestiges of the divine image which he himself wove into the fabric of the human race at the Creation.

As with St. Paul at Athens, there is a real sense in Orthodoxy that men and women of good will who are historically and culturally bound up in their native religions can still be apprehending the Divine Logos whom the church knows and serves as the sole gateway to God.[140]

Question: What are the theological arguments presented in the text in support of the indeterminate position on the salvation of non-Christians?

Assessment: The *indeterminate view* has some merits. It reminds Christians that God alone knows who will be saved and how they will be saved. The *indeterminate view* also serves to remind Christians to move with caution on how to speak of the eternal destiny of people who do not share the Christian view of the world. Some theologians are uneasy with the "reverent agnosticism" of the indeterminate position. Clark Pinnock, for example, criticizes John Stott for evading an important theological question. Theology, Pinnock insists, is supposed to address serious questions

140. McGuckin, *Orthodox Church*, 427.

that Christians face. He also notes that since the Bible is not utterly silent on the issue, the indeterminate position is really unhelpful to Christians.[141]

Exercise 3.2

Case Study: Although Angela's parents, who were adherents of an African indigenous religion, died without seeing the Bible or hearing about Jesus Christ, Angela heard about Jesus through a friend in the university and chose to become a Christian. She is, however, worried about the salvation of her parents.

Student's assignment: Explain to Angela, using your choice of one of the views on Christian theologies of religions and doctrine of salvation, whether or not her parents will be saved.

Concluding Reflections on Christian Theologies of Religions and the Doctrine of Salvation

The traditional Christian teaching that Jesus is God incarnate requires giving Jesus the liberty to critique all religions, including Christianity. Karl Barth wisely uses the double-edged word *Aufhebung*—which can mean "abolition" or "negation" *and* "elevation" or "sublation"—to highlight how Jesus Christ, the revelation of God, deconstructs and at the same time reconstructs religions.[142] Barth's intention may have been, as Daniel Migliore argues, to show that Jesus Christ "brings not only judgment on all religion but also the power to transform human beings and their religious life."[143]

If indeed Jesus is truly God and truly human, as some of the early ecumenical councils taught,[144] the significance of his life and work extends beyond Christianity's theological parameters. Two major soteriological implications of the doctrine of God incarnate and of how this doctrine bears on Christian theologies of religions should be highlighted. First, *God's salvation is not contingent upon Christian evangelism*. God *saves* (that is, undertakes the mission of reconciling, reclaiming, healing, and pruning of God's creation) with or without human structures and activities. God can

---

141. Pinnock, *Wideness in God's Mercy*, 150–51.

142. For extensive discussion of Barth's view of religion and its relation to God's revelation, see Barth, *CD* I/2, 280–361.

143. Migliore, *Faith Seeking Understanding*, 304.

144. For discussion of the doctrine of the incarnation and the early ecumenical theological positions on the person and work of Jesus Christ, see Ezigbo, *Introducing Christian Theologies*, vol. 1, ch. 5.

use "religious people" (the community of individuals who live in obedience to God as taught in their religious traditions) to bring to light God's salvific work in the world. Christianity's teaching about sin, of course, entails that human beings often misconstrue and misappropriate God's salvific work. Christians must rethink their motives of evangelism. Christians ought to engage in evangelism (or missions) in obedience to Jesus' command to all his disciples to *evangelize*—that is, to proclaim the good news about God's reign. Christians are to present Jesus, the embodiment of God's good news, as one whose "vision" of God and humanity corrects human's misunderstandings of God, humanity, and God's relationship with humanity. Christians who fail to do evangelism are therefore not only disobedient to Christ's command but also deprive non-Christians of the opportunity to hear Christianity's unique contributions to the discussions about God, God's expectations from humanity, and God's salvific work in the world. But Christians must not engage in evangelism for fear that their failure to preach the gospel to people who have not heard it would entail God's inability to save such people. We also know that hearing and understanding the gospel do not always result in an exercise of faith in Jesus Christ as the savior of the world. Some people hear, understand, and sometimes teach the gospel without truly accepting it as true or as the only valid path to enter into a relationship with God.

Second, *the knowledge of people who are the recipients of God's salvation escapes humans.* There is a profound wisdom in Paul's words in Rom 11:32–36. Speaking about salvation, Paul says, "For God has consigned all to disobedience, that he may have mercy on all" (Rom 11:32 ESV). Paul perhaps knew that some of the recipients of his letter would have been bewildered by these words, and therefore quickly added, "Oh, the depth of the riches and wisdom and knowledge of God! How unsearchable are his judgments and how inscrutable his ways!" (Rom 11:33 ESV). Humans' finitude prevents them from knowing the "secret things" that belong to God (Deut 29:29). In the beginning of the section titled "Christian Theologies of Religions and the Doctrine of Salvation," I told a story from the book of Acts. I would like to end this chapter with another story from the book of Acts. Luke in Acts 1 narrates a story about Jesus' conversation with his disciples on one occasion. Jesus' disciples wanted to know from him the details about God's salvific plan for the world, and for Israel in particular. They had anticipated that the time had come for Jesus to "restore the kingdom to Israel" (Acts 1:6). Jesus responded with an awkward answer, as if he were telling them, *mind your own business and stay out of God's prerogatives*: "It is not for you to know the times or dates the Father has set by his own authority. But you will receive power when the Holy Spirit comes on you; and you will be my witnesses in

Jerusalem, and in all Judea and Samaria, and to the ends of the earth" (Acts 1:7–8 NIV). When placed in the larger context of his life and proclamation of the kingdom of God (Acts 1:3), Jesus' answer to his disciples' question should be a reminder to Christians that God has been redeeming, healing, pruning, and reclaiming God's creation—this is the heart of Jesus' preaching about God's kingdom or reign. These salvific acts of the Triune God have been made manifest in the life (teaching, miraculous works, and experience) of Jesus Christ. Also, Jesus' answer should remind Christians that they have a role to play in God's salvific work in the world. Their role is not to be concerned about the details of God's salvation: when or how God will restore God's world. Their role is to proclaim and embody Jesus' message of God's kingdom within and beyond their communities.

Glossary

Apokátastasis: Greek word that means "restoration"; used by some theologians to support the claim that God will ultimately restore all people into divine fellowship (see Acts 3:19–21).

Exclusivism: broad term used by some theologians to describe the view that hearing the gospel and exercising faith in Jesus Christ are necessary for salvation.

fides ex auditu: Latin expression that means "faith comes from hearing" the gospel.

Inclusivism: broad term used by some theologians to describe the view that although no one can be saved in isolation from the salvific work of Jesus Christ, hearing the gospel and exercising faith in Jesus Christ are not necessary for salvation.

Universalism: umbrella term used for the theological positions that teach that God will save all people in the end.

Review Questions

1. What are the differences in the approaches Christian theologians use in their interreligious conversations?

2. Discuss the interface between the Christian doctrine of salvation and theologies of religions. Which of the models discussed in this chapter

183

do you consider the most theologically sound? Explain the theological rationale for your choice.

3. What ought to be the relationship between the objectives of Christian theologies of religions discussed in this chapter?

Suggestions for Further Reading

Anderson, Norman. *Christianity and World Religions: The Challenge of Pluralism.* Downers Grove, IL: InterVarsity, 1984.

Clendenin, Daniel B. *Many Gods, Many Lords: Christianity Encounters World Religions.* Grand Rapids: Baker, 1995.

Cohn-Sherbok, Dan. *Interfaith Theology: A Reader.* Oxford: Oneword, 2001.

D'Costa, Gavin, ed. *Christian Uniqueness Reconsidered: The Myth of a Pluralistic Theology of Religions.* Maryknoll: Orbis, 1990.

————. *Christianity and World Religions: Disputed Questions in the Theology of Religions.* Oxford: Wiley-Blackwell, 2009.

Jones, Charles B. *The View from Mars Hill: Christianity in the Landscape of World Religions.* Cambridge: Cowley, 2005.

Kereszty, Roch A. *Christianity among Other Religions: Apologetics in a Contemporary Context.* Edited by Andrew C. Gregg. New York: Society of St. Paul, 2006.

Küng, Hans, et al. *Christianity and World Religions: Paths of Dialogue with Islam, Hinduism, and Buddhism.* Translated by Peter Heinegg. Maryknoll, NY: Orbis, 1993.

Muck, Terry, and Frances S. Adeney. *Christianity Encountering World Religions: The Practice of Mission in the Twenty-First Century.* Grand Rapids: Baker, 2009.

Peace, Jennifer Howe, et al., eds. *My Neighbor's Faith: Stories of Interreligious Encounter, Growth, and Transformation.* Maryknoll, NY: Orbis, 2012.

4

Church

The vast majority of people with no formal theological training associate the term "church" with a physical building. The expression "I am going to church" is commonly understood to mean attending a Christian gathering in a church building or in a space marked out for worship and prayer. The New Testament idea of the "church" (*ekklesia* in Greek), however, refers to the assembly of Christ's followers—a community that is brought into existence and is sustained by the Triune God. This chapter focuses on *ecclesiology* (discourse about the church).

Christian Ideas of the Church

In one of the famous conversations Jesus had with his disciples about his identity, he announced his goal to build his "church" (Matt 16:17). Jesus' announcement to build his church was provoked by Peter's answer to his earlier question "Who do you say I am?" Peter responded: "You are the Christ, the Son of the living

FOCUS QUESTION:

How may we understand the nature, scope, and mission of the church?

God" (Matt 16:15, NIV). On hearing Peter's answer, Jesus said: "Blessed are you, Simon son of Jonah, for this was not revealed to you by man, but by my Father in heaven. And I tell you that you are Peter, and on this rock I will build my church, and the gates of Hades will not overcome it" (Matt 16:17, NIV). Several questions come to mind when one explores what it is exactly that Jesus meant by the word "church" and how he intended to accomplish the task of building it. As one schooled in the Jewish religious tradition, Jesus most likely had in mind the idea of an "assembly" (*qāhāl* in Hebrew). Jesus seemed to announce his mission to create a community of God's people whose lives would be governed by his own lifestyle, experience, and teaching.

Two introductory comments are necessary before discussing different conceptions of the church. First, Jesus' announcement to build his church was recorded only by Matthew.[1] Some argue that since the other two Synoptic Gospels (Mark and Luke) omitted the announcement, Jesus did not actually say it. But it is also plausible, as some theologians have argued, that Jesus made the statement but Luke followed Mark in omitting it.[2] Second, the play on words contained in Jesus' response to Peter's confession should be noted. Jesus most likely used the word "Peter" (*pétros* in Greek, which means "rock" or "stone"; *Kēphás* in Aramaic) as a nickname (not a proper name) for Simon. Jesus might have used the nickname to highlight Peter's future role in the *church* he planned to build. Jesus in fact said to Simon, the rock (Peter): "on this rock [*petra* in Greek] I will build my church" (Matt 16:17).

One question that has gotten the attention of many Christians is this: Did Jesus promise to build his church on Simon (Peter) or did he promise to build his church on Peter's confession that he was "the Christ"? For some theologians, Jesus promised to build his church on Simon. Cyprian

---

1. See the parallel passages in Luke 9:18–27 and Mark 8:27–30.

2. Keener, *Commentary on the Gospel of Matthew*, 425.

of Carthage (ca. 200–258) argued that Jesus built his church on Peter.[3] In this view, the parallelism between *pétros* (you are the "rock") and *pétra* (on this "rock") shows that Simon, the "rock," is exactly the same rock on which Jesus promised to build his church.[4] By calling Simon "Peter," Jesus was indicating the foundational work he would commission Peter to do in the early life of the church (John 21:15–19). As we now know, Peter became the major leader of the church in Jerusalem after Jesus' earthly ministry (see Acts 1:15; 2:14–40). Some church traditions (like Roman Catholicism) have developed the idea of an *apostolic succession* (continuity of church bishops) in which they trace their overseeing bishops (such as popes) back to Peter's apostleship. In the Roman Catholic Church, the apostolic succession is sometimes used to defend the primacy, infallibility, and authority of popes. The Roman Catholic Church's association of the ministry and authority of the papacy with the early church leaders going back to Peter indicates that a pope is the spiritual shepherd of all Christian communities or churches.[5] Not all theologians who hold the view that Jesus promised to found his church on Peter, however, accept the Roman Catholic teaching on the Infalliblity of the pope. Also, some theologians, particularly Protestants, argue that Jesus only promised to build his church on Peter's confession ("you are the Christ") or on Peter's faith in Jesus as the Christ.

Another issue that arises when discussing Jesus' church is its birthday. The question about the birthday of the church Jesus promised is more complex than it appears. For example, one cannot simply cite Pentecost as the church's birthday (Acts 2). This is because if "church" is defined broadly as the *community of Christ's followers*, then, Pentecost cannot be its birthday because prior to Pentecost Jesus gathered and attracted followers and disciples. Pentecost is best described as the official "inauguration" of the church. But the question about the church's birthday raises another question: What are the criteria for becoming a member of the community of Christ's followers? Theologians have approached this question with caution, which is evident in the classification of the church by some into two kinds: the "visible church" (members of identifiable local Christian communities) and the "invisible church" (usually understood as the true or genuine followers of Christ, some of whom may not be part of an identifiable Christian community).

The word "Church," in theological terms, is a complex reality in all of its ramifications: its composition, scope, task, and destination. Regarding its

---

3. Cyprian, *Epistles* 70.3 (*ANF* 5:377).

4. Cullmann, "Pétros, Kēphás," 5:108.

5. For more discussion of the papal primacy, see Fahey, "Church," 50–58.

form (including its composition, scope, and membership), we can speak of three types of church. For lack of better expressions, I name them the "local church," the "global church," and the "cosmic church." The *local church* refers to the members of identifiable Christian congregations located in specific locales. The members of ecclesiastical denominations (such as Roman Catholicism, the Greek Orthodox Church, Pentecostalism, Baptists, etc.) and members of specific congregations (such as Five Oaks Community Church in Woodbury, the Church of All Saints in Jerusalem, etc) make up the *local church*. The second church's type, the *global church*, comprises all of the local churches or all identifiable Christian communities, which can be found in all parts of the world. The *cosmic church*, the third type, is comprised of both the local and global church. But its scope extends beyond the local church and global church. The *cosmic church* includes also all the *people of God*— those whom the Triune God has called and will call into divine fellowship. As we saw in the last chapter, many who belong to God's family may or may not have identified with Christianity. While the *local church* and the *global church* require their members to identify with both Jesus Christ and Christianity, an explicit knowledge of Christ and a commitment to Christianity are not a requisite for being a member of the *cosmic church*. This chapter will focus only on the *local church* and the *global church*. Therefore, unless stated otherwise and with the exception of when I am quoting other theologians, I will use the term "church" to refer both to the *local church* and the *global church* as defined above.

The early church, especially in the fourth and fifth centuries CE, was known for its groundbreaking theological work and conciliar decisions on Christology and the Trinity. Today new Christologies and Trinitarian theologies are usually measured in the light of their faithfulness or non-faithfulness to such ecumenical councils' decisions. The early church, however, did not have an official and ecumenically endorsed doctrine of the church. All that the early Christian communities left behind are disparate ecclesiologies of individual theologians who addressed peculiar issues facing their local communities. Theologians sometimes within the same church denomination have held competing ecclesiologies. In what follows, I will describe some of the major models of the church developed and employed by different Christian communities around the world.

Church as the Triune God's Mode of Presence in the World

The "church," as argued by the Orthodox Church theologian Alexander Schmemann (1921–83), "does not exist" if by existence we mean an independent "thing."[6] Schmemann's point is that the church "cannot be defined, apart from the very content of her life." The church's life is dependent on the Triune God's work in the world. The church is God's new creation and God's mode of being present in the world. As Schmemann writes, "The church is first of all and before everything else a God-created and God-given reality, the presence of Christ's new life, [and] the manifestation of the new eon of the Holy Spirit."[7] The church is the presence of Christ's life in the world. "The church . . . is not an 'essence' or 'being' distinct, as such, from God, man, and the world, but is the very reality of *Christ in us* and *us in Christ*, a new mode of God's presence and action and His creation, of creation's life in God."[8] For Schmemann, what happened at Pentecost was not merely "an establishment of an institution endowed with specific powers and authorities." Rather Pentecost was the "inauguration of the new age, the beginning of life eternal, the revelation of the kingdom which is 'joy and peace in the Holy Spirit.'"[9]

The church has both cosmic and eschatological dimensions: it is a "new creation" (cosmic) that must live in the present world with the expectation of the life to come (eschatological). The church is the continuing presence of *Pentecost*—the inauguration of the creation as "renewed by Christ and sanctified by the Holy Spirit." As an eschatological reality, the church must live in this present world with the constant expectation of a future life with Christ.[10] In other words, the church as a *called out* community cannot be completely at home in this present world. As God's new creation, the church embodies rejection of the world's self-sufficiency and must thirst and hunger for God's consummation of all things. The church is God's vehicle for manifesting God's reign or kingdom in the world.[11] Schmemann also sees the church as a *mystery*.[12] This mystery, of course, has a context: the church represents the divine-human union, a union that is symbolized in the Eucharist. Through this mystical union all life is transformed and returned to what God intends for humans in paradise. The church is a *eucharistic assembly*. In the celebration of the Eucharist, the church both *ascends to the throne of God* for purification and for the "reconciliation of the whole creation to God" and *returns to the world* for its mission—to transform the world.[13]

6. Schmemann, "Ecclesiological Notes," 35.

7. Schmemann, "Missionary Imperative in the Orthodox Church," 197.

8. Schmemann, "Ecclesiological Notes," 35. Emphasis in original.

9. Ibid., 36.

10. Ibid.

11. Schmemann, "Missionary Imperative in the Orthodox Church," 197.

12. Schmemann, "Ecclesiological Notes," 36.

13. Schmemann, "Missionary Imperative in the Orthodox Church," 200–201.

As an *institution*, the church is a visible community that must constantly "fulfill [its] oneness, holiness, catholicity, and apostolicity." Schmemann distinguishes *the* "Church" (One, Holy, Catholic, and Apostolic Church) from "churches," which are the local manifestations of the one universal Church. On the one hand, each church is both a "part" and a "whole." Each church is a "part" because it is "only in unity with all churches and in obedience to the universal truth can it be the Church." On the other hand, each local church is also a "whole" because in it "the whole Christ is present, the fullness of grace is given, and the catholicity of new life is revealed."[14] The relationship of the "Church" and its manifestations as a "plurality of churches" is integral. Therefore, there is no need to separate the "invisible church" from the "visible church."

Other theologians that associate the church with the life of the Triune God have highlighted the Holy Spirit's relation to the church. John D. Zizioulas notes that some Orthodox Church theologians are dissatisfied with the Second Vatican Council's ecclesiology because of its lack of emphasis on the work of the Holy Spirit. Zizioulas accuses the Second Vatican Council (hereafter Vatican II Council) of bringing the Holy Spirit into its discussion on ecclesiology after constructing an "edifice of the Church . . . with Christological material."[15] Zizioulas cautions Christian theologians against the danger of allowing Christology (discourse about Jesus Christ) to dominate pneumatology (discourse about the Holy Spirit) in their discussions on the nature and mission of the church.[16] While Zizioulas contends there is no need to disrupt the unity between Christ's and the Holy Spirit's work in the church, he argues that the Holy Spirit is the one who brings the church into existence. He writes, "The Spirit is not something that 'animates' a Church which already exists. The Spirit makes the Church *be*."[17] Simon Chan, a Pentecostal theologian, shares a similar understanding of the Holy Spirit's relation to the church. Chan writes that in the Trinitarian economy, it is the Holy Spirit's role to give the church its distinct identity. For him, the Holy Spirit both brings the church into existence and into relationship with the Triune God's life.[18] The Holy Spirit indwells the church, uniting its members with Christ.[19]

14. Schmemann, "Ecclesiological Notes," 37–38.

15. Zizioulas, *Being as Communion*, 123.

16. Ibid., 129.

17. Ibid., 132.

18. Chan, *Pentecostal Ecclesiology*, 50.

19. Ibid., 64.

The idea of the "church" as the *Triune God's mode of presence in the world* is a powerful reminder that God enacts and sustains the life of the community of Christ's followers. The relationship of the members of the church, as Miroslav Volf has argued, should be modeled after the pericho-retical life of mutuality and interdependence of the Triune God.[20] In the words of Dumitru Stăniloae, "The Holy Spirit continues the revelation of Christ . . . through the act of bringing the Church into existence and through the practical organization of her structures, that is, through the initial putting of them into practice."[21] The presence of the church in the world shows that God has not left the world without a continuing witness—a prophetic voice that calls humans beings, as God's creatures, to live in obedience to God. When the church is derailed from this prophetic mission by denominational rancor, distractions from within secular cultures, and theological debates, the church undermines its existence and relevance in the world. A potential danger of seeing the church as the Triune God's mode of presence in the world is the likelihood of mistaking it for God, a mistake that amounts to what can be described as "ecclesiolatry"—the act of giving an excessive and undue reverence to the church. While the church is called to be God's mouthpiece, it cannot replace God or receive honor due to God.

Church as Institution

Dorothee Sölle rightly notes that the vast majority of people (both Christians and people of other religions) "experience the church as a great institution which publicly administers the traditions of religion, fulfills an external role by organizing certain rituals, and represents a factor of political power."[22] The concept of the church as an *institution* highlights the structure, organization, and governance that preserve and enforce the identity markers of Christian communities. To become a member of a church is in a sense to enter into a "social contract" or a relationship with an organized ecclesiastical body. Members of a church should be prepared to comply with the church's social, political, and religious guidelines or laws. Such members are to order their lives in accordance with the church's defined way of life.[23] For some theologians, the external structures of the church are intended to "express part of its inner reality."[24] The visible representations of the community of

20. Volf, *After Our Likeness*, 220.
21. Stăniloae, *Experience of God*, 57.
22. Sölle, *Thinking about God*, 136.
23. Congar, *Mystery of the Church*, 44.
24. Fahey, "Church," 31.

Christ's followers require order and form. It may be impossible for churches to carry out their ministries to the world and to their members effectively without some stable structures and forms. Many churches have translated the necessity of order and form into hierarchical structures.

A church's form of government, number of elected leaders and offices, and the relations of officeholders to the laity and non-ordained leaders will vary from denomination to denomination and also from place to place. To cite a few examples, some churches use the *Presbyterian* form of church government in which a council of elders (*presbytérion* in Greek) governs the church and oversees its affairs. In this type of church government, there is less emphasis on an individual leader (such as the Moderator of the Church of Scotland or the Presbyterian Church of Nigeria). Members of local churches appoint or elect their representatives who attain to the social, doctrinal, teaching, and other needs of the church. Some of the elected leaders represent their churches at synods, councils, and general assembly meetings. The Reformed church traditions, some Evangelical churches, and Pentecostal churches use variant forms of the *Presbyterian* form of government.

Some churches adopt an *Episcopalian* form of church government in which the office of a bishop (*episcopē* in Greek) is assigned an enormous power. In this form of government, the overarching bishop like the pope in the Roman Catholic Church, the archbishop of Canterbury of the Church of England, and patriarch or (archbishop) of Alexandria of the Orthodox Coptic Church play significant roles in decision-making that concern the teaching, leadership, and identity of their churches. In both Presbyterian and Episcopalian forms of church government, a local church does not have an absolute autonomy. For instance, the official decisions of a Roman Catholic pope regarding doctrines will have (or is expected to have) an effect on the local Roman Catholic churches worldwide.

Other churches use the *Congregational* form of church government. This form of church government emphasizes the democratic responsibility of members of a local church in choosing or deposing their leaders. Also, this form of government places emphasis on the autonomy of local congregations or churches.[25]

Users of these three forms or models of church government appeal to the Bible for support.[26] In some cases, local churches adopt a combination of two or more of these forms. Churches can abuse any of these forms

25. Grenz, *Theology for the Community of God*, 554–57.

26. For the Presbyterian model, see 1 Tim 4:14 and Jas 5:14. For the Episcopalian form of government, see Acts 1:16–26 and 1 Tim 3:1. For the Congregational model, see Acts 6:1–5.

of government; any one can be conscripted to ungodly and dehumanizing purposes. When a church's style of governance destroys the fellowship of its members or destroys the dignity of any member, the church must change or modify its form of government. In some church denominations, some ecclesiastical structures are believed to be divinely ordained or sanctioned. For instance, the Vatican II Council argued that the Holy Spirit has bestowed upon the church "varied hierarchic and charismatic gifts" through which the Holy Spirit directs the church.[27] In the Roman Catholic Church, the office of the pope is believed to be divinely instituted. Also, the official doctrine (the *ecclesiastical magisterium*), sacraments, and governmental structures are believed to be founded on divine revelation.[28] Some founders of Pentecostal churches who also serve as the General Overseers of their churches usually exert enormous influence on the theology, form of worship, organizational structures, and vision of their churches. Many of these founders believe (and also teach their members to believe) they are acting under the Holy Spirit's direction and leadership. In sub-Saharan Africa, as Ogbu Kalu notes, many founders of Pentecostal churches appeal to the Holy Spirit's guidance to justify their leadership decisions. In so doing they discourage many of their members from questioning their decisions and judgments.[29]

Three major criticisms of the concept of the church as an *institution* are noteworthy. First, the model of the church as an *institution* usually leads to a bureaucratic mode of operation that destroys the interconnections and equality of relations, which ought to characterize the relationship between all the members of a local church. Second, seeing the church as an *institution* with defined and codified rules and guidelines sometimes makes it extremely difficult to view the church as a reality that is "becoming"—moving towards its intended purpose rather than as having achieved its intended purpose.[30] Churches that operate with the institutional model are usually reluctant to change their doctrines even when such changes are necessary. Third, some theologians argue that the church is not primarily an institution but rather a community that is governed by a life of sharing, witnessing, and fellowshipping.[31] A church's institutional elements are, therefore, secondary to the church's mode of being and nature.

---

27. Vatican Council II, *Lumen Gentium* 4, in Flannery, *Vatican Council II*, 352.

28. Dulles, *Models of the Church*, 42.

29. Kalu, *African Pentecostalism*, 124.

30. Corcoran, "Introduction: The Emerging Church," xv.

31. Dulles, *Models of the Church*, 45.

Church as Communion

How the term communion (*koinōnía* in Greek and *communio* in Latin) is to be understood in relation to the church remains an open question. What is clear is that many theologians who construe the church as "communion" aim to distinguish the communities of Christ's followers from the rigidity and structures associated with the institutional church. When used in relation to the church, communion refers to three related types of fellowship: *intra-fellowship* of the members of a local Christian community, *inter-fellowship* among various Christian communities, and *personal fellowship* between a believer and the Triune God.[32] What these three realities share is an emphasis on a life of participation that derives its impetus from the Triune God who generates the church and also forms it according to the image of Jesus' person and work. Paul in his first letter to Christians in Corinth reminded them that God called them "into fellowship with his Son Jesus Christ" (1 Cor 1:9 NIV), which they are to commemorate in the sharing of the eucharistic meal or Lord's Supper (1 Cor 11:14–22).

The German theologian Dietrich Bonhoeffer (1906–45) divides the New Testament's ideas of the church broadly into two categories: that of Jerusalem, which is hierarchical in nature, and that of Paul, which is organic in nature and focuses on the local assembly of Christ's followers.[33] Bonhoeffer argues that Paul moved the early Christians away from the concept of the church as a hierarchical intuition.[34] For Bonhoeffer, the church is given its communal identity by the Holy Spirit; he argues that the Holy Spirit uses human social life, bonds, and will to form relationships in the church.[35] As a member of the church, an individual belongs both to Christ (who unites all members) and to the community of God.[36] As an assembly of the communion of saints, the church is a social organism in which each member lives for others and is willingly to share in the lives of others.[37] The French Roman Catholic theologian Yves Congar shares a similar understanding of the church. For him, the church is the mystical body of Christ that is grounded in communion—a communion that is lived out as the members of the body of Christ grow in Christ in charity "so that the whole body benefits from the advance of each" other.[38]

32. Fahey, "Church," 34–37.

33. Bonhoeffer, *Communion of Saints*, 97–98.

34. Ibid., 98.

35. Ibid., 99–100.

36. Ibid., 102.

37. Ibid., 130–36.

38. Congar, *Mystery of the Church*, 84.

Several African theologians have argued that the idea of the church as "family," which brings to light the communion of Christ's followers, resonates with most Africans. The notions of *ubuntu,* which include communion, communality, and interrelatedness, are at home with the traditional values of African societies.[39] Izunna Okonkwo uses a traditional saying of the Igbos of southeastern Nigeria, *onye aghana nwanne ya* (which means literally, "do not forsake your sibling") to highlight the community orientation of many African communities.[40] The word "sibling," of course, does not do justice to the richness and scope of the meaning of the Igbo word "nwanne," which extends beyond the nuclear family to include the extended family and kindred, both the living and the dead. For Okonkwo, the saying *onye aghana nwanne ya* can enrich African Christians' ecclesiologies because of the profundity of its emphasis on solidarity, fellowship, and communion.[41]

The idea of communion does not rule out using intuitional structures to guide members of the church in their worship, manner of living, and relationship with people both within and outside of the church. Yet when communion, and not institutional structures, is made the heartbeat of a church, it can help the church guard against the threat of individualism and private spirituality. Also, when communion is made the heartbeat of the church, Christians of a given denomination may begin to address the need of engaging ecumenically with other Christian communities that may not share their theologies and modes of worship. A life of communion can motivate a Christian to refrain from exercising his or her rights "if it means offending a brother or sister. For that person is a member of *one's own body*, and deserves the care and respect that the eye, ear, hand . . . owe each other."[42] Christians will become aware of the need to join other Christians in fellowshipping with God.[43]

Critics of communion ecclesiologies warn that the concept of the church as *communion* when likened to the perichoretical life of communion in the Trinity may lead to the divinization of the church. Theologians that adopt a communion ecclesiology must shoulder the responsibility of working out the implications of the idea of the church as communion of members of Christ's body without ascribing to the church an undue

---

39. See Tutu, *God is Not a Christian*, 22; Orobator, *Church as Family*, 35–36.

40. Okonkwo, "Sacrament of the Eucharist (as Koinonia)," 100–101.

41. Ibid., 101.

42. Mangina, "Cross-Shaped Church," 70.

43. Dulles, *Models of the Church*, 58.

divine status.[44] The communion model can also discourage the use of firm structures that are sometimes necessary to define a church's identity and way of life.

Church as Emerging

In the twentieth century, Christians (mainly of Protestant traditions) in the Western world witnessed some ecclesiological movements that were driven by the quest to reimagine *how to be* the church in a postmodern world. From the late 1980s, Christians in Europe and North America began to question the static and institutional life of the church. Although they did not abandon the idea of the church entirely, they sought to recast the traditional conception of the church in the new light provided by some insights drawn from postmodernism and advancement in media communication. For most leaders of the movements, contemporary Christians must rediscover the *pilgrimaging* characteristic of the church. As Doug Gay observes, "The Church's pilgrimage as a journey through space and time involves it in a continuing negotiation between the faith once delivered to the saints and the incarnation of that faith in each new context."[45] The movements resulted in what is now known as "alternative worship" in the United Kingdom and the "emerging church" in the United States.[46] In the United Kingdom, individuals such as Jonny Baker and Ian Mosby led the reconfiguration of the church from what *is* to what is *becoming*.[47] The Nine O'Clock Service, based in an evangelical Anglican congregation in Sheffield, with its "hybrid" style that combined traditional and contemporary charismatic modes of worship, ornamented with media, graphical designs, and projected visuals, may be legitimately termed the forbear of alternative worship.[48] Beginning in the early 1990s, the emerging church flourished in the United States, attracting both critics and those who welcomed it as a breath of fresh air in Christianity.

Members of the alternative worship and emerging church movements learn from both philosophical and cultural postmodernist discourses. From *philosophical postmodernism*, they have learned to be suspicious of intellectual arrogance, which is the consequence of one's failure to acknowledge that human beings' grasp of reality "is always partial, incomplete,

44. Ibid., 60.

45. Gay, *Remixing the Church*, 72.

46. Ibid., 6.

47. Corcoran, "Introduction: The Emerging Church," xi–xii.

48. Gay, *Remixing the Church*, 7–8.

and fragmentary."[49] Humans cannot explain the reality of God's creation and God's work in creation exhaustively or formulate theologies that are supra-cultural, unbiased, and always universally useful. The products of *cultural postmodernism*—advancements in telecommunications and other technologies, connectivity, and globalization—have been put to use by the advocates of alternative worship and emerging churches.[50] Technologies are used not only to reach contemporary Christians or inquirers about Christianity but also more importantly to decentralize ecclesiastical power, which is usually reserved for a few elite in the traditional churches.

Aesthetically, the alternative church and emerging church communities are deeply rooted in contemporary culture and art.[51] They retrieve and modify the contents of some traditional forms of worship such as liturgy and ritual, while resisting the temptation to fix the order of worship in scripts.[52] The conception of "tradition" as static and irrevocable is greatly opposed. Movement, flexibility, and fluidity are embraced in the alternative worship and emerging church communities. They steer away from speculative theologies that detract from the responsibility of the church to this-worldly affairs. Taking a cue from the doctrine of the incarnation—God's eternal Word becoming human in Jesus of Nazareth—they argue that just as God entered the world to heal and liberate it, the church should likewise be attentive to the needs of the world. The church in particular must become God's voice against oppression "on behalf of all of those excluded."[53]

What is known as alternative worship in the United Kingdom and the emerging church in the United States may have been preceded by the *Mukyōkai* ("Non-Church") movement in Japan that began with individuals such as Kanzō Uchimura (1861–1930).[54] One assessor of Uchimura's influence described him as an individual who "nearly performed the task for Japan that John Knox did for Scotland, Luther for Germany, and Calvin for France and Switzerland."[55] While these movements are not to be confused with each other, they share the same dissatisfaction with the traditional church's fixation on static and intuitional structures. Uchimura was dissatisfied with the Methodist Church's intuitionalism and the Methodist missionaries' unwillingness to contextualize Christianity in Japan. In the 1900s,

49. Corcoran, "Who's Afraid of Philosophical Realism?," 11.

50. Ibid.

51. Gay, *Remixing the Church*, 13.

52. Ibid., 21.

53. Rollins, "Worldly Theology of Emerging Christianity," 36.

54. Norman, *Interim Report on Non-Church Christianity*, 3.

55. Ibid.

Mukyōkai communities aimed to be a church or a Christian assembly without institutional structures and without a priestly class. The true church, for Uchimura, was not an organized institutionalized church but rather an assembly of people who gather in the name of Christ (Matt 18:20). Therefore, he rejected the liturgical, sacramental, and traditional models of church as suitable for his Japanese context.[56] For Uchimura, the sacraments should not be a requirement for church membership but rather should be an outward expression of the fellowship that Christ's followers enjoy among themselves and with Christ.[57] He envisioned a church that was deeply shaped by small groups that met regularly to study the Bible and for fellowship.

Returning to the alternative worship and emerging church movements, their members are ecumenically minded. They are open to fellowshipping with people from diverse church denominations. This openness to ecumenism should be celebrated, because Christians are to take seriously Jesus' prayer to God the Father regarding the unity of his followers (John 17:20). The alternative worship and emerging church congregations, however, have attracted many critics. Some worry that their ecclesiologies' close affinity with postmodernism's incredulity towards absolute truth claims endangers traditional Christian metanarratives and truth claims. D. A. Carson, for example, accuses some advocates of alternative worship and emerging church of rejecting modernism (and its assumption of the possibility of attaining a universal non-contextual truth) but failing to provide a penetrating criticism of postmodernism.[58] Carson's concern is that failing to have a universally binding "frame of reference" that is rooted in the Bible, which he believes is "authoritative precisely because it is God-revealed and true," leaves the church open to all sorts of false teachings.[59] Another criticism of alternative worship and emerging church concerns their construal of the church as a fluid or liquid phenomenon.[60] These congregations' emphasis on the fluidity or liquidity of the church's mode of being or operation may be the Achilles' heel that will undermine their focus on forming "tight communities."[61] A liquid church, which has the potential of attracting a massive network of people through the use of media resources, may focus on issues at the macro level and ignore people's needs at the micro level.

---

56. For his contextual theologies and ecclesiologies, see Uchimura, *The Complete Works of Kanzo Uchimura*.

57. Kärkkäinen, *Introduction to Ecclesiology*, 169.

58. Carson, *Becoming Conversant*, 125–38.

59. Ibid., 142.

60. Gibbs and Bolger, *Emerging Churches*, 113–15.

61. Ibid., 115.

Church as Christ's Multicultural and Cross-Generational Body

"After this I looked," writes the author of Revelation, "and behold, a great multitude that no one could number, from every nation, from all tribes and peoples and languages, standing before the throne and before the Lamb, clothed in white robes" (Rev 7:9 ESV). In his letter to Christians living in Ephesus, Paul used the word "body" (*sōma* in Greek) to describe the church (Eph 1:22). Andrew F. Walls argues that the description of the church as Christ's body is the key to Paul's ecclesiology in the Ephesian letter.[62] The church is multicultural, cross-racial, and multi-charismatic. To put it differently, the church is comprised of "different races (Jew and Gentile), different lifestyles (Hebraic and Hellenistic), and different people with different gifts and functions."[63] Walls recognizes that the depictions of the church's diversity of cultures, peoples, and modes of living are essential to the metaphor of the "body." However, Walls takes the metaphor in a more intriguing direction. He focuses on the temporality of the body. A body, he writes, "functions in time as well as in space; time is also an element in which salvation is worked out: its various manifestations across time are necessary for its completion, for 'the completion of him who himself completes all things everywhere.'"[64]

For Walls, the temporality of the body indicates two related realities about the church. First, the church belongs to Christ; it is Christ's body. As people from different parts of the world and generations receive Christ, they will interpret him with the intellectual tools available to them in their own societies and cultures. And as they appropriate Christ to their cultures, he is "formed in local Christian communities whose ways of life" are distinct from one another. Although the communities of Christ's followers who form part of Christ's body differ in looks and lifestyles, they "belong together; they are part of the same story."[65] Second, the diverse and cross-generational communities of Christ's followers are also incomplete in themselves. They need the life (so to speak), vision, knowledge, and relationship of each other to explore the depth, width, and length of the Triune God's work in the world.

The church's existence (which is actualized by the work of the Holy Spirit) is grounded in the Christ-event. The metaphor of the "body of Christ" signifies a covenant relationship between Jesus Christ and the community of people that the Triune God has created in response to the life and work

62. Walls, *Cross-Cultural Process in Christian History*, 74.

63. Ibid.

64. Ibid.

65. Ibid.

of Jesus Christ. In the words of Stanley Grenz, the early followers of Jesus Christ "saw themselves as a special people, a people united together because they had been called out of the world by the gospel to belong to God."[66] John Zizioulas notes that the church "is one because Christ is one and she [the church] owes her being to this one Christ."[67] However, this one church, one body of Christ, in its visible representations takes different modes of being—the local churches. Seeing the visible representations of the one catholic or universal church as a multicultural and cross-generational body of Christ prepares us for the surprises of the diversity that characterizes local churches.

Students of ecclesiology who travel around the world to observe the communities that bear the label "church" will encounter many communities that differ from their ecclesiastical beliefs and practices. For example, an English member of the Church of England who resides in London will be shocked by the conspicuous white or blue garment required of members of the Celestial Church of Christ in Nigeria. Andrew Walls has noted that the differences in the forms of worship and liturgies of local Christian communities, which are deeply shaped by their contexts, may mean "Christians of different times and places must often be unrecognizable to others, or indeed even to themselves, as manifestations of a single phenomenon."[68] A major problem with seeing the church as *Christ's multicultural and multigenerational body* is how to arrive ecumenically at the nonnegotiable beliefs and practices that should govern all communities bearing the name "Christian." Allowing each church to take different forms of meanings as it encounters new cultures can open doors to false Christian identities.

---

66. Grenz, *Theology for the Community of God*, 480.

67. Zizioulas, *Being as Communion*, 132.

68. Walls, *Missionary Movement in Christian History*, 7.

Table 4.1
Summary of the Ideas/Models of the Church

Model	Concept of the Church	Assessment
Triune God's Mode of Presence in the World	• A community of people whose existence and subsistence are dependent on the Triune God. • A community that is constantly purified by the Triune God and also commissioned to represent the Triune God in the world.	• Strength: This model reminds us that the life of mutuality should characterize the fellowship of the members of the church. • Weakness: This model can lead to "ecclesiolatry"—giving to the church the honor that is due to God alone.
Institution	• A church is a society that requires order and structure.	• Strength: The institution model is extremely helpful for protecting a church's identity against external pressures and internal doctrinal detractors. • Weakness: The institution model is susceptible to an autocratic form of governance that protects the interest of the elite and ignores the concerns of the laity.
Communion	• A church is by nature an assembly that is primarily governed by fellowship and sharing in people's experiences.	• Strength: This model helps guard the church against individualism that can destroy the communal life of Christians. • Weakness: This model may discourage the use of structures, which in some cases are necessary to guide Christians in their worship and beliefs.
Emerging	• A church is a living organism that, on the one hand, remains faithful to its roots, and on the other hand adapts to the changes in its environment.	• Strength: This model is open to ecumenism. It also reminds Christians to strive to engage contemporary issues with contemporary "secular" resources available to them. • Weakness: Not having a static or firm point of reference makes it difficult to define the social and doctrinal identity of the church.

Christ's Multicultural and Multigenerational Body	• A church is the body of Christ that must follow the footsteps of the Incarnate Son of God in taking new forms of expression as Christian communities are formed in different cultures.	• Strength: This model is very helpful in understanding the complexity of the phenomenon of global or world Christianity. It helps to facilitate cross-cultural conversations among Christian communities. It also promotes contextual theologizing. • Weakness: This model can open doors to false Christian identities.

Concluding Reflections on the Ideas of the Church

As an assembly called into existence by the Triune God, the *church* (the people of God who are empowered by the Holy Spirit to commit to Jesus' vision for the world and his understandings of God-human relations) should be characterized by a life of fellowship that facilitates the faith, dignity, well-being, and morality of its members. The doctrine of the Trinity teaches mutual dependence and respect among the three divine persons. This perichoretical life of the Triune God must serve as a model of living for the church. Just as the individuality of the members of the Trinity is preserved in their relationship, the individuality of all the members of the church is to be maintained, protected, and celebrated notwithstanding their social status, social location, commitment, and ethnicity.

Like the Trinitarian life of interdependence, the church should promote the life of interdependence of its members. When a member is suffering in sin, the rest of the members should also suffer in solidarity with the sinner. When a member celebrates God's blessings and provisions, the rest of the members should celebrate as well. To put it rather bluntly, good news for one member of the church is good news for all the members of the church. Bad news for one member of the church is bad news for all members of the church. The diversity in the roles, modes of operation, and modes of being of the Trinity should also teach the church of the necessity of celebrating diversity—in terms of ethnicity, modes of doing God's work, and modes of worship. This diversity, however, has a context—the church, the community or assembly of Christ's followers called into existence by the Triune God. As a "community," the church must embody and exhibit communal relations in which, to use the words of Miroslav Volf, a Christian embraces "concrete relations with other Christians."[69]

As a community being transformed by God into the image of Jesus Christ through the ministry of the Holy Spirit, the church should strive to *hear* the voice of Jesus, the shepherd who calls all members of the community of God into fellowship. Jesus in a parabolic fashion speaks of himself as a good shepherd who gives himself sacrificially for the welfare of his sheep (John 10:11; 17–18). Jesus also expects his sheep to heed his voice, depending on him for protection, guidance, provision, discipline, and restoration (John 10:14). *Heeding* the voice of Jesus Christ entails embodying his vision in the world—a vision that comprises the healing of the world of its social and spiritual wounds, being an agent of reconciliation that brings human beings back to divine fellowship, and proclaiming God's good news to all

69. Volf, *After Our Likeness*, 134

people irrespective of their religious affiliations, ethnicity, social status, and social location (Matt 28:19–20; Luke 4:16–22; Acts 1:8). Local church congregations cannot completely abandon "organizational" structures, such as rules for networking, forms of governance, membership guidelines, and modes of fellowship. But these should not inhibit the church from working towards addressing the needs of the members of the church.

Exercise 4.1

What do you consider to be the peculiar issues facing the church in your community? Which of the models (or combination of the models) discussed above can be useful to you in identifying and tackling those issues?

Church's Relation to Its Members

The Church exists for the Triune God's *glory* but also for the *benefit* of God's entire creation, human beings in particular. I will discuss the church's

FOCUS QUESTION:
What sort of relationship should exist between the church and its members?

relation to the nonmembers of the church in the final chapter under the heading "The Christian Life and Christian Communities' Relation to the World." In this section, I will focus on the church's relation to its members (that is, Christ's followers). Four themes will be discussed: namely, ecumenism, sacraments, spiritual gifts, and gender and ecclesiastical leadership.

Ecclesiastical Ecumenism

The word "ecumenism" is used here to describe the pursuit of unity of relationships, doctrines (teaching), and praxis (practice) among adherents of Christianity. But the question, "Which Christianity?" is one of the major questions a Christian who wishes to preach the gospel message to people of other religions or to people with no religious affiliation should be ready to answer in our contemporary world. Christianity is more than ever fraught with competing beliefs and practices that most times undermine any quest to achieve unity of expression, identity, mission, and purpose among Christians. J. M. R. Tillard (1927–2000) described divisions within Christianity as "the greatest scandal of the Church's history" and as the "greatest obstacle to evangelization."[70]

Two issues, which are neither mutually exclusive nor equally weighed, govern discourses on ecumenism. These are (*a*) the issue of how to interpret and appropriate Jesus' prayer for the unity of his followers in John 17, and (*b*) the issue of how to interpret and appropriate the Nicene-Constantinopolitan conception of the church as "one, holy, apostolic, and catholic." Although some Christians use the word "ecumenism" to describe the pursuit of fellowship or dialogue between Christians and non-Christians, in this chapter I use the term "ecumenism" to describe the sort of relationship that ought to exist among Christian communities.[71]

Given the divisions among Christians, one may ask, has God the Father not answered Jesus' prayer for the unity of his followers, as recorded in John 17:20? Jesus prayed to the Father to enable all of his followers to "be one." Clearly, Christians do not show the sort of unity that Jesus had desired for them. Christians are not only divided in their theologies and forms of worship; they sometimes persecute or dehumanize each other because of their differences. On the Nicene-Constantinopolitan description of the church as *one*, *holy*, *apostolic*, and *catholic*, theologians have disagreed on how to parse these features of the church. For some, "one," "catholic," and "apostolic" imply there is only one true church with one human headship—a human leader that can be traced back via the apostolic succession to Peter's headship. For many Roman Catholics, the Roman Catholic Church and the pope are the true representatives of the one, catholic, and apostolic church. Some theologians, however, contend that the primary issue in apostolic succession is the *teaching* of the apostles and not *individuals* who occupy the office of a bishop. Theologians of other church denominations reject the Roman Catholic understandings of the Nicene-Constantinopolitan language of *one, holy, apostolic*, and *catholic church*.[72] Martin Luther, for instance, viewed the church's catholicity as referring to the "community or number of assembly of all Christians in the all the world." Also, he viewed ecclesiastical offices such as bishops and priests as servants in and of the church and not the heads or lords of the church because Jesus Christ is the "only head" of the church.[73] Consequently, he argued that the church "exists not only in the

---

70. Tillard, *I Believe, Despite Everything*, 15.

71. For discussion on Christians' dialogue with non-Christians, see ch. 3 of this book.

72. Braaten, *Mother Church*, 27–30.

73. Luther, *Confession Concerning Christ's Supper—Part III (1528)*, 57.

realm of the Roman Church or pope, but in all the world, as the prophets foretold that the gospel of Christ would spread throughout the world."[74]

Several other issues condition the discourse on ecclesiastical ecumenism. I will highlight two: theological identity and diversity.

Theological Identity

For some people, ecclesiastical ecumenism is a project that is doomed to failure from the start because of the competing theological identities within Christianity. The differences of these theological identities are so glaring that only a careless student of Christianity can miss their impact on Christian communities. Most people who are unsympathetic to ecclesiastical ecumenism usually defend their stance on the issue by appealing to the necessity of maintaining the purity of Christian doctrines. They fear that striving for an ecumenical church will entail accepting or tolerating some doctrines that (in their judgment) will not pass the test of the Scriptures and sound theological reasoning. Purity of doctrine, however, may only be an *apparent* reason for such people's suspicion of the necessity of ecumenism. The secret underlying reason may be the quest to defend their own denomination's theological identity, their interpretation of the Scriptures, and their understandings of the classical ecumenical conciliar theological positions. Many such theologians, of course, see their church's theological positions as the most Christian and biblical vis-à-vis the theological positions of churches that differ from theirs.[75]

In the context of ecclesiastical ecumenism, discussions about "theological identity" should be attentive both to disparate theological ideas and positions of the *local church* and to the implications of those ideas and positions for the *global church*.[76] Working out the details of the relationships between disparate and sometimes competing theological identities of the *local church* and also their implications for the *global church* is not an easy task. Christians have pursued these relationships from different angles. Some have focused on ecumenically driven theological projects that bring people from two or more church traditions to discuss specific theological issues.[77]

74. Ibid.

75. *Ecumenism among Us*, 12–14.

76. As stated earlier, the local church refers to the members of identifiable Christian congregations in specific locales. The global church is comprised of all the local churches that can be found in all parts of the world.

77. For example, see the theological discussions on Christian spirituality undertaken by Orthodox Church theologians, mainline Protestant theologians, and Evangelical

Other theologians and church leaders pursue the project of ecclesiastical ecumenism through conciliar meetings. Historically, conciliar meetings have been the most used avenues in Christianity. The earliest of such meetings can be traced back to the Jerusalem Council recorded in Acts 15. In our time, the World Council of Churches (WCC), which began in the twentieth century, has led the way in the use of a conciliar meetings' approach to address ecumenical issues.[78]

How can the issues relating to theological identity that raise problems for ecclesiastical ecumenism be addressed? What is required is the creation of a "theological circumference" within which the discussions can take place. The "theological circumference" will serve as the markers for identifying the theologies that pass the test of Christianity and those that do not, and therefore, should be discarded or revised. Having such "theological circumference" will foster healthy conversations and also mutual criticisms. Also, the "theological circumference" will create a *common and shared context* within which Christians can variously iron out their theological beliefs, practices, modes of worship, and so on. The *common and shared context* may require Christian communities to tweak but not abandon their unique history and their own theological identities. Also, perhaps more importantly, the *common and shared context* should be revisable. Present and future generations must have the freedom to modify the *common and universally binding context* as the need arises and becomes necessary. But how do Christians arrive at such "theological circumference"? Who should determine the components of the theological circumference? These are the questions that many ecumenically minded theologians dread to ask or to answer. But they are too important to be ignored.

For some theologians such as Carl Braaten, the only viable option for addressing these questions is to return to the "Scripture, creedal, and confessional traditions of the church."[79] Braaten is saddened by the unfortunate outcome of the Protestant Reformation. The protest against Rome, which for him was necessary for the sake of the one (catholic) church and which was originally intended to be a temporary arrangement, has now become the permanent state of affairs that divide the church. Braaten sees this unintended outcome of the sixteenth-century Protestant Reformation as tragic.[80] Contemporary Christians must return to the original purpose of the Prot-

---

theologians that resulted in the publication of Demarest, ed., *Four Views on Christian Spirituality*.

78. For more information about the history, vision, and goals of the WCC, see its official website: http://www.oikoumene.org/en.

79. Braaten, *Mother Church*, 10.

80. Ibid., 12–13.

estant Reformation (that is, to Luther's original intention), which was "a call to catholicity and away from the Romanization of the Western Church."[81] Christians must strive for a reunion of the divided *global church*. Achieving such unity and reconciliation requires rethinking the meaning of "catholicity" as used in the ancient Christian creeds. Braatan argues that the word "catholic" cannot mean "Roman Catholic" as many Roman Catholics assume.[82] Protestants in their search for the meaning of "catholicity" should be open to accept the necessity of *episcopal structures* ("the historic episcopacy and papacy"), albeit without ignoring the abuses of these structures that led to the Protestant Reformation.[83] For Braaten, the vision for a reunited church should not be disregarded as wishful thinking, as unattainable. On the contrary, Christians are to strive for a reunited church even though they may not yet know exactly what it will look like when it is achieved. For him, seeking the "evangelical truth" or the truth of the gospel must "take priority over ecclesiastical unity."[84] Braaten suggests the following as that which ought to govern Christians' search for a reunited, catholic, and evangelical church. He contends that Christians should

> long for a church that will be both evangelical and catholic, continuous with the faith of the apostles, and coterminous with all that is universally valid in the experience of Christ's body on earth. We long for a church in which the members will be one with Christ and one with one another, even as the Son is one with the Father. We long for a church that will be one and catholic, so that the mission of Christ through his church unto all nations might be accomplished; unity and mission belong together. Let us work for the church we long for. Christ will accomplish his will, indeed, without our help, but we pray that he may accomplish it through us.[85]

While Braaten has focused on the divisions within Christians of the West, other theologians have focused on the reconciliation of Christians of the *West* (Roman Catholics and Protestants) and Christians of the *East* (Orthodox Churches). To highlight one such project, the Lausanne-Orthodox Initiative founded in 2010 aims to foster mutual respect, learning,

---

81. Ibid., 12.

82. Ibid., 22.

83. Ibid., 23–24

84. Ibid., 32.

85. Ibid., 24.

and theological exchanges between Evangelical and Orthodox Christians.[86] The mission statement of the Lausanne-Orthodox Initiative states,

> The goal of the Lausanne-Orthodox Initiative is to reflect con-
> structively on the history of relationships between Orthodox
> and Evangelicals in order to work towards better understanding,
> and encourage reconciliation and healing where wounds exist.
> Through this process Evangelicals and Orthodox will be mutu-
> ally enriched and strengthened in the work of mission, working
> towards mutual respect, support and cooperation in the spirit of
> our Lord's Prayer for His Church in John 17.[87]

The question of how to arrive at a *shared* "theological identity" should not be resolved by appealing only to the Scriptures and classical ecumenical council's theological decisions. While recognizing that these texts cannot be ignored in contemporary discussions on theological identity in an ecu-menical context, Christian theologians of each century must take the risk of developing theologies that are both faithful to the Scriptures and at the same time relevant to issues of their time. In other words, a nostalgic mindset that quickly moves present-day theologians back to the classical ecumeni-cal councils' theological positions whenever a new theological need arises may do more harm than good to present-day Christianity. The classical ecu-menical councils should guide contemporary theologians into developing new (and when possible ecumenical) theological positions that are attentive to the peculiar needs of present-day Christians. For example, merely cit-ing the position of the Councils of Nicaea (325 CE) and Constantinople (381 CE) on the doctrine of the Trinity in discussions of women's leadership roles in twenty-first-century Christian communities will not take us very far. This is partly because the councils' context was different from today's context, and the sorts of theological issues that conditioned the attendees of both councils are foreign to the sorts of issues that condition contempo-rary discourses on women's leadership roles in churches. But as we will see later in this chapter, theologians use insights from the classical doctrine of the Trinity to develop theologies of men-women relations in the church. Contemporary Christians have the responsibility to develop ecumenical theological boundaries that may guide future Christian generations, who should in turn develop their theologies with intent to provide guidance for future generations.

---

86. For more information about the Lausanne-Orthodox Initiative, visit the official website: http://www.loimission.net.

87. Ibid.

Diversity

Ecclesiastical ecumenism as I imagine it in this book is not about creating a single global church with a single universal leader. The church already has a universal leader, namely Jesus Christ, whom the Apostle Paul described as the "head of the church" (Eph 5:23; see also 1 Cor 1:10–17; 12:12–31; Col 1:18). As shown in the preceding section, the goal of ecclesiastical ecumenism is rather to create a *common theological context* defined by a theological circumference within which Christians can variously appropriate their theological beliefs, practices, and modes of worship. Diversity should be celebrated. In 1994, the Institute for Ecumenical and Cultural Research argued that "diversity as such is not the problem to overcome." It also stated that the goal of ecclesiastical ecumenism is not to achieve "uniformity or structural streamlining."[88] As Christianity encounters new cultures and contexts it will take new forms of expressions, which undoubtedly will result in diverse interpretations and appropriations of the Christian Scriptures, teachings, beliefs, and practices. In this sense, diversity can lead us to new vistas of the Triune God's providential work in places beyond our immediate communities. Each Christian community will exhibit its distinctiveness and particularity that are shaped by their peculiar contexts and aspirations. Diversity can also promote healthy dialogues among Christians.

Yet diversity in the church should neither be rooted in divisiveness nor should it promote destructive conflicts. Sometimes the diversities that characterize local Christian congregations are rooted in demonic values and assumptions such as racism. I continue to be amazed at how racism shapes the membership of churches in the United States of America. Most people in the United States attend churches where the vast majority of people come from the same ethnic backgrounds. Although the number of churches that genuinely welcome people from diverse ethnic backgrounds is increasing, such churches remain in the minority. Only careless students of Christianity can miss the divisive languages and actions that are present in Christian communities. In some societies, fellowship between Roman Catholics and Evangelical churches are prohibited. For example, in Nigeria, many Evangelical parents forbid their children from marrying from Roman Catholic families. While Christians must celebrate diversity of membership, forms of worship, and even theologies, they must reject all forms of divisiveness.

That the Apostle Paul spoke about the *supremacy of love* (1 Cor 13) to highlight the divisive Corinthian Christian communities (1 Cor 3) is noteworthy. Love, here, of course, should not be understood as mere affections

88. *Ecumenism Among Us*, 5.

210

that are grounded in selfish desires and expectations. Neither should love be understood as what stands in opposition to the quest for truth or purity of doctrines. Paul himself on many occasions warned early Christians of the danger of bad or wrong theologies (see Gal 1:6–10; 2 Tim 2:15). Still, Paul was convinced that *love*—the act of self-giving—must govern all Christian activities, including their quests for purity of doctrines, theologies, and spiritual development. To quote Paul: "If I speak in the tongues of men and angels, but have not love, I am only a resounding gong or a clanging cymbal. If I have the gift of prophecy and can fathom all mysteries and all knowledge, and if I have a faith that can move mountains, but have not love, I am nothing. If I give all I possess to the poor and surrender my body to the flames, but have not love, I gain nothing" (1 Cor 13:1–3 NIV). The supremacy of love of which Paul speaks is a call to Christian communities to return to the unity that Jesus desires for his followers.

Church and the Sacraments

The word "sacrament" (*sacramentum* in Latin) is used theologically to express a *sign* (an external object or element) and *what is signified* (non-external signification). For example, in the sacrament of the Eucharist or the Lord's Supper, the *bread and wine* are "signs" (external elements), while *God's gracious healing and restoration that flow from Jesus' death and resurrection* (non-external) is what is signified. The sacraments are liturgical rituals performed for different purposes by different Christian communities. The sacraments are a form of "communion worship or liturgy."[89] Some churches like the Orthodox Church use the word "sacrament" less frequently but use alternate terms such as "mysteries." In many Orthodox Churches, the term mystery (*mysterion* in Greek) is preferred because of its connotation of what "produces awe in the hearts and minds of those who witness it, and understand it." Also, the term *mystery* has the capacity to accentuate the need for people to be silent in acknowledgement and awe of the "consecration that has taken place, as God in his mystery has 'passed by.'"[90]

Depending on the church, the number of the sacraments (or mysteries) ranges from one to seven. Many Protestants churches recognize two sacraments (Eucharist or the Lord's Supper and baptism) mentioned by Jesus Christ. The Roman Catholic Church contends there are seven sacraments (Eucharist, baptism, marriage, holy orders, penance or confession, extreme unction, and confirmation). The Orthodox Church recognizes

89. Fahey, "Sacraments," 268.
90. McGuckin, *Orthodox Church*, 277.

seven mysteries, which are sometimes classified into great initiation experiences (Eucharist, baptism, and chrismation), two mysteries of healing (anointing and confession or *metanonia*), and two mysteries of vocation (holy orders and matrimony).[91] Protestant churches that limit the use of the term "sacraments" to baptism and the Lord's Supper use the term "ordinances" to describe the remaining five rituals that the Roman Catholic and Orthodox Churches include in their sacraments or mysteries respectively. In the sixteenth century CE, the Council of Trent (1545–63) pronounced anathemas on those who taught that there were more or less than seven sacraments (baptism, confirmation, Eucharist, penance, extreme unction, order, and matrimony).[92]

A major source of theological debate on the sacraments since the early church period was the nature of the relationship between a "sign" and "what is signified." In a sacramental ceremony, do signs "cause" divine grace (that is, do they make divine grace possible)? Or do the signs "symbolize" divine grace that is already present in the celebrants and also draw them to the divine grace? In the fourth century CE, questions regarding the sacraments were phrased to capture the contextual issues facing Christians of North Africa who negotiated Christian identity in the light of persecutions and abandonment of faith. For example, they asked the question, what makes a sacrament efficacious? Since the Protestant Reformation the central question about the nature of the relationship between a "sign" and "what is signified" has been phrased along the lines of whether or not the elements of the sacraments are substantively identifiable with what they signify. I will focus only on baptism and the Eucharist because of the importance given to them in most, if not all, Christian communities and also because theological debates on the sacraments have primarily focused on them.

Baptism

Several years ago one of my students wrote a theological position paper on the requirement of water baptism for church membership. Her decision to write on this topic was occasioned by the experience of her parents who were baptized as infants in their previous church. Her parents' new church practiced believer's baptism and required all who desire to become full members to undergo believer's baptism. Her parents who rejected what they saw as re-baptism neither desired to leave the church nor settle as casual

91. For more on these seven mysteries, see ibid., 277–346.

92. Council of Trent, The Canons and Dogmatic Decrees of the Council of Trent, "On the Sacraments in General," canon 1, in Schaff, *Creeds of Christendom*, 2:119.

members. Historically, the nature, criteria, mode, and purpose of baptism have been hotly debated by Christians. I will focus on some major theological positions, highlighting in some cases how such positions have been adopted or modified by present-day churches.

DONATISTS' POSITION

For the Donatists, baptism (or any other sacrament) is null and void if performed by a priest who renounced his faith during persecutions or who was not in a good moral standing. The term "Donatists" is used here to describe the followers of Donatus who was appointed to the position of bishop to lead the church founded by North African Christians who refused to recognize the leadership of those who apostatized or recanted their faith during persecutions. The Donatists' ecclesiology emphasized the purity of doctrines and practices. In the late third century and early fourth century CE, as the persecutions of Christians intensified in North Africa, many Christians began to abandon their faith in Christ in order to save their lives. Some not only renounced their faith but also betrayed other Christians by cooperating with the Roman officials, pointing them in the direction of other Christians who had not renounced their faith. Some of those who forsook their faith brought out their Bibles and other important Christian literature to be burned as a sign of their sincerity. They were later labelled *traditores* (people who handed the Bible over to be destroyed) by those who did not renounce their faith.[93] Around 312 CE, the Donatists founded a new church for the "pure" largely in reaction to the appointment of Caecilian as the bishop of Carthage who was rumored to have been consecrated by Felix of Aptunga, a *traditor*.[94] The Donatists were appalled by Caecilian's consecration. They refused to recognize his pastoral leadership and the legitimacy of the sacraments administered by him or other *traditores*. The Donatists were uncompromising in their insistence on the separation of the "wheat" and "tares" in the church. The church, in their judgment, must remain holy and free from contamination with sinners.

The founding of a competing church by the Donatists caused controversies and schisms in North African Christianity as many people (willingly or by compulsion) accepted the Donatists' ecclesiology.[95] For the Donatists, the effectiveness of a sacrament is contingent upon the ecclesiastical and moral standing of the priest that administers it and/or the moral standing

93. Davidson, *Public Faith*, 26.
94. Ibid., 26.
95. McGrath, *Christian Theology*, 478.

of recipients of the sacraments. In the medieval era, the Donatists' belief was expressed in Latin as *ex opere operantis*, "by the work of the doer or performer." The emphasis on preserving the purity of the church reigned supremely in the Donatists' ecclesiology. For the Donatists, those who received the sacrament of baptism from priests that renounced the faith or gave the Scriptures over to the Roman authorities must be rebaptized by priests in good moral standings. To them, any baptism administered by a priest who was a *traditore* was null and void.

The Donatists appealed to Cyprian of Carthage (ca. 200–258) as an ally. In his ecclesiology, Cyprian wanted to maintain both the unity and purity of the church.[96] He judged those who renounced the faith under persecution to have apostatized and therefore demanded their excommunication from the church. The excommunication was necessary to maintain the church's purity and to discourage other Christians from forsaking the faith. Cyprian also taught that a sacrament was valid and efficacious if done within the Catholic Church. Priests who have been excommunicated are by definition without the ecclesiastical authority to administer the sacraments. If they administer the sacraments, the sacraments are invalid or null and void.[97] In his letter to Epictetus, Cyprian admonished the church at Assurae against allowing Fortunatianus, a former priest who lapsed, back into the pastoral leadership. According to Cyprian, "Those . . . who have brought grievous sins upon themselves, that is, who, by sacrificing to idols, have offered sacrilegious sacrifices, cannot claim to themselves the priesthood of God, nor make any prayer for their brethren in [God's] sight."[98] Cyprian was, however, willing to allow the lapsed bishops back into Christian fellowship, but without returning to their former ecclesiastical positions. He wrote, "Let the lapsed . . . who acknowledge the greatness of their sin, not depart from entreating the Lord, nor forsake the Catholic Church, which has been appointed one and alone by the Lord; but, continuing in their atonements and entreating the Lord's mercy, let them knock at the door of the Church, that they may be received there where once they were, and may return to Christ from whom they have departed."[99]

The Donatists' ecclesiology and doctrine of the sacraments followed Cyprians' view on denying the returning lapsed priests the right to perform priestly duties. The Donatists, however, disregarded Cyprians' call to extend a hand of fellowship to them by readmitting them into the church.

96. Cyprian, *Epistles* 69.3 (*ANF* 5:376).

97. Ibid., 70.1 (*ANF* 5:377).

98. Ibid., 63.2 (*ANF* 5:364).

99. Ibid, 63.5 (*ANF* 5:365).

For Cyprian, the problem of lapses and heresy are to be resolved through excommunication (when the offenders are unrepentant) and not through the establishment of a parallel church. This is because, for him, the idea of a "parallel church" is theologically meaningless since "baptism is one and the Holy Spirit is one, and the Church founded by Christ the Lord upon Peter, by a source of principle of unity, is also one."[100] If Cyprian were alive during 312 CE, he most probably would have not approved of the Donatists' choice of establishing a parallel church as a way to purge the church of ungodly people. Cyprian's emphasis on the unity of the church, as Augustine pointed out in his criticism of the Donatists, would have prevented him from supporting the Donatists' schismatic ecclesiology.

AUGUSTINE'S POSITION

Augustine (354–430), the bishop of Hippo (in modern-day Algeria), was one of the loudest critics of the Donatists. Unlike the Donatists, Augustine believed that God made the sacraments efficacious irrespective of the moral standings of the priests that administered them. For Augustine, the sacraments are self-authenticating: their effectiveness depends on what God does through them and not on the moral standing of the one who administers the sacraments or the moral standings of their recipients. His theology of the sacraments is expressed in Latin as *ex opera operato* (literally "by the work worked"). As one who believed it was his duty to defend orthodoxy, Augustine devoted the large majority of his pastoral life to rigorous theological reflections and writings that were polemical in nature. He provided an astute *apologia* (defense) for what he believed to be the church's orthodoxy (right teaching) against *Donatism* (different strands of theological positions that are associated with the Donatists' beliefs and practices). Augustine's attack on the Donatists' ecclesiology was motivated by his determination to stop the spread of Donatism's influence on Christian communities in North Africa and beyond.[101] During Augustine's episcopal tenure, the Donatists constituted the majority of the members of the church in several North African locales. The term "Donatist" was used to describe the church of the Donatists, whereas the term "Catholic" (which was intensively debated) was used to describe other churches that rejected the Donatists' ecclesiology.[102]

Like Cyprian of Carthage, Augustine was determined to maintain the unity of the church and as such was intolerant of schism. Augustine

100. Ibid., 69.3 (*ANF* 5:376).

101. Harrison, *Rethinking Augustine's Early Theology*, 127–28.

102. Davidson, *Public Faith*, 172.

appealed to Cyprian's writings in his refutation of the Donatists' teaching.[103] For Augustine, schism (an offense committed by the Donatists) was a serious sin. In *On Baptism, against the Donatists*, Augustine wrote,

> Answer me this, ye ravening wolves, who, seeking to be clad in sheep's clothing, think that the letters of the blessed Cyprian are in your favor. Did the sacrilege of schismatics defile Cyprian, or did it not? If it did, the Church perished from that instant, and there remained no source from which ye might spring. If it did not, then by what offense on the part of others can the guiltless possibly be defiled, if the sacrilege of schism cannot defile them? Wherefore, then, have ye severed yourselves? Wherefore, while shunning the lighter offenses, which are inventions of your own, have ye committed the heaviest offense of all, the sacrilege of schism?[104]

Augustine cited Cyprian as an ally in his contention that the unity of the church should take precedence over clerical misconducts.[105]

Augustine employed several tactics in his attack on the Donatists, including public debates with Donatists' representatives, polemic writings, preaching, and also the use of imperial legislation.[106] He argued that the Donatists' ecclesiology made God powerless in the face of clerical immorality or lapses. God is sufficiently powerful and gracious to forgive repentant sinners. As Augustine saw it, Christians who failed to maintain a steadfast testimony during the persecution and who later repented would not be rejected by God. For Augustine, all sins require repentance and sinners are objects of God's forgiveness. Therefore, the sin of the *traditores* and the sin of theft, while different in form and stature, need repentance and are forgivable by God.[107] Augustine argued that the Donatists have no theological justification for fellowshipping with Christians who commit other forms of sin but deny fellowship to *traditores*. Also, Augustine scolded the Donatists for arrogating to themselves an authority that is God's prerogative—the authority of separating the wheat and tares (Matt 13). He believed there were false Christians within the church. He wrote: "So, too, as long as she is a stranger in the world, the city of God has in her communion, and bound to her by

103. Augustine, *On Baptism, against the Donatists* 1.1 (*NPNF*[1] 4:411); see also ibid., 3.1 (*NPNF*[1] 4:436).

104. Augustine, *On Baptism, against the Donatists* 2.11 (*NPNF*[1] 4:430).

105. Augustine, *On Baptism, against the Donatists* 2.15 (*NPNF*[1] 4:434).

106. Davidson, *Public Faith*, 175.

107. Augustine, *Letters of Petilian, the Donatist* 2.52–54 (*NPNF*[1] 4:443–545).

the sacrament, some who shall not eternally dwell in the lot of the saints."[108] Yet he was convinced it was God's prerogative to separate false Christians and true Christians at the consummation of all things when God will judge God's creation.[109]

VATICAN COUNCIL II

In the official Roman Catholic Church's ecclesiology, baptism is required for the remission of (original) sin and for initiating a person into the church.[110] In agreement with the Council of Trent (1545–63), the Vatican II Council (1962–65) defended the necessity of infant baptism for salvation. As an instrument of salvation made possible by the Triune God, baptism's effectiveness is not dependent on one's cognitive assent or personal faith. Yet the Council argued that the church is the "sole and necessary gateway to which is Christ."[111] One of the aims of the Vatican II Council was to show that a person's relationship with Christ should not be imagined as what happens outside the community of Christ's followers or the church. The mystery of a personal union with Christ is not an individual affair but a communal one. As the Vatican II Council wrote in *Lumen Gentium*, "For by communicating his Spirit, Christ mystically constitutes as his body those brothers of his who are called together from every nation." The Council went on to say, "In that body the life of Christ is communicated to those who believe and who, through the sacraments, are united in a hidden and real way to Christ in his passion and glorification. Through baptism we are formed in the likeness of Christ. . . . In this sacred rite fellowship in Christ's death and resurrection is symbolized and is brought about . . . [Rom 6:4–5]."[112]

There is a great lesson to learn from the Vatican II Council about the communal nature of the church. In some strands of Protestantism, individual salvation and personal relationship with Christ are placed above the communal life of the church. Working out the nature of the relationship between a *personal union* with Christ and *a community's (or the church's) union* with Christ will most likely be conditioned by people's context. Christians living in societies that emphasize community as the point of departure in discussions on the identity and worth of human beings will most likely appropriate fully the scriptural teaching about the church as a community or

108. Augustine, *City of God* 1.35 (*NPNF*¹ 2:21).

109. Ibid.

110. Duffy, "Baptism and Confirmation," 221.

111. Vatican Council II, *Lumen Gentium* 6, in Flannery, *Vatican Council II*, 353.

112. Ibid., 7, in Flannery, *Vatican Council II*, 355.

body of Christ's followers (see Eph 4). Although individual persons make up the church, it is not individuals' personal agenda and aspirations that ought to govern the church's mission to itself and to the world. On the contrary, the collective will and good of all the members of the church must occupy the pride of place.

In the official Roman Catholic Church's ecclesiology, baptism, like other sacraments, causes what it signifies. Karl Rahner and Herbert Vorgrimler describe baptism as what causes the incorporation of a person "into the Church" and also causes or bestows new life, which is the result of "rebirth into the life of Christ."[113] The Vatican II Council emphasized the importance of other sacraments such as Confirmation and the Eucharist for the spiritual welfare of members of the body of Christ, especially infants who have been baptized.[114]

> Incorporated into the Church by Baptism, the faithful are appointed by their baptismal character to Christian religious worship; reborn as sons of God, they must profess before men the faith they have received from God through the Church. By the sacrament of Confirmation they are more perfectly bound to the Church and are endowed with the special strength of the Holy Spirit. Hence they are, as true witnesses of Christ, more strictly obliged to spread the faith by word and deed. Taking part in the eucharistic sacrifice, the source and summit of the Christian life, they offer the divine victim to God and themselves along with it.... They, strengthened by the body of Christ in the eucharistic communion, manifest in a concrete way that unity of the People of God which this holy sacrament aptly signifies and admirably realizes.[115]

Eucharist

The Eucharist or Lord's Supper is a ritual instituted by Jesus Christ. The Gospel of Luke tells a story of a conversation Jesus had with his disciples during a celebration of the Jewish feast of Passover. Jesus told them it was the last time he would celebrate the feast before his death and "until it is fulfilled in the kingdom of God" (Luke 22:16 ESV). Jesus "took bread, gave thanks" and said to his disciples, "This is my body, which is given for you"

113. Rahner and Vorgrimler, *Dictionary of Theology*, 38.

114. Vatican Council II, *Pueros Baptizatos* 1–2, in Flannery, *Vatican Council II*, 254.

115. Vatican Council II, *Lumen Gentium* 11, in Flannery, *Vatican Council II*, 361–362..

(Luke 22:19 ESV). He also instructed them to celebrate the feast in his absence "in remembrance of him" (Luke 22:19). Does Jesus in this passage teach that the "bread" *becomes* his body and the "wine" *becomes* his blood during the eucharistic celebration? Or did he intend the bread and wine to serve merely as symbols for his body and blood? The Apostle Paul complicated the issue further when he told the Corinthian Christians many of them were "weak and ill, and some have died" because they participated in the Lord's Supper in an "unworthy manner" (1 Cor 11:17–34). How can Christians celebrate the Eucharist or the Lord's Supper in a *worthy manner*? The theological positions discussed below will highlight different answers to these questions.

MARTIN LUTHER'S POSITION

During the Protestant Reformation and Roman Catholic Counter-Reformation, theologians' discussions on the Eucharist centered on the nature and purpose of the elements (bread and wine) used in the celebration. Disparate and competing views of the sacraments undermined the alliance the Protestant communities desperately needed to engage in theological and ecclesiological battles against the Roman Catholic Church. Martin Luther (1483–1546) construed the elements used in the sacrament of the Lord's Supper as "the true body and blood of Christ [that] are orally eaten and drunk in the bread and wine."[116] For Luther, the nature and efficacy of the "sacrament of the altar" (or the Lord's Supper) do not change irrespective of the moral condition or faith of the person who administers it or of its recipient.[117] Luther, however, has an exception: the bread and wine used in the sacrament of the altar may remain mere bread and wine and not become the "true body and blood of Christ" when people misinterpret the Word of God and perform the sacraments outside the "instituted ordinance of God" as written in the Scriptures.[118] To Luther, the Lord's Supper signifies a union of human elements (bread and wine) and divine elements (body and blood of Jesus Christ). This union does not imply the mixture of two natures or the transformation of bread and wine into the real body and blood of Jesus Christ.

In what way exactly, according to Luther, is Christ's body present in the Eucharist and consumed by the recipients? This was a question that defined and divided the sacramental and liturgical theologies of German Protestant

116. Luther, *Confession Concerning Christ's Supper—Part III (1528)*, 57.

117. Ibid.

118. Ibid.

theologians such as Martin Luther and Martin Bucer (1491–1551). For non-theologians, the technicality that saturated the theologies of the sacraments produced during the Reformation period can be cumbersome. Of particular interest is the way in which Protestant theologians in the Reformation period understood the preposition "in." For Luther, when applied to the presence of Christ *in* the Lord's Supper, the preposition "in" should be understood in the sense of "above," "beyond," "beneath," and "everywhere."[119] Luther's aim is to show that Christ's presence in the Lord's Supper cannot be measured because Christ is present incorporeally in the elements (bread and wine) of the Lord's Supper.

Luther's sacramental theology is deeply christological. For example, he uses the christological concept of "the communication of properties" (*communicatio idiomatum* in Latin)—the idea that two natures (divine and human) co-existed in Jesus Christ, with each nature sharing the properties of the other—to buttress his view of the spiritual presence of Christ's body in the Lord's Supper. If we cannot measure the manner in which the two natures dwelled in Jesus Christ, we also cannot measure the manner in which Christ's body is present in the Lord's Supper. But since, as most Christians believe, God the Son entered into the womb of Mary and was nourished by her, it is also possible for God's Son to enter into the bread and wine used for the Lord's Supper.[120] Also, since Jesus Christ is fully divine and fully human, he can choose to be *present* either in corporeal or incorporeal forms.[121]

In his criticism of the Swiss Protestant theologian Ulrich Zwingli, Luther contended that since Christ's resurrected body dwells in heaven, we must understand his words "This is my body" as indicating his ubiquitous presence. He writes, "Christ's body is everywhere because the right hand of God is everywhere."[122] For Luther, Christ's "real presence" (*realis praesentia* in Latin) in the Lord's Supper should be understood "in an uncircumscribed manner."[123] Just as the risen Lord came through a closed door to meet his disciples without altering the physical appearance of the door so also is the risen Lord's body present in the Lord's Supper without altering the physical appearance of the bread and wine.[124] Christ's *definitive* or *incorporeal* mode of presence in the Lord's Supper cannot be measured. Therefore, for Luther, theologians who reject Christ's presence in the Lord's Supper on the

119. Luther, *Confession Concerning Christ's Supper—from Part I (1528)*, 399.

120. Luther, *Sacrament of the Body and Blood of Jesus Christ*, 317.

121. Luther, *Confession Concerning Christ's Supper—from Part I (1528)*, 387.

122. Ibid., 376.

123. Ibid., 385.

124. Ibid.

grounds that the bread used in the celebration remains bread to the visible human sight are in error. Such people like Zwingli, Luther reasoned, have failed to recognize that God is omnipotent and "can do more than we see" with our physical eyes.[125] He accused Zwingli of reducing Christ's presence in the Lord's Supper only to a circumscriptive or corporeal mode. Luther argued that we require the "eyes of faith" to be able to see beyond the circumscribed mode of presence.[126] Sometimes Luther's critics have used the term "consubstantiation" (i.e., coexistence of two substances, implying the inclusion of the real presence of Christ in the consecrated bread and wine) to describe his view.[127] Other critics contend that Luther's view was merely a modified version of Roman Catholics' doctrine of "transubstantiation" (i.e., the substance of the consecrated bread and wine are transformed by God's power into the real body and blood of Jesus Christ).

The excerpts below highlight Luther's view of the Lord's Supper and the manner in which we can speak of Christ's presence in the Lord's Supper.

> Just as little as you are able to say how it comes about that Christ is in so many thousands of hearts and dwells in them—Christ as he died and rose again—and yet no man knows how he gets in, so also here in the sacrament, it is incomprehensible how this comes about. But this I do know, that the word is there: "Take, eat, this is my body, given for you, this do in remembrance of me." When we say these words over the bread, then he is truly present, and yet it is a mere word and voice that one hears. Just as he enters the heart without breaking a hole in it and he is comprehended only through the Word and hearing, so also he enters into the bread without needing to make any hole in it.[128]
>
> My grounds, on which I rest in this matter, are as follows: The first is this article of our faith, that Jesus Christ is essential, natural, true, complete God and man in one person, undivided and inseparable. The second, that the right hand of God is everywhere. The third, that the Word of God is not false or deceitful. The fourth, that God has and knows various ways to be present at a certain place, not only the single one of which the fanatics prattle, which the philosophers call "local" [physical mode of presence].

125. Ibid., 378.

126. Ibid., 390. Luther labeled Zwingli "un-Christian" and judged him to be "seven times worse than when he was a papist" for denying that Christ is present in the elements used for the Lord's Supper. See Luther, *Confession Concerning Christ's Supper—from Part I (1528)*, 400.

127. Strong, *Systematic Theology*, 3:968–69.

128. Luther, *Sacrament of the Body and Blood*, 320.

> Christ can be and is in the bread, even though he can also show himself in circumscribed and visible form wherever he wills. For as the sealed stone and the closed door remained unaltered and unchanged, though his body at the same time was in the space entirely occupied by stone and wood, so he is also at the same time in the sacrament and where the bread and wine are, though the bread and wine in themselves remain unaltered and unchanged.
>
> Consider our physical eyes and our power of vision. When we open our eyes, in one moment our sighy is five or six miles away, and simultaneously present everywhere within the range of those six miles. Yet this is only a matter of sight, the power of the eye. If physical sight can do this, do you not think that God's power can also find a way by which all creatures can be present and permeable to Christ's body?[129]
>
> **Questions**: Why does Luther appeal to God's omnipotence in support of his view of Christ's mode of presence in the Lord's Supper? What theological arguments does Luther present to justify his view of the manner of Christ's presence in the Lord's Supper?

ULRICH ZWINGLI'S POSITION

The Swiss theologian Huldrych (or Ulrich) Zwingli (1484–1531) argued that the words "This is my body given for you" should be taken metaphorically and also should be read in the light of the words "flesh counts as nothing" (John 6:63). Zwingli was not suggesting that the physical body of Jesus had no salvific value or that there was no sense in which Jesus could be present in the Lord's Supper. Rather, for him, Jesus' body is beneficial "by being slain, not eaten" during the celebration of the Lord's Supper.[130] Jesus is present *symbolically* and the recipients of the Lord's Supper do not eat the body of Christ or drink his blood. The bread used in the Lord's Supper symbolized the body of Christ and the wine symbolized the blood of Christ. Zwingli contended, for example, that the word "eating" is a metaphor for "believing" in Jesus Christ.[131] He insisted that the Lord's Supper, like all the sacraments, was only a *sign* for what God accomplishes in the lives of those who partake in the sacrament.[132] The word "Eucharist" (*eucharistia* in

---

129. Luther, *Confession Concerning Christ's Supper—from Part I (1528)*, 383, 385–86.

130. Zwingli, *Commentary on True and False Religion*, 209.

131. Zwingli, *On the Lord's Supper*, 199.

132. Ibid., 188.

Greek) conveys the ideas of rejoicing, showing gratitude, and giving thanks. For Zwingli, the Lord instituted the Lord's Supper as a reminder to his followers to rejoice together in giving thanks to God as they commemorate and reflect on the salvific significance of his death.[133] Zwingli also reasoned that if Jesus Christ in his resurrected body was seated at the right hand of God, he could not be *in* or *under* the elements of the Lord's Supper. He opposed the idea of appealing to God's omnipotence to defend a view that is glaringly contradictory.

Against people who claim the elements of the Lord's Supper are mysteriously transformed into the body and blood of Christ when the priest blesses the elements and says the words "This is my body," Zwingli marshaled these arguments. First, Zwingli argued that a priest's words are not to be equated with Jesus' own words. Zwingli made this distinction because he held that God's Son had the power to change the substance of anything through his words just as God spoke things into existence according to Genesis. But since priests are merely reciting the words of Jesus, their pronouncement of Jesus' words does not have the same power as Jesus' words.[134] Second, Zwingli contended that a good biblical exegesis requires identifying the genre of a speech or text. For example, a figurative speech should not be taken literally. For him, Jesus spoke figuratively when he said "This is my body" just as he spoke figuratively when he said in John 15 "I am the vine."[135] To him, the word "is" in this context should not be taken substantively or literally, which will imply that Jesus is "literally and essentially present" in the elements of the Lord's Supper.[136] He argued that if the elements were literally transformed into the body and blood of Jesus Christ then the change should be perceptible. Zwingli also faulted Luther and Lutherans who held that the elements remained physically unchanged even though Christ was really present *in* and *under* the elements. For him, transubstantiation was more attainable than Luther's position. If the words of Jesus "This is my body" were to be taken literally, then transubstantiation made more sense.[137] Zwingli also read the passages that speak of the Lord's Supper *evangelistically*. For him, the passages point us to Jesus as the one who saves the world through his passion. The short text below captures some of the main themes in Zwingli's view of the Lord's Supper.

133. Zwingli, *Commentary on True and False Religion*, 200.

134. Zwingli, *On the Lord's Supper*, 189.

135. Ibid., 190.

136. Ibid.

137. Ibid., 191.

A sacrament is the sign of a holy thing. When I say: The sacrament of the Lord's body, I am simply referring to the bread which is the symbol of the body of Christ who was put to death for our sakes. The papists all know perfectly well that the word sacrament means a sign and nothing more, for this is the sense in which it has always been used by Christian doctors. Yet they have still allowed the common people to be deceived into thinking that it is something strange and unusual, something which they cannot understand and which for that reason they have come to equate with God himself, something which they regard as holy in that sense. But the very body of Christ is the body which is seated at the right hand of God, and the sacrament of his body is the bread, and the sacrament of his blood is the wine, of which we partake with thanksgiving. Now the sign and the thing signified cannot be one and the same. Therefore the sacrament of the body of Christ cannot be the body itself.

If [Jesus] is present literally and essentially in the flesh, then in the flesh he is torn apart by teeth and perceptibly masticated. We cannot evade the issue by saying: "With God all things are possible." [It] is not possible that the light which he created by the Word should not be a literal and perceptible light. On the contrary, when he spoke the Word, the light was there, a literal, perceptible, present and visible light, as it still is. In the same way, if we take the word "is" [in the expression "This *is* my body"] literally, it is not possible that the flesh should not be perceptible, for the light was not an imperceptible light.

And if we say that although the bread is flesh and the flesh is literally eaten, this takes place miraculously so that the flesh and blood are not perceived, is it not evident that we are lying and deceiving ourselves? For God never performed miracles or manifested them to the world without someone either seeing them or in some way perceiving them.[138]

Questions: How does Zwingli interpret the expression "This is my body given for you"? What are the theological conclusions he drew out from his interpretation? Where does his view differ from Luther's?

COUNCIL OF TRENT'S POSITION

For the theologians of the Roman Catholic church who met intermittently between December 13, 1545, and December 4, 1563, at Trent (Italy), the theological war on the sacraments among the Protestants is precisely a reason to avoid ecclesial schisms. Although they recognized that the church

138. Ibid., 188, 190, 195.

should undergo reform from within, they opposed the establishment of parallel or competing church denominations. The Council of Trent believed it was necessary to provide counter arguments against the theologies of some prominent Protestant leaders.

On the relationship between Jesus and the elements of the sacrament of the Eucharist, the Council of Trent taught that the consecrated bread and wine changed into the true body and blood of Jesus Christ. This position is labelled the doctrine of *Transubstantiation*: the conversion of human elements, when consecrated for the feast of the Eucharist, into the real body and blood of Jesus given for humanity's salvation.[139] The Council of Trent pronounced a curse on those who rejected the doctrine of Transubstantiation. It also stressed that the sacraments were objectively efficacious, siding with Augustine in his argument that the effectiveness of the sacraments was not contingent upon the moral standings of the recipient or the priest that administered them.

In the twentieth century, the Vatican II Council stressed the importance of the communal life of the church in its discussion on the Eucharist. When members of the church share "in the body of the Lord in the breaking of the eucharistic bread," they are "taken up into communion with him and with one another."[140] Jean-Marie Roger Tillard has cautioned against focusing on the celebration or ceremony of the Eucharist but ignoring what the sacrament really accomplishes. For Tillard, the Eucharist is *the* primary sacrament of the church because "the full incorporation in Christ and in the church is effected in Eucharistic communion."[141] The issue Tillard raises is the sacraments' ability to cause grace or whatever else they signify. For example, the Eucharist does not merely show that a union between Christ (the head of the church) and the church (the body of Christ) already exists. More importantly, the sacrament of the Eucharist causes this union between Christ and his church. The sacraments, as the Vatican II Council noted, are necessary for the spiritual health and well-being of the church. The Roman Catholic theologian Yves Congar describes the Eucharist as the sacrament that contains, gives purpose, and significance to all other sacraments. The Eucharist merits this status because in it the "redeeming Body and Blood of Christ are really present and so . . . substantially contains the common spiritual food of the whole Church."[142]

139. Council of Trent, Canons and Dogmatic Decrees of the Council of Trent, "Decree Concerning the Most Holy Sacrament of the Eucharist" 4, in Schaff, *Creeds of Christendom*, 130.

140. Vatican Council II, *Lumen Gentium* 7, in Flannery, *Vatican Council II*, 355.

141. Tillard, "New Roman Catholic Insights," 433.

142. Congar, *Mystery of the Church*, 70.

Some Protestant critics of the Tredentine teaching on the Eucharist argue that the belief that the Eucharistic elements (bread and wine), when blessed or consecrated, are turned into the real body and blood of Christ is foreign to Jesus' and Paul's teaching. A. H. Strong, for example, argues that since "Christ was with the disciples in visible form at the institution of the Supper, he could not have intended them to recognize the bread as being his literal body."[143] Some Roman Catholic theologians have also pointed out that the Council of Trent's focus on the change in the substance of the elements of the Eucharist encourages "adoration and devotion but not communion and active participation in the ritual memorial."[144]

The excerpts below underscore the main theological decisions of the Council of Trent on the sacrament of the Eucharist.

In the first place, the holy Synod teaches, and openly and simply professes, that, in the august sacrament of the holy Eucharist, after the consecration of the bread and wine, our Lord Jesus Christ, true God and man, is truly, really, and substantially contained under the species of those sensible things. For neither are these things mutually repugnant,—that our Savior himself always sitteth at the right hand of the Father in heaven, according to the natural mode of existing, and that, nevertheless, he be, in many other places, sacramentally present to us in his own substance, by a manner of existing, which, though we can scarcely express it in words, yet can we, by the understanding illuminated by faith, conceive, and we ought most firmly to believe, to be possible unto God....[145]

And because that Christ, our Redeemer, declared that which he offered under the species of bread to be truly his own body, therefore has it ever been a firm belief in the Church of God, and this holy Synod doth now declare it anew, that, by the consecration of the bread and of the wine, a conversion is made of the whole substance of the bread into the substance of the body of Christ our Lord, and of the whole substance of the wine into the substance of his blood; which conversion is, by the holy Catholic Church, suitably and properly called Transubstantiation.[146]

143. Strong, *Systematic Theology*, 3:965.

144. Power, "Eucharist," 263.

145. Council of Trent, Canons and Dogmatic Decrees of the Council of Trent, "Decree Concerning the Most Holy Sacrament of the Eucharist" 1, in Schaff, *Creeds of Christendom*, 126–27.

146. Ibid., 4, in Schaff, *Creeds of Christendom*, 130.

If anyone denieth, that in the sacrament of the most holy Eucharist, are contained truly, really, and substantially, the body and blood together with the soul and divinity of our Lord Jesus Christ, and consequently the whole Christ; but saith that he is only therein as a sign, or in figure, or virtue: let him be anathema.

If anyone saith, that, in the sacred and holy sacrament of the Eucharist, the substance of the bread and wine remains conjointly with the body and blood of our Lord Jesus Christ, and denieth that wonderful and singular conversion of the whole substance of the bread into the body, and of the whole substance of the wine into the blood—the species only of the bread and wine remaining—which conversion indeed the Catholic Church most aptly calls Transubstantiation: let him be anathema.[147]

Questions: How does the Council of Trent interpret these words of Jesus: "This is my body"? How does Luther's view differ from the Council of Trent's view?

JOHN ZIZIOULAS' POSITION

The Orthodox Church theologian (and the Metropolitan of Pergamon) John Zizioulas has argued that the church (*ekklesia* in Greek) is a "eucharistic assembly."[148] Therefore, when we speak about the "catholicity" or universality of the church, we must recognize the importance of local assemblies.[149] Zizioulas' primary concern is not Christ's mode of presence in the celebration of the sacrament of the Eucharist. Rather, he focuses on the relationship between the Eucharist and unity of the *church*. For Zizioulas, the Eucharist is the key to understanding Paul's usage of the term "church" in his epistles. He notes that Paul used the word "church" to describe Christians in a specific city (for example, the church in Corinth) and used words such as "saints" to refer to Christians in a larger geographical areas (for example, saints in Achaea). Zizioulas argues that the most appropriate explanation for Paul's linguistic choice is that when Paul used the word "church" he had in mind "the faithful united in their eucharistic assembly." Zizioulas concludes, "It was natural that for Paul and his readers the Church should be not in Achaea

---

147. Council of Trent, Canons and Dogmatic Decrees of the Council of Trent, "On the Most Holy Sacrament of the Eucharist," canons 1–2, in Schaff, *Creeds of Christendom*, 136–37.

148. Zizioulas, *Eucharist, Bishop, Church*, 46.

149. Zizioulas, *Being as Communion*, 143, 253–57.

or some other areas wider than the city, but in Corinth, i.e. in a specific city, because it was there that the assembly took place during which his epistles would be read."[150] When Paul addressed an assembly as "church" he expected that they would gather together to perform the Eucharist.[151] In Zizioulas' ecclesiology, it is the Eucharist that makes an assembly "the Church of God." He goes to a great length to buttress his claim by distinguishing the gathering of a "Christian family" or a Christian household (*oikos* in Greek) and the "church." The celebration of the Eucharist makes the gathering of a Christian family "church in the household."[152] The celebration of the Eucharist is what unites many people from different backgrounds and cultures. In other words, where there is *Eucharist* there is the *church*.

Zizioulas discusses Christ's presence in the celebration of the Eucharist in the context of his role as the minster *par excellence*—the one ruler, priest, bishop, and teacher of the church.[153] The authority of Christ over the church, however, is reflected through ministers of the church. He writes, "As the one Lord and ruler of the Church, Christ does not govern in parallel with an ecclesiastical administration on earth, but *through it* and *in it*."[154] To Zizioulas, the church is a "theocentric unity" because human ministers (such as bishops) have no authority in the church except as representatives of Christ, the only minister *par excellence*.[155] The unity of the church, which is made possible by the Eucharist, requires "order." This order is characterized by the "order of leaders" (the clergy) and the "order of respondents" (laity)—who are to respond to the leading of the ministers in the Eucharist with "Amen."[156] Zizioulas notes that the primary task of the ministers, particularly the bishops, from the earliest beginning, is "liturgical consisting in the offering of the Divine Eucharist."[157]

Some theologians have pointed out two potential weaknesses in Zizioulas' ecclesiology. First, by privileging the Eucharist in his discussion on the formation and existence of the church, Zizioulas overlooks or under-emphasizes other important components of ecclesiology such as monasticism and spirituality. Second, Zizioulas' identification of the church with Jesus

150. Zizioulas, *Eucharist, Bishop, Church*, 47.

151. Ibid., 48.

152. Ibid., 52.

153. Ibid., 60.

154. Ibid.

155. Ibid., 60–61.

156. Ibid., 65.

157. Ibid., 66.

Christ leads to a weak Pnuematology (discourse about the Holy Spirit).[158] The excerpt below is taken from Zizioulas' *Eucharist, Bishop, Church.*

The characterization of the Church as the "body of Christ," which has provoked much discussion among modern scholars, cannot be understood apart from the eucharistic experience of the Church, which was most likely the source of the use of this term.

The characterization of the Church as a "building" or "house" does not imply something inanimate, but an organism living and growing to "mature manhood," "to the measure of the stature of the fullness of Christ." This is not unrelated to the Divine Eucharist. In the spirit of the unity of the "many" in the One, we can also have a right understanding of the description of the Church as "bride of Christ," through which the faithful are understood as "members of Christ" in a manner analogous to the union of husband and wife "into one flesh."

But the point relevant to the very close connection of the Divine Eucharist with the primitive Church's consciousness of unity, is this: that all these images become meaningless outside the ontological unity of the "many" in Christ. Deeply rooted . . . in the historical foundations of Christianity, this unity found its fullest expression through the Divine Eucharist. The ancient Church was fully aware of this when she declared, through the first theologian of her unity [the Apostle Paul], "we who are many are one body, for we all partake of this one bread" [1 Cor 10:17].[159]

Questions: In Zizioulas' ecclesiology, what role does the Eucharist play in the formation of the church and in maintaining the church's unity? How does Zizioulas discuss Christ's presence in the Eucharist?

Concluding Remarks on the Sacraments

Three major implications of the sacraments are noteworthy. First, the sacraments have a *social implication*: they ought to remind Christians that the church is a social assembly comprised of people of diverse cultures, history, and worldviews. In many church denominations, people become members of a local Christian assembly through the sacrament of baptism. The Lord's

158. For more discussion on these issues, see Berger, "Does the Eucharist Make the Church? An Ecclesiological Comparison of Staniloae and Zizioulas."

159. Zizioulas, *Eucharist, Bishop, Church*, 57–58.

Supper should not only remind us of the place of Jesus in God's economy of salvation but also should facilitate deeper fellowship among members of the church. When the sacraments are repeated ceremoniously without serious reflections on their theological meanings they will lose their worth in making, forming, and nourishing the church. The sacraments bring to the fore the equality of all Christians in the church. The minster who leads the sacraments and the congregation must see themselves as equal parts of the body of Christ. All must be actively involved in sacramental worship. As the Pentecostal theologian Simon Chan has argued, sacramental or liturgical worship should not be "a drama in which the worship leader acts and the congregation [merely] watches and responds to the cues from the leader." On the contrary, "the congregation's response is a constitutive part of liturgical drama."[160]

Second, the sacraments have a *spiritual implication*: they ought to remind Christians that although the church exists in the world it does not exist for itself but for the glory of the Triune God. When Christians come together to celebrate the sacraments they must be reminded that they are the church called out by God to partake in divine fellowship. It is divine fellowship, and not worldly affairs (such as material possessions and denominational rancor), that ought to characterize the life of the church. The sacraments should not be reduced to a meaningless and routine commemoration. They must invoke in the members of the church their spiritual benefits. For example, while water baptism may not be what *brings* the Holy Spirit into the life of a person or *causes* a person to receive the Holy Spirit,[161] it should inspire the members of the church to seek a life of purity that is grounded in the person of Jesus Christ and empowered by the Holy Spirit.

Third, the sacraments have a *kerygmatic implication*: they ought to remind Christians, as the church, to proclaim God's gospel or good news to the world. Our theologies of the sacraments must be judged partly by how they facilitate Christians' reflection and appropriation of their meanings. The Lord's Supper, for example, must become *kerygmatic*: in celebrating the feast of the Eucharist the church must also proclaim the gospel, that is, how the death and resurrection of Jesus Christ are relevant for God's reconciliation of the world to God's self. In his reflection on Paul's usage of the word "body" to describe the church's relationship with Jesus Christ, Robert Jenson notes: "to say that the church is the body of the risen Christ is straightforwardly to affirm that the church is his availability in and for the world." As members of the church share in the eucharistic bread and cup,

160. Chan, *Pentecostal Ecclesiology*, 119.
161. Fee, *God's Empowering Presence*, 860–64.

they share in the one body of Christ.[162] As the mode of existence of the risen Christ, the church must continue to proclaim Christ as God's gospel to the world.

Church and Spiritual Gifts

Theological discussions on the spiritual gifts (*charismata* in Greek) and how the Holy Spirit operates both within and through people endowed with spiritual gifts have followed different paths. Some churches that are concerned with the question of how to identify and use spiritual gifts available to them focus on spiritual gifts' inventories.[163] Many Christian communities including Protestants and Roman Catholic Churches encourage their members to identify (most times through the use of questionnaires) and use their spiritual gifts. The problem with taking an inventory of spiritual gifts is that it is extremely difficult to distinguish a person's "special" abilities from "natural" abilities (acquired through training and practice). For example, do great teachers have a "special" gift of teaching or do they become great teachers by developing, through practice, their natural teaching abilities?[164] Several Protestant theologians have focused primarily on the set of gifts that continue to exist in the church today and those they believe have ceased to exist today. In his 1996 *Are Miraculous Gifts for Today?*, Wayne Grudem put together four competing views on the spiritual gifts, each view represented by its advocate.[165] I will describe and critique these views.

Cessationist View

The *Cessationist view* teaches that certain spiritual gifts are to be classified as "miraculous gifts" or "sign gifts." Such gifts will include the gifts of prophecy, tongues (*glossolalia* in Greek), and healing. These gifts ceased to exist with the early apostolic church. Some of the early advocates of the *Cessationist view* include B. B. Warfield and Jonathan Edwards. For both theologians, the claim that the gift of prophecy has continued to exist in the postapostolic era poses a threat to the authority of Scripture. This is because the existence of the gift of prophecy implies the possibility of additional revelatory

162. Jenson, "Bride of Christ," 2.

163. See Wagner, *Your Spiritual Gifts Can Help Your Church Grow*; Wagner and Keefauver, *Your Spiritual Gifts Can Help Your Church Grow: Group Study Guide*.

164. For more discussion, see Berding, *What Are Spiritual Gifts?*; Page, "The Assumptions behind Spiritual Gifts Inventories," 39–59.

165. Grudem, *Are Miraculous Gifts for Today? Four Views.*

message that would add to the closed biblical canon.[166] Some Cessationists may also appeal to John Calvin as an ally. Calvin described the offices or functions of prophets (those who received revelation from God), apostles, and evangelists as temporary offices. He wrote: "these three functions were not established in the church as permanent ones, but only for that time during which churches were to be erected where none existed before, or where they were to be carried over from Moses to Christ." Calvin quickly qualified his claim by noting that the risen Christ can still appoint people to any of these three offices or endow them with the gifts associated with the offices on special occasions. "Still, I do not deny that the Lord has sometimes at a later period raised up apostles, or at least evangelists in their place, as has happened in our own day [most likely referring to Martin Luther.]"[167]

Richard Gaffin, a Cessationist, argues that while God continues to heal miraculously today the gift of healing has ceased to exist. The gift of healing and other sign gifts marked the ministry of the apostles in the apostolic era. Such gifts were designed for the foundational period of the life of the church. The prophetic gifts were temporary in function because they served as the "canonical principle" that governed the church in its foundational period.[168] Since the foundation of the church has already been laid by the apostles and prophets who were authorized by Christ to be witnesses to his person and work, the special gifts they were endowed with are neither in existence nor necessary for the church today.[169] Gaffin contends that the miraculous gifts along with the event of the Pentecost must be located within the context of the "history of salvation" (*historia salutis* in Latin), the non-repeatable events that are "part of Christ's once-for-all accomplishment of his word of earning our salvation."[170] Like Warfield and Edwards, Gaffin believes that the continuation of prophetic gifts stands in tension with the Scripture, which is a closed canon.[171] For Gaffin, the Scripture is God's written revelation, which is a "completed historical organism, a finished redemptive-revelatory process."[172] However, Gaffin notes that John 3:8 is a warning to theologians that their theologies of the Holy Spirit "will be left with a certain remainder, a surplus unaccounted for, [and] an area of mystery."[173] But Gaffin proceeds

166. See Edwards, *Charity and Its Fruits*; Warfield, *Counterfeit Miracles*.
167. Calvin, *Institutes of the Christian Religion*, 4.3.4
168. Gaffin, "Cessationist View," 61.
169. Ibid., 42–43.
170. Ibid., 31.
171. Ibid., 44.
172. Ibid., 53.
173. Ibid., 25.

to contend that the Scripture must govern what we say about the Holy Spirit: the patterns of the Holy Spirit as revealed in the Scriptures, "and not what the Holy Spirit may choose to do beyond them, ought to be the focus and [also] shape the expectations of the church today."[174] In response to the criticism that the *Cessationist view* puts the Holy Spirit in a box, Gaffin argues that the Holy Spirit has chosen the "box," namely, the Scripture.

Critics of the *Cessationist view* have pointed out that that its limitation of the scope of the operation of the Holy Spirit in the church to the apostolic era is both theologically and exegetically unsustainable. For example, Robert Saucy, who largely agrees with Gaffin but holds a position he describes as "An Open but Cautious View," contends: "Scripture does not clearly teach the cessation of prophecy. While it links prophecy to the foundation period, it does not show that all prophecy is foundational . . . . We must be open to what God desires to do, but seek to evaluate all phenomena by biblical criteria."[175] Gordon Fee argues that the scope of the duration of the Holy Spirit's operation in the church cannot be limited to the apostolic period. For him, Paul did not anticipate that the Holy Spirit's operation and the manifestations of spiritual gifts will cease during his lifetime. Therefore, we can expect that the Holy Spirit's operation in the church "will continue as long as we await the final consummation."[176]

Open but Cautious View

The other three views discussed in *Are Miraculous Gifts for Today?* allow for the continuation of miraculous gifts, albeit with different degrees of openness. In defense of the *Open but Cautious view*, Saucy makes a distinction between "special manifestations of miraculous gifts," which were confined to the apostles and prophets and were not intended to be the permanent experience of the church, and the "miraculous gifts" distributed among other members of the church.[177] Saucy concedes that the Bible is unclear about the relationship of these types of miraculous gifts. The gifts of prophecy and healing belong to the "special" category. The presence of a biblical canon required a "decrease in the prophetic activity" since the biblical canon gradually became the rule for measuring acceptable doctrines. On the gift of healing, Saucy argues: that people in the early church brought their sick loved ones to the apostles was an indication the gift of healing was not given

174. Ibid.
175. Saucy, "Open but Cautious Response," 69.
176. Fee, *God's Empowering Presence*, 893.
177. Saucy, "Open but Cautious View," 121.

to Christians who were not apostles. But Saucy maintains that the ceasing of tongues (*glossolalia*), knowledge, and prophecy when the "perfection comes" that Paul spoke about in 1 Corinthians 13:8–10 does not "expressly teach the cessation of these gifts during the church age."[178] For Saucy, "perfection" in this context refers to the Second Coming of Christ. Therefore, the passage should not be used to support the view that claims certain gifts have ceased to exist in the church era and before the coming of Christ. Also he notes that even when perfection arrives, it is not the functioning of the gifts that will pass away but the "imperfect knowledge that is obtained through them."[179] Yet Saucy argues that since the Bible neither explicitly teaches the cessation of the miraculous gifts nor explicitly teaches their continuation, "we must be open at all times to what God desires to do."[180] Even if people no longer possess these gifts permanently, the Holy Spirit can act temporarily through people to accomplish miraculous work such as healing.

Sam Storms criticizes both Gaffin and Saucy for assuming that "apostleship" or being an "apostle" is a spiritual gift. He writes, "Spiritual gifts, such as those described in 1 Corinthians 12:7–10, are divinely energized deeds that are performed. But how does one do *apostle-ing*? I have no problem with how one might do prophecy or show mercy or give encouragement. But apostleship, it would seem, is not an inner working of the Holy Spirit through a human vessel, but an office to which one is called by Christ Jesus himself."[181] Storms' point is that the confinement of miraculous gifts to the apostolic age has no theological merit. Douglas Oss has also argued that Saucy's appeal to the infrequency of discussion about miraculous healing in the New Testament epistles as an indication the gift diminished is deeply problematic. For Oss, Saucy fails to acknowledge that healing was not a major pastoral problem requiring the attention of the New Testament writers, with the exception of James. Therefore, Saucy's argument from silence does not carry much weight.[182]

Third Wave View

Sam Storms defends the *Third Wave view*. The term "Third Wave" here refers to the renewal movement that began in North America in the 1980s. The movement is designated "Third" because it follows the rise of North

178. Ibid., 123.
179. Ibid., 124.
180. Ibid., 126.
181. Storms, "Third Wave Response," 157.
182. Oss, "Pentecostal/Charismatic Response," 171.

American Pentecostalism in 1901 (first movement) and the Charismatic renewal movements in the 1960s and 1970s (second movement). According to the *Third Wave view*, all of the spiritual gifts mentioned in the New Testament exist today. Christians, Storms argues, should ask for the Holy Spirit's work in their midst and also should expect the Holy Spirit to minister to them "*through* God's people by means of the full range of *charismata* listed in such passages as 1 Corinthians 12:7–10, 28–30."[183] Storms, who used to be a Cessationist, contends that upon a closer look at the Scriptures, one must conclude that the spiritual gifts do exist and that Christians are to use their gifts in their ministries.

Storms, like Saucy, is critical of Pentecostal/Charismatic theologians who hold the *doctrine of subsequence*.[184] This doctrine teaches that "Spirit baptism" is an event that is subsequent to the reception of the Holy Spirit at conversion. This is a traditional Pentecostal/Charismatic teaching. As Simon Chan contends, "Spirit-baptism with *glossolalia* as its initial evidence" defines Pentecostals' ecclesiology and Pnuematology.[185] Although Pentecostal and Charismatic Christians do not deny that, for the purposes of evangelism, the Holy Spirit can enable Christians to speak in "tongues" (in this context, referring to *xenolalia*—speaking in a recognized human language that is unknown to the speaker),[186] many hold that *glossolalia* is an initial evidence of Spirit baptism. Storms argues that what Pentecostals describe as baptism in the Spirit (or Spirit baptism) is better described as *a daily filling* in which the Holy Spirit empowers them to live righteously and to put their spiritual gifts to use (Luke 1:15–17, Acts 9:17). There is one Spirit baptism (which occurs at conversion) and multiple *fillings* of the Holy Spirit.[187]

Returning to the issue of the continuance of the "revelatory gifts" (such as prophecy, tongues, and interpretations of tongues), Storms argues that all spiritual gifts are operative today. Since the primary purpose of the spiritual gifts is to edify (build up) the church, Storms argues that they must remain in existence. As long as the church requires edification, these gifts will remain in operation in the church.[188] Speaking of the gift of prophecy, which is sometimes confused with the gift of teaching, Storms argues that *prophecy* is the "human report of divine revelation" while teaching is based on what is

---

183. Storms, "Third Wave View," 175.

184. Ibid., 176.

185. Chan, *Pentecostal Ecclesiology*, 93. For more discussion on the concept of Spirit baptism in Pentecostalism, see Ezigbo, *Introducing Christian Theologies*, 1:215–16.

186. Ferguson, "Separating Speaking in Tongues from Glossolalia," 40.

187. Storms, "Third Wave View," 180.

188. Ibid., 192–93.

already revealed and documented orally or textually. All spiritual gifts and their usages are subject to God's will and not humans' will. But if people still possess the gift of healing why does illness continue to kill people who have prayed for healing? Storms answers this question by noting that it is God's prerogative to know when and how the spiritual gifts are used. .[189]

Some critics of the *Third Wave view* espoused by Storms reject his description of spirit-baptism as what God does in believers without them praying for it and also as what is not followed by a dramatic experience such as *glossolalia*.[190] Some criticize Storms for defining prophecy as a "report" of God's revelation, which the recipient may misunderstand or communicate erroneously to God's people. Saucy, for example, argues that Storm's definition lacks biblical support. To Saucy, prophecy is not a report of God's revelation but God's actual word (here understood in a propositional sense). He writes, "Storm's definition of prophecy fails to see that Spirit's work of inspiration in prophecy goes all the way to the actual prophecy, that is, the words spoken or written."[191]

The Pentecostal/Charismatic View

Pentecostal and Charismatic churches continue to play vital roles in the expansion of Christianity in the world, especially in places where Christianity is nonexistent or in decline.[192] As Allan Anderson argues, many Pentecostals' integration of their "experience of the Spirit with their mission . . . resulted in thousands of transnational missionaries going out to plant churches and cause the fastest expansion of a new Christian movement in the history of Christianity."[193] In Africa and some parts of Asia, for example, the Pentecostal theology of the Holy Spirit's empowerment, which is exercised through the use of *charismata*, has been a major reason for people's conversion to Christianity. In many Pentecostal and Charismatic churches, spiritual gifts are believed to be given for the purpose of waging spiritual warfare. This belief propels Pentecostal and Charismatic churches' conception of a theology of "power encounter": the act of waging a spiritual war against the kingdom of darkness. Most Pentecostal and Charismatic churches attribute believers' empowerment for witness and service to a post-conversion reception of the

189. Ibid., 212–15.

190. Oss, "Pentecostal/Charismatic Response," 235–36.

191. Saucy, "Open but Cautious Response," 230.

192. See Anderson, *To the Ends of the Earth*. See also Kalu, *African Pentecostalism: An Introduction*; Kay, "Where the Wind Blows," 128–48.

193. Anderson, *To the Ends of the Earth*, 165.

Holy Spirit. As Allan Anderson observes, Pentecostals use biblical passages such as Acts 1:8 and Mark 16:15–18 as evidence to show that "the primary purpose of the outpouring of the Spirit was to send countless witnesses for Christ out to the farthest reaches of the globe."[194]

According to Robert Oss, the classical *Pentecostal view* of Spirit baptism teaches that it is an "empowering work of the Holy Spirit" that is subsequent to conversion experience. While the Holy Spirit indwells all believers at conversion, believers are to pray to "receive" the Holy Spirit in a post-conversion experience. The reception of the Holy Spirit in a post-conversion experience empowers believers "in 'charismatic' ways for witness and service."[195] For Oss, the expression "second experience" is misleading because Spirit baptism is in actuality the "first experience of the Spirit's empowering work, which inaugurates a life characterized by continued anointings with the Spirit."[196] Oss argues that Luke's pneumatology, as expressed in the Gospel of Luke and in Acts, shows that the Holy Spirit's empowerment of believers for service is different and subsequent to conversion or salvation.[197] Believers who receive the post-conversion Spirit baptism will know they have had such experience because of its *initial physical evidence,* namely, speaking in tongues (*glossolalia*).[198]

The book of Acts, for Oss, presents *glossolalia* as the initial evidence of the authenticity of Spirit baptism. Regarding the reason for concluding that a post-conversion Spirit baptism is intended to be the experience of all Christians in the postapostolic era, Oss argues that the nature of the "narratives" in Luke-Acts implies that such was the intention of Luke. Why does a narrator "narrate" (or retell) as story? For Oss, it is to describe the origin of the story and how it shapes or ought to shape the community of its immediate audience. Oss notes that while classical Pentecostalism sees *glossolalia* as the initial physical evidence of Spirit baptism, some Charismatic churches reject this characterization and conversely see *glossolalia* as a spiritual gift that is not necessarily associated with Spirit baptism.[199]

Richard Gaffin criticizes the *Pentecostal/Charismatic view* (along with the *Third Wave view*) for assuming that since Jesus and the apostles exercised miraculous gifts, it followed that such gifts must be present in the postapostolic era of the church. For Gaffin, Oss fails to take seriously

---

194. Ibid., 164–165.

195. Oss, "Pentecostal/Charismatic View," 242.

196. Ibid., 243.

197. Ibid., 259. See also Chan, *Pentecostal Theology,* 85–96.

198. Oss, "Pentecostal/Charismatic View," 260.

199. Ibid., 263.

the discontinuity between "biblical history" (chronicles of the once-for-all salvific events) and "church history" (appropriation of the biblical history by Christians in all eras). As a result the *Pentecostal/Charismatic view* (espoused by Oss) and the *Third Wave view* (espoused by Storms) have failed to see there are temporary miraculous gifts confined to the Old Testament period, in the ministry of Jesus, and in the apostolic era, which belong to the salvific "biblical history."[200] Other critics of the *Pentecostal/Charismatic view* and the *Third Wave view* on the practice of *glossolalia* as the Holy Spirit–endued activity are wary of how to distinguish *glossolalia* in Christianity from the practices of *glossolalia* in non-Christian religions. Is the Holy Spirit operative in those religions? Some critics also see *glossolalia* as *aphasia* (a language disorder caused by damage to the hemisphere of the brain that deals with the production of human language.) To some, *glossolalia* is a form of pathology or manifestations of schizophrenia. Others dismiss *glossolalia* as meaningless gibberish that people can learn through practice.[201]

Concluding Remarks on the Spiritual Gifts

There is no sufficient theological or exegetical evidence to conclude that certain spiritual gifts are confined to the apostolic era and others are operational in the postapostolic era. The argument of the threat to the finality of the closed biblical canon is not entirely relevant. The nonexistence of the gift of prophecy, for example, is not a guarantee that Christians will always agree on the books that are to be included in the canon or how the books included in the canon can be interpreted. Also, a prophetic message does not always need to be for the benefit of the whole church. Prophecy may be for an individual's benefit. For instance, an individual may receive a prophetic message (from someone endowed with the gift of prophecy) that God is calling him or her to become a medical missionary in a foreign land. While the whole church should be encouraged to pray for discernment, it does not mean that the prophetic message is for the entire church. Focusing on the classes of spiritual gifts that are in existence today and those that have ceased to exist today does not really move the conversation on spiritual gifts forward. A helpful way to conclude the discussion on "Church and Spiritual Gifts" is to answer the question: What are the *purposes* of the spiritual gifts for the church? I will highlight only two purposes here: *edification of the church* and *empowerment of the church for evangelism.*

200. Gaffin, "Cessationist Response," 285–88.

201. For more on the criticisms of glossolalia, see Ferguson, "Separating Speaking in Tongues from Glossolalia," 39–49.

The Holy Spirit gives spiritual gifts (Rom 12:4–8; 1 Cor 12:8–10, 28–30; Eph 4:11) to the church for the purpose of building it up and moving it gradually to perfection as intended by the Triune God. In Paul's words, these gifts are designed "to prepare God's people for works of service, so that that the body of Christ may be built up, until we all reach unity in faith and in the knowledge of the Son of God and become mature, attaining to the whole measure of the fullness of Christ" (Eph 4:13 NIV). I use the word "edification" here broadly to describe the holistic nurturing of the church to develop spiritually, intellectually, socially, and materially. The gifts of teaching (Eph 4:11) and discernment (Acts 17:11), for example, are designed to help Christians make sound theological judgments regarding what Christians ought to believe and how they ought to act. Miroslav Volf has noted the following as the characteristics of *charismata*: universal distribution to the church (which implies common responsibility and mutual subordination), interdependence (since no single Christian has all *charismata*), and the Holy Spirit's prerogative (the Spirit is the one that allots the gifts).[202] Edification of the church through the use of *charismata* should lead to a reimagination of the church's identity in the light of the changing human cultures. Christian communities must make the necessary adjustments to remain effective in their ministries to the unique needs of individual members and the collective needs of the church.

Evangelism—the proclamation and embodiment of Jesus as God's good news (gospel)—is a requirement for Christ's followers. Jesus was always willing to send his disciples out to proclaim and embody the good news (Matt 28:16–20; Luke 10:1–12; John 17:20–21). Evangelism, however, is one of the most difficult responsibilities of Christ's followers. Jesus was well aware of this and forewarned his disciples. To highlight some of the difficulties: Jesus sends his followers out "as lambs in the midst of wolves" (Luke 10:3); they will be hated by the world because they are not of the world (John 15:18–19; 17:14); and they are to bear the cross, which involves putting Christ ahead of their own interests and the interests of their families (Luke 14:25–27). Reflecting on these difficulties associated with evangelism, one may begin to fully appreciate the significance of Jesus' promise to his disciples as noted by Matthew: "Go therefore and make disciples. . . . And behold, I am with you always, to the end of the age" (Matt 28:19–20 ESV). Although it is not clear from Matthew's text, it is likely that Jesus envisioned the necessity of his presence among his disciples (as they undertake the work of evangelism in a treacherous world) to serve a similar purpose like God's presence in the life of the Psalmist. Like

202. See Volf, *After Our Likeness*, 228–33.

the Psalmist, perhaps Jesus wanted his disciples to know that he would be with them "even though [they] walk through the valley of the shadow of death." They are to "fear no evil" for he will be with them. They also should expect that Christ will comfort them, which involves both discipline and restoration (Ps 23:4) They are not to be ruled by unbelief but rather are to be emboldened by Christ's presence, with the expectation to do great things in the name of Christ (Mark 16:14–20).

How exactly are we to imagine Christ's presence among his followers, and how does he equip them to do the work of evangelism? Jesus Christ acts in and through the gifts of the Spirit given to the people of God, the church.[203] Jesus himself was empowered by the Holy Spirit to do his ministry (Acts 10:38). Christians are equipped for evangelistic work through the teaching of the Scriptures and the empowerment of the Holy Spirit. The Scriptures provide information about the content of the gospel. The Scriptures are necessary for teaching people "to obey" what Christ commands (Matt 28:20). But Christians must also seek the empowerment of the Holy Spirit for the boldness and courage to proclaim the gospel in this hostile world (Acts 1:8). Great lessons can be learned from some Pentecostal and Charismatic churches on how Christians are to rely on the empowerment of the Holy Spirit through *charismata* to do evangelism. While other non-Pentecostal and Charismatic Christians do not deny that the Holy Spirit empowers Christians to wage war against principalities and powers, they rarely emphasize it. The de-emphasis of spiritual warfare is also more common in the Western world (with the exception of Pentecostal churches and some non-Western Christian communities in Diaspora). The Lutheran theologian Carl Braaten invites Western Christians "to reconsider whether [their] enlightened sophistication has not rendered [them] oblivious to the demonic."[204] Johann Christoph Blumhart, as Christian Collins Winn notes, perceived Christians' role in God's kingdom as transforming "the spiritual and physical conditions of humanity."[205] Evangelism should be a reminder to Christians to participate in God's transformation of God's world, healing it of its social-economic and spiritual diseases.

---

203. Ibid., 228.
204. Braaten, *That All May Believe*, 116–17.
205. Collins Winn, *"Jesus is Victor!"*, 95.

Gender and Ecclesiastical Leadership

The nature of male-female relationships has caused major theological problems and schisms in Christianity. Are women who are church leaders, who

FOCUS QUESTION:
What ought to be the primary criterion or criteria of ecclesiastical leadership?

serve in positions of authority over men, in violation of God's law regarding male-female relationships? Are the sacraments administered by ordained women valid? These are some questions that usually awaken the curiosity of my theology students. The students also become more curious when I broaden "women's authority" beyond the context of ecclesiastical leadership to include women who teach pastors or people training to become pastors in seminaries, schools of Divinity, and theological colleges.

Some contemporary Christian theologians accuse the early church of failing to deal adequately with the problems associated with the Roman concept of *paterfamilias* ("head of household"), such as patriarchy, misogyny, and child abuse. For these critics, *paterfamilias* assigned to men (or husbands) the status of "owners of the house" and reduced women (or wives) and children to subsidiary helpers whose chief goal was to serve the needs of men (or fathers and husbands). In ancient Roman society, the head of the household "held complete authority over the entire *familia* [household] and was, legally speaking, the sole possessor of its property."[206] Also, the head of the family possessed *patria potestas* (legal "paternal power"), "which gave him the right of life and death over his family."[207] The fathers had the responsibility to preserve the honor of the family. They had absolute authority over their family within the limits granted by the state law. In the judgment of many contemporary critics of the influence of *paterfamilias* on Christianity, early Christians uncritically adopted this Roman cultural value. Consequently, women were not permitted to "teach or exercise authority over a man" but were enjoined "to remain quiet" (1 Tim 2:11). Also, from an early period, women were taught to believe that "a woman is the glory of man" (1 Cor 11:7), that a woman is "made for man" and not vice versa (1 Cor 11:8–10), and that wives are to submit to their husbands in everything because "the husband is the head of the wife even as Christ is the head of the church" (Eph 5:23). Other theologians see these roles as culturally conditioned and therefore not God's intended purpose for male-female relationships in a Christian community.

---

206. Backman, *Cultures of the West*, 177.
207. Ibid.

Some Christian theologians believe that the roles assigned to males are divinely given and therefore irrevocable. Martin Luther held the view that men can be trained to be "bishops, pastors, and other servants of the church," whereas women can be trained to be "fine, respectable, learned" people who are "capable of keeping house and rearing children in a Christian way."[208] In Roman Catholicism, women are barred from the priesthood. As Phyllis Zagano has noted, some Roman Catholic theologians who might have been open to the ordination of women to the diaconate fear that such a move could lead to the quest for the ordination of women into priesthood.[209]

In what follows, I will discuss two major theological positions on the criteria of ecclesiastical leadership. One of the positions contends that women are not to have any authority over men in the church. The other positon argues that spiritual gifts and vocational calling, and not biological sexes or gender differences, should be the criteria for deciding on who is qualified to hold an ecclesiastical position. Note that there are different views within each of the broad positions. The views discussed below will highlight the complexity of appropriating concepts such as "hierarchical relations" and "submission" in the context of church leadership.

Sexes as a Defining Criterion of Ecclesiastical Leadership

Description: The views that belong to this category argue that in the divine order of creation men have authority over women (1 Tim 2:11–12), which they must exercise with prudence and with love. Women are to submit to their husbands and must learn from men in silence in the church. Such views uphold male leadership and female submission. Women's position in the hierarchical relations of the family and the church are divinely ordained. To violate these hierarchical relations is to disobey God's law. Some views emphasize female complementarity to male headship. They also emphasize the ontological equality of males and females as God's creatures. Some of these views have been labeled "complementarianism" or "hierarchical complementarianism."

Theological Rationale: I will describe three major theological rationales that are put forward by some theologians in support of the views that see biological sexes as an essential criterion of ecclesiastical leadership. First, *male headship and female submission are the pre-fall divine order*. Against some critics who interpret the submission of women to men's authority as the consequence of the fall (Gen 3), some theologians who see biological

208. Luther, *Confession Concerning Christ's Supper—Part III (1528)*, 54.
209. Zagano, "Catholic Women's Ordination," 126.

sexes as a defining criterion of ecclesiastical leadership contend that the submission of women is part of God's pre-fall and originally intended creation order.[210] They accuse those who approve of women in ecclesiastical leadership positions of departing from the teaching of the Bible and also of succumbing to the pressure coming from secular feminist discourse.

If male headship and teaching authority are a pre-fall divinely ordained will of God, then the question about whether Paul could have commanded women to learn in quietness if he lived in a century where women were theologically educated would be irrelevant to the discussion about women's pastoral role in the church. John Piper has argued that the difference in biological sexes are not "mere physiological prerequisites for sexual union." Rather, they are God-designed differences that define personhood.[211] For Piper, God has assigned different responsibilities and roles to men and women. He writes, "Our understanding is that the Bible reveals the nature of masculinity and femininity by describing diverse responsibilities for man and woman while rooting these differing responsibilities in creation, not in convention."[212] This is God's pre-fall plan for humanity. Men are divinely called to show *loving* and *strong* leadership in relation to women, and in *joyful* response, women are to show support for men's leadership.[213] Headship of men (1 Cor 11:3), which is interpreted as implying *having authority over* women, should be understood functionally and not ontologically. Just as Jesus is *functionally* subordinate to the Father, so also are women *functionally* subordinate to men.

Second, *Jesus did not appoint female apostles.* In the Roman Catholic Church, two major arguments are presented against the ordination of women. The first argument is that since Jesus was male, only male priests can act *in his place* as sacramental and teaching leaders in the church (the *Iconic argument*). Some theologians in the Orthodox Church make similar arguments against women's ordination to priesthood. For these theologians, as Nonna Verna Harrison notes, "priesthood is specifically christological and therefore masculine."[214] Put differently, priesthood should be reserved for males. The second argument is that Jesus exemplified the necessity of male ecclesiastical leadership by choosing only male disciples. By choosing only males, Jesus appears to endorse different roles for men and women

210. Hurley, *Man and Woman in Biblical Perspective*, 215–16; see also Clowney, *Church*, 218–21.

211. Piper, "Vision of Biblical Complementarity," 32.

212. Ibid., 35.

213. Ibid., 52.

214. Harrison, "Orthodox Arguments against the Ordination of Women," 169.

in the church.[215] Some theologians also argue there is no evidence that the apostles chose women apostles (the *apostolicity argument*).[216] They argue that the absence of women priests in the earliest Christian communities should serve as a reminder for present-day churches to be cautious about rushing to ordain women into priesthood.[217]

Three, *Scripture prohibits women from being authoritative teachers in the church*. For some theologians and biblical exegetes, Paul is unequivocal is his prohibition of women from teaching men God's Word in the church (1 Cor 11:1–16; 1 Tim 2:12).[218] James Hurley in his discussions on 1 Timothy 2 argues that Paul's instructions on how Christians are to conduct themselves when they gather for worship is cross-generational. For him, Paul would have expected all Christians in all cultures and generations to abide by the instructions.[219] Hurley argues that Paul commands women to learn from men and to do so in quiet receptivity and submission.[220] For him, Paul's use of the word "quietness" (*hēsychia* in Greek) in 1 Tim 2:11–12 indicates that Paul prohibits women from being "authoritative teachers in the church."[221] On Paul's reasons for commanding women to learn in quietness and submission and not to have authority over men in the context of the teaching office of the church, Hurley states that Paul references the order of creation and women's susceptibility to deception.[222] Eve was an "innocent but deceived person," while Adam was" a deliberate rebel."[223] Hurley concludes: "The man, upon whom lay responsibility for leadership in the home and in religious matters, was prepared by God to discern the serpent's lies [See Gen 3]. The woman was not appointed religious leader and was not prepared to discern them. She was taken in. Christian worship involves re-establishing the creational pattern with men faithfully teaching God's truth and women receptively listening."[224] Some theologians have argued that Paul's words in Gal 3:28 should be understood in a soteriological context: all Christians enjoy equal salvific status before God. This soteriological equality does not

215. See Borland, "Women in the Life and Teaching of Jesus," 120.

216. Sacred Congregation for the Doctrine of the Faith, "Declaration *Inter Insigniores*."

217. Harrison, "Orthodox Arguments against the Ordination of Women," 167.

218. See Schreiner, "Women in Ministry," 265–66.

219. Hurley, *Man and Woman in Biblical Perspective*, 196–97, 202–4.

220. Ibid., 200.

221. Ibid., 201.

222. Ibid., 202.

223. Ibid., 215.

224. Ibid., 216.

overturn the different responsibilities of men and women in the context of the teaching office of the church.[225]

Criticism: One of the criticisms of the views that teach that women are not to have teaching and/or leadership authority over men is how to define the scope of "authoritative teaching." For example, can male pastors and theologians learn from the works of female scholars? Other theologians have noted that there is a difference between the eternal divine Son's functional subordination (more appropriately, submission) to God the Father and women's functional subordination to men as imaged in hierarchical complementarianism. For example, Grenz and Kjesbo note that the difference lies in the nature of the submission. In the case of God the Son (who became Jesus of Nazareth), it was a *personal voluntarily* decision, which he made for the purpose of accomplishing the Triune God's salvific work. In contrast, the subordination of women is a subordination of a whole group (women and wives) without taking into considerations their "abilities, giftedness or mission."[226] On Jesus' selection of only males disciples, some argue that it was a culturally conditioned practical decision: choosing females disciples could have hindered the expansion of his message in a patriarchal society.

Charismata as the Defining Criteria of Ecclesiastical Leadership

Description: The views (sometimes called "egalitarianism" or "Evangelical feminism") described below argue that *charismata*—the spiritual gifts, which the Holy Spirit gives to Christians indiscriminately and universally (1 Cor 2:11–15)—ought to determine the areas of service of both men and women in the church. Also, they argue that mutual submission should govern male-female relationships (Eph 5:21).

Theological Rationale: Three major theological rationales are used to buttress the claim that *charismata* (and vocational calling) should be the primary criteria for ecclesiastical leadership. First, *male domination is the consequence of the fall*. For some theologians, male dominance and female subordination are contrary to God's original intention for men and women. They argue that Genesis 1 and 2 indicate that God gave men and women the same responsibility: they are to rule the earth and cultivate the ground together (Gen 1:28–31). The fall (Gen 3) had a negative effect on male-female relationships. After the fall, Adam and Eve (along with their posterity) lived in the bondage of sin. The desire to control and dominate others is a major

225. Johnson, "Role Distinctions in the Church," 163–64.
226. Grenz and Kjesbo, *Women in the Church*, 114–15.

manifestation of the fall. The language of men's rule over women is a post-fall judgment (Gen 3:16). As Carroll Osburn argues, "Gen 1–2 . . . teach that originally man and woman shared an equality in a pristine world designed by God. The Fall in Gen 3 shattered this equality and began a long history of gender conflict based upon male hierarchy. Patriarchy is an unfortunate result of the Fall, not something designed by God."[227]

Second, *the Bible is equivocal on male-female responsibilities in the context of ecclesiastical leadership.* For example, as in Old Testament times, the New Testament women and men *prophesied*, which was the most common way of "declaring God's word" to God's people.[228] Some theologians cite Paul as an ally in arguing that the new status of the church, which is achieved by Christ, dissolves male domination and headship over women. They recognize that Paul's view on male-female relationships is ambivalent.[229] Some like Paul Jewett contend that Paul did not unpack the full ecclesiastical ramifications of the unity and equality of all believers in Christ. Jewett sees Gal 3:28 as the Magna Carta of humanity. He argues that for Paul, Christ has destroyed the social issues that threaten human fellowship. Paul's language of female subordination should be explained as his lingering, unresolved Jewish culture and rabbinic training.[230] Jewett argues that Christ has not abolished biological sexes or human sexuality but rather "the immemorial antagonism between the sexes."[231] Paul's favorable attitude of women and their service to the church (Rom 16:1–16) is indicative of his movement toward the social implication of the salvation that Jesus Christ achieved for humanity.[232] Stanley Grenz and Denise Kjesbo also share a similar reading of Paul. They argue that Paul's actions and writings overall point to the dissolution of the social-economic issues that bring divisions in the church, highlight the reconciliation of males and females as equal members of the church, and indicate that believers' new status in Christ caries them "beyond creation, not by destroying it but by lifting creation to God's redemptive intent."[233] Some theologians have also pointed out that the concept of the priesthood of all believers reclaims the original pre-fall

227. Osburn, *Women in the Church*, 124.

228. Keener, "Women in Ministry," 207.

229. See Scanzoni and Hardesty, *All We're Meant to Be: A Biblical Approach to Women's Liberation*.

230. Jewett, *Man as Male and Female*, 112–13. Jewett's claim is misleading. For example, one may assume that Judaism is irredeemably patriarchal. Also, his claim suggests that Christianity should replace Judaism.

231. Ibid., 143.

232. Ibid., 145.

233. Grenz and Kjesbo, *Women in the Church*, 105.

intention of male-female relationship that is grounded in mutual responsibility and mutual submission. In this context, God's redemptive work is
emphasized without minimizing God's creation. Richard Longenecker, for
instance, contends that Christians are to "stress the redemptive notes of
freedom, equality and mutuality that are sounded in the New Testament."[234]

Third, *Christianity should be rescued from the shackles of patriarchy.*
Carroll Osburn defines patriarchy as a "strict hierarchy of male leadership
and women submission."[235] Rosemary Radford Ruether sees patriarchy as
largely responsible for the exclusion and subordination of women in the
church. For Ruether, the church must reclaim an alternative understanding
of male-female relationships, which was present, although it did not rise to
prominence, in early Christianity. In this alternative understanding, women
are viewed as "equal with men in the divine mandate of creation, restored to
this equality in Christ; the gifts of the Spirit poured out on men and women
alike; the church as the messianic society, not over against creation but over
against the systems of domination."[236] The *church*, for Ruether, is "where the
good news of liberation from sexism is preached" and "where the Spirit is
present to empower us to renounce patriarchy." The church is also a community of God's people that is governed by a life of mutuality, interdependence, and the vision to oppose dehumanization.[237]

Criticism: Some critics of the views that give spiritual gifts and vocational calling the pride of place argue that the advocates of such views are
diminishing the authority of the Bible. Some such advocates have been accused of disagreeing with Paul's reading of Genesis 1 and 2 as teaching male
leadership and women submission. Wayne Grudem, for instance, contends:
"if the Bible is the Word of God, then these interpretations [Gen 1–2] are
not just Paul's; they are also God's interpretations of his own Word. There
might be times when I cannot understand an interpretation of the Old Testament by a New Testament author, but that does not give me the right to
disagree with his interpretations."[238] Some critics also argue that egalitarians
fail to acknowledge that the subjugation of women is not an unavoidable
consequence of male headship. They argue that the subjugation of women
is only the result of an ungodly appropriation of male headship. When male
leaders exercise their authority over women in a godly manner they will
not subjugate or dehumanize women. Other critics argue that *prophesying*

234. Longenecker, "Authority, Hierarchy, and Leadership," 84.

235. Osburn, *Women in the Church*, 32.

236. Ruether, *Sexism and God-Talk*, 195.

237. Ibid., 213.

238. Grudem, *Evangelical Feminism*, 47.

should not be equated with the "regular teaching and preaching of God's word," which will require women having authority over men.[239] Therefore, early Christian women who prophesied should not be used to justify the ordination of women into priesthood.

Concluding Remarks on Gender and Ecclesiastical Leadership

The Apostle Paul occupies center stage in theologians' discussions about male-female relationships in the context of ecclesiastical leadership. Theologians who argue that women are not to be in a position where they will have authority over men appeal to Paul as an ally. Also, those who argue that spiritual gifts and vocational calling, rather than biological sexes, should be the criteria for ecclesiastical leadership cite Paul in support of their views. In 1 Cor 14:34–35, Paul says, "The women are to keep silent in the churches; for they are not permitted to speak, but are to subject themselves, just as the Law also says. If they desire to learn anything, let them ask their own husbands at home; it is improper for a woman to speak in church" (NASB). In his epistle to Christians in Galatia, Paul argues that Christ has redeemed those who were under the Law (Gal 4:4–6), therefore, they were no longer governed by the Law (Gal 3:23–25). The way of life of the church, as an assembly of those who have been redeemed, should no longer be governed by social, racial, and gender walls of separation, for they have been "baptized into one Christ" (Gal 3:27). Therefore, those who are redeemed must recognize that in Christ "there is neither Jew nor Greek, there is neither slave nor free man, there is neither male nor female; for you are all one in Christ Jesus" (Gal 2:28 NASB).

One way of interpreting Paul is to dismiss his view on male-female relationships as wishy-washy. This reading of Paul, however, is too simplistic. It fails to take into account Paul's intellectual development and also his contextualized messages that were attentive to both the general cultures of his recipients and their level of spiritual maturity. The Church in Corinth was spiritually immature and Paul was well aware of it. "And I, brethren, could not speak to you as to spiritual men, but as to men of flesh, as to infants in Christ. I gave you milk to drink, not solid food; for you were not yet able to receive it. Indeed, even now you are not yet able, for you are still fleshly" (1 Cor 3:1–3 NASB). To the same church in Corinth, speaking about Christian liberty, Paul says, "If food causes my brother to stumble, I will never eat meat again, so that I will not cause my brother to stumble" (1 Cor 8:13 NASB). These texts show that Paul was meticulously attentive

239. Schreiner, "Women in Ministry," 127.

to his audience's specific *context*: their spiritual maturity, social location, cultures, political milieu, and so on.

One of the central issues in the discussions about male-female relationships in the context of the church is the authority of Scripture. Of course, the main matter is not whether the Bible should be used as the final authority in making theological judgments on male-female relations in the context of the church. The main matter is rather how to discern what the Scriptures teach about the *ideal vision* of the church and the relationship of its members. Using Paul as an example, people who dismiss his view as being self-contradictory or as advocating patriarchy have judged him incorrectly. Max Turner has noted that the New Testament presents us with varied portraits of how the earliest Christian communities celebrated "implications of the Christ-event *contextually*."[240] A more appropriate way to read Paul's writings and theologies is to construe him *as a missionary-theologian who imagined an ideal way of life for the church and who worked cautiously, albeit progressively, to move some early Christian communities he served towards the ideal.* But what exactly is the "ideal way of life" that Paul imagined for the church? This is a complex question and no answer will be completely free from denominational biases. Yet Paul's dialectical treatment of men-women relationships (1 Cor 11:11–12) and his counter-cultural ecclesiology (Gal 3:28–29) provide sufficient clues. One way of summarizing what is most likely Paul's conception of the *ideal way of life* of the church is: the church is a new community of God's people whose life must be governed by Christ's life, the only head of the church who acts through the Holy Spirit's giving of spiritual gifts to members of the church. When approached from what I have summarized as Paul's ideal view of the church's life, the question driving the criteria of ecclesiastical leadership should not be: Which occupies pride of place, male headship or mutual submission? Rather, the question should be: What should be the criterion for judging male headship or mutual submission of men and women? And the answer is: the *ideal way of life of the church* as imagined by early Christians such as the Apostle Paul.

Our discussions about male-female relationships in the context of ecclesiastical leadership should be contextual. This requires being faithful to Scriptural teaching on the life of the church as a community that must be governed by Christ's life (Phil 2:5) and the spiritual works of the Holy Spirit through the use of *charismata* Rom 12:4–8; 1 Cor 12:8–10, 28–30; Eph 4:11). The church today, like the church of Paul's era, must continue to strive for the *ideal of way of life* of the church. Being contextual also means that each community must proceed with caution on how to appropriate the *ideal way*

240. Turner, *Holy Spirit and the Spiritual Gifts*, 145. Italics in original.

of life of the church. In societies and cultures where ordaining women into priesthood will be a stumbling block for the proclamation of the gospel, the church must act wisely, patiently, and if necessary delay the appointment of women in ecclesiastical leadership positions. Paul himself operated with this principle as Stanley Grenz and Denise Kjesbo have noted: "There is a good reason to conclude that Paul's pervasive concern for evangelism is also operative. . . . Believers must always act with a sense of propriety which prevents their conduct from becoming a source of offense to those outside of the faith."[241] This, of course, does not mean that the church in such societies should not press on and move towards the Christian ideal in which people's gifts and vocational calling function as the principal criteria for serving in the church in all capacities.

Exercise 4.2

Jenna was determined to act on her desire to become a pastor of a local church. Tony, Jenna's husband, asked her not to do so because he believed the Bible prohibits women from becoming pastors. Jenna, however, insisted on acting on her desire because she was convinced that *spiritual gifts* and not biological sexes should be the criteria for leadership in the church.

Question for discussion: Would you advise Jenna to go ahead with her decision to become a pastor in a local church? Discuss your answer and the theological (and other) reasons for your answer with other students.

Glossary

AICs: acronym for African Independent (or Instituted Churches).

Consubstantiation: term rejected by many Lutherans but used by some critics of Luther's doctrine of the real presence of Christ in the elements of the Lord's Supper. For such critics, Luther's view implies the coexistence or commingling of divine and human substances in the consecrated bread and wine used for the celebration of the Lord's Supper.

Ecumenism: when used in reference to the church, *ecumenism* refers to the initiative that is geared toward restoring the unity but not uniformity of Christian churches.

241. Grenz and Kjesbo, *Women in the Church*, 115.

Glossolalia: term used to describe a form of prayer inspired by the Holy Spirit in which a worshipper speaks "in tongues" or in languages that are not in use in any human society.

Sacraments: broad term used to describe sacred rituals of the church, which some Christians believe *convey* God's grace to people and other Christians see as mere *signs* of God's grace that is already present in the lives of the celebrants.

Transubstantiation: the view that the elements (bread and wine) used in the celebration of the Eucharist become the real body and blood of Christ when consecrated by the priest.

Review Questions

1. What are the major views of the Eucharist or the Lord's Supper? Compare and critique them, highlighting what you consider to be the most appropriate way of understanding the Eucharist.

2. In what ways have Christians understood the nature of spiritual gifts? What class of gifts has caused controversies in Christianity? What are the purposes of such spiritual gifts?

3. What theological arguments are used to support male headship or leadership and female subordination in ecclesiastical assemblies? What counterarguments have been presented against this position?

Suggestions for Further Reading

Anderson, Allan Heaton. *To the Ends of the Earth: Pentecostalism and the Transformation of World Christianity*. New York: Oxford University Press, 2013.

Braaten, Carl E. *Mother Church: Ecclesiology and Ecumenism*. Minneapolis: Fortress, 1998.

Evans, Abigail Rian. *The Healing Church: Practical Programs for Health Ministries*. Cleveland: United Church Press, 1999.

Gibbs, Eddie, and Ryan K. Bolger. *Emerging Churches: Creating Christian Community in Postmodern Cultures*. Grand Rapid: Baker Academic, 2005.

Osburn, Carroll D. *Women in the Church: Reclaiming the Ideal*. 2nd ed. Abilene, TX: Abilene Christian University Press, 2001.

Tillard, J.-M. R. *I Believe, Despite Everything: Reflections of an Ecumenist*. Translated by William G. Rusch. Collegeville, MN: Liturgical, 2000.

Volf, Miroslav. *After Our Likeness: The Church as the Image of the Trinity*. Grand Rapids: Eerdmans, 1998.

Zizioulas, John D. *Being as Communion: Studies in Personhood and the Church.* Crestwood, NY: St. Vladimir's Seminary Press, 1985.

5

Christian Eschatological Hope

CHAPTER OUTLINE

Ideas of Christian Eschatological Hope
Christian Eschatological Hope: Its Nature and Scope
Time and Christian Eschatological Hope
Christian Eschatological Hope and Models of Interpretative Framework
Theories of Millennialism
Postmillennialism
Amillennialism
Premillennialism
Scientific Challenge to the Christian Views of Cosmic Consummation
Describing the Scientific Challenge
Christian Theological Responses to the Scientific Challenge
Major Themes in the Doctrine of Christian Eschatological Hope
Kingdom of God
Resurrection
Second Coming
Final Judgment
Hell
Heaven
Concluding Reflections on Christian Eschatological Hope
Glossary
Review Questions
Suggestions for Further Reading

This chapter discusses the topic that is traditionally known as *eschatology* (from the Greek *eschata*, "last things"; *eschatos*, "last" or "end"). Theological discussions of Christian eschatological hope (or "eschatology") cover issues relating to the ultimate destiny of individuals (individual eschatology), the ultimate destiny of the community of the people of God (*communal eschatology*), and the ultimate destiny of the universe (*cosmic eschatology*).[1] Many theologians reserve the last chapter for eschatology in their systematic theology books. Some of such books focus primarily on future events such as people's destinies either in hell or heaven. In many texts on Christian eschatology, a careful reader can discern two related trajectories in theologians' conception of the *eschaton*. Some follow the trajectory of *telos*—the purpose, goal, and fulfillment of all things. Others follow the path of *finis*—the finale or ends of all things.[2] The following topics will be discussed: ideas of Christian eschatological hope, theories of millennialism, scientific challenges to the Christians views of cosmic consummation, and some major theological themes in the doctrine of Christian eschatological hope.

Ideas of Christian Eschatological Hope

I chose to title this chapter "Christian Eschatological Hope" rather than "Eschatology" because the term "eschatology" has the tendency to nudge people into thinking about the *very last things* that will bring human history and salvation history to an end or completion. For example, Alister McGrath notes that in a broad sense, the "term 'eschatology' is 'discourse about the end.' The 'end' in question may refer to an individual's existence or to the closing of the present age."[3] But the themes that are discussed under the heading "eschatology" should not be entirely about the events that will happen near or during the time of God's *final* remaking of the present world.[4] Rather, theologians should also be attentive to the ongoing work in this present world. Although the terms "hope" and "eschatology" look toward the future, hope underscores what *is happening* in the present and also how it conditions or ought to condition what *will happen* in the future. In this section, I will discuss the nature and scope of Christian eschatological hope, the place of "time" in theological discussions on Christian eschatological hope, and the major interpretative frameworks in the discourse on Christian eschatological hope.

1. Macquarrie, *Principles of Christian Theology*, 353.
2. Moltmann, *Coming of God*, 134.
3. McGrath, *Christian Theology*, 553.
4. Hellwig, "Eschatology," 349–50.

Christian Eschatological Hope: Its Nature and Scope

Christian eschatological hope should not be treated as an addendum in Christian theology. On the contrary, Christian hope should permeate other aspects of Christian doctrines beginning from creation. For instance, our doctrine of creation must account for Christian beliefs about God's continuing involvement in creation and also God's ultimate intention for the creation. The fear of nuclear war, incurable diseases, and terrorism have "proved fertile soil for renewed eschatological speculation" in all parts of the world.[5] Advancements in science and economy in some parts of the world have constituted a major threat to the doctrine of Christian eschatological hope. In some parts of the Western world, the discourse on Christian eschatological hope has been trapped between optimism and pessimism. However, in the parts of the world where there is limited advancement in the scientific, political, and economic arenas, the doctrine of Christian eschatological hope remains central to the life and aspiration of many Christians.

The author of the Epistle to the Hebrews was one of the most imaginative biblical writers who reflected on "hope." Two texts in particular are noteworthy. In Heb 6:19–20, the author wrote, "We have this hope as an anchor for the soul, firm and secure. It enters the inner sanctuary behind the curtain, where Jesus, who went before us, has entered on our behalf" (NIV). In Heb 11:1, the author also wrote, "Now faith is being sure of what we hope for and certain of what we do not see" (NIV). Christian eschatological hope is not "grounded in projections based on current trends nor merely on fantasies about what could or should be, but rather on what God has done, is doing, and will do through Christ."[6] Christian hope derives from God's promise of redemption, providence, and sovereign rule over God's creation. In the midst of dehumanization, marginalization, the grave threats posed by weapons of mass destruction, poverty, terrorism, and disease, Christians continue to speak of their hope in God's providence and reign. This is because the *hope* of which they speak does not promise that God will always "shield Christians from disappointments and hardships, nor does it provide neat solutions to the world's problems; but it does give courage, energy, and confidence to persist in the struggle for life and God's transformation of creation."[7]

The Apostle Paul in his letter to Christians in Ephesus also outlines helpful frameworks for understanding Christian eschatological hope. Paul

---

5. Fergusson, "Eschatology," 227.

6. Barr, "Christian Hope," 475.

7. Ibid.

writes, "I pray that the eyes of your heart may be enlightened, so that you will know what is the hope of His calling, what are the riches of the glory of His inheritance in the saints and what is the surpassing greatness of His power toward us who believe" (Eph 1:18–19 NASB). The hope that Paul speaks of here is not rooted in wishful thinking. It is the hope that is rooted in a historical event: the life, ministry, death, and resurrection of Jesus of Nazareth (Eph 1:20). For Paul, the Christian hope is grounded not only in God's power by which God raised Jesus from the dead but also in God's commission to Jesus to have authority over God's creation (Eph 1:20–23).

In theological terms, Christian eschatological hope may be described as the discourse about the Triune God's ongoing work of remaking or making anew this present world that is "perishing from its sin and its injustice"[8] with the intent of bringing it to its ultimate fulfillment. Therefore, the two major components of Christian eschatological hope are (*a*) God's remaking of this world, and (*b*) God's drawing of this world to its ultimate fulfillment. Many Christian theologians use the expression "already-not-yet" to describe two interrelated components in the doctrine of Christian eschatological hope. The "already" refers to what has occurred and is occurring and the "not-yet" refers to future things, which include God's final decision regarding the destiny of God's creation. Of course, we need to be conscious of the interconnectedness of all the events that are included in the *already-not-yet* events. The theological content of Christian eschatological hope, therefore, cannot be totally futuristic. On the contrary, it must properly account for God's reign that is already underway and God's ongoing drawing of God's creation to its ultimate fulfilment. As Monika Hellwig notes, "As Christians . . . we see all of human history moving toward a very definite goal—the reign of God fully extended in all creation through the reconciliation of individual human beings and of human society as a whole."[9] Christians are to pay close attention to *this* present world and should also participate in the Triune God's ongoing work of renewing this world and moving it toward its ultimate fulfillment.

Time and Christian Eschatological Hope

Since I discussed technical matters relating to philosophical and theological conceptions of time in volume 1, chapter 7, I will not rehearse such matters here. Instead, I would like to highlight the idea of "future" and how it relates to time in Christian eschatological hope. "Future" is intrinsic to time

8. Moltmann, *Coming of God*, 29.
9. Hellwig, "Eschatology," 370.

whether a person construes time as cyclical or linear. The primary issue here, as Ted Peters points out, is whether the "future" is open to newness or simply a return to "an eternal point of origin."[10] Peters notes that it is too simplistic to associate openness and newness to the linear concept of time and to associate recurrence (or returning to the point of origin) with the cyclical view of time. For Peters, the idea of linearity does not guarantee an openness and newness of future events or human actions. As I also showed in volume 1, chapter 7, some theologians who operate with the linear concept of time imagine God's predestination in a manner that rules out genuine newness and openness of future human actions. Similarly, in some cultures where time is construed as cyclical, future human actions are not seen as *merely playing out* a predetermined will of God or the gods.[11]

What is of primal importance to this chapter vis-à-vis the concept of time is whether God is moving the world to a future, to a purposeful end. What are Christians to make of the growing scientific claim that the universe is biologically "predestined" to an entropic end—catastrophic disorder deprived of any purpose or meaning? The concept of time is crucially important for discussions about the Christian eschatological hope. As we shall see below, a theologian's view of divine action and God's involvement in the future of the world will be largely determined by the theologian's perception of time, especially its "future" element.

Christian Eschatological Hope and Models of Interpretative Frameworks

Human beings always *hope*, which can be an anticipation of a better or worse condition. Hope can be broadly construed as "perceiving rays of light amidst a cloudy sky." In an age in which humans, animals, and entire ecosystems are threatened by incessant religiously motivated wars, gun violence, infectious diseases such as Ebola and AIDS, poverty, derelict neighborhoods, and homelessness, many people understandably may have fears about a potentially disastrous end to their lives. Many religious people have had the audacity to hope for a better life beyond this present world. What and how people hope undoubtedly will shape their actions and manner of living in *this* world. For example, Ernst Conradie notes that poverty and disease drive some South Africans to live in a manner that endangers the environment as they struggle to provide food for their families. Conradie proposes that the Christian hope of the future of the earth offers a way out

10. Peters, "Terror of Time," 58.

11. See Mbiti, *New Testament Eschatology*, 24–32.

of the environmental crisis. This is because, as Conradie argues, "Without any hope, without any vision of a future for the earth itself, an environmental praxis will soon lose its impetus. It will consciously be fighting a losing battle."[12] Such hope can deter people from living in a manner that destroys the environment. It will also inspire them to act to preserve the earth and to work against injustice and oppression. Yet Conradie argues that the transformation of the world into a better future does not lie entirely in the hands of humans. Such transformation, to Conradie, requires the intervention of God. He writes, "Hope for the earth remains in God's hands, not in ours. This calls for attention to be given to the involvement in the world of a God who is also beyond human limitations in space and time."[13]

Careful readers of the Scriptures will notice the expressions "this age" or "this world" (Matt 12:32; John 14:30; 2 Cor 4:4; 2 Tim 4:10; 1 John 2:15–17) and "the age to come" (Matt 12:32; Eph 1:21). The meanings and relationship of these expressions have fascinated Christian theologians. To some, "this age" refers to the present world as we know it (and as the authors of the Bible knew it), while "the age to come" points to a future world (which is most likely to be a renewal of the present world). Some theologians have cautioned against construing "the age to come" primarily as referring to "the end of time." For some of these theologians, identifying "the age to come" with "the end of time" distorts scriptural teaching on the relationship between the "ages." To highlight the differences and relationship between both ages (and worlds), some theologians speak of the *ethical* relations and *chronological* relations. Ethically, the two ages are set in sharp antithesis analogous to death and life.[14] "This age" represents human rebellion and sin against God—a world that will "pass away under God's judgment." On the contrary, "the age to come" represents the rule or reign of God, which is uniquely exemplified in the person and work of Jesus of Nazareth, the Christ.[15] Chronologically, "this age" and "the age to come" intersect: they "coexist with a measure of interpenetration" and are experienced simultaneously even though they differ in characteristics.[16]

Theologians deal differently with eschatological and apocalyptic materials. Some theologians approach biblical apocalyptic literature as texts that use metaphorical terms to describe the experiences of the people that wrote them and/or the experiences of the audience for whom they wrote the texts.

12. Conradie, "Eschatology in South African Literature," 6.

13. Ibid., 21.

14. Wells, "The Future," 292.

15. Ibid.

16. Ibid.

This eschatological outlook is called *Preterism* (or the Preterist view). Some theologians who adopt *Preterism* as their primary interpretive framework, for example, hold that Jesus' predictions were "fulfilled" during the lifetime of his contemporaries.[17] Other theologians use a futuristic hermeneutic (called *Futurism*). Theologians that use this model argue that the apocalyptic predictions pertaining to the ultimate destiny of the world, particularly the destiny of human beings, will take place in the future "before the end of times."[18] Two trajectories are present in the discourse on Christian eschatological hope that has adopted *Futurism* as a primary interpretive framework. I will call the first trajectory the "non-calendarist model" and the second trajectory the "calendarist model."

Theologians that use the *non-calendarist model* emphasize the metaphorical nature of the languages used by the biblical writers to express their understandings of the events that have begun to happen in *this* age but will extend to "the age to come." They rarely speak of the timing and sequences of the events in "the age to come." They focus rather on eschatological themes emerging from prophetic and apocalyptic writings in the Bible. On the contrary, theologians that use the *calendarist model* understand eschatological events literally. Some such theologians outline eschatological events periodically and sequentially. Dispensationalists are examples of such theologians that have adopted the calendarist model.[19] Many such theologians employ a literalistic theological hermeneutics in their interpretations of biblical passages and metaphors that relate to Christ's Second Coming as shown in their *millennial* theories.[20] Underlying the *calendarist model* is the assumption that through a careful reading of the Bible a reader can identify the sequence of events that will lead to the final consummation of this world.

Theories of Millennialism

In Christian theology, the idea of one thousand years of divine reign in this present world, which is associated with Jesus Christ as the prime divine representative or ruler, is called *millennialism* (from the Latin *mille*, meaning "thousand") or *chiliasm* (from the Greek *chilias*, meaning "thousand").[21]

17. DeBruyn, "Preterism and 'This Generation,'" 180.

18. Weber, "Millennialism," 366.

19. A good survey of dispensationalism is Bass, *Backgrounds to Dispensationalism: Its Historical Genesis and Ecclesiastical Implications*.

20. See Ryrie, *Basic Theology: A Popular Systematic Guide to Understanding Biblical Truth*.

21. For a survey of the history of millennialism, see Weber, "Millennialism," 369–83.

Although Rev 20:1–6 is the primary biblical text cited in support of the belief in the millennium, as Timothy Weber notes, theologians sometimes cite other biblical passages that speak of God's peaceful kingdom on earth, the writing of God's law on human hearts and transformation of human society, and God's supernatural intervention to control evil forces (Isa 2; Jer 31–33; Ezek 36–37; Mic 4; Zech 1–6; Matt 24; etc.).[22] American Protestant theologians popularized the millennial theories in the nineteenth and twentieth centuries. It should be borne in mind that within each position, there are different nuances. Theologians disagree on the timing and the sequence of the events as the positions described below will show. I will focus on the main distinctive features of each position.

In the millennial theories, the doctrine of the Second Coming (the *Parousia*, a Greek word that means "presence" or "coming") of Christ is also a pivotal issue. Four related questions have generally informed the millennial theories. First, would there be a *millennium*—that is, a period of time (whether or not it is a literal one-thousand-year period) in which Christ's presence will be increasingly felt in the world (whether or not Christ is physically present on the earth)? Second, is the millennial reign of Christ (*a*) the *Parousia*, or (*b*) the period that ushers in the *Parousia*, or (*c*) the period that is inaugurated by the *Parousia*? Third, in what way would Jesus be actively present on earth? Fourth, is the millennium a literal one thousand years?

Postmillennialism

Postmillennialism holds that Jesus would *physically* return to the earth (the *Parousia*) *after* the millennial reign.[23] For postmillennialists, the millennium precedes the *Parousia*. Postmillennialists contend that the millennium is not literally a thousand-year period (as in the case of 2 Pet 3:8) but rather an unspecified period of time that is marked by a gradual increase in the knowledge and also acceptance of the Triune God's work in the world brought about by the church's proclamation of the gospel. Some postmillennialists see the millennium as the entire period between the first coming and the second coming of Christ. They argue that Jesus Christ established the millennium during his first coming, which indicates that we are currently in the millennial era at least since the resurrection of Jesus Christ. Others think of the millennium as a golden period (perhaps still in the future) leading to Christ's Second Coming.

22. Ibid., 365.
23. Walvoord, "Postmillennialism," 149.

Postmillennialists share the belief that the millennium will usher in Christ's Second Coming and that the millennial period is (or will be) characterized by the "spread of the gospel and the conversion of a great number of persons" to Christianity.[24] For some postmillennialists, Jesus Christ is not the rider on a white horse mentioned in Rev 19:11–16. On the contrary, they argue that Rev 19:11–16 speaks figuratively of the victory of the forces of good over evil that will be brought about through the church's proclamation of the gospel message of Jesus Christ. According to Stanley Grenz, that the event described in Rev 19:11–16 will take place in heaven and not on the earth (Rev 19:11) clearly shows that the writer of the book of Revelation did not have the Second Coming in mind.[25] Many postmillennialists, however, distance themselves from *utopianism*—an optimism of the progressive penetration and spread of the Christian message in the world that will (*a*) result in the abolition of evils in the world, and (*b*) bring about total social transformation.[26]

For some critics of postmillennialism, failure to see the rider of the white horse of Rev 19:11–16 as the risen Christ is a biblical blunder. Other critics of postmillennialism point out that historically, while the Christian gospel is spreading throughout the world, as scholars of World Christianity have shown, evils have continued to thrive in the world. The world has become increasingly strife-ridden due to religiously motivated wars (e.g., Boko Haram in Nigeria, ISIS in Iraq and Syria), the persistence of poverty, terrorism, and the threat posed by the acquisition of weapons of mass destruction by wealthy nations, to name a few factors. For some critics, the fact that the world is getting worse and not better indicates that the postmillennialist view is empirically untenable.[27] Some biblical passages (such as Matt 24) suggest there will be an increase, and not a decrease, in immorality and disbelief in God in the last days. Other critics question the biblical justification for postmillennialism. One critic, George Eldon Ladd, dismissed postmillennialism with these words: "There is so little appeal to Scripture that I have little to criticize."[28]

24. Grenz, *Millennial Maze*, 68.

25. Ibid., 72–73.

26. Ibid., 66.

27. Hoyt, "A Dispensational Premillennial Response."

28. Ladd, "Historic Premillennial Response," 143.

Amillennialism

In Greek, placing the letter *a* before a word negates it. Literally, *amillennium* means "no millennium." This definition of amillennium, however, is misleading since it suggests that amillennialism teaches there is no millennium. Amillennialism, however, contends that there will be no future literal one thousand years reign of Christ on the earth, which either precedes or follows the Second Coming. For the amillennialists, the millennium spoken about in Revelation 20 is "now in process of realization."[29] Given that amillennialism does not deny the idea of a millennium per se but rather the idea of a future period of time that precedes or immediately follows the Second Coming, some amillennialists have argued in favor of the term "realized millennialism" as a replacement for the term "amillennialism"[30] Amillennialists distinguish the millennium (which is happening now) from the *Parousia*, a future event. Amillennialists identify the *church age*—the period between Christ's first coming and the *Parousia*—with the millennium. Unlike the postmillennialists, amillennialists argue that the millennium should not be understood as a period of time in the future that will be clearly marked by a gradual moving of the majority of people in the world towards knowledge and acceptance of the Christian teaching about God, especially God's salvific work in Christ. On the contrary, as Anthony Hoekema writes, one thousand years in Revelation 20 should be understood as an unspecified long period, which began with Christ first coming and will end "just before his Second Coming."[31] Hoekema also argues that the binding of Satan (Rev 20:2) entails that he "cannot deceive the nations in such a way as to keep them from learning about the truth of God."[32] Unlike the postmillennialists, amillennialists argue that both Jesus Christ and the church have fulfilled the prediction of a golden age in the Old Testament.[33] In amillennialism, the Parousia is followed by God's summoning of all humans for the final judgment on their deeds and response to God's offer of salvation.

Some critics of amillennialism fault its advocates for using a "spiritualizing hermeneutic" that ignores the apocalyptic events described in both the Old and New Testaments, which require a literal understanding. For example, some argue that the church must be distinguished from the people of Israel. Another criticism of amillennialism that relates to the issue

29. Hoekema, "Amillennialism," 156.
30. Ibid., 155.
31. Ibid., 161.
32. Ibid., 162.
33. Weber, "Millennialism," 368.

of spiritualizing hermeneutics is the tendency of amillennialism to nudge people in the direction of *supersessionism*—the belief that God brought the church into existence as a replacement for the people of Israel. In the concept of supersessionism, God acted primarily through the people of Israel in the old covenant. But in the new covenant, God acts through the church. Increasingly, Christian theologians have become critical of supersessionism as an adequate way of understanding the relationship between Judaism and Christianity and also the relationship between the nation of Israel and the church.

Premillennialism

Premillennialism holds that the *Parousia* precedes the millennium. In other words, it is the Second Coming that will usher in a literal period of one thousand years of the reign of Christ on the earth. For premillennialists, the millennium will be a "golden age of civilization" in which the risen Christ will rule with righteousness.[34] As Charles Ryrie writes, the reign of Christ on the earth will be a theocratic rule: Jesus will establish God's reign (see Isa 9:6 and Rev 19:11–16).[35] Jesus Christ will return as a divine agent who will defeat the Antichrist (Rev 19:17–21) and then establish a peaceful reign on earth for a millennium. Some premillennialists hold the *pretribulation rapture* theory, which argues that (*a*) God will miraculously remove Christians from the world (i.e., the rapture) before the Antichrist unleashes an unprecedented tribulation, and (*b*) Christ will return with the raptured Christians to establish God's kingdom on earth for a period of one thousand years. The theological rationale for this theory is that the great tribulation will be a time when God will unleash immense wrath on the sinful world for a period of seven years (see Dan 9; 1 Thess 5; Rev 3:10).[36]

In contrast to his first coming (the humble servant of God; see Phil 2), in his Second Coming, Jesus will return as a divine warrior in power and glory to conquer the Antichrist and Satan, restraining these evil forces for a millennium.[37] This "temporal" restraining or binding will ensure Christ's peaceful reign for one thousand years. After the end of the one thousand years, they will be released from imprisonment. They will launch a final onslaught against Christ, who will in turn crush them in a final battle,

34. Hoyt, "Dispensational Premillennialism," 63.

35. Ryrie, *Basic Theology*, 522.

36. For a good survey of the different theories on the rapture and tribulation, see Archer et al., *Three Views on the Rapture*.

37. Ladd, "Historic Premillennialism," 18.

known as Armageddon (2 Thess 2:8; Rev 20:7–10). This final defeat of Satan and satanic evil forces will be followed by resurrection and final judgment. Note that while amillennialists see Rev 20 as a recapitulation of Rev 19, premillennialists see them as separate events, with events of Rev 19 (Christ's Second Coming) following the events of Rev 20 (the millennial reign).[38]

While some premillennialists may describe the church as the "spiritual Israel," they insist that the church has not replaced the nation of Israel as the chosen community of God. This means that the nation of Israel has a future role to play when God's kingdom is established on the earth at Christ's Second Coming. Some forms of premillennialism emphasize both God's ongoing reign in the world and the future establishment of God's kingdom on the earth (historic premillennialism) and others stress the future reign of God during the millennium (dispensational premillennialism).

Premillennialism is criticized by amillennialists for seeing the church as the "spiritual Israel" (a position held by most historic premillennialists) but at the same time refusing to concede that the church has indeed replaced the nation of Israel in God's salvific plan.[39] Other critics of premillennialism (in all of its forms) point out that using a literalist hermeneutic is problematic for dealing with biblical apocalyptic materials. The genre of apocalyptic and prophetic writings is characterized by metaphoric and figurative languages.[40] Therefore, understanding such writings literally betray their genre. Other critics argue that premillennialism (especially its dispensational form), gives a special privilege to the Jewish people, assuming they still hold a special place in God's salvific plan as those "divinely favored above all others in the world."[41]

Scientific Challenge to the Christian Views of Cosmic Consummation

In this section, I will describe the nature of the challenge some scientific predictions about the world pose to Christian eschatological hope. I will also discuss the varied theological responses marshalled out by contemporary theologians.

> **FOCUS QUESTION:**
> How should Christian theologians deal with scientific predictions about the nature of the ultimate fate of the world in their theologies of eschatological hope?

38. Riddlebarger, *Case for Amillennialism*, 231–32.

39. Grenz, *Millennial Maze*, 140.

40. Migliore, *Faith Seeking Understanding*, 340.

41. Boettner, "Postmillennial Response," 52.

Describing the Scientific Challenge

Does it still make sense to speak about eschatological hope in Christian terms in a world overwhelmingly impacted by some science-religion discourses that seek to rid the world of God and of ultimate purpose? Many students of theology (particularly in Europe and North America) know too well that they cannot ignore the serious challenges that scientific predictions of a doomed world pose to Christian theologies, especially the theology of hope. Many Christian theologians argue that humans and also the cosmos in its entirety (or some aspects of it) await final divine transformation. God's future transformation of the world will involve the gift of eternal life to God's creatures, which will foster new relationships between humans and the whole creation.[42] The Apostle Paul anticipated this sort of cosmic relationship between humans and the whole creation. He writes,

> For the creation waits in eager expectation for the children of God to be revealed. For the creation was subjected to frustration, not by its own choice, but by the will of the one who subjected it, in hope that the creation itself will be liberated from its bondage to decay and brought into the freedom and glory of the children of God. We know that the whole creation has been groaning as in the pains of childbirth right up to the present time. Not only so, but we ourselves, who have the firstfruits of the Spirit, groan inwardly as we wait eagerly for our adoption to sonship, the redemption of our bodies. For in this hope we were saved. But hope that is seen is no hope at all. Who hopes for what they already have? But if we hope for what we do not yet have, we wait for it patiently. (Rom 8:19–25 NIV)

Paul's eschatological hope for the cosmos will baffle many scientists today who predict its catastrophic and non-purposeful end. Increasingly, many Christian theologians have begun to take very seriously the challenge such scientific prediction poses to a Christian theology of hope. What is at stake is not only the reliability of the Christian Scriptures on cosmological matters but also the veracity of most of Christian doctrines, such as the doctrines of creation, divine providence, salvation, and hope.

Many contemporary scientists expect that all life on our planet will "inevitably and remorselessly be extinguished." While some expect a "cosmic freeze," others anticipate a "cosmic fry."[43] Conversely, based on their reading of the Scriptures, Christian theologians have traditionally held that God is

---

42. Moltmann, *Coming of God*, 131.

43. Russell, "Eschatology and Scientific Cosmology," 999.

moving God's creation towards a specific *end*—a purposely and meaningful renewal of the old and sin-ridden world. The scientific predictions about a non-purposeful catastrophic end of the world and the Christian theology of hope that anticipates God's deliberate and purposeful renewal of God's creation are in direct conflict. William Stoeger summarizes this conflict as follows: "From the indications we have from the neurosciences, biology, physics, astronomy, and cosmology, death and dissolution are the final words. There is no scientifically supportable foundation for the immortality of the soul, the resurrection of the body and the person after death, a transformed new heavens and new earth."[44] Although the scientific predictions about entropic catastrophe or death, which is awaiting the cosmos, are quite remote and "of long time-scale occurrence," many scientists believe they are bound to happen.[45]

Christian Theological Responses to the Scientific Challenge

Christian theologians have approached the challenge scientific predictions of a catastrophic end of the world pose to Christian eschatological hope in three different ways. First, some theologians ignore the scientific predictions as matters of no theological consequence since, for them, scientists are finite humans who operate with finite knowledge of God's creation. They conclude that scientific predictions of cosmological futility and Christianity's teaching about eschatological hope and a purposeful end of God's world are locked in an irreconcilable conflict. Second, for some theologians, science and religion are two separate ways of inquiry that are bound to provide parallel interpretations of the world. For such theologians, it is best to let science and religion (in this case Christianity) pursue their different courses and interpretations of the future of the world. Third, some theologians heed the warnings of scientists and seek to reimagine a traditional Christian theology of hope in the light of new scientific discoveries and insights. I will focus on these three responses to the "scientific challenge." Each of these three responses is discussed further and critiqued below.

44. Stoeger, "Scientific Accounts of Ultimate Catastrophes," 19.
45. Ibid., 21.

Retaining Christian Theology of Hope in Contradiction to Scientific Predictions of Cosmological Disaster

Some theologians argue that if the scientific predictions of an ultimate and non-divinely governed demise of the cosmos were true, Christian eschatological hope, particularly the teaching about the resurrection of the dead and future fulfillment of the world, would be illusions at best. Theologians that adopt this strategy contest the reliability of scientific predictions of a doomed world. For example, the Scottish theologian John Macquarrie (1919–2007) has argued that Christian eschatology should be imagined as a "continuous consummation" in which the creation finds its "completion and fulfilment in God."[46] Against the scientific predictions of a cosmic freeze or fry, Macquarrie contends that the Christian teaching about creation and divine providence entails hoping that God will eternally draw God's creation to God's self. For Macquarrie, the creation (humans in particular) depends on God for existence and its meaning. He understands God's providence as God's activity in preserving (which involves *establishing* and *advancing*) "the being of the creatures in the face of the risk of dissolution."[47] Macquarrie concedes the difficulty of holding on to the view of the continuous preservation of creation in the awake of some scientific predictions of a catastrophic end of the cosmos. He insists that if it were to be shown convincingly that the scientific predictions of a disastrous end (either through a freeze or fry) of the universe are true, Christian eschatological hope would be a false teaching. The excerpt below captures some of the main ideas espoused by Macquarrie.

> [An] eschatological doctrine does not necessarily imply an end of the world of time. Theologically, the doctrine of creation was understood as meaning that man and the world are dependent upon holy Being, and this creaturely status is compatible with the possibility that there always has been a world. In a parallel way, the doctrine of eschatology means theologically that man and the world are destined for holy Being and will find their completion and fulfillment in God, but this is quite compatible with the possibility that the world may continue to endure forever. Indeed, if we are to think of Being as not only stable but dynamic (and we must think of it in this way if it is to be taken as holy Being and thus as God), then it is hard to see how there ever could be an end to the world; for then God (Being) would have retired into

46. Macquarrie, *Principles of Christian Theology*, 355–57.
47. Ibid., 364.

undifferentiated Being as a kind of motionless uncarved block, and it is only Being that pours itself out through expressive Being that can claim adoration and allegiance, and that can rightly be named "God." An end in time, in the sense of a stopping, would be a kind of death, even if something like a perfection had been achieved. So just as we have thought of creation and reconciliation as continuous ongoing activities of holy Being, so we must try to conceive of consummation as likewise continuous.

Let me say frankly, however, that if it were shown that the universe is indeed headed for an all-enveloping death, then this might seem to constitute a state of affairs so wasteful and negative that it might be held to falsify Christian faith and abolish Christian hope.[48]

Questions: How does Macquarrie explain the relationship between creation and eschatology as God's ongoing activities? What theological reasons does he present to justify his claim that the world will exist continuously?

Criticism: The near misses of asteroids and comets happen continually. Some space objects have the capacity to wipe out all life and thus are a constant threat to the future of life on earth. For some scientists, asteroids and comets pose the danger of triggering global catastrophes.[49] The sun poses a greater danger to life on earth. Some scientists predict that if the sun exhausts its hydrogen fuel (a process that is several billions of years away), it will expand and become a "red giant," which will envelop and destroy all the habitable planets within our solar system.[50] Theologians cannot ignore these scientific predictions, hoping they are wrong or assuming that if they are right, they are irrelevant to God's providential work. Also, ignoring scientific predictions and insights about the world does a disservice to theology. It makes theology an obsolete field of study that has no relevant, new insights to offer to the world. Many pastors in the West know that they cannot successfully ignore such predictions and the challenges they pose to Christian doctrines. Many of their members remind them that such challenges are here to stay and cause a great deal of anxiety to their faith.

48. Ibid., 355–56.

49. Gritzner et al., "Asteroid and Comet Impact Hazard," 361–73.

50. Stoeger, "Scientific Accounts of Ultimate Catastrophes," 25; Polkinghorne, "Eschatology," 31.

Christian Hope of Purposed Future of the Cosmos and Scientific Predictions of Cosmological Futility as parallel Interpretations

Increasingly, theologians have begun to see *nature* as a "text" that is open to multiple ways of viewing, seeing, and interpreting. This manner of construing nature implies that there is no "self-evidently valid way of reading" and interpreting it.[51] For such theologians, proposing God as the creator of nature is one of the many competing ways of interpreting nature and the cosmos.[52] While some of the theologians that see nature in this manner are open to dialogue between science and religion, others see the product of such dialogue as inconsequential since science and religion are two disparate fields. What these theologians, however, share is the belief that the world does not have the capacity to bring itself on its own to a complete destruction.

Kathryn Tanner explores a strategy that compels theologians to speak of a future hope of the world in Christian terms, which allows theologians to "cope with and make sense of the end of things" as contended by scientists.[53] Tanner's strategy requires theologians to drop the importance of *how* exactly God will bring the world to its end. Theologians can still argue that God will bring the world to an end without confronting the scientific prediction about *how* the cosmos will bring itself to a futile end.[54] Recognizing that her strategy implies rendering theology irrelevant to questions about the future of the world, Tanner states that her aim is to propose "an eschatology for the world without a future."[55] What is important to Tanner is a view of Christian hope that drops a predominantly future-oriented eschatology and in its place upholds a holistic view that presents God as the redeemer of the world and also accounts for the past, present, and future history of the world. For Tanner, biological death and life should be understood within the framework of one's relationship to God who is the giver of life. Also, death and life should not be taken strictly in a literal sense. She appeals to the metaphorical usages of the terms "death" and "life" in the Old Testament. "Life" refers sometimes to "fruitfulness and abundance, longevity, communal flourishing, and individual well-being," while "death"

---

51. McGrath, "Origins of a Scientific Theology," 262.

52. Ibid.

53. Tanner, "Eschatology with a Future?," 224.

54. Ibid.

55. Ibid., 226.

is employed sometimes to describe "suffering, poverty, barrenness, oppression, social divisiveness, and isolation."[56]

Tanner's eschatology also requires reimagining the Christian concept of "eternal life" in the context of being in fellowship with God. Since death is not beyond God's reach and is also within God's providential sphere, it has no "power to separate one from God."[57] Theologically, eternal life has both spatial and nonspatial aspects. In its nonspatial sense, eternal life refers to living in God or God indwelling in us before and after biological death. In spatial sense, eternal life refers to God's reign or kingdom in this present world, in which God through us confronts suffering, oppression, and hopelessness in order to bring about a new pattern of relationship "marked by life-giving vitality and renewed hope."[58]

If there is no defined "future" for the world that is not *this-worldly*, does it really matter how one leads his or her life in this present life? Tanner acknowledges the importance of this question and the threat it poses to her eschatology. She responds to the question by arguing that eternal life, which is God's unconditional gift to humanity, calls for action. It requires us to be holy people and to show willingness to enter into the "realm of God's life-giving being."[59] The holy life should not be grounded in the fear of a future judgment but rather in one's gratitude to God for the gift of eternal life. The excerpts below show how Tanner works out her eschatology.

> In a move that is typical for most modern theological struggles with scientific description of the world's beginnings, creation . . . is detemporalized, one might say, so that it becomes a relation of dependence on God that everything that exists enjoys in every respect that it is. Such a relation of dependence holds whether the world has a beginning or not. . . . If being created means to depend on God, the world that is created is not just the world of the beginning but the world as a whole, across the whole of its duration however long or short that may be, whether with or without a beginning or end.
>
> There is life in God (in Christ) that we possess now and after death. Ante- and post-mortem do not, then, mark any crucial difference with respect to it. Death makes no difference to that life in God in the sense that, despite our deaths, God maintains a relationship with us that continues to be the source of all benefit. Even when we are alive, we are therefore dead insofar as we are

56. Ibid., 226–27.

57. Ibid., 228.

58. Ibid., 230–31.

59. Ibid., 234.

dead in Christ. Separation from Christ (and from one's fellows in Christ) is a kind of death despite the apparent gains that might accrue to one in virtue of an isolated, simply self-concerned existence. Eternal life, moreover, is one's portion or possession despite all the sufferings of life and death in a way that should comfort sufferers of every kind of tribulation. In all the senses of death, including the biological death, we therefore live even though we die if we are alive to Christ. "If we live, we live to the Lord, and if we die, we die to the Lord; so then, whether we live or whether we die, we are the Lord's" (Rom 14:8).

Thus, in my account of the eschaton, it is the very mortal body as scientists describe it that takes on the immortality of God as it lives in God through Christ.[60]

Question: How does Tanner's eschatology explain the following theological themes: death, life, and eternal life?

Criticism: One of the difficulties with Tanner's eschatology is how to account for the resurrection of Jesus Christ, which many theologians believe is linked to God's promise of a future resurrection of those who have died.[61] Would there be a resurrection? If yes, would it be bodily resurrection? Also, her eschatology appears to dismiss the relevance of the science-theology dialogue in which both fields can mutually enrich each other. If human action does not bring about life in God because eternal life is God's unconditional gift to humanity,[62] why is it really important to focus our attention on how we are to live in this present life? How does one explain the biblical passages that speak of God's future judgment (for example, see Rom 14:12; Heb 9:27)?

Re-conceiving Christian Eschatological Hope in the Light of Scientific Predictions of Cosmological Catastrophes

For some theologians, God will use the unpleasant cosmological catastrophes (which are part of the evolutionary process) to transform God's creation. As Stoeger notes, "although the human species, life, the earth, the sun, and the universe will end, that end is not ultimate but somehow leads to a

60. Ibid., 225, 228–29, 237.

61. Peters, *Anticipating Omega*, 32; see also Greer, *Christian Hope and Christian Life*, 60–61.

62. Tanner, "Eschatology with a Future?," 234.

fuller, transformed reality, to which the natural sciences provide no access, and to which our human experience gives us only obscure, nevertheless real, intimations and indications."[63] The universe is tinkered into its present condition by *nature*, which is both self-destructive and life-generating. Asteroids, comets, and the sun pose great danger not only to the earth but also to other planets. Yet nature has the capacity to continue to fashion new forms of life by taking life, replacing the old with new forms of objects and beings.[64] God is retained as the Creator of the universe who patiently works through the evolutionary process that brings about death and new or transformed forms of life.

British theologian-physicist John Polkinghorne holds the view that God is moving God's creation toward its fulfillment through natural processes. He rejects the idea of "non-overlapping magisteria" that nudges science and religion into two separate ways. On the contrary, he contends, using the Christian idea of divine *kenosis* (or emptying), that God relinquishes certain powers of creating to the creatures, allowing the "creatures to be made and to make themselves."[65] For Polkinghorne, when God's relation to creation is understood in this way, science and religion cannot be seen as mutually exclusive or antagonistic. Christian theologians must incorporate valid scientific insights about the world into their understandings of the world's origin and its movement towards God's intended purpose.[66] Polkinghorne argues that the future of the present world will be conditioned by God's transformation (through the natural evolutionary process) into something new, which, of course, will bear the marks of both continuity and discontinuity. To him, if God's will and action lie behind the evolving changes in the cosmos, it follows that it is beyond the competence of science to say exactly what the new creation would look like.[67] The uncertainty of cultural evolution has made it extremely difficult, if not impossible, to predict biological evolutionary process and the future of biotic life with precision. Yet science has an important role to play in theological understandings (and predictions) of the future of the world: it poses to theology "with considerable sharpness, the question of what meaning there could be in the hopeful belief that 'in the end all will be well.'"[68]

63. Stoeger, "Scientific Accounts of Ultimate Catastrophes," 20.

64. Ibid., 28.

65. Polkinghorne, "Continuing Interaction of Science and Religion," 43; Polkinghorne, *God of Hope*, 114.

66. Polkinghorne, "Continuing Interaction of Science and Religion," 43.

67. Polkinghorne, "Eschatology," 29.

68. Ibid.

Polkinghorne grounds the cosmic eschatological hope in the resurrection of Jesus Christ, an event that, he argues, is the origin and guarantee of human hope and universal hope.[69] God will not bring the "new creation" (Rev 21) into existence *ex nihilo* ("out of nothing"); rather, the "new creation" will be the result of the transformation of this present creation. In Polkinghorne's words, it will be a "resurrected world created *ex vetere* ["from the old"]."[70] Consequently, the new creation will bear the marks of both continuity and discontinuity with this present world. Death is a necessary cost of life that is part of God's providential care for the creation, which God has given the "space" it requires to make and remake itself through the evolutionary process.[71] The excerpt below highlights Polkinghorne's understandings of how both the Christian theology of hope and scientific predictions about impending cosmological catastrophe can enrich our view of the ultimate ends of the world.

God must surely care for all creatures in ways that accord with their natures. Therefore, we must expect that there will be a destiny for the whole universe beyond its death, just as there will be a post mortem destiny for humankind. [Two] remarkable New Testament passages (Rom 8:18–25; Col 1:15–20) do indeed speak of a cosmic redemption. Just as we see Jesus' resurrection as the origin and guarantee of human hope, so we can also see it as the origin and guarantee of a universal hope. The significance of the empty tomb is that the Lord's risen and glorified body is the transmuted form of his dead body. Thus matter itself participates in the resurrection transformation, enjoying thereby the foretaste of its own redemption from decay. The resurrection of Jesus is the seminal event from which the whole of God's new creation has already begun to grow.

This current universe is a creation endowed with just those physical properties that have enabled it to "make itself" in the course of its evolving history. A world of this kind, by its necessary nature, must be a world of transience in which death is the cost of life new life. In theological terms, this world is a creation that is sustained by its Creator, and which has been endowed with a divinely purposed fruitfulness, but which is also allowed to be at some distance from the veiled presence of the One who holds it in being and interacts

69. Polkinghorne, *God of Hope*, 113.
70. Polkinghorne, "Eschatology," 30.
71. Ibid., 38–39.

in hidden ways with its history. Its unfolding process develops with the "space" that God has given it, within which it is allowed to be itself.[72]

Questions: What are the roles of God and the evolutionary process in Polkinghorne's account of a complementary view of science and theology on the subject of Christian eschatology? Why does Polkinghorne hold that Jesus' resurrection is the ground for cosmic transformation and redemption?

Exercise 5.1

Imagine that you were invited as a Christian to a public conversation on the ultimate destiny of the world. As preparation for the conversation, write a one-page theological reflection on the topic "Living for God in the face of scientific predictions of cosmic non-purposeful disintegration." The paper should show clearly your view of the relationship between science and religion (with a focus on Christianity).

Major Themes in Christian Eschatological Hope

The following themes are covered in this section: the kingdom of God, Christ's Second Coming, resurrection, and judgment (focusing on hell and heaven).

Kingdom of God

While some see the kingdom of God as the quintessence of Christian eschatological hope, others see it as a phenomenon with specific scope and timeframe, limiting it to the period between Jesus' first coming and second coming, and distinguishing it from apocalyptic events such the final judgment. The biblical concept of the "kingdom of God" (*basileia tou theou* in Greek) shapes Christians' conception of hope. But what exactly does the expression "kingdom of God" mean? Theologians as well as biblical scholars have devoted enormous efforts to unpacking its meanings, focusing primarily on how Jesus Christ used it. Two views of the "kingdom of God" discussed below have gained prominence in many theological circles.

72. Polkinghorne, *God of Hope*, 113, 114.

God's Kingdom as Territory

For some, the term "kingdom of God" and its Matthean equivalent, "the kingdom of heaven" (*basileia tōn ouranōn* in Greek), refer to a divine *territory*, one with geographical boundaries.[73] For some who interpret the phrase "kingdom of God" in terms of a geographical boundary or territory, the kingdom of God is a future event that is part of God's reclaiming of the world as God's created work. Such theologians argue that God's kingdom refers to the *Parousia* of Jesus and the millennial era. In his reflections on the ethics of God's kingdom, Lewis Chafer writes, "The teachings of the kingdom have not been applied to men in all ages; nay, more, they have not yet been applied to any man. Since they anticipate the binding of Satan, a purified earth, the restoration of Israel, and the personal reign of the King, they cannot be applied until God's appointed time when these kingdom laws will be addressed to Israel and beyond them to all the nations which will enter the kingdom."[74] For those who see God's kingdom in terms of a *territory*, it will be a future event in which God will rule through God's risen Son (Jesus Christ) over the world, executing judgment on the world (2 Tim 4:8; see also Ps 72). For such theologians, the ethics of God's kingdom does not pertain to the Christian life but rather refers to a legal code of conduct that will govern the lives of people in the future earthly kingdom of God. People will earn the blessings of the kingdom through their own work.[75]

One criticism of the conception of God's kingdom as a physical territory is that it fails to take serious Jesus' proclamation that the kingdom of God is "at hand" or "has come near." In Mark 1:15 Jesus says, "The time is fulfilled, and the kingdom of God is at hand; repent and believe in the gospel" (NASB). Many biblical scholars have shown that the notion of a physical territory is foreign to Jesus' understanding of God's kingdom.[76] In Christ, we encounter the "breaking in" of God's kingdom into this present world.

---

73. Matthew's preference for the "kingdom of heaven" over the "kingdom of God" should be understood as a typical Jewish honorific way of avoiding the use of God's name.

74. Chafer, *Systematic Theology*, 4:207.

75. Ibid., 4:211–12, 216.

76. For more discussion, see Ladd, *Theology of the New Testament*, 60–65.

God's Kingdom as Divine Sovereignty and Reign

Other theologians describe the "kingdom of God" as God's *reign*, highlighting God's "rule and living power over the world."[77] Unlike those who see the phrase "kingdom of God" in terms of a geographical boundary or territory, those who construe the kingdom of God as God's reign contend that it is not merely a future event but rather a175 divine activity that is already ongoing in this present world. People become part of God's kingdom when they accept God's rule over their lives.[78]

Theologians that construe the kingdom of God as divine sovereignty and reign usually understand the expression "at hand" dialectically: God's reign is both present and absent in this world. The term "already not-yet" is used by theologians to describe this dialectical tension. This tension means, as Joseph Ratzinger notes, "Jesus is speaking not of a heavenly reality but of something God *is doing* and *will do* in the future here on earth."[79] In the words of the Kenyan theologian John Mbiti, the kingdom of God has come in Jesus Christ (Matt 12:28), "but this is only the beginning which points towards the future consummation (Matt 24:14) also in him."[80] The task of theologians is to work out how God's reign is simultaneously present and absent.

> "The *basileia* is here, and yet it is not here; it is revealed, yet also hidden; it is present, but always future; it is at hand, indeed in the very midst, yet it is constantly expected, being still, and this time seriously, the object of the petition: Thy kingdom come."
>
> —Karl Barth, *CD* III/3, 156

The Triune God and the Kingdom of God

God the Father as the Sovereign Governor

When understood as sovereignty and reign, God's kingdom can be said to be presently ongoing in the world. The Bible presents God as one who reigns and rules over God's creation (see Ps 103:19; Jer 10:7–10). In his commentary on Matt 6:5–16, Augustine of Hippo (354–430 CE) argues that God has always had a kingdom in as much God rules over God's creation. He writes, "For God hath a kingdom always; neither is He ever without a kingdom,

---

77. Ratzinger, *Eschatology*, 26.
78. Ladd, *Theology of the New Testament*, 79–80.
79. Ratzinger, *Eschatology*, 26; emphasis mine.
80. Mbiti, *New Testament Eschatology*, 42.

whom the whole creation serveth."[81] One particular way to unpack the rule of God in the world is through the discourse on *divine providence*—God's act of governing, providing, healing, pruning, and redeeming God's creation. Of course, it is very difficult to measure or even detect God's providential work in the world that is filled with evils and gratuitous sufferings.

The penetrating words of the Hebrew prophet Habakkuk sum up the difficulty of assessing God's sovereign rule over God's creation in the midst of evil and suffering in the world: "How long, O LORD, will I call for help, and You will not hear? I cry out to You, 'Violence!' Yet You do not save. Why do You make me see iniquity, and cause me to look on wickedness? Yes, destruction and violence are before me; strife exists and contention arises. Therefore the law is ignored and justice is never upheld. For the wicked surround the righteous; therefore justice comes out perverted" (Hab 1:1–4 NASB). Habakkuk also cautions against moving too quickly to the conclusion that God is absent from the world or is not actively involved in its affairs (Hab 1:5–11). Yet theologians should not ignore the force of the question about how God is really bringing God's kingdom to this present world, in the present time. Some early Jewish leaders (such as the Zealots) sought to make God's kingdom visible through political means. Some religious leaders (especially the rabbis) taught people to bring God's kingdom nearer "through repentance, keeping the commandments and good works."[82]

But if God's reign has been ongoing (even before the Christ-event), how should we understand Jesus' words "your kingdom come" (Matt 6:10)? For Augustine of Hippo, it is the entrance of God's kingdom in people. In other words, the kingdom of God, which has always existed, can come afresh in people when they consciously accept God's reign and surrender their lives to God. He writes, "We pray that it [God's kingdom] may come *in us*; we pray that we may be found *in it*. For come it certainly will; but what will it profit thee, if it shall find thee at the left hand."[83] Craig Blomberg extends the meaning of "your kingdom come" beyond the scope of an individual to include the cosmic sphere. For him, to pray "your kingdom God" is to acknowledge God's reign over God's creation. It is also to desire for God to accomplish God's purposes for the world.[84] If we define God's providence broadly to include God's making, remaking, and renewing of God's creation, we can conceive of the expression "your kingdom come" as a theological address to humans. To pray for the arrival of God's kingdom,

81. Augustine, *Sermons on New Testament Lessons* 6.6 (*NPNF*[1] 6:275).

82. Ratzinger, *Eschatology*, 28.

83. Augustine, *Sermons on New Testament Lessons* 6.6 (*NPNF*[1] 6:276).

84. Blomberg, *Matthew*, 119.

therefore, is to acknowledge and accept God's summons to humans to live in expectation of God's providential care and also to become involved in God's reign in the world by embodying the sort of life that characterizes the kingdom.

God the Son as the Embodiment of God's Reign: Jesus' Role in God's Kingdom

In christological terms, Jesus Christ is the divine-human agent whose life concretizes God's kingdom. Although the idea of God's reign in the world permeates the Hebrew Scripture, it was Jesus who popularized the expression "kingdom of God." In the 122 times the expression "kingdom of God" (*basileia tou theou* in Greek) appears in the New Testament, Jesus used it ninety times.[85] Theologians and New Testament scholars are in agreement that the concept of God's kingdom figures prominently in the teaching of Jesus Christ. But what exactly is the relationship between Jesus Christ and God's kingdom?

As the Messiah, Jesus could not be a spectator in God's reign. Jesus was not merely a proclaimer of the kingdom of God. The German theologian Martin Luther (1483–1546) argued that one of Jesus' missions in the world was to "begin and establish" God's kingdom. He went on to say that true believers in Christ serve under Jesus Christ, the King.[86] Jesus Christ embodied God's reign by announcing its continuing *presence*

> "Without the kingdom Jesus would be little more than an abstract object of study; without Jesus, however, the kingdom would only be a partial reality."
>
> —Jon Sobrino, *Christology at the Crossroads*, 37

(indicating God's kingdom is not something that is merely in the future), by demonstrating its *characteristics* (showing that God's kingdom is not merely an abstraction), and exemplifying its *way* (charting out the course of the kingdom and the role of humans in it). For Jesus Christ, God's kingdom is "near" (*ēggiken* in Greek; see Mark 1:15) and is "upon" (*ephthasen* in Greek; see Luke 11:20) us. Here, it seems that Jesus expected that his audience would become increasingly aware of God's reign in their communities and beyond. Therefore, Christopher Rowland's suggestion that the phrase "kingdom of God" refers to "a future age of glory, when the divine will would be revealed in human affairs" is misealding.[87] If the kingdom of God, as Row-

---

85. Ratzinger, *Eschatology*, 25.

86. Luther, *Temporal Authority*, 662.

87. Rowland, "Eschatology of the New Testament," 59.

land acknowledges, "was already at work in Jesus' ministry," the idea of the kingdom as "a future age of glory" would be a contradiction. His miraculous works highlight and make more glaring the continuous presence and manifestation of God's kingdom in the world in which he lived.

Jon Sobrino has noted that in order to understand what Jesus means by the phrase the "kingdom of God" we must consider what "he *says* and *does* in the service of the kingdom of God."[88] After the arrest of John the Baptist, the one who popularized the Jewish expectation of the Messiah, he sent his disciples to inquire of Jesus whether he was indeed the expected one, the Messiah (Matt 11:2). Jesus sent the following words back to John: "The blind receive sight, the lame walk, those who have leprosy are cured, the deaf hear, the dead are raised, and the good news is preached to the poor" (Matt 11:4–5 NIV). Jesus' message to John provides two important clues about the nature of God's kingdom. First, God's kingdom is not primarily political in the sense of acquiring political spheres and maximizing political influence through the use of force. Rather, God's kingdom brings about the well-being of God's creatures. Second, God's kingdom is equally not *apolitical* because bringing about the well-being of God's creatures requires exposing and confronting the forces that oppose their well-being. It requires preaching the good news to the poor, proclaiming freedom to those under the imprisonment of evil structures, liberating the oppressed and empowering them to stand up against oppression (see Luke 4:18; cf. Isaiah 61:1–2).

God's kingdom requires *conversion*—an enduring redirection of human beings toward God's visions for the world as embodied by Jesus Christ. It is not a coincidence that Jesus, after announcing that God's kingdom is at hand, immediately adds, "Repent and believe the good news!" (Mark 1:15 NIV). We can construe Jesus as the good news, that is, as the embodiment of God's reign. Followers of Jesus Christ "enter" into God's reign by repenting of their sins and turning toward God, which entails accepting Jesus' understanding of the relationship between God and God's creation. It is to follow Jesus Christ in making God's reign more visible by confronting the structures and forces that oppose God's reign—God's remaking, renewing, and reconciling of God's creation. Given, as I have argued earlier, that God's kingdom is not about acquiring political territories, the Christian teaching about God's kingdom should not be used to justify holy wars (such as the Crusades), imperialism, and colonization of "non-Christian" territories. In fact one may argue, as Richard Horsley does, that Jesus' exorcism (expulsion

---

88. Sobrino, "Jesus and the Kingdom of God," 108.

of an occupying alien force) is a critique of imperialism.[89] Also, given that God's kingdom is not *a*political, Christians must become actively involved in transforming their societies; they must follow in Jesus' footsteps, denouncing and confronting unjust social systems and structures.[90]

God the Holy Spirit as the Facilitator of God's Reign

Two of the visible ways in which God's kingdom is made manifest are through the *Christ-event* (the being, person, and work of Jesus Christ) and the *Church-event* (the community of God's people). The Holy Spirit is indispensable to the successful kingdom-work of both Jesus Christ and the church. Jesus Christ demonstrated God's rule (*regnum Dei* in Latin) through his obedience to God the Father and through miraculous healings and good works, which he performed by the power of the Holy Spirit (Matt 12:22–37; Acts 10:38). During his earthly ministry, Jesus, through the power of the Holy Spirit, embarked on the mission of demonstrating what a world under God's reign would look like. It is a world governed by God's providence, forgiveness, giving of life, and bringing of humanity into divine fellowship—all of which come through repentance (Matt 6:9–14). The risen Jesus Christ continues to make God's kingdom visible in the world through his disciples who are empowered by the Holy Spirit (John 20:21–23; Acts 1:4–5, 8). We can say, therefore, that *regnum Christi* (Christ's rule) is ongoing as a result of the Holy Spirit's regenerative work and empowerment of God's people to embody Jesus Christ as God's good news to the world.

In chapter 4, we saw that the "church" is an *assembly* called into existence by God the Father, governed by the person and work of Jesus Christ, and empowered by the Holy Spirit. In other words, the church derives its existence from the Triune God. The Holy Spirit makes the reign of God possible in the lives of God's people. The members of the church, as Christ's disciples, are not mere spectators in God's kingdom. According to Martin Luther, people who belong to God's kingdom (as opposed to belonging to the kingdom of the world), are ruled by the Holy Spirit who enables them to do justice and also restrain them from doing injustice to no one.[91]

In his commentary on the pastoral work (especially on exorcism) of the German pastor and theologian Johann Christoph Blumhardt (1805–80), Christian Collins Winn argues that for Blumhardt "the struggle and call of the Christian is to both wait on and hasten towards the presence of

89. Horsley, *Jesus and the Empire*, 107.

90. Sobrino, "Jesus and the Kingdom of God," 114–15.

91. Luther, *Temporal Authority*, 663.

Christ—which is also the kingdom of God in the world—through identification with the suffering of the world."[92] Christians are to "groan on behalf" of all people, especially those who are sick and suffering."[93] James Cone argues that to enter into the kingdom is to "enter into salvation." For him, the Christian concept of salvation should be understood in the light of human historical contexts. For example, for those suffering injustice, salvation means liberation from oppression and from oppressors. Cone's point is that the hope which is offered to those who are suffering in this life should not be futuristic but rather must be concretized and exemplified in this life.[94] The Triune God calls the people of God to exhibit and make visible the *regnum Dei* by acting in a manner that fosters forgiveness, healing, justice, peace, and well-being, which are the hallmarks of God's kingdom.

Christ' Second Coming

According to the Gospel of Mark, Jesus made the following prediction about himself: "And then they will see the Son of Man coming in clouds with great power and glory" (Mark 13:26 ESV). Many Christians have interpreted these words as referring to the return of the risen Christ to earth—his "Second Coming." The earliest Aramaic-speaking Christian communities prayed "Our Lord, come" (*Maranatha* in Aramaic; see 1 Cor 16:22). As stated earlier, *parousia* ("presence" or "coming") is the Greek word from which the doctrine of the Second Coming is developed (see 1 Cor 15:23; 1 Thess 4:15). The Nicene Creed says the following about Christ's Second Coming: he "will come to judge the living and the dead." This understanding of the Second Coming derives from the literal reading of some biblical passages such as Matt 24:30–31, John 14:1–4, Acts 1:9–11, 1 Thess 4:15–18, 2 Thess 1:5–10, and 2 Pet 1:16–18. The doctrine of the Second Coming is a form of political Christology: it relativizes human political powers and points Christians in the direction of the risen Lord who will rule supremely above all human powers and authorities.

The expression "second coming," of course, presupposes a "first coming." The first coming refers to the *incarnation* (God's eternal son becoming a human being in the person of Jesus of Nazareth) and the entirety of Jesus' earthly life, which includes his teaching, miraculous work, his death on the cross, his resurrection, and his ascension. A person's view of each of these aspects of the first coming, especially the resurrection, will greatly impact

92. Collins Winn, "Groaning for the Kingdom," 58.

93. Ibid., 73.

94. Cone, *Black Theology of Liberation*, 124–25.

the person's view of the second coming. For example, if a person denies the bodily resurrection of Jesus Christ, the person will reject his physical return to earth to rule as God's co-regent.

The beliefs in Jesus Christ's Second Coming and his millennial reign have informed certain behaviors of Christians. Examples of such behaviors are the truancy of some Christians in Thessalonica (2 Thess 3:6–15), protest against social oppression in Latin America and South Africa, terrifying sermons as seen in the "end time" sermons in the United States and beyond, zeal for evangelism, especially among Pentecostals,[95] and withdrawal from social and economic activities, as seen in the actions of some members of Last Days Deliverance Ministries in Nigeria following the founder's prophecy that Jesus was returning before or by the end of 2001.[96] Some biblical scholars have argued that the earliest followers of Jesus expected his second return during their lifetime. The belief in and hope for Jesus' Second Coming has been an impetus for Christians to seek to live continuously in conformity to the life of Christ. Ralph Martin argues that from the "standpoint of Scripture, living in expectancy of Christ's coming—indeed longing for it!—is an essential element of Christian life itself."[97] In the remainder of this section, I will explore the question, what is the nature of Jesus' Second Coming? I will describe two related theological answers to this question.

The Second Coming as a Physical and Personal Event

According to N. T. Wright, Jesus' presence in the lives and communities of his followers must be distinguished from the Second Coming. He argues that Jesus' Second Coming is a future event in which he will meet with people who have known and loved him. It will be a meeting analogous to "meeting face to face" with "someone we have only known by letter, telephone, or perhaps e-mail."[98] Also, when Jesus appears, he will execute God's judgment. Unlike his present mode of being the lord of the world, Jesus in the future, as a judge, will confront "the world personally and visibly" (Phil 2:10–11).[99] Wright distances his view of the Second Coming from theologians who associate the Second Coming with the doctrine of *rapture*—Christ's meeting of Christians halfway in the air. Wright contends that the idea of "rapture" is foreign to the New Testament.

95. Ma, "Pentecostal Eschatology," 97–100.
96. Ojo, "Eschatology and the African Society," 95.
97. Martin, *Is Jesus Coming Soon?*, 55.
98. Wright, *Surprised by Hope*, 123.
99. Ibid., 142.

Against those who argue that Jesus predicted his Parousia,[100] Wright contends that the concept of the Second Coming cannot be traced back to Jesus Christ. Commenting on Mark 13:26, he argues that Jesus' words "the Son of man coming on the clouds," when it is understood in the context of Daniel 7, refers to God's vindication of him by raising him from the dead and other events that would take place after his resurrection such as "the destruction of the Temple, the system that opposed him and his mission."[101] For Wright, the concept of the Second Coming was developed by Jesus' disciples after the resurrection and ascension, particularly the Apostle Paul.[102] He goes on to argue that Paul uses the metaphor of *parousia* (royal presence) to convey his belief that the risen and exalted Jesus Christ "will be personally present, the dead will be raised, and the living Christians will be transformed."[103] The *coming* or *appearing* of Jesus, therefore, does not refer to his descending from the sky. For Wright, God's world (what we call heaven) and our world (earth) intersect in different ways. In the future, "when heaven and earth are joined together in the new way God has promised," Jesus will "appear to us—and we will appear to him, and to one another, in our own true identity."[104]

The Second Coming as Already Not-Yet Event

On how to understand the word "soon" usually associated with the Second Coming, Ralph Martin contends that the timing of Jesus' return is a mystery.[105] To him, knowing when Jesus Christ will come is "not the most significant thing" about the Second Coming. What is most significant, Martin argues, is to be attentive to the different ways in which Jesus is coming to people. Martin notes that Jesus has already come into people's lives, is coming into people's lives, and will come in the future physically in glory to reign over the human race.[106] He writes that Jesus "surely is present now and wanting to come to each and every one of us as we open our hearts and minds to him and surrender to the grace he offers to us all. He is coming. He is truly coming in so many ways to all of us."[107]

100. See Schweitzer, *Quest of the Historical Jesus*, 332.
101. Wright, *Surprised by Hope*, 125.
102. Ibid., 127–28.
103. Ibid., 133.
104. Ibid., 135.
105. Martin, *Is Jesus Coming Soon?*, 150.
106. Ibid., 53.
107. Ibid., 153.

Construing the Second Coming as an already-not-yet event has several important theological implications. First, when the Second Coming is not understood primarily as a future event, it can help Christians move away from focusing on the exact timing of Jesus' return to earth. It may shield Christians from misleading predictions and speculation about the exact year, day, and time of the event. Second, if the Second Coming is not construed merely in futuristic terms, it can help Christians avoid the temptation to live primarily for the future rewards they will receive at the coming of Jesus and to focus instead on making Jesus present in the lives of people (especially people who do not share the Christian faith and the downtrodden in our societies) through their actions. Third, imagining the Second Coming as an already-not-yet event can help Christians avoid the unwarranted conflict between the "physical" and "nonphysical" ways Jesus *is* and *will be* present in the world.

Resurrection

"Resurrection" makes sense only when it is understood within the horizon of "death." If we define biological death as the loss of a biological life, then,

> FOCUS QUESTION:
> In what ways have Christians understood the meaning of resurrection?

resurrection as the "giving of a new life" to people who are dead can be construed as a solution to death or as the evidence of death's defeat (for those who see death as an enemy). This is perhaps the reason the Apostle Paul mockingly asks, "Where, O death, is your victory? Where, O death, is your sting?" (1 Cor 15:55 NIV; cf. Isa 25:8). Many Christians see resurrection as God's act of giving a new life to those who are dead, albeit with transformed bodies. Theologians who write on the doctrine of resurrection, like many other eschatological themes, speculate about what will happen in the future. Since most of the *future* eschatological events are not natural and analogous to common human experience, we cannot speak precisely about their nature or timing.

In spite of the difficulties surrounding the doctrine of resurrection, many Christians continue to see it as an essential doctrine to Christian eschatological hope. Some Christians live in cultures where the scientific knowledge that points to the finality of death reigns supremely. Others live in cultures where the hope for a future resurrection of humans is what inspires them to endure sufferings and evils in this present world. And some live in cultures where the hope for a future resurrection is the foundation on which they establish the veracity of Christianity's teaching about Jesus of

Nazareth as God incarnate. Christians who trust in Jesus as God's salvific agent and who believe that God raised him from the dead—a divine act of vindication of Jesus' relationship with God—must shoulder the responsibility of articulating the *meaning* of Jesus' resurrection and its *significance* for Christian eschatological hope.

Traditionally, the hope that God will raise people from the dead is grounded in the belief that God bodily raised Jesus Christ from the dead in the power of the Holy Spirit (Rom 1:3-4; 8:11; 1 Cor 6:14; 1 Pet 3:18-19). The Apostle Paul expressed this belief in his instruction to Christians at Corinth who were anxious about the reasonableness of hoping for a bodily resurrection. "But if it is preached that Christ has been raised from the dead," Paul asked rhetorically, "how can some of you say that there is no resurrection of the dead? If there is no resurrection of the dead, then not even Christ has been raised." Paul was so convinced that God raised Jesus from the dead that he was willing to stake the creditability and relevance of Christianity on it. He wrote, "And if Christ has not been raised, our preaching is useless and so is your faith. More than that, we are then found to be false witnesses about God, for we have testified about God that he raised Christ from the dead. But he did not raise him if in fact the dead are not raised. For if the dead are not raised, then Christ has not been raised either. And if Christ has not been raised, your faith is futile" (1 Cor 15:12-17 NIV). Theologians face the difficulty of showing that Jesus was raised bodily from the dead since rising from the dead is not a normal human experience.

Would people who die be resurrected? Our personal experience and our knowledge of the laws of nature tell us that people who die do not rise from the dead. Even if one grants to Christians that Jesus' (bodily) resurrection was an isolated exception—a random anomaly—they still must explain how this unusual event is relevant for the Christian hope of bodily resurrection of human beings in the future. Therefore, the belief that someday in the future people who have died will be raised from the dead still poses a serious theological difficulty for Christians. This difficulty has made some theologians to take the *subjectivist* option that states that Jesus Christ was only raised from the dead metaphorically in the faith of his disciples. Many theologians have also remained unconvinced that Jesus was not *bodily* raised from the dead by God. It should be noted that these two positions (subjectivist and bodily resurrection) are grounded in Jesus' physical death. Some theories of resurrection-belief have been proposed, which are not grounded in the physical death of Jesus, as we will see later.

Before discussing the subjectivist and bodily views of Jesus' resurrection, I would like to note that any theological explanation of the Christian doctrine of resurrection, which hopes to appeal to people, should account for the role of "faith"—belief in God who has the ability to interfere in the natural process of life and death. Merely appealing to the biblical texts to speak of Jesus' resurrection as the only evidence for belief in God's resurrection is not sufficient for giving a full account of the Christian theology of resurrection. Neither will it do to take common human experience of the natural process of life and death as the only reliable criterion for evaluating the belief in resurrection. Explanation of what became of Jesus after his death, if it includes the Easter faith—that he was raised bodily from the dead—must be placed in a broader theological context: God, the giver of life, gave him a new life and body.

The Subjectivist Resurrection Position

Description: The laws of nature, physicists tell us, show that death is the end of biological life and that dead people stay dead. The Bible, theologians remind us, speaks of God's future transformation of this world in which dead people will be given new lives and bodies. For some of these theologians, the most sensible way to address the conflict between what the laws of nature and the Bible tell us about death is to reformulate the Christian concept of resurrection to fit into the knowledge we can scientifically gather from nature. As a result, these theologians reject the view of a future bodily resurrection of the dead.

Theological Warrants: The subjectivist view of resurrection states that the language of resurrection is a theological metaphor employed by the earliest followers of Jesus to communicate the *continuing presence* of the crucified Jesus in their minds and hearts. One way to encounter this continuing presence of Jesus Christ is through the Christian *kerygma*— the proclamation about Jesus Christ's person, work, and significance by his followers. This implies that Christians, as Rudolf Bultmann contends, should not concern themselves with the historicity of the resurrection for that would mean to "tie [their] faith in the word of God to the results of historical research."[108] In the subjectivist view, the post-resurrection appearance (or apparition) of Jesus Christ also points to his "continuing presence" in his followers.

One advocate of "the subjectivist resurrection position" is the American theologian Sallie McFague. Her understanding of the meaning of Jesus' resurrection is deeply shaped by the metaphor of the world as "God's body"—a theological way of speaking of God's presence in the world. The short excerpt below, taken from *Models of God*, highlights her conception of Jesus' resurrection, post-resurrection appearances, and ascension narratives.

108. See Bultmann, "New Testament and Mythology," 41.

The resurrection is a way of speaking about an awareness that the presence of God in Jesus is a permanent presence in our present. The appearance stories capture this awareness better than do the empty-tomb narratives with the associated interpretation of the bodily resurrection of Jesus and his ascension to glory.... Whatever the resurrection is, if interpreted in light of the appearance narratives, it is inclusive; it takes place in every present; it is the presence of God to us, not our translation into God's presence.

But what if we were to understand the resurrection and ascension not as the bodily translation of some individuals to another world—a mythology no longer credible to us—but as the promise of God to be permanently present, "bodily" present to us, in all places and times of our world? In what ways would we think of the relationship between God and the world were we to experiment with the metaphor of the universe as God's "body," God's palpable presence in all space and time?

[To] imagine the world *as* God's body . . . is not to say that the world *is* God's body or that God is present to us in the world. Those things we do not know; all that resurrection faith can do is imagine the most significant ways to speak of God's presence in one's own time. And the metaphor of the world as God's body presents itself as a promising candidate.[109]

Criticism : Critics of the subjectivist view of the resurrection of Jesus argue that it fails to account for the earliest Christians' devotion to Jesus as one whom God has vindicated by giving him a new life and a new body. The belief that God raised Jesus from the dead moved his earliest disciples at an astonishingly early period to devote to him as one whom God has exalted.[110] Since the New Testament presents God as the one who is responsible for Jesus' resurrection (Acts 2:32–33; Rom 4:24–25; 10:9; 1 Cor 6:14; 1 Cor 15; 1 Thess 4:4–15), denying his bodily resurrection has serious christological and theological consequences. Theologically, to deny Jesus' resurrection can be seen as a form of blasphemy since it is brought about by God the Father through the power of the Holy Spirit (Rom 1:3–4; 1 Pet 3:18–19). It amounts to a denial that Jesus was the beneficiary of God's power. Christologically, denying that God has raised Jesus from the dead entails denying his divine vindication as the Messiah and also as one who holds a unique status in God's redemptive work (Acts 2:32–36; Phil 2:9–11).[111] Jesus himself clearly

109. McFague, *Models of God*, 59–61. Emphasis mine.

110. Hurtado, "Resurrection-Faith and the 'Historical' Jesus," 35–52.

111. Ibid., 41–42.

anticipated that God would resurrect the dead (Mark 12:24–27). Denying Jesus' resurrection and his teaching about the future resurrection of the dead implies a denial of the authenticity of his message about God. Daniel Migliore cautions against two extreme views of the resurrection. First, he argues that the Easter message—Christ is risen!—cannot be demonstrated by modern historical research. Second, the view of resurrection as something that did not happen *to* Jesus but rather something that happened *in* his disciples, as argued in the subjectivist view, does not adequately account for scriptural testimonies about what *really* happened to Jesus on Easter morning.[112]

The Bodily Resurrection Position

Description: According to this position, Jesus of Nazareth was "really" dead, buried, and raised from the dead in a bodily recognizable form. Gerald O'Collins argues that the verbs used in 1 Cor 15:3–5 to describe Jesus' experience—namely, *died, buried, raised*, and *appeared*—convey "factual information about what happened to Jesus as well as expressing or at least implying the religious significance of what happened."[113]

Theological Warrants: Some theologians contend that holding a bodily resurrection position is not irreconcilable with the laws of nature. For them, what is required is a reimagining of the laws of nature to accommodate the future bodily resurrection of the dead. Some philosophical theologians argue that the laws of nature should be defined loosely to make room for God's infrequent interference in its operation. Without denying the "deterministic principle" of the laws of nature, Richard Swinburne argues that the laws of nature predictably determine things that happen in the universe "unless God (or some other supernatural agent) intervenes to set the law aside temporarily."[114] When understood in this way, the resurrection of Jesus Christ was an isolated event that was not the result of chance or arbitrary randomness (which is possible given the principle of indeterminacy as quantum mechanics or physics shows), but rather an event that could be traced back to God's intentional interference in the normal operation of the laws of nature. That God intervened in the process of the laws of nature to resurrect Jesus, for many theologians, is sufficient to hope that God will raise people from the dead in the future. The bodily resurrection of Jesus Christ was a peculiar event and a fore-

---

112. Migliore, *Faith Seeking Understanding*, 191–92.

113. O'Collins, *Christology*, 84.

114. Swinburne, *Resurrection of God Incarnate*, 18, 22.

taste of what will become of all people who are dead (1 Cor 6:14; 1 Thess 4:14–16).[115] The resurrection of Jesus Christ has no "true precedent," writes Larry Hurtdao. He goes on to argue that it is "not another example in a series of essentially similar events already known, but instead a *novum*. It is not simply another miracle, or even a grander miracle, but instead *sui generis*, an exercise of divine power and purpose that comprises a unique manifestation of eschatological reality."[116]

Other arguments presented in support of the bodily resurrection of Jesus Christ are the *empty tomb* where Jesus was buried, the *post-resurrection bodily appearances* of Jesus to his followers, and the *subsistence and expansion* of Christianity after the crucifixion of Jesus. On the argument of the empty tomb, theologians that hold the bodily resurrection view argue that Jesus' burial tomb was empty because he was raised from the dead by God. They reject suppositions that the tomb was empty either because his disciples stole his body and buried it in a secret location or that his corpse was devoured by scavenging animals.[117] They contend that God physically raised him from the dead, giving him a new body.[118] In the excerpt below, we see the summary of the arguments for the bodily resurrection view articulated by the British New Testament scholar N. T. Wright.

> Far and away the best historical explanation is that Jesus of Nazareth, having been thoroughly dead and buried, really was raised to life on the third day with a renewed body (not a mere "resuscitated corpse," as people sometimes dismissively say), a new *kind* of physical body, which left an empty tomb behind it because it had used up the material of Jesus' original body and which possessed new properties that nobody had expected or imagined but that generated significant mutations in the thinking of those who encountered it. If something like this happened, it would perfectly explain why Christianity began and why it took the shape it did.
>
> I do not claim . . . that I have hereby proved the resurrection in terms of some neutral standpoint. I am offering, rather, a historical challenge to other explanations and to the worldviews within which they gain their meaning. Precisely because at this point we are faced with worldview-level issues, there is no neutral ground, no island in the middle of the epistemological ocean as yet uncolonized by any of the warring continents. Historical argument alone

115. See Peters, *Anticipating Omega*, 40–44.

116. Hurtado, "Resurrection-Faith and the 'Historical' Jesus," 39.

117. Crossan, *Who Killed Jesus?*, 187–88.

118. Mbiti, *New Testament Eschatology*, 174.

> cannot force anyone to believe that Jesus was raised from the dead, but histori-
> cal argument is remarkably good at clearing away the undergrowth behind,
> which scepticisms of various sorts have long been hiding.[119]

Criticisms : Theologians who reject the bodily resurrection of Jesus contend that it is a myth and a nonhistorical narrative that is no longer credible.[120] The critics argue that the language of resurrection is metaphoric in the sense that it does not say in factual terms what really happened to Jesus' dead body. Rather, the resurrection language speaks metaphorically about God's continuous activity through Jesus' disciples (Rom 8:11). When construed in this way, the narratives about Jesus' resurrection presented in the New Testament say more about the experience and life of the early church than they say about Jesus' post-death experience.

Concluding Remarks on the Theological Meaning of Jesus' Resurrection and Its Eschatological Implications

Whether or not a theologian believes that God in the power of the Holy Spirit raised Jesus of Nazareth in a bodily form from the dead, the theologian should explicate the *theological implications* of Jesus' resurrection. I would like to conclude this discussion on the resurrection by highlighting some such theological implications.

First, Jesus' resurrection points us to *God's providence*, which in this context must be understood broadly to include God's remaking of the world, gradually bringing it to its fulfillment and meaning. Jesus' resurrection gives new meaning to the world as the creation of God. As Daniel Migliore notes, the hope for resurrection, which is grounded in the resurrection of Jesus Christ, extends to the "whole cosmos groaning for release from bondage to death (Rom 8:18–25)."[121] Resurrection, therefore, should be viewed in an eschatological already-not-yet context. Jesus' resurrection is indicative of God's continuing love for God's creation and God's ongoing redemptive work in the world. The resurrection of Jesus Christ, for example, shows that God cares about human life in this world. Christians, therefore, should oppose actions and structures that destroy human life or obstruct the flourishing of human life.

---

119. Wright, *Surprised by Hope*, 63–64; empahsis in original.

120. McFague, *Models of God*, 60.

121. Migliore, *Faith Seeking Understanding*, 196.

Second, Jesus' resurrection reveals *God's ruling against human beings' quest for ontological freedom.* The death of Jesus Christ exposes the height of human beings' quest for "ontological freedom"—that is, the desire to be human in a way that God does not desire for them (their determination to live apart from God). Jesus' resurrection shows that human rejection of God will not have the final word. God will overrule such rejection by accomplishing God's purpose for humanity. God's "ruling" should be construed broadly to include (*a*) the declaration of God's lordship over God's creation, (*b*) the showering of love and grace on humanity, and (*c*) God's determination to hold human beings accountable for their actions.

Finally, Jesus' resurrection points to *humans' responsibility within the scheme of God's activity in the world.* The belief in the resurrection should not lead Christians to live in abandonment of earthly matters. In other words, they should not live passively through *this world* in the assumption that God will make all things new in *the world to come.* For example, Christians should not have a nonchalant attitude toward evils and sufferings in this world. On the contrary, they must participate in God's providential activity by confronting evils. As Jon Sobrino puts it, "the resurrection sets in motion a life of service designed to implement in reality the eschatological ideals of justice, peace, and human solidarity. It is the earnest attempt to make those ideals real that enables us to comprehend what happened in Jesus' resurrection."[122]

Judgment

Many Christians live with the expectation that God will someday in the future pass definitive *judgment* on all humans. In *The City of God*, Augustine of Hippo (354–430 CE) writes that

FOCUS QUESTION:
What are the nature, scope, and purpose of God's final eschatological judgment?

people who accept the Scriptures as divinely inspired texts and who take the biblical passages that speak of God's judgment at "face value" cannot deny that God will at some point in human history judge all human beings.[123] Augustine avoids speculation about the time and duration of God's final judgment because of the metaphorical usage of the word "day" in the Bible. Also, Augustine contends that no one knows exactly the sequence of the events that will occur during the final judgment. Yet he speculates that the events may come in the follow-

122. Sobrino, *Christology at the Crossroads,* 255.

123. Augustine, *City of God* 20.1 (Walsh et al., 483).

ing order: Elijah the Thesbite will return, the Jews will believe, Antichrist will persecute the Church, Christ will be the Judge, the dead will rise, the good will be separated from the wicked, the world will suffer from fire but will be renewed.[124]

One of the issues that figures prominently in the final judgment discourse is "eternal life." The Apostle John, like some other New Testament writers, expects "eternal life" for those who "believe" in Jesus Christ (John 3:16). As we will see in the discussion on hell, some Christian theologians believe that eternal life is God's gift to people who accept God's offer of salvation. Those who reject God's offer of salvation will be destroyed or eliminated by God. But what is the nature of eternal life? Does eternal life have both *present* and *future* dimensions? If the Christian idea of "eternal life" is bound by finitude and temporality of this present life—the *now* of pre-mortem life—it follows that the hope of joining the resurrected Christ in the future and also of reigning with him in the life to come (2 Tim 2:11–12) is at best an illusion. While some theologians construe eternal life as *attaining the ultimate purpose* of human history without conceding an unending biological existence, others see eternal life as a new form of life, albeit in a different form of biological existence. Paul Tillich holds the former position while Ted Peters holds the later. According to Tillich, eternal life should be understood in the context of the "end" (*telos* in Greek, *finis* in Latin) of history. In biological terms, then, human history, the earth, and human life will be terminated. Theologically, God will bring human history to its intended end (purpose or aim)—this is eternal life. He writes, "Eternal life . . . includes the positive content of history, liberated from its negative distortions and fulfilled in its potentialities. . . . Life universal moves toward an end and is elevated into eternal life, its ultimate and ever present end."[125] For Tillich, the ultimate or final judgment consists in God's act of elevating the positive (good) in existence into *eternal life* (ever present fulfillment) and annihilating the negative (evil) in existence.[126] When eternal life is construed as *telos*, one can discard the notion of the "eternal destiny of the individual either as being everlastingly condemned or as being everlastingly saved."[127] Ted Peters argues that Tillich fails to give a complete picture of the dimensions of eternal life as imagined by the biblical writers. He agrees with Tillich that eternal life has a present dimension. But unlike Tillich, Peters insists that eternal life also has a future dimension.[128] Peters contends

124. Augustine, *City of God* 20.1 (Walsh et al., 492).

125. Tillich, *Systematic Theology*, 3:397–98.

126. Ibid., 398–99.

127. Ibid., 407.

128. Peters, "Eschatology," 352–53.

that the biblical teaching on resurrection points in the direction of life after biological death (1 Cor 15:20). For Peters, "The New Testament answer to the existential question posed by our own temporal end is not resignation to the present now but rather hope for future renewal."[129]

Returning to the theme of divine judgment, the notion of a future final judgment does not mean that God is not exercising judgment in the present. Augustine contends that God has been temporally judging the world since the *fall*—Adam's and Eve's sin. God, for Augustine, judges humans and angels collectively as well as individually.[130] Unlike God's ongoing judgment in this world, the final or last judgment will be God's ultimate act of dealing permanently with evil and of separating sinners and saints.[131] Augustine presents the risen Christ as the primary executor of God's final judgment. He argues that on the day of God's final judgment, "Christ will come from heaven to judge the living and the dead."[132] Augustine concedes it is not clear that the Old Testament passages (e.g., Isa 48:12–16) that speak of the "Day of the Lord" point ultimately to the risen Christ. He believes that when the risen Lord returns in his glory and power to judge the living and the dead, the Spirit of God will enable the living Jews to recognize him as the Messiah, repent, and believe in him.[133] What is of paramount importance to Augustine's discussion on the final judgment is that God the Father will execute the final judgment "by the means of the coming Son of Man."[134]

The Christian talk about God's eschatological judgment has both *immediate* and *remote* purposes. Its immediate purpose is to magnify the seriousness of sin and to deter people from living in sin. John Polkinghorne notes that the biblical language of God's definitive judgment is an "acknowledgement of moral seriousness" of sin. Also, it reminds us that "sin is no trivial matter, but in fact a deadly matter (Romans 6:23)."[135] The remote purpose of Christian talk about God's eschatological judgment is to highlight God's moral rectitude and authority to bring God's creatures to justice. In the remainder of this section, I will discuss two major themes—hell and heaven—that are traditionally associated with God's final judgment.

129. Ibid., 352.

130. Augustine, *City of God* 20.1 (Walsh et al., 484).

131. Ibid.

132. Augustine, *City of God* 20.1 (Walsh et al., 483).

133. Augustine, *City of God* 20.1 (Walsh et al., 489–90).

134. Augustine, *City of God* 20.1 (Walsh et al., 490).

135. Polkinghorne, *God of Hope*, 129.

Hell

It is commonplace in Christian theology to see *hell* as a form of evil, if not the greatest evil. Wilko van Holten notes two ways in which hell can be construed as a form of evil. First, hell entails being "separated from God forever." Second, hell is associated with an elongated "mental and/or physical suffering inflicted" upon those who are outside of God's beatific vision.[136] Traditionally, Christians have spoken of hell as a future experience of people who reject God and refuse God's offer of salvation. I classify the major Christian theories of the nature, purpose, and duration of hell into three broad categories: the punitive eternal theory, the punitive temporal theory, and the purgative temporal theory.

Punitive Eternal Theory of Hell

Theological and Biblical Arguments: In the "punitive eternal theory," unbelievers—those who reject God and God's offer of salvation—will be consigned to hell, where they will suffer eternally (Rev 14:9–12; 20:10). The second-century theologian Justin Martyr (died ca. 165 CE) wrote the following words regarding the final destiny of all rational creatures of God who died in their rebellion against God: "[Satan] would be sent into the fire with his host, and the men who follow him, and would be punished for an endless duration, Christ foretold."[137] Douglas Moo shares a similar view. He asserts that God's punishment of people in hell is irreversible. People who are sent to hell by God will remain there eternally because a person can only escape it and its consequences in this present life by accepting Jesus Christ as the Savior.[138] Citing 2 Thess 1:8–9, Moo states that the word "destruction" (*olethros* in Greek) in verse 9 does not necessarily imply "extinction."[139] He argues that when the word is placed in a broader context of Paul's teaching on God's final judgment of sinners, *olethros* (destruction) should be understood as "ruin" rather than "extinction." In other words, for Moo, God will not annihilate people in hell. That this is the case, Moo argues, is evident in Paul's usage of the word "eternal" (*aiōnios* in Greek) alongside *olethros* (2 Thess 1:9). He concludes that people in hell will live unceasingly away from God's presence.[140] For R. Albert Mohler, rejecting or revising the view that unrepentant sinners will

136. Holten, "Eschatology with a Vengeance," 182.

137. Justin Martyr, *First Apology* 28 (*ANF* 1:172).

138. Moo, "Paul on Hell," 96, 102.

139. Ibid., 104–5.

140. Ibid., 108–9

suffer "everlasting conscious punishment" undermines both Christianity's teaching about God and the salvific value of the Christian gospel. He cautions Evangelicals against succumbing to the pressure coming from modern cultures concerning the scandal of hell.[141]

Augustine of Hippo is one of the earliest holders of the punitive eternal theory of hell. For him, the Bible plainly teaches that unbelievers will suffer eternally in hell. The following excerpts are taken from *The City of God*.

> It is not easy to find a proof that will convince unbelievers of the possibility of human bodies remaining not merely active, alive, and uncorrupted after death, but also of continuing forever in the torments of fire.[142]
>
> Why should God be unable to raise bodies from the dead and allow the bodies of the damned to suffer in eternal fire, seeing that He made a universe filled with uncounted miracles in the heavens and on earth, in the air and in the ocean—a universe, therefore, which is a greater and nobler miracle than any of the miracles of which it is full?[143]
>
> Suffice it to say . . . first, that living creatures can continue in fire without being consumed and in pain without suffering death; second, that this is in virtue of a miracle of the omnipotent Creature; and third, that anyone who denies the possibility of this miracle is simply unaware of the Source [God] of all that is wonderful in all natures whatsoever.[144]

Criticism of the Punitive Eternal Theory: Critics of this theory argue that the idea that God will torture people in hell eternally is not only offensive but also a contradiction to the biblical teaching about God. The Bible, they argue, presents God as a just and omnibenevolent being whose nature is love. Also, some critics point out that the word "eternal," which sometimes is associated with God's judgment of impenitent sinners, refers to the permanency of their judgment rather than the state and duration of their physical sufferings in hell.[145]

---

141. Moehler, "Modern Theology," 40–41.

142. Augustine, *City of God* 21.2 (Walsh et al., 495).

143. Augustine, *City of God* 21.7 (Walsh et al., 499).

144. Augustine, *City of God* 21.9 (Walsh et al., 503–4).

145. Pinnock, "Annihilationism," 466.

Punitive Temporal Theory of Hell

Theological and Biblical Arguments: Annihilationism and conditionalism (also called "conditional immortality") are two major views that belong to the punitive temporary theory of hell. *Annihilationism* teaches that the suffering of people in hell will be cut short by means of extinction. John Stott, the British Evangelical theologian, has urged his fellow Evangelicals to be open to the possibility of the annihilation of people who ultimately reject God's offer of salvation as a "legitimate, biblically founded alternative" to the "eternal conscious torment" position.[146] For annihilationists, those who are objects of God's wrath will suffer temporarily because God will withdraw the gift of life from them. Unlike conditionalism, annihilationism holds that human beings are created immortal and can only cease to exist when God the Creator withdraws life from them. God will destroy unrepentant sinners (Ps 37:9–18; Matt 10:28; 2 Thess 1:9; Rev 20:14–15). The excerpts below highlights the argument for annihilationism put forward by Clark Pinnock, one of its major advocates.

> Annihilationism represents the conviction that the finally impenitent have no real life after death, save to be raised temporally only to be condemned. The choices which they have made in life will be respected, which means that they will have no part in the kingdom of God and, being severed from the source of life, they will exist no more as persons. The biblical terms which may point to this are death, destruction, perishing, and the like. The term annihilation, which sounds rather technical, may be a distraction. (Elimination might be a better word than annihilation . . .) The chief point is just that persons who choose hell by their actions will not live any longer as human beings. The issue is that, once the gift of life is withdrawn by God, the lost will cease to exist as persons. . . . There is a road that leads to life and another that leads to destruction. After this first death, there is the resurrection, but after the second death, there is only destruction for the finally impenitent.[147]

Conditionalism teaches that people who are objects of God's wrath will not live forever because they have not accepted God's gift of eternal life, which comes through faith in Jesus Christ. Exponents of conditionalism argue that human beings are created "only potentially immortal" and

146. Edwards and Stott, *Evangelical Essentials*, 320.
147. Pinnock, "Annihilationism," 464.

that those who are united with Christ (mystical union) will inherit immortality.[148] Since those who reject Jesus Christ will not experience the mystic union, they will cease to exist. Both annihilationism and conditionalism share the view that the life and suffering of unrepentant sinners will be temporal in hell. Edward William Fudge argues that God alone is immortal (1 Tim 6:16); therefore, only God can give human beings the gift of immortality. For him, God will raise those who died without accepting Christ for destruction and not to torment them forever. In other words, they will not be given the gift of eternal life, which God reserves only for people who accept the gift of salvation. The purpose of hell is to consume unrepentant sinners. Below is an excerpt from his essay in *Two Views of Hell*.

> The notion that the wicked will live forever in inescapable pain contradicts the clear, consistent teaching of Scripture from Genesis to Revelation.
>
> Jesus Christ warns his hearers of the terrible consequences of rejecting God's gift of eternal life. The alternative, he says, is to be condemned and destroyed, to lose one's life and to perish. People should fear God's wrath, Jesus warns, because God is able to destroy both body and soul in hell. Jesus compares such a fate to that of dead trees or weeds that are burned up, to that of a house destroyed by a hurricane, to that of someone crushed by a huge, falling boulder.
>
> Paul's epistles present the final choices of salvation and wrath, life and death. Paul says that the lost will "die," "perish" and be "destroyed." Paul explains the "eternal punishment" of which Jesus warned and specifies that it will be "eternal destruction." Once destroyed, the lost will never be seen again.[149]

Criticism of the Punitive Temporal Theory: Some critics of annihilationism and conditionalism point out that the word "destruction," which is used in the Bible to describe the condition of those whom God has not saved, should not be taken literally—as *ceasing to exist*. Robert Peterson, for example, contends that exponents of annihilationism (and also conditionalism) defend these positions not from a clear teaching of the Scriptures. He insists that the Scriptures never clearly say that God will exterminate unrepentant sinner in hell. He warns against the danger of formulating argument for annihilationism and conditionalism from silence.[150] Other critics

148. Morgan, "Annihilationism," 196.

149. Fudge, "Case for Conditionalism," 80–81.

150. Peterson, "Case for Traditionalism," 85.

also argue the views of hell that deny eternal suffering of sinners will weaken the force of the gospel and also can discourage people from accepting Jesus as the Savior of the world.[151]

Purgative Temporal Theory of Hell

Theological and Biblical Arguments: Some theologians argue that God punishes sinners with the aim of saving and restoring them to fellowship. For such theologians, the punitive theories of hell present God's punishment as what has no salvific value for those who are being punished. On the contrary, they argue that hell is a metaphor that describes God's process of purifying sinners before they are brought back into divine fellowship.

The "purgative temporal theory of hell" should be distinguished from the doctrine of *purgatory*, which is one of the traditional teachings of the Roman Catholic Church.[152] According to this doctrine, there are two *final* destinations of people—heaven or hell. Purgatory is somewhat like an intermediary "state, place, or condition" of purgation for the people whose sins on the one hand have prevented from entering into heaven, but on the other hand are not sufficient to earn them a place in hell.[153] This entails that the purification process of some members of the church takes place not only in this life but also in a post-mortem period that lasts until God's final judgment, when people in purgatory will transition to heaven. Yet the existence of purgatory, as Jerry Walls argues, is a reminder to Christians that "there is no shortcut to sanctity."[154] John Thiel has argued that purgatory "has fallen off the eschatological map" of many Roman Catholics since the Second Vatican Council. Thiel assigns a partial blame to the Second Vatican Council for the vanishing of the doctrine of purgatory in many Roman Catholics' repertoire of doctrines. For Thiel, the Second Vatican Council's emphasis on the power of God's grace to bring believers to salvation may have "undermined the detailed accounting of personal virtue and sin" that was emphasized by the Council of Trent.[155]

Protestant critics of the doctrine of purgatory argue that it has no biblical basis (by biblical, of course, they mean the teaching that can be

151. Wenham, *Goodness of God*, 39.

152. For a survey of the historical development of the doctrine of purgatory in the Roman Catholic Church, see Le Goff, *The Birth of Purgatory*.

153. Hayes, "Purgatorial View," 93.

154. Walls, *Heaven*, 58.

155. Thiel, *Icons of Hope*, 58.

grounded in the Protestant canon).[156] They contend that the doctrine of purgatory is derived from 2 Macc 12:41–46, which is excluded from the Protestant canon. Also, some Protestant critics argue that the doctrine of purgatory implies that God's salvation is based on human works. They insist the Bible consistently teaches that God's salvation is based on God's grace and not on human works (Eph 2:8–9).[157] Some attack the doctrine of purgatory from the perspective of the cult of the saints. Many Roman Catholics venerate the saints as those who are interceding on behalf of both the living and people in purgatory. The critics fear that the veneration of the departed saints diminishes the intercessory work of Jesus Christ and the Holy Spirit.[158] In defense of the intercessory work of the saints, Thiel argues that "the saints' engagement in supernatural forgiveness is not an escapist alternative to this-worldly obligation but instead offers a way of imagining a continuity in achieved solidarity in the communion that surpasses a solidarity of mere intention and hope."[159]

Returning to the "purgative temporal theory of hell," one of its theological consequences is *universalism*—that God will ultimately purify and redeem all people. In chapter 3, I discussed universalism. Rather than rehearsing the arguments for universalism (or the universalist position) here, I will focus on how the Greek Orthodox theologian Kallistos Ware brings the idea of universalism to bear on the biblical language of hell. Ware is convinced that there is sufficient evidence in the Scriptures that point us in the direction of a universal restoration of all human beings to divine fellowship. Ware argues that the Apostle Paul did not merely speak of the possibility of God's restoration of all humans to divine fellowship. On the contrary, he argues that Paul was "confident" that God would do so (see 1 Cor 15:22, 28; Rom 5:18; 11:32; 1 Tim 2:4).[160] Ware also argues that the idea of God punishing people eternally in hell is incommensurate with the scale of humans' sins against God. He writes, "It is blasphemous to assert that the Holy Trinity is vengeful. In any case, it seems contrary to justice that God should inflict an infinite punishment in requital for what is only a finite amount of wrongdoing."[161] Ware finds Origen's view of God's restorative judgment deeply fascinating and helpful for dealing with the problem

---

156. For discussions on the biblical canon, see Ezigbo, *Introducing Christian Theologies*, 1:80–86.

157. Erickson, *Christian Theology*, 1186.

158. Thiel, *Icons of Hope*, 16.

159. Ibid., 182.

160. Ware, *Inner Kingdom*, 194–97.

161. Ibid., 203.

of hell. For Ware, God should be seen as a physician who heals the world. Hell, therefore, should be construed as a temporary instrument God will use to purify sinners. He concludes: "Hell exists as a possibility because free will exists. Yet trusting in the inexhaustible attractiveness of God's love, we venture to express hope—it is no more than a hope—that in the end . . . we shall find that there is nobody there."[162]

Criticism of the Purgative Temporal Theory: Critics of this theory argue that it disregards the seriousness with which the Scriptures speak about God's final punishment for those who reject Christ. For them, God's personal judgment on sinners is eternal.[163] For criticism against universalism, see chapter 3.

Heaven

In a highly emotive speech, Jesus said to his disciples, "In my Father's house are many rooms; if it were not so, I would have told you. I am going there

> FOCUS QUESTION:
> What does "heaven" mean in Christian eschatological hope?

to prepare a place for you. And if I go and prepare a place for you, I will come back and take you to be with me that you may be where I am. You know the way to the place where I am going" (John 14:2–4 NIV). As a child, I learned in Sunday school that heaven is the place Jesus has gone to prepare a place for his disciples. I was taught to live and long for heaven. The idea of not going to heaven was terrifying, especially since the only alternative was hell. Belief in heaven has continued to thrive among Christians, even those living in parts of the world that are deeply influenced by atheism and the scientific predictions about cosmic dissolution. For example, many American adults still believe in heaven. A 2013 poll conducted by Harris Interactive showed that 68 percent of adults in America believe in heaven and 58 percent believe in hell.[164] What these statistics do not show, of course, is what exactly those who participated in the polling mean when they hear the word "heaven." Jerry Walls contends that a major reason belief in heaven has declined is that people "think they can make moral and spiritual sense of their lives without it."[165] In parts of the world in which Christianity remains a prominent force, such as in sub-Saharan Africa, the hope for heaven is not seen as a prescientific

162. Ibid., 215.

163. See Horton, *Christian Faith*, 984.

164 Shannon-Missal, "Americans' Belief in God, Miracles and Heaven Declines."

165. Walls, *Heaven*, 11.

and antiquated belief that has no relevance to human questions about the ultimate meaning of life.

The word "heaven" (*shamayim* in Hebrew; *ouranos* in Greek) is one of the most used terms in Christian eschatology. "The notion that this life is no more than preparation for a life beyond," Jürgen Moltmann writes, "is the story of a refusal to live, and a religious fraud. It is inconsistent with the living God, who is a 'lover of life.' In that sense it is a religious atheism."[166] Moltmann makes this claim as a counter theological move against the temptation to see life in this present world as a mere passage to a future otherworldly life. Seeing life in the present world in this way, Moltmann argues, can lead people to squander the treasures of the world, an act that amounts to selling the treasures of this world "off cheap to heaven."[167]

In Christianity, the discourses about heaven have followed different paths, resulting in competing positions on its nature and purpose. I will describe briefly the literal view and the symbolic view. In the literal view, heaven is a real place, whereas in the symbolic view, heaven is a state of *being* or *living* in the beatific vision of God.

Literal View: Heaven as a Physical Locale: God's Abode

The view that describes heaven as a physical place has a long history in Christianity. Tertullian (ca. 160–ca. 220 CE), for instance, spoke about heaven as a place "where Christ is already sitting at the Father's right hand."[168] Many Christians continue to imagine heaven as a place in which God resides. Writing about the prominence of the word heaven in American Christianity, Gary Scott Smith notes that many American theologians have perceived heaven as "a physical place" of beauty and ending joy.[169] In his study of the usages of the word heaven in the Old Testament and the New Testament, Wilbur Smith, notes that it refers to three major realms: atmospheric heaven, celestial heaven, and the abode of God. He concludes that in eschatological terms the notion of heaven as *God's abode* or place of dwelling is what those who are saved hope for in the future (Luke 24:50–51; Acts 7:54–56).[170] For Robert Yarbrough, we can deduce from Jesus' teaching that heaven is "a place of blessing and of unending joy in the presence of the Lord."[171]

166. Moltmann, *Coming of God*, 50.

167. Ibid.

168. Tertullian, *Treatise on the Soul* 55 (ANF 3:231).

169. Smith, *Heaven in the American Imagination*, 4.

170. See Smith, *Biblical Doctrine of Heaven*, 28–75

171. Yarbrough, "Jesus on Hell," 76.

Some theologians that construe "heaven" as a literal place prefer to speak of the "new heaven and new earth" (Isa 65:17; 2 Pet 3:13; Rev 21). For them, those whom God has saved will enjoy a life of fellowship with God in a renewed or renovated world. The excerpts below capture some of the arguments made by Wayne Grudem in defense of the view of heaven as an identifiable place.

> When referring to this place, Christians often talk about living with God "in heaven" forever. But in fact the biblical teaching is richer than that: it tells us that there will be new heavens *and a new earth*—an entirely renewed creation—and we will live with God there.
>
> What is Heaven? During this present age, the place where God dwells is frequently called "heaven" in Scripture. The Lord says, "Heaven is my throne," (Isa 66:1) and Jesus teaches us to pray, "Our Father who art in heaven." (Matt 6:9) Jesus has "has gone into heaven, and is at the right hand of God." (1 Pet 3:22). In fact, heaven may be defined as follows: *Heaven is the place where God most fully makes known his presence to bless.*
>
> Heaven is a place, not just as state of mind.... [Stephen] did not see mere symbols of a state of existence [Acts 7:55–56]. It seems rather that his eyes were opened to see a spiritual dimension of reality which God has hidden from us in this present age, a dimension which nonetheless really does exist in our space/time universe, and within which Jesus now lives in his physical resurrection body, waiting even now for the time when he will return to earth.[172]

Some critics of this view contend that the Bible uses metaphorical language to describe the joyous experience of people whom God has saved. Heaven, therefore, should not be understood as an identifiable place or location.[173]

Symbolic View: Heaven as the Fullness of God's Presence in the World— Experiencing the Beatific Vision

For some theologians, heaven is to be understood as a future event in which God will bring to completion God's salvific work in the world. This consummation of God's salvific work, to Alister McGrath, will be marked by the replacement of "presence, penalty, and power of sin" by God's total presence

---

172. Grudem, *Systematic Theology*, 1158–59.

173. Russell, *History of Heaven*, 8–10.

in "individuals and the community of faith."[174] When thinking about heaven, then, Christians should not imagine entering into or occupying a specific location where God resides, which is different from the human world. Rather, they should imagine it as "entering" into total fellowship with one another in the presence of God. McGrath sees heaven as a "spiritual sphere or realm which coexists with the material world of space and time."[175] Being in heaven means experiencing the fullness of the beatific vision of God. In this mystical experience, God embraces people, enabling them to "see" fully who they are in Christ.[176]

Donald Guthrie notes that the concept of heaven has increasingly decreased in its importance in the works of scholars of the New Testament. However, he insists that heaven "is essential for a complete picture of NT theology."[177] Guthrie, however, argues that the idea of heaven as a physical place is foreign to the writers of the Bible. For him, in examining the "localizing expressions" like "above" or "up" or "ascend" that are used to describe heaven, it should be borne in mind that they reflect "the limitations of human language to express the surpra-mundane."[178] Guthrie goes on to contend that the Apostle Paul "does not think of heaven as a place, but thinks of it in terms of the presence of God."[179] The Kenyan theologian John Mbiti also imagines heaven and the concept of the "New Jerusalem" as metaphors employed by some biblical writers to express a state of being in a perfect relationship with God. The passage below highlights Mbiti's theological reflection on the book of Hebrews in his discussion of the concepts of heaven and the "New Jerusalem." He imagines these concepts contextually in order to engage the eschatological yearnings of the Akamba people of Kenya.

> Through faith and baptism the saints now "stand before Mount Zion and the city of the living God, heavenly Jerusalem" (Heb 12:22).
>
> The New Jerusalem belongs to the rejuvenated order of existence, realized by God through his Son. It is not simply the Messianic capital of Jewish apocalyptic: it is the symbol of perfect fellowship between God and His people. And this experience is a reality so intense that it has dimensions for the

---

174. McGrath, *Christian Theology*, 571.

175. Ibid.

176. Russell, *History of Heaven*, 3.

177. Guthrie, *New Testament Theology*, 874.

178. Ibid., 875.

179. Ibid., 880.

present (Heb 4:6) and the hereafter. The Way to that "city" is none other than Jesus Christ (John 14:1–7; 10:7, 9).

When Akamba Christians come across the notion of the heavenly city (*musyi*), their concept of it is strongly colored by both traditional and modern ideas of *musyi* [city]. Through the emphasis on an exclusively futurist eschatology and a prolongation of the future dimension of time, many Christians have come to believe in a physical and colossal city hanging up somewhere in the distant heavens, waiting for them to go there just as Nairobi and Mombasa [two Kenyan cities] wait for young people to go there when they finish their schooling. The physical city promises and provides all the good material things that people cannot acquire in this life. . . . Jesus is brought into the picture as the Agent conveying believers from this earth to the city in Heaven; and the Christian faith is the only passport to that city of prosperity.

An eschatological country is spoken of in Hebrews. OT saints sought it (11:14, 16), and by faith "greeted it from afar" (11:13). But what was promised in the OT is, in a temporary context, now realized and fulfilled in Christ, the leader or pioneer . . . of faith (12:2). Consequently, the pilgrims have arrived at their fatherland (12:18ff.), and the writer can plead with those who, through faith, participate in Jesus, to "be grateful for receiving a kingdom which cannot be shaken" (12:28). But, because this is an eschatological experience, it is only a foretaste in expectation: Christians can go "to Him outside the camp" (13:13), but they are still pilgrims (13:14). Jesus Himself, having initiated the eschatological era (9:26), will "appear a second time" to unveil and bring salvation to a consummation (9:28).[180]

Concluding Reflections on Christian Eschatological Hope

There is profound theological wisdom in the words "vanity of vanities" uttered by an ancient Jewish sage. He went on to say, "I have seen all the works which have been done under the sun, and behold, all is vanity and striving after wind" (Eccl 1:2, 14 NASB). The most important lesson to draw from the words of the message, however, is not that human beings' desire for happiness or even joy cannot be quenched through material possessions. Rather, it is that human beings thirst and search for the *meaning of existence* that cannot be satisfied by human accomplishments or any form of answers generated within the human spheres of existence. According to Paul, it is

180. Mbiti, *New Testament Eschatology*, 75–76, 78.

only in God that "we live and move and have our being" (Acts 17:28 NIV). The doctrine of Christian hope should be understood within the context of Christian teaching about the Triune God's relation to the world. For Augustine, the satisfying answer to humans' questions about the ultimate meaning of existence can be found in God. He wrote, "You [God] have made us for yourself and our hearts find no peace until they rest in you."[181] Christian eschatological hope proposes that humans, and indeed the whole creation, will attain their meaning in God.

We should not approach the *future* eschatological events as "calendarists"—as people who can say with precision the time, location, duration, and characteristics of such events. The metaphorical language employed by the biblical writers to describe such events makes this task impossible. Here, the word "metaphoric" does not suggest that events will not happen but rather that the description of such events should not be taken literally. What is of importance to a theologian is not the literal descriptions of such events but the "theological meanings" of such events—that is, what the events say about God's activity in the world. Finally, as I said in the beginning of the chapter, Christian eschatological hope should be understood in terms of an already-not-yet framework. Christian eschatological hope should not be construed as referring only or even primarily to events that will happen toward the end of the world. On the contrary, in so far as God is actively at work in the world, gradually bringing it to its *telos* (or meaning, purpose, and fulfillment), Christian eschatology comprises events in *this* world and in the world to come. These words of David Tracy are helpful for grounding Christian hope in God's action in the present world as it is moved toward its fulfillment in God: "The hope of human beings is not merely life after death but a hope for history itself. For the God who raised Jesus from the dead is the God who acted in the history of Israel and the history of Jesus. That same God will act in history and beyond it to save the living and the dead. The fact that God—the origin, sustainer, and the end of all reality—acts in history becomes the heart of Christian faith and thereby hope in history."[182]

Glossary

Annihilationism: View of hell that teaches God will end the life and suffering of the impenitent sinners whom God sentences to hell.

---

181. Augustine, *Confessions* 1.1 (Pine-Coffin, 21).
182. Tracy, *On Naming the Present*, 47.

Apocalyptic: Body of literature that is deeply metaphorical and that speaks vividly about eschatological acts of God in the world.

Conditionalism: Term used to describe the view that humans are created *potentially* immortal and that only those who are saved and are given eternal life by God *actually* experience immortality. As a view of hell, conditionalism teaches that the unsaved will cease to exist because God has not given them eternal life or because they have not accepted God's offer of eternal life.

Dispensationalism: Term that derives from the Greek word *oikonomia*, "dispensation." As a theological system, dispensationalism classifies God's activity in the world in epochs or periods, from the beginning of creation to its consummation.

Millennialism: Term used for the views that are grounded in the theological meaning of the one-thousand-year reign of Christ.

Review Questions

1. In what ways have Christians imagined the idea of Christian eschatological hope?

2. What challenges do scientific predictions for the future of the cosmos pose to Christian eschatological hope? In what ways have Christian theologians responded to these challenges?

3. What does it mean to say that Christian eschatological hope is characterized by *already-not yet* events?

4. What are the millennial theories? What do they share in common? What are their distinctive features?

5. What are the arguments against the doctrine of hell? Articulate and critique them.

6. What are the main views on heaven described in this chapter? What is heaven's relation to the "new heaven and new earth"?

Suggestions for Further Reading

Crockett, William, ed. *Four Views on Hell*. Grand Rapids: Zondervan, 1992.
Polkinghorne, John, and Michael Welker, eds. *The End of the World and the Ends of God: Science and Theology on Eschatology*. Harrisburg, PA: Trinity, 2000.

Walls, Jerry L., ed. *The Oxford Handbook of Eschatology*. New York: Oxford University
    Press, 2008.

6

Christian Life

This chapter focuses on *Christian identity formation*—what it is to be a Christian, who a Christian is, and how a Christian should live. In a narrower sense, Christian identity formation may be called the "Christian life." But what does it mean to say that Christians are to live the *Christian life*? Broadly, the Christian life can be viewed as the purpose of Christian theology. Theological discussions and doctrines ought to consummate in the type of life that Christ's followers live—a life that is deeply conditioned by Christian doctrines such as divine revelation, Scripture, the Trinity, sin, salvation, and eschatological hope. This is the primary reason

I have made the "Christian life" the last chapter of this two-volume book. Construing the Christian life in this way disrupts the common perception of it as a non-theological spiritual exercise. Also, it questions the assumption that "theology" is a dry and boring intellectual exercise that hinders Christians from truly living a Christlike life. This, of course, does not mean that theology, when wrongly conceived and appropriated, cannot hinder the spiritual growth of Christians.

I recall on several occasions during my undergraduate days in a theological seminary in Nigeria when some of my Pentecostal friends told me to beware of the danger that theology posed to the practice of the Christian life. Those well-meaning friends were concerned that my preoccupation with rigorous theological thinking would prevent me from "walking the walk"—living in the manner Jesus expects of his followers. They were quick to point out to me that some of our brilliant theology professors used theological skills to justify their "non-Christian" lifestyles. What I was not truly convinced of then was the possibility of knowing what Jesus really expects of his disciples without engaging in some theological reflection. Put another way, I was not entirely convinced that it was possible to conceptualize and practice the Christian life without ever engaging in theological thinking and also making some theological judgments. Over the years through my study of theology, I have learned that it is not only impossible to successfully imagine the Christian life in isolation from some theological reflection but also, and more importantly, that all Christian theological reflections about God, humans, the world, and so on ought to culminate in the Christian life. A theology that does not shape the *life* (manner of thinking, living, believing, behaving, hoping, etc.) of followers of Christ may be irrelevant to Christians in their journey to live a life of obedience to the Triune God

The Christian life deals with the manner of living of Christians. It is a manner of living that focuses on the life of Jesus Christ. The Christian life, therefore, is a form of living that is molded after the life of Jesus Christ. But to say that the *Christian life* is a "manner of living" evokes three important issues. First, the Christian life is a daily *form of existing*: it is a way of life. Second, the Christian life requires *formation* of character. Third, the Christian life is *directed toward some ends*: to resist the power of sin, to glorify the Triune God, and to transform the fallen world. These three issues will serve as guides to my discussion in the remainder of this chapter.

Imagining the Christian Life

Five conceptions of the Christian life, which are not mutually exclusive, are discussed below. They are Christian life as *putting off the old self*, Christian life as *spiritual exercise*, Christian life as *thanksgiving*, Christian life as *sanctification*, and Christian life as *moving toward glorification*. These should be viewed as partial descriptions of the phenomenon of the Christian life.

Christian Life as Putting Off the "Old Self"

Jesus calls his disciples to "take up the cross and follow" him (Mark 8:34). What does Jesus really mean? Certainly, his words cannot be taken literally in this context. Here, Jesus summons his disciples to undertake a life of self-denial: not *living for self* (that is, glorifying their selfish desires) but *living for him* (that is, being transformed into a life of obedience to God as Jesus exemplifies through his actions). Jesus' words invoke mortification: we must deliberately and continually "put to death the old nature and its evil desires" and embrace resurrection, which "leads to a new life of righteousness in fellowship with God."[1] Inward spirituality involves two related actions: living actively and living contemplatively. The Orthodox Church theologian Kallistos Ware describes these two actions in the following way. The "active life" (or living actively) requires repentance and exercise of the power of the will with God's help to escape from enslavement to ungodly passionate impulses. Living for Christ entails attaining the purity of heart and also involves growing in awareness of God's desire for humanity as embodied by Christ. The second action—living contemplatively—involves two interrelated stages. In the first stage, as Christians live the life of contemplation, they will sharpen their perception of God's presence in and around them. In the second, they will begin to experience God not only through the "intermediary of conscience or created things" but also by meeting God "face to face in an unmediated union of love."[2]

Being a Christian does not merely entail learning about Christianity's teachings. Being a Christian requires crucifying the "old self"—a metaphor for the power of sin within human nature. "You were taught," Paul wrote "to put off your old self, which is being corrupted by its deceitful desires" (Eph 4:22 NIV; see also Col 3:5–17). Dealing with the "old self" entails, to use the words of Sinclair Ferguson, "crucifying sin" that is within us. For Ferguson, being united with Christ does not mean that "sin has died" permanently

1. Stott, *Cross of Christ*, 280.
2. Ware, *Orthodox Way*, 106.

in the life of believers. On the contrary, what has changed is the believers' relationship to sin. Believers are no longer slaves to sin. This means that believers can engage in the daily struggle against sin, the struggle to crucify or put to death sin, from "a perspective of victory," which is won for them by Christ.[3] In practical terms, according to Ferguson, crucifying sin is "the constant battle against sin which we fight daily—the refusal to allow the eye to wander, the mind to contemplate, the affections to run after anything which will draw us from Christ. It is the deliberate rejection of any sinful thought, suggestion, desire, aspiration, deed, circumstances or provocation at the moment we become aware of its existence."[4]

Christian Life as Spiritual Exercise

The Christian life is not formed *ex nihilo* (out of nothing). To be a Christian is to be a disciple of Jesus Christ. A good disciple is like an apprentice who learns from his or her teacher. Jesus required his disciples to "follow" him, which implied heeding his voice, accepting God's chastisement or spiritual pruning, and welcoming God's forgiveness (John 10:27–30; 15:1–5; Matt 6:9–15). Following Jesus Christ is a daily practice of taking upon oneself Jesus' *way of life*—his manner of living, behaving, thinking, hoping, and relating to God, human beings, and the entire creation. Spiritual exercises are designed to help Christians develop the stamina for redirecting their desires: from pleasing self to pleasing God. The Spanish monk Ignatius of Loyola (1491–1556) wrote that spiritual exercises can help Christians gain "deeper knowledge" of their sins and acquire "a greater understanding of and sorrow for sins."[5]

One example of the conception of the Christian life as a spiritual exercise can be found in Christian monasticism. Christian monks understood the Christian life as a form of life modeled by Jesus Christ, empowered by the Holy Spirit, and practiced through contemplation, asceticism (exercise in self-discipline and self-denial), prayer, and manual work. In some early Christian communities, monks typically followed either a hermit lifestyle (*eremitic monasticism*) or a communal lifestyle (*coenobitic monasticism*). Eremitic monks such as the Egyptian Anthony the Great (ca. 251–356 CE) lived mostly solitary lives in exclusion in the desert. However, some of them, like Anthony the Great, occasionally left their solitude to minister among

3. Ferguson, *Know Your Christian Life*, 138.

4. Ibid., 143.

5. Ignatius of Loyola, *Spiritual Exercises*, 44.

people in the towns and cities around them for a period of time.[6] Coenobitic monks, unlike the eremitic monks, lived a communal lifestyle, with well-defined structures governing the pattern of life and leadership of each community. The Italian monk St. Benedict of Nursia (480–547) is celebrated as one of the primal leaders of coenobitic monasticism. He wrote a handbook (known as the *Rule of St. Benedict*) to govern the pattern of living of the monks in the monastery he founded at Monte Cassino, Italy.[7] Benedictine monastic life emphasized moderation between physical labor and study, personal contemplation and communal worship.[8] Christian monasticism exerted a great influence on Christianity and the world at large from the fifth to the ninth century CE. For example, monks devoted large amounts of time to copying manuscripts and writing commentaries on religious and secular texts.[9]

The Orthodox Churches and Roman Catholic Church have preserved Christian monasticism to the present era, albeit with significant modifications (as can been seen in different monastic orders such as the Franciscan order). The emphases on "sacred reading, manual work, and liturgical prayer" have remained central to the lifestyles of Christian monastic communities.[10] The Protestant Churches have also joined in this tradition as can been seen in what is called "new monasticism." This form of monasticism is labelled "new" because it moves away from some of the restrictions of the "old" form of monasticism such as "celibacy" and "taking lifelong vows."[11] People who follow the path of "new monasticism," like the traditional monks, "choose to live in a Christian community with a focus on service, especially with the poor and marginalized."[12] What all forms of Christian monasticism share is a commitment to live out in practical ways the life of Christ, which is a form of spiritual exercise aimed at living obediently to God. Writing about Ethiopian Orthodox monasticism and how it can inspire Christians to live responsibly in preserving the ecosystem, Joachim Persoon notes that the monks of Mahbere Selassie's choice of life of poverty and prohibition against owning private property "is a sign of embracing asceticism and calling the wider population to repentance." Persoon goes on to argue that the monks' lifestyle is a prophetic address to all Christians "to

6. Ward, "Anthony the Great," 1.

7. Backman, *Cultures of the West*, 278.

8. Ibid.

9. Ibid.

10. Cummings, *Monastic Practices*, 7.

11. Heath and Duggins, *Missional, Monastic, Mainline*, 33.

12. Ibid.

practice voluntary self-divestiture, recalling the great saints and asceticism of early Christianity. This could be described as a need for eco-asceticism, voluntary self-denial, freeing from the technologies that destroy God's good earth."[13]

Christian Life as Thanksgiving

The Christian life is an expression of thanksgiving to the Triune God for acting to redeem fallen humanity. The Second Vatican Council in *Lumen Gentium* summoned all those "baptized, by regeneration and the anointing of the Holy Spirit" to remember that they have been consecrated by God "to be a spiritual house, a holy priesthood," that they may "offer spiritual sacrifices and proclaim the perfection of him who has called them out of darkness into his marvelous light (1 Peter 2:4–10)."[14] Christians are to live their daily lives as an act of thanksgiving to God for saving them and bringing them into fellowship.

The act of thanksgiving provides dual services to the practice of the Christian life, namely, "motivation" for Christian living and "deterrence" from living in a manner that does not conform to the life of Christ. Almost every human culture cherishes "thanksgiving" as a good virtue. Unthankful people are considered in many cultures as irresponsible people. Luke narrates a story that shows Jesus values thankfulness and expects his followers to be thankful to God (Luke 17:11–19). If not being thankful to God is a sinful act, then thanksgiving can serve as a form of "deterrence" from not living the Christian life. The desire to be thankful to God can push us toward Christ and also can empower us to conform to his life, as the one who models for us what it is to be *human* in the manner God expects of us. Living the Christian life as an act of thanksgiving to God is an acknowledgement that God is the center of our life and existence.

Living the Christian life as an act of thanksgiving to God also amplifies the role of prayer in Christian living. What is important here is not the right practice or method of Christian prayer. Instead, when prayer is correlated with thanksgiving in the context of the Christian life, we see more clearly how having a relationship with the Triune God is the foundation of Christian living. Like thanksgiving, prayer entails living before the *presence* of God. Prayer should not be seen primarily as an activity a Christian pauses to engage in for a period of time. On the contrary, prayer is a way of living that

13. Persoon, "Towards an Ethiopian Eco-Theology," 223.

14. Vatican Council II, *Lumen Gentium* 10, in Flannery, *Vatican Council II*, 360–631.

entails a deep commitment to a relationship with God. Prayer, as Lawrence Cunningham and Keith Egan note, signals "communication with an Other and, simultaneously says, in effect, that a person is not totally self-sufficient and does not regard himself or herself as totally autonomous or alone."[15] Karl Barth stretches the concept of prayer further by imagining it as Christians' vocative response to God's command "call upon me" (Psalm 50:15). This response to God's command, for Barth, is the heart of the Christian life. He writes: "we regard invocation according to this command ["call upon me"] as the basic meaning of all human obedience. What God permits man, what he expects, wills, and requires of him, is a life of calling upon him. This life of calling upon God will be a person's Christian life: his life in freedom, conversion, faith, gratitude, and faithfulness."[16]

Prayer, broadly speaking, means living before the presence of God. When understood in this way, prayer is a form of living that requires making daily and momentary decisions such as decisions about how to use our resources, about telling the truth, and so on. When we live the life of prayer as a form of a life of thanksgiving to God, we will become more aware that God's presence is not something we should dread as if God is looking over our shoulders waiting to punish us when we sin. On the contrary, God's presence should bring us comfort even in our darkest moment. Of course, God's comfort may come through divine correction and discipline. This is this wisdom of Ps 23:4, "Even though I walk through the valley of the shadow of death, I will fear no evil, for you are with me; your rod and your staff, they comfort me" (NIV). In the Christian life, therefore, Christians should not *run away from* God when they sin. Conversely, they should *run toward* God for the forgiveness of their sins and to draw encouragement to continue in their struggles to live faithfully to God with thanksgiving for their salvation.

Christian Life as Sanctification

The word sanctification signifies a state of "being holy" or to "make holy." It can be associated with God, human beings, and objects. Sanctification (from the Hebrew root *qds* and the Greek root *hágios*) denotes sacredness, holiness, and awe. In theological terms, when the Greek word *hágios* or the Hebrew *qds* is applied to God, holiness is construed as the nature of God (Isa 6:3; John 17:11; Rev 6:10).[17] In this sense, holiness signifies the "otherness"

15. Cunningham and Egan, *Christian Spirituality*, 67.

16. Barth, *Christian Life*, 44.

17. Procksch, "Hágios," 1:100–101.

of God. In other words, holiness, as an essential nature of God highlights God's majesty, distinctiveness, uniqueness, and apartness. God is distinct from human beings (Hos 11:9) and all other creatures of God. But holiness also sometimes refers to God's moral rectitude (Ps 145:17; 1 Pet 1:13–16). The biblical writers used the word "holiness" in this sense to express the belief that God is morally pure, perfect, and "free from the pollution of sin."[18] In Christian theology, the moral rectitude of God is the ground for speaking of human sanctification. Since God is holy, the people of God are called to be holy. The Apostle Peter makes this clear when he says, "But just as he who called you is holy, so be holy in all you do" (1 Pet 1:15 NIV). For Paul, the church is holy and set apart by God to become "a holy temple" and to "do good works, which God has prepared in advance for" its members (Eph 2:10, 21–22). Also, the members of the church are to offer their bodies as "living sacrifices, holy and pleasing to God," for this is their "spiritual act of worship" (Rom 12:1 NIV).

Theologians, especially those belonging to the Protestant camp, sometimes speak of "positional sanctification" and "progressive sanctification" when describing the purity of human beings in relation to God. In the *positional* (or definitive) sense, Christians are sanctified by God because they are in Christ. By virtue of being in Christ, God sets believers apart. Those who are *in Christ* are justified by God, declaring and making them saints (Rom 1:7). In the positional sense, sanctification has nothing to do with human moral improvement: it is not the result of the righteous works of Christians. On the contrary, it is God's act of seeing those who are in Christ as "holy" on the basis of Christ's work. As Michael Horton notes, "All that is found in Christ is holy, because it is in Christ. He is our sanctification—'the LORD is our righteousness' (1 Cor 1:30; 6:11), our Holy Place."[19] Before God, the status of a believer in Christ has changed from that of "unholy" to "holy."

Progressive sanctification refers to the "work" of being holy to which God has called those who have been justified. Admittedly, the power to live a holy life that is pleasing to God comes from God: it is a gift from the Triune God. The responsibility of Christians is to seek the gift of empowerment for Christian living. As Thomas Merton notes, "If we are called by God to holiness of life, and if holiness is beyond our natural power to achieve (which it certainly is) then it follows that God himself must give us the light, the strength, and the courage to fulfill the task he requires of us. He will

18. Feinberg, *No One Like Him*, 342

19. Horton, *Christian Faith*, 652.

certainly give us the grace we need. If we do not become saints it is because we do not avail ourselves of his gift."[20]

Christian Life as Moving toward Glorification

In the chapter on salvation (see chapter 2), I discussed the Eastern Orthodox Church's theology of *theosis* or deification. I will not repeat what was said in that chapter in this section. I will focus my attention on the importance of the doctrine of deification in the Orthodox Church's views on Christian living or spirituality. The Lebanese theologian Bradley Nassif has written extensively on the spirituality of the Eastern Orthodox Church. For him, the idea of spirituality in the Orthodox Church is "less taught than caught. It is a whole way of life, not a list of regimens for developing the spiritual life." Spirituality is grounded in a loving relationship with the Triune God who calls humans to participate in the divine life. The excerpt below is taken from one of Nassif's works on spirituality.

The definition and destiny of the human person is to become divine. Communion with God is the goal of creation and salvation. The church calls this goal christificaiton or, more commonly, deification (from the Greek *theosis*). Deification is the goal that integrates all Eastern Orthodox theology and spirituality. While acknowledging the term has Greek philosophical origins, it is nevertheless thoroughly biblical. The Gospel of John and the Epistles of Paul clearly speak of a mystical union between Christ and the believer and a personal dwelling of the Holy Spirit. The church fathers and ecumenical councils . . . base their understanding of deification on the reality of the incarnation. By participating in Christ, who united our humanity with his divinity, believers "participate" in the very life of God himself. It is by such intimate union that we "are being transformed into the same image [of the Lord] from one degree of glory to another" (2 Cor 3:18 ESV). The best biblical term that is equivalent to the Greek theosis or deification is probably glorification.

The goal of glorification is seen in the creation account in Genesis 1–2. Orthodox Christians believe that at creation Adam and Eve were fashioned after a Trinitarian likeness. . . . *Theosis* includes growth in the characteristics of God, such as love, compassion, and mercy. But it also includes the idea of growing in communion with God, resulting in a continued state of immortality. Accordingly, the fall into sin was not a drastic withdrawal from a perfected

20. Merton, *Life and Holiness*, 17.

state. Instead, it was a failure to achieve the original purpose God had set for humanity. It was a departure from the path of deification.[21]

Question: What does this text say about the nature and purpose of Christian spirituality as understood in the Orthodox Church?

Forming the Christian Life

Any Christian who seeks to live like Jesus Christ will soon discover that it is extremely difficult to say no to a manner of living that pulls people away from the way of Christ. The manner of life Jesus lived sometimes goes against our "natural" way of responding to things and people that threaten our interests. For example,

> **FOCUS QUESTION:**
> Who and what is involved in the formation of the Christian life?

it is not natural to love those who hate us. Our "natural" response to those who hate us is to hate them even more. It is "natural" to exact revenge on those who have done harm to us rather than to forgive them. Like the Apostle Paul, many Christians discover through the practice of the Christian life that what they want to do in order to please Christ they rarely do; instead, they find themselves doing what they do not desire to do (Rom 17:15–20). The Christian life requires making a decision: choosing between satisfying our "natural" desires and pleasing God by following the life Jesus exemplifies for his disciples (Rom 8:1–15). Christians, as Nigel Cameron writes, should move from "the passive idea of 'discerning guidance' to the active one of 'making Christian decisions.'"[22] Making such decisions, however, is an ongoing spiritual struggle—a struggle we *gradually* overcome by drawing insights and empowerment from the Triune God, from the Scriptures, and from the church.

The Triune God's Role in the Christian Life

In Gal 2:20, the Apostle Paul tells his readers, "I have been crucified with Christ. It is no longer I who live, but Christ who lives in me. And the life I now live in the flesh I live by faith in the Son of God, who loved me and gave himself for me" (ESV). What exactly did Paul mean by "Christ who

21. Nassif, "Orthodox Spirituality," 53–54.

22. Cameron, *Are Christians Human?*, 57.

lives in me" and "I live by faith in the Son of God"? Is Paul suggesting that his role in the practice of spirituality or Christian living is passive and that Jesus is the principal actor who produces Christlike qualities in him? One of the passages that may come to mind as one ponders these words of Paul is John 15, in which Jesus tells his disciples, "Abide in me, and I in you. As the branch cannot bear fruit by itself, unless it abides in the vine, neither can you, unless you abide in me. I am the vine; you are the branches. Whoever abides in me and I in him, he it is that bears much fruit, for apart from me you can do nothing" (John 15:4–5 ESV). Could Paul have heard these words of Jesus through oral tradition (the epistles were most probably written before the Gospel of John)? There is no need to be delayed by the historical connections between Jesus' words and the Apostle Paul's words. What is of paramount importance is how to understand Jesus' role (and by extension the role of God the Father and the Holy Spirit) in Christian living.

Returning to Paul's words to Galatian Christians highlighted earlier, three major theological lessons that can impact Christian living are noteworthy. First, Christian living is a "new life" that requires putting the "old self" to death. For Paul, those whom God has justified should no longer live their lives to satisfy their selfish interests or desires. Second, the "new life" is made possible by God's justification of a sinner on the account of Christ's righteousness. Those who are justified by God have been crucified and also raised from the dead (metaphorically speaking) along with Christ. In other words, the "new life" they have received is grounded in their identification with the passion, death, and resurrection of Jesus Christ.[23] Third, the Christian life requires living *for* God. But how is this possible? Paul attributes his ability to live for God to the indwelling Christ. In his words, "It is no longer I who live, but Christ who lives in me" (Gal 2:20 ESV).

How can Christians apply these three lessons from Paul's discussion on Christian living? Unsurprisingly, Christians have understood and moved Paul's words in different directions. For some, Paul's words indicate that perfectionism is attainable in this life. Others, on the contrary, argue that perfectionism is foreign to Paul's theologies. Yet for some other theologians, Christian living or spirituality ought to be understood as communion between the Triune God and humans, a life of communion that requires Christians to continually draw the strength for Christian living from the Triune God. For these theologians, Christians must avoid the danger of reducing spiritual life "to a set of emphases and practices each believer is to follow."[24]

23. George, *Galatians*, 199.
24. Nassif, "Orthodox Spirituality," 28.

The Triune God makes the Christian life possible. In Christian soteriology (doctrine of salvation), the Triune God is believed to be responsible for restoring human beings into divine fellowship. God the Father through the work of the Holy Spirit brings people into union with Christ. This union (in theological terms, the "mystical union") is the foundation (*a*) for entering into fellowship with the Triune God and (*b*) for living the Christian life. The mystical union changes people's (positional) status from being an "old creation" to being a "new creation." In 2 Cor 5:17, the Apostle Paul writes, "Therefore, if anyone is in Christ, he is a new creation; the old has gone, the new has come!" (NIV). Those who are united with Christ should, in Paul's language, "fulfill the law of Christ," which includes carrying the burdens of other believers (Gal 6:2). They should also "live by the Spirt," which entails not gratifying sinful desires (Gal 5:16–18). The mystical union, therefore, can be described as the foundation of the Christian life and the fountain from which Christians draw power and encouragement for Christian living. When understood in this way, Jesus Christ is not merely a model of moral living that his followers can imitate (like imitating a movie star). Rather, the Christian life, in so far is it is ground in the mystical union, is the Triune God's work *within* Christians that produces *outward* lifestyles—what Paul calls the fruit of the Sprit (Gal 5:22–23). John Calvin imagined the implication of one's union with Christ for Christian living in this way: "We ought not to separate Christ from ourselves or ourselves from him. Rather we ought to hold fast bravely with both hands to that fellowship by which he has bound himself to us. So the Apostle teaches us: 'Now your body is dead because of sin; but the Spirit of Christ which dwells in you is life because of righteousness' (Rom 8:10)."[25] The Christian life necessitates a "visible act of obedience" to Christ.[26] In his typical dialectical and christocentric fashion, Karl Barth sees the Christian life or what he calls "special ethics" as concerning itself with God's *goodness*, which demands *human good action* as exemplified by Jesus Christ. He writes,

> In God's Word, then, we are dealing both with God and with man: with God acting in relation to man and with man acting in relation to God; or, to put it in terms of the ethical problem, with the sure and certain goodness of the divine action and the problematical goodness of human action. At every point in true church proclamation it must and will be a matter of both. And the Word of God is the command of God to the extent that in it the sure and certain goodness of God's goodness confronts the

25. Calvin, *Institutes of the Christian Religion*, 3.2.24.
26. Bonhoeffer, *Cost of Discipleship*, 209.

problematic goodness of man's as its standard, requirement, and direction.

At issue is the relation of human action to *God's* command. God himself, God alone is good, and he decides what human action may be called good or not good.

Who the commanding God is and who the responsible man is—God in the mystery of his commanding and man in the mystery of his obedience or disobedience—is not hidden from us but is revealed and may be known in the one Jesus Christ: God and man, if not in their essence, at least in their work and therefore in their manner; God and man, accessible to human apprehension, if not expressible in human words, at least describable and attestable.[27]

Barth's point is that the Christian life does not primarily refer to personal piety but rather to what makes Christians "Christian"—namely, their relation to Jesus Christ and the "obligation and commitment that derives from this relation."[28] While Barth is typically christocentric in his theological reflections, he is also deeply Trinitarian. Christians' obedience to God, for Barth, entails recognizing that God is the Father of Jesus Christ, which they are able to do by the power of the Holy Spirit.[29]

Those who are received into divine fellowship through faith are to live faithfully. They are to continuously "crucify" the gratification of self in order to live a new life in Christ through the power of the Holy Spirit. The life of Christians, Dietrich Bonhoeffer writes, "is marked by a daily dying in the war of the flesh and the spirit, and in the mortal agony the devil inflicts" upon them daily.[30] In Rom 8:15–17, Paul told his readers that people become children of God by the power of the Holy Spirit. It is also the same Spirit of God, Jesus told his disciples, that would bring people to him, convicting them of their sins (John 16:8). The Holy Spirit is so central to the Christian life that Paul reminded his readers to rely on the Holy Spirit who would help them in their weakness and intercede for them "in accordance with the will of God" (Rom 8:26). It is not only in spiritual things that the Holy Spirit aids Christians. Even in mundane things such as standing before a magistrate, Christians are to depend on the Holy Spirit for the ability to speak in a manner pleasing to God (Mark 13:11). Kendra Hotz and Matthew Mathews argue that the Holy Spirit "enlivens" the church through the process of purifying and illuminating the lives of the members of the church. To them,

27. Barth, *Christian Life*, 3, 4, 5.

28. Ibid., 49.

29. Ibid., 52.

30. Bonhoeffer, *Cost of Discipleship*, 273.

the Holy Spirit's *purification* (the Spirit's act of empowering Christians to crucify sin in their lives) and *illumination* (the Spirit's act of empowering Christians to live as new creatures in Christ) are central to the Christian life. The daily Christian movement of dying to sin and rising as new creatures in Christ are brought about by the sanctifying work of the Holy Spirit.[31]

The paramount issue in discussing the role of the Triune God in the Christian life is not merely the issue of *character formation* (John 14:15–25). While the transformation of character is an essential part of the Christian life, enjoying a fellowship with the Triune God is the focal issue of the Christian life. Samuel Powell puts it this way: the Christian life "is not equivalent to a life of moral development. It is not simply equivalent to a life of self-discipline and spiritual exertion, although self-discipline and exertion are required. It is, in addition to these things, a life in God, not a life that springs spontaneously out of human nature."[32]

The Scriptures' Role in the Christian Life

Dietrich Bonhoeffer in *The Cost of Discipleship* writes that Christians hear the call, which the risen and living Lord addresses to them, through "the testimony of the Scriptures."[33] Bonhoeffer goes on to note that one's encounter with Christ through the Scriptures occurs in the church: "The preaching of the Church and the administration of the sacraments is the place where Jesus is present."[34] The role of the Bible (or the Scriptures) in the formation of the Christian life may appear obvious to merit discussions; after all, it is the sacred text that guides what Christians believe and how they live. But at a closer look, the role of the Bible in Christian living is a much more complex issue. To highlight the complexity, one may ask *which* Bible? As I discussed in chapter 3 of volume 1 of *Introducing Christian Theologies*, Christians use different canons—lists of books considered sacred and authoritative. Since some of these canons contain competing texts and teaching, it is to be expected that the role of the Bible in Christian living is not an easy issue to address. Another question that can be raised is, *how much influence* should the Bible have on the formation of Christian living? Even if we answer the question about the difference in the biblical canon by saying "to each Christian community in their own choice of a biblical canon," this answer does not really take us very far. This is because Christian communities also need

---

31. Hotz and Matthews, *Shaping the Christian Life*, 50–51.
32. Powell, *Theology of Spirituality*, 66–67.
33. Bonhoeffer, *Cost of Discipleship*, 201.
34. Ibid.

to deal with the issue of *hermeneutics* (how to interpret) and the issue of *appropriation* (how to make theirs the meaning they arrive at after interpreting a biblical text). Since Christians within the same denomination (especially within the Protestant churches) rarely agree on their interpretations of several biblical passages, we ought to expect more difficult discussions on the Bible's role in Christian living.

Notwithstanding the differences in Christian understandings of biblical hermeneutics and the ways the Scriptures can be used to define Christian beliefs, many Christians read the Bible with the expectation to hear how they are to live as those whom God has called in Christ and are being sanctified by the Holy Spirit. If they are reading diligently and attentively, they will hear of God's grace, judgment, and forgiveness. They will hear that repentance is required of them. They will hear that they are required to journey in a "continuing transformation of life" concretized in the "practice of love of God and love of neighbor."[35] In the Scriptures, they will also hear about the struggles of the earliest Christians to live in conformity to the life of Christ and also about their determination to please Christ even when doing so meant risking their lives. In sum, the practice and conceptualization of the *Christian* life cannot be successfully imagined in isolation from the teaching of the Scriptures. Rejecting the Scriptures as an indispensable resource that should inform and shape the Christian life is tantamount to rejecting the Scriptures' primary purpose as texts that are "able to make [people] wise for salvation" and are "useful for teaching, rebuking, correcting and training in righteousness" (1 Tim 3:15–16 NIV).

Two theological reasons can be given in support of the claim that Christians cannot successfully imagine the practice of the Christian life in isolation from the Scriptures. First, the Scriptures are to be read by a Christian community as *the community's* sacred writings. By association, becoming a Christian and a member of a local church entails accepting the Scriptures as the written texts that inspire, govern, and empower Christians' beliefs and practices. Second, by accepting the Scriptures as sacred texts, a Christian community can maintain and accentuate the *continuity* of all Christian communities. The church is a work in progress: the Triune God is building, assembling, and purifying the diverse local communities that make up the church. Each local community should shoulder the responsibility of showing that it belongs to the "single" history of the church. Two related ways the community can accomplish this task are through its acceptance of the *normative status* of the Scriptures in the formation of the Christian life and through its interpretation of the Scriptures in dialogue

35. Migliore, *Faith Seeking Understanding*, 241–42.

with other Christian communities. When Christian communities interpret the Scriptures, as Rowan Williams notes, they are invited to identify themselves in the story being completed, to re-appropriate who they "are now and shall or can be, in terms of the story."[36]

Church's Role in the Christian Life

In the preceding section, it is argued that reading the Bible as a community's text is essential for understanding the role it plays (or its function) in the formation of the Christian life. In this section, I focus on the church's role or function in the lives of its members as they seek to practice the Christian life. As we shall see below, the Scriptures provide a model for the church that can help each individual member live the Christian life. Christians cannot successfully live the Christian life in isolation from the Triune God, from the Scriptures, and from the community of Christ's followers (the Church). In the words of Dietrich Bonhoeffer, when a person is united with Christ he or she loses the world but gains a new community—the visible church. This means that Christians are to "live in the visible community of Christ."[37] But how exactly can the church help each Christian to live the Christian life? This is a broad question that can be answered in a number of ways. I will limit my discussion to three concrete ways the church can come to the aid of each member as he or she negotiates, struggles, and pursues the Christian life. The three ways are teaching, correcting, and sharing.

Church's teaching role: One of the major tasks of the church is to produce leaders who are equipped to expound the word of God, to declare the whole counsel of God, and to help the members of the church on how they are to act and live. Paul's advice to pastor Timothy to "correctly handle the word of truth" should encourage Christian leaders to devote themselves to the study of the Scriptures and sound doctrines.

I have encountered some leaders in Pentecostal churches and African Indigenous Churches (AICs) who do not take theological and biblical studies seriously because they believe the Holy Spirit will teach them all things. For these leaders, pastors (and all Christians) should read the Bible devotionally and also rely on the Holy Spirit to direct them on what they are to say to the church. For them, Christians should rely on the prophetic words of the Holy Spirit given to their church through prophets and prophetesses. But we can ask: Do theological and biblical studies inhibit one from hearing from the Holy Spirit? One of the perennial issues that arises each time spontaneous

36. Williams, *On Christian Theology*, 50.
37. Bonhoeffer, *Cost of Discipleship*, 209.

prophetic utterances are heard by the church through a prophet or prophetess is how to determine when a given prophetic utterance is truly inspired by the Holy Spirit. What is at stake here is not simply *how* to know when the Holy Spirit is speaking spontaneously to the church but also the *criterion* of theological judgment or discernment. A church that is devoid of sound teaching, which is ironed out through deep theological reflections, will have no form of reference to judge the truthfulness or falsehood of a prophetic utterance. Anyone who reads the Scriptures closely will know that some of the texts are not easy to understand. The Apostle Peter, for example, writes that some of Paul's words are "hard to understand, which ignorant and unstable people distort, as they do the other Scriptures, to their own destruction" (2 Pet 3:16 NIV). Kevin Vanhoozer correctly notes that true Christian doctrine supplies "true knowledge" and encourages "sound habits" that are necessary to keep Christians *spiritually fit*.[38]

Church's correcting role: Another important role the church plays in the practice of Christian living is that of correcting sinning Christians with the purpose of nudging them back into the path of righteousness (Matt 18:15). Churches deal with the issue of sinning members differently, depending on the nature of the sins and their ecclesiastical traditions. The ministry of correcting a sinning member of the church can sometimes take the form of church discipline or excommunication. There is no need to assume, as some of the medieval church leaders had assumed, that excommunicating a sinning member from the church amounts to the loss of the person's salvation. As argued in chapter 2, salvation is a divine prerogative and the church has no power to make a decision on people's salvation. Excommunicating a sinning member from the fellowship of the church (Matt 18:15–17; 1 Cor 5) should be driven by the desire to bring the sinner back to fellowship.

A sinning member of the church can render two *positive* services to the church. Of course, I am not suggesting that churches *necessarily* need sinning members, but rather that the presence of a sinning member can become helpful to the church in two ways. First, a sinning member puts the church on its toes against becoming complicit in sinful acts. Paul scolded the members of the church of Corinth for their complicity in the sin of sexual immorality (most probably incestuous sexual acts between a man and his stepmother).[39] The church of Corinth failed to deal decisively with the sin. Paul was astonished at the behavior of the church: "Shouldn't you rather have been filled with grief and have put out of fellowship the man who did this?" The church, as a community, has the responsibility to stand

38. Vanhoozer, *Drama of Doctrine*, 376.
39. Keener, *1–2 Corinthians*, 48.

up against sinners irrespective of the position of the sinner in the church. The second positive service a sinning member can render to the church is to test its exercise of grace. The goal of disciplining or excommunicating sinning members is not to destroy them but rather to correct them. The church should work relentlessly to help them repent of their sins and return to fellowship. In Gal 6:1 Paul wrote: "If someone is caught in a sin, you who are spiritual should restore him gently."

Church's sharing role: Paul instructed Christians living in the region of Galatia to "carry each other's burdens," for in doing so they would "fulfill the law of Christ" (Gal 6:1). The church is to share in the burdens (spiritual, physical, social, material, and so on) of its members. This act of sharing involves *empathizing* with the suffering of each member. Deserting a sinning member does more harm than good, both to the sinner and to the whole church. Loneliness can provide fertile ground for a sinning Christian to go on sinning. The church that abandons a straying member is irresponsible: it has failed to perform its job of nurturing. The church should be like a good shepherd that does not give up on the strayed sheep but works relentlessly until he finds it (Luke 15:4–7). Sharing also includes *giving resources* to help the members that are in need. When a member is burdened by sin or need, the other members are to identify with the suffering, pathos, and pain of that member. We may not search for a long time in our nearby churches to encounter people who have engaged in sinful acts because they are struggling to feed themselves and their families. James made it clear that it was not enough to wish a person in need well without being willing to give sacrificially to help the person (Jas 2:15). John was even more direct in his rebuke of Christians whose faith lacked right practice: "If anyone has material possessions and sees his brother in need but has no pity on him, how can the love of God be in him? Dear children, let us not love with words or tongue but with actions and in truth" (1 John 3:17–18 NIV). Sharing the burdens of other Christians also involves *accountability*. Christians need each other to become aware of the threat or presence of sin. Our spiritual blind spots, which are conditioned by our cultures and personal experiences, may prevent us from seeing a potential circumstance in which we may be led to sin. Christians owe it to each other to be watchful of such circumstances and to point them out to those who may be unaware of them. In this sense, Christians are to be a light to each other's path.

The Christian Life and Christian Communities' Relation to the World

In this section, I focus on *how* Christian communities are to act "Christianly" in the public space, that is, in the world. Some Christians live in a predominantly "secular" society, while others live in a predominantly "religious" society. I use the word "secular" in this context along the lines of Charles Taylor's definition: a society in which belief in God is no longer "unchallenged and indeed, unproblematic." Belief in God in a secular society is understood as "one option among others, and frequently not the easiest to embrace."[40] North America and Europe are the best candidates for being examples of a secular society. A predominantly "religious" society is the opposite of secular society. It is a society, to reverse the order of Taylor's description of a secular age, in which belief in God is rarely critically introduced into daily conversations and also where belief in God is the easiest option to take. Examples of a "religious" society in this sense can be found in Africa and the Middle East.

Successfully bringing the Christian life—way of thinking, living, and behaving—into the public sphere will largely depend on whether the society is "secular" or "religious." I have come into contact with several people who shared with me how difficult it has been for them to live the Christian life in North America and Western Europe. On closer examination, I learned that such people were expressing how the contexts of North America or Western Europe negatively impact their practice of the Christian faith. For example, those who prayed daily for their meals when they were living in Africa increasingly found it difficult to pray to God to provide their daily meals in societies where food is not scarce. In Africa, the issue may be how to survive diseases that are caused by hunger and malnutrition. In North America, the issue may be how to survive the diseases that are caused by the consumption of too much food, especially junk food, which is readily available. But it will be utterly naïve to assume that living in a "religious" society does not pose any difficulty to the Christian life. Sometimes people living in a religious society fail to critically examine their religious commitments; they may do bizarre things because their pastors tell them to do so. For example, some members of a church in South Africa ate grass, as if they were animals, after their pastor, Lesego Daniel, asked them to do so. Daniel also asked his members to drink petrol (gasoline) after claiming that it would be turned miraculously into pineapple juice—and some members trustingly drank it.[41]

40. Taylor, *Secular Age*, 3.
41. Martinez, "After South African Pastor Makes Church Members Eat Grass."

The issue of how Christians should relate to the world is unsurprisingly complex. Christians must clarify what they mean when they confess that they are called to be the "salt of the earth, and the light of the world" (Matt 5:13–16) as a way of expressing the church's relation to the world. Throughout the history of the church, Christians have tried to imagine the church-world relation without colluding with uncritical attitude towards the world, on the one hand, and without compromising the church's religious identity, on the other hand. One way of sorting the complex web of Christians' understandings of the church's relation to the world is through the use of "models" to classify the *mode of operation* and the *nature of the church's mission* to the world. I will categorize Christians' understandings of the church's relation to the world into three major models: the antithetical model, the empire model, and the dialectical model. Within each of these three broad models, I will highlight different, albeit related, views. Also, note that in practice some of these models intersect.

Antithetical Model

Description: Some Christians see "Christian identity" as being at war with other competing identities (such as "national identity" and "political identity") and as such treat them with hostility. Such Christians' attitudes fit the antithetical model, which sees the Christian life as living in opposition to or in direct confrontation with the world. For some of these Christians, the church must be ready to choose martyrdom when it is confronted by the forces of the world.

Example of the Antithetical Model: We can distinguish two trends in the antithetical model, namely, the strict type and the moderate type. Christian monasticism represents the *strict version* of the antithetical model. Some early Christian monks left the cities and moved to the desert to live in solitary or to form a community—a move that signaled their rejection of the ways of the world. As H. Richard Niebuhr has noted, many monks withdrew from the "institutions and societies of civilization, from family and state, from school and socially established church, from trade and industry."[42] The *moderate version* of the antithetical model differs from the *strict version* primarily because of its rejection of the idea of withdrawing physically from the society and living in a sort of Christian enclave. For theologians whose views of the church's relation to the world fit the *moderate version*, the church should not withdraw from society but rather should steer away from the "way" of the world—that of violence,

42. Niebuhr, *Christ and Culture*, 56.

war, and coercive power. The name of the African American civil rights activist and American Baptist minister Martin Luther King Jr. (1929–68) comes to mind as an exemplar of nonviolent protest. Outside of the Christian religion, the Indian Mahatma Gandhi (1869–1948) remains one of the preeminent figures involved in nonviolent movements. I will use the Mennonite theologian John Howard Yoder (1927–97) as an example to illustrate the moderate version of the antithetical model. For Yoder, Jesus Christ and his earliest disciples radically resisted the violent and coercive structures of their day through nonviolent means. Yoder insists that the way of Jesus—a radical nonviolent resistance of coercive powers—should be the foundation of Christian social ethics. To him, when the cross-event is understood in the context of its relation to "enmity and power," what comes to light is that "servanthood replaces dominion, forgiveness absolves hostility."[43] Like Christ, Christians are to voluntarily submit to violent oppressive structures and should do so without resentment.[44] Below is a collection of passages taken from *The Politics of Jesus*.

> It is . . . a fundamental error to conceive of the position of the church in the New Testament in the face of social issues as a "withdrawal," or to see this position as motivated by the Christians' weakness, by their numerical insignificance or low social class, or by fear of persecution, or by scrupulous concern to remain uncontaminated by the world. What can be called the "otherness of the church" is an attitude rooted in strength and not in weakness. It consists in being a herald of liberation and not a community of slaves. It is not a detour or a waiting period, looking forward to better days which one hopes might come a few centuries later; it was rather a victory when the church rejected the temptations of Zealot and Maccabean patriotism and Herodian collaboration. The church accepted as a gift being the "new humanity" created by the cross and not by the sword.
>
> The liberation of the Christian from "the way things are," which has been brought about by the gospel of Christ, who freely took upon himself the bondages of history in our place, is so thorough and novel as to make evident to the believer that the givenness of our subjection to the enslaving or alienating powers of this world is broken. It is natural to feel Christ's liberation reaching

43. Yoder, *Politics of Jesus*, 131
44. Ibid., 185.

into every kind of bondage, and to want to act in accordance with that radical shift.

[Jesus'] motto of revolutionary subordination, of willing servanthood in the face of domination, enables the person in a subordinate position in society to accept and live within that status without resentment, at the same time that it calls upon the person in the superordinate position to forsake or renounce all domineering use of that status.[45]

Assessing the Antithetical Model: Living in seclusion may be helpful for protecting some Christians from the circumstances that can tempt them to sin. In other words, living in a Christian "enclave" can be beneficial to some Christians' personal growth. But should the Christian life be reduced to a personal piety? How can Christians understand and help tackle the needs of the world if they withdraw from the world? Christians who adopt the *strict version* of the antithetical model are in danger of seeing themselves as mere "outsiders" in the world and consequently may never be open to learning from non-Christian communities and cultures of their societies. Former president of Tanzania Julius Nyerere argues that the church must side with the victims of poverty and oppression, which for him entails active "involvement and leadership in constructive protest against" their condition. He goes on to state that "the Church has to help men rebel against their slums; it has to help them to do this in the most effective way it can be done." Without fearing the consequences, Nyerere continues, churches must fight all "institutions and power groups which contribute to the existence and maintenance of the physical and spiritual slums."[46]

Against the *moderate version* of the antithetical model it can be argued that it disempowers the oppressed from fighting back in a manner necessary to prevent or contain the evil actions of oppressive governments, groups, individuals, and institutions. In our present world, without the use of any sort of violence or coercive power (such as bombing a terrorist cell), evil actions may never be prevented or contained. Calling on people in superordinate positions to abandon their acts of domination without taking a well-regulated violent action against them may amount to an empty rhetoric that does not deter people from carrying out massive and sustained evil acts in the world. Some critics of pacifism (such as Oliver O'Donovan) argue that pacifism rules out the possibility that God providentially may act through a powerful and legally constituted authority to deter evil or bring

45. Ibid., 148, 149, 185–86.
46. Nyerere, "Christian Rebellion," 83–84.

penetrators of evil to justice with the use of force or violent means such as war. Pacifism appears to be "morally overambitious and impracticable" in *this* violent world.[47]

Empire Model

Description: The empire model sees the church as God's co-regent in the world and seeks to introduce Christianity as the predominant religion that should shape people's pattern of life both in the church and in the world at large. Christian values are infused with a government's political power and military agenda to control the economy, social life, and vision of the state. To put it another way, empire is justified through Christian theological means, such as by invoking the idea of God's *mediated* providence in the world through human instruments, especially Christian institutions.[48]

Example of the Empire Model: The empire model gradually became prominent in the Roman Empire during the latter stage of the reign of the Emperor Constantine the Great (r. 306–37 CE). During the medieval era, Christendom provided the impetus for the Crusades—the so-called Holy Wars. From the sixteenth century to the twentieth century, during the European exploration and missionary expeditions, Christian mission and theology were largely constructed after the likeness of what may be described as "Christian imperialism." The missionaries saw it as the duty of their powerful nations to Christianize and "civilize" other nations.[49] A neo-Constantinian imperial mindset has appeared in the writings of some American Christian theologians in the twenty-first century. I will highlight the work of Stephen Webb.

> Jesus commands his followers not to stand back from history but to change it. Christianity was animated from the beginning by a universal impulse. Only when the whole world is filled with God's Word will the biblical story of history come to its rightful conclusion. Given this command, the most pressing task of a theology of providence today clearly is to interpret the connection between globalism and Christianity, especially as America mediates that connection.

47. For more on this critique of pacifism, see O'Donovan, *Just War Revisited*, 7–12.

48. See Avram, *Anxious about Empire: Theological Essays on the New Global Realities*.

49. Oikotree, "Mission in the Context of Empire: Putting Justice at the Heart of Faith." Oikotree is a group that seeks "to live faithfully in the midst of economic injustice and ecological destruction." See http://www.oikotree.org/about-us/.

Providence asks Christians to get off the sidelines and into the game of history. It does not ask Christians to be uncritical in their expressions of national loyalty. *American Providence* is intentionally not entitled *Providential America*, because keeping the focus on providence as the constant and America as the variable is important. I do not mean to say that America is uniquely providential, nor that the doctrine of providence should be reconsidered only in the light of American history. Nevertheless, I do mean to take the risk of reflecting on what God might be doing through America today. God's providence is, no doubt, universal but all theology is concrete.

American Christians have a significant measure of responsibility not only for America but also for the fate of democracy worldwide. Modern democracy is, to a large extent, a product of Christian ideals and values, so that Christians of any nationality have a stake in America's attempt to support the growth of democracy abroad.

American providence is an interpretation of American history set in a global, indeed cosmic, context. In the end, American providence is not really about America. America's heart is so often in the right place because the American government was designed as a safe harbor for the Christian faith. If America were to stop providing the safe harbor, the providence would cease being, in any sense of the term, American.[50]

Assessing the Empire Model: The church will enjoy freedom of worship and policies that favor Christianity if it exists in a context where the empire model is implemented. The empire model, however, appears to do enormous harm both to Christians and people who do not share the Christian faith. During the time of Constantine's reign and the period immediately following, when Christianity gradually became the official religion of the Roman Empire, many Christians lost the zeal for morality and commitment to live the life of obedience to Christ. The church became powerful, had wealth, and enjoyed freedom but lacked moral power. The immoral church became the impetus for people to join the monastic movement as a way of escaping the worldly church.

When the church enjoys an imperial romance, its leaders tend to support the imperial power and become less critical of its colonial projects. Two examples can be used to buttress this claim. First, in the case of the experience of American Indians in the 1500s, as Clara Kidwell, Homer Noley, and George "Tink" Tinker have argued, some European Christian missionaries sometimes participated, implicitly or explicitly, in "oppression and cultural

50. Webb, *American Providence*, 6, 10, 168.

genocide."[51] Kidwell, Noley, and "Tink" Tinker are also critical of the christological expression "Jesus is Lord" because it was used in a way that had a devastating effect on the Native American people. For them, some European missionaries used it as justification for their colonization of American Indians. The church of the empire colonizes and erases difference rather than embodying Jesus Christ as God's good news to the world. The second example can be drawn from the experiences of many sub-Saharan African communities during the period of Western missionaries' expeditions in the 1800s and 1900s. African Instituted (or Independent) Churches (AICs) were birthed in the 1800s as some African church leaders rose up to the challenge posed by imperial Western Christianity and also by the *foreignness* of Western Christianity to the sensibilities of many African Christian converts. Western missionaries' Christianity—with its distinctive Western theologies, modes of worship, rituals, costumes, and unsympathetic attitudes toward many indigenous religious beliefs and practices—threw into an intriguing light the need to contextualize Christianity in sub-Saharan Africa.[52] Some African leaders such as the Nigerian James Johnson (1840–1901), the Liberian William Wade Harris (ca. 1860–1929), and the Malawian Yesaya Zerenji Mwasi (ca. 1869–1955), to name a few, resisted what they considered the tyrannical forms of leadership of Western missionaries. They resolved to establish local churches that attended to the social, spiritual, and theological needs of Africans and at the same time remained critical of imperialism and colonialism that ruined the image of Christianity in Africa.[53] The empire model is usually accompanied by the mindset of invasion, aggression, and colonization of non-Christian communities.

The empire model fails to account properly for the presence of non-Christian religions and their place in God's providential work in human history. Also, the version of providential imperialism proposed by Stephen Webb assumes that democracy is a neutral form of governance and assumes that it is the ideal, or should be made the ideal, form of governance in all societies. J. Akin Omoyajowo, who favors the use of Christian values to unify or control cultures, warns that "The Church that will help to integrate a developing nation cannot identify itself with a particular social class, prefer a particular political philosophy and party."[54] Webb's concept of "American providence" is in the end more about *American* political and economic val-

51. Kidwell et al., *Native American Theology*, 65.

52. For a concise historical account of the rise of indigenous African churches, see Sanneh, *Translating the Message*, 130–72.

53. See Mwasi, *My Essential and Paramount Reasons for Working Independently*.

54. Omoyajowo, "Christianity as a Unifying Factor," 97.

ues and agendas than about God's providence. As one reviewer of Webb's *American Providence* has noted: "Apart from justifying and guaranteeing American dominance, God is surprisingly absent from the book. . . . He proclaims faith in the trinity of Christianity, Democracy, and Capitalism, not the Father, Son, and Holy [Spirit]."[55]

Dialectical Model

Description: This model rejects both the empire and antithetical models. For theologians that adopt the dialectical model, the church is commissioned by Christ to be "in the world" but not "of the word." Rather than seeing Christians as those who are to escape from the world (the antithetical model) or as those who are to control all aspects of the world (the empire model), the dialectical model forces Christians to negotiate their existence in a movement of yes and no as they dialogue with other communities and cultures.

Examples of the Dialectical Model: Two examples of the dialectical model can be seen in the concepts of the church as *missional* and the church as God's *healing balm*. The shift in Christians' understandings of "mission" as one of the tasks of the church (what the church *does*) to the idea that mission is the church's heartbeat (what the church *is*) has changed the landscape of ecclesiology (doctrine of the church). The idea of the church as an assembly *sent* by God into the world to embody God's gospel is central to the notion of a *missional* church. The emphasis is on God's *sending* of the church as "Apostle" to the world. I will highlight the work of a team of scholars and church leaders (Lois Barrett, Inagrace T. Dietterich, George R. Hunsberger, Alan J. Roxburgh, Craig Van Gelder, and Darrell L. Guder) who have produced a helpful text on the concept of the missional church. For them, the church's role is not to control the world but rather to engage it with the intention to embody a life characteristic of God's kingdom or reign. The passage below is taken from their book *Missional Church: A Vision for the Sending of the Church in North America*.

> The Bible sometimes describes the missional church as being in the world but not of the world. That is, the church is in the midst of the world, both geographically and culturally, but it is not of the world. It does not have the same values as the world, the same behaviors, or the same allegiances. The missional church differs from the world because it looks for its cues from the One who has sent it out, rather than from the powers that appear to run the world.

55. Beach-Verhey, review of *American Providence*.

The church always lives in and among a culture or group of cultures. The vast majority of the church's particular communities share with their neighbors a primary culture or cultures, which include their language, food, perhaps styles of dress, and other customs. But they are called to point beyond that culture to the culture of God's new community.

This does not mean that the church or the gospel it preaches is somehow outside of culture. There is no cultureless gospel. Jesus himself preached, taught, and healed within a specific cultural context. Nor is it the case that the gospel can be reduced to a set of cultureless principles. . . . One of the tasks of the church is to translate the gospel so that the surrounding culture can understand it, yet help those believers who have been in that culture move toward living according to the behaviors and communal identity of God's missional people—in the language of the New Testament, God's *ethnos* (1 Pet 2:9).

The church's particular communities live in the context of the surrounding culture, engage with the culture, but are not controlled by the culture. The faithful church critiques its cultural environment, particularly the dominant culture; affirms those aspects of culture that do not contradict the gospel; speaks the language of the surrounding cultures and of the gospel; [and] constantly tries to communicate the gospel in the surrounding culture. . . .[56]

The dialectical model is also exemplified in the view of the church as God's *healing balm* in the world. Abigail Evans has argued that the church's "healing ministry" should not be relegated to a subset of the church's mission to the world but rather seen as what "should permeate every part of its mission."[57] For Evans, the scriptural concept of salvation entails *healing*—restoration of the well-being of God's creation. She argues that the miraculous healings of Jesus and as well as the early Christians' emphasis on overcoming principalities and powers (Eph 6:12) point the church's responsibility and concern toward the health of God's creation.[58] Christians, however, must trace the need of healing God's creation back to God's own work in the world. "Where there is healing," Evans writes, "there is God; God is the source of all healing."[59] Christians must also expect that God's healing work in the world may not fit their categories. Again she writes, "God is not limited to our understanding of how God works. God uses a variety of

56. Barrett, "Missional Witness," 110, 114–15.
57. Evans, *Healing Church*, 1.
58. Ibid., 2–7.
59. Ibid., 51.

means to heal including faith as testified by Christ's healing miracles."[60] For Evans, *conventional medicine*, which must pass double-blind and placebo-controlled studies, should not rule out the possibility of *faith healing* or deter Christians from seeking *faith healing*. Theology, in Evans' judgment, has something relevant to offer to the project of health, of healing God's creation.[61]

The Indian Preparatory Group that participated in the discourse on Asian spirituality organized by Asian scholars, which met in Suanbo, South Korea, in 1989, under the auspices of the Ecumenical Association of Third World Theologians (EATWOT), emphasized the role of Christians in bringing healing to their societies. Writing specifically about social problems in India, the Indian Preparatory Group argues that Christian spirituality requires healing the wounds of Indian societies caused by social inequality and injustice.

Spiritual is all that the Spirit of God originates, gives, guides, and accompanies; all that the Spirit can bless, accept, and work with. It is all that can contribute to the balance and blossoming, the healing and wholeness of India, of the human race, the earth, the cosmos. It may be described as the *Godwardness* of life, the experience of seeing God in all things and all things in God; or, as a sustained search for meaning, depth, transcendence, and comradeship, overcoming mental and social inertia and determinisms in order to grow in freedom and to be able to relate to reality.

History is contemplated to discern the signs of the times, what God is doing in our days, and to what collaboration God is summoning us. Contemplation may, in fact it must, deepen into probing and analysis of social reality with a view to a finer response.

It goes without saying that the response must be relevant. If it does not correspond to the need at hand, to the cry of the situation, to the call of God that comes through the people, it is no response at all. In the Samaritan story [Luke], what the two religious men did is no response, even if they hurried to the temple to pray for the man who was broken and left on the roadside.[62]

Healing the world requires hearing the questions the world addresses to Christianity and to the church in particular. The church should not *teach* the "world" (in this context, used broadly to include people, religions, political and social communities that are not grounded in the life and teaching of

60. Ibid., 51.

61. Ibid., 53–62.

62. Indian Preparatory Group, "Indian Search for a Spirituality of Liberation," 76–77.

Jesus Christ) without being willing to *listen* to the world, that is, to what the "world" is saying about the church. To become a Christian is to commit to the "way of Christ": to see the world, to relate to people, and to understand oneself in the light of the life and teaching of Jesus Christ. The Christian life has consequences for how Christians are to act responsibly in their societies.

Criticism of the Dialectical Model: The dialectical model should be applauded for preserving the complexity of the Christian vision of the living "in the world but not of the world." But while the dialectical model may sound nice on paper, how it is implemented in the face of any specific context will largely determine how exactly it is to be judged. For example, some theologians who favor *healing* a society through the use a violent revolution may be criticized by Christian pacifists for using an evil strategy to accomplish a good deed.

Concluding Remarks on the Christian Life

I conclude this chapter by highlighting three dimensions of the Christian life: the worldview dimension, relational dimension, and ethical dimension. Regarding the *worldview dimension*, the Christian life can be construed as a "way of seeing" that involves interpreting the meaning of life, events that happen in the world, humans' place and responsibility in the world, and the *telos* (ends, goal, and fulfillment) of the world. In Ephesians 4:17 Paul writes, "I tell you this, and insist on it in the Lord, that you must no longer live as the Gentiles do, in the futility of their thinking" (NIV). The Christian life is a particular *way of seeing*, which has its own distinctive features. The central question here is: What does it mean to "see" the world the Christian way? This is a very difficult question to answer given the different forms Christianity has taken in different contexts around the world. This difficulty is glaring in the face of competing understandings of Christianity that are represented in the disparate forms of expressions Christianity takes as it encounters new and different peoples and cultures. There are no easy solutions to these difficulties.

Two observations are in order in the context of this difficulty. First, the Christian "way of seeing" must be grounded in the life, experience, and teaching of Jesus of Nazareth as expressed and interpreted in the Scriptures. The worldview dimension of the Christian life, therefore, can be summarized as *seeing* and *living* in the world through the perspective of Jesus of Nazareth as represented and interpreted in the Scriptures. As an "intellectual" exercise, the Christian life must be measured against Jesus' life, experience, and teaching. Jesus is the *content* of the Christian life: to live a Christian life is to be "crucified with Christ" and to no longer live for *self* but rather to allow Jesus Christ to live through and transform *self* (Gal 2:20). The person being transformed, a process governed by the Holy Spirit (Gal 5:5–25), should seek to embody Jesus' vision of how to relate to God, to fellow humans, and to the entire creation. Second, the content of our understandings of the life, experience, and teaching of Jesus Christ must be rooted in communal reflections. This means that no single individual can on his or her own decide on what constitutes the content of Jesus' life, experience, and teaching. But more importantly, the communal reflection should also become an exercise in ecumenical conversations. No single Christian community can on its own know, grasp, and appreciate "how wide and long and deep is the love of Christ" (Eph 3:18–19) and his significance for the Christian understanding of God and God's relationship with the world. Christian communities should enter into dialogic communication with each other with the aim of discovering in common what it means to *see* the world in the *Christian way*. The Christian life is a form of living that is governed by the "mind" of Christ—that is, his way of thinking, pattern of behavior, and understanding of God's relationship to God's creation.

The Christian life also has a *relational dimension*. The Christian life flows from the Triune God's reception of human beings into divine fellowship. Here, it should be noted that the governing factor of this relationship is "love." The relational view of the Trinity makes clear that love is central to the perichoretical (i.e., interpenetrative and mutually giving) life of the persons of the Trinity. The God who is love (1 John 4:8, 16) pursues a relationship with God's creation (John 3:16; 1 John 4:9–10). The communities of God's people also are to live a life governed by love, however inadequate it may be compared to the type of love exemplified by the Triune God. The relational dimension of the Christian life, therefore, requires that Christians live a life of fellowship governed by love with both God and their fellow humans. As the Apostle John writes, "This is how we know who the children of God are and who the children of the devil are: Anyone who does not do what is right is not a child of God; nor is anyone who does not love his brother" (1 John 3:10 NIV; see also 1 John 4:7–21). Living the Christian life is not merely a matter of ticking boxes, nor is it adhering to a list of dos and don'ts. It is a *life*, which means that the Christian life is negotiated in dialogical relationship with both God and our fellow humans. This sort of relationship is perhaps part of what Isa 1:18 aims to communicate: "'Come now, let us reason together,' says the LORD. 'Though your sins are like scarlet, they shall be as white as snow; though they are red as crimson, they shall be like wool'" (NIV).

The *ethical dimension* of the Christian life focuses on practice—the daily act of living out the life of Christ in the power of the Holy Spirit. This dimension of the Christian life includes both motives and actions. Samuel Powell writes that the Christian life requires "embodied practices." Samuel's aim is to show that the Christian life opposes any dichotomy between "right intentions" and "faithful practice." Christians' good or right intentions must be embodied in their actions. The Christian life, therefore, is not an abstraction but what is continually lived out through concrete actions.[63] It is a gradual process that continues throughout a Christian's lifetime. On the one hand, the doctrine of the Christian life should remind Christians that they are always in need of God's "repeated forgiveness and of final transformation in the resurrection."[64] On the other hand, the Christian life should remind Christians they are not to "go on sinning" so that God's grace for them may increase (Rom 6:1).

Exercise 6.1

Topic: The church and preventable infectious diseases

Question: Does the church have a *responsibility* to address preventable infectious diseases? Discuss your answer to this question along with the theological reasons for your answer. Give some practical examples of how people can implement your answer.

Glossary

Asceticism: Term used to describe "spiritual exercise"—a form of spiritual training (from the Greek word *askesis*) that is rooted in denying one's self of worldly desires that hinder people from devoting themselves completely to God.

Monasticism: Christian monasticism refers to the movements that focus on the practice of the Christian life (either in solitude or community), involving rejection of worldly affairs (such as accumulation of wealth), spiritual exercises (such as asceticism), service to the poor, manual labor, and worship.

63. Powell, *Theology of Christian Spirituality*, 26–31.
64. Gunton, *Christian Faith*, 142.

Pacifism: Term used to describe the position of people who reject violent acts as a means to deter, contain, or solve any form of conflict or a threat to one's life.

Sanctification: Term used by some theologians to describe a life of holiness that is grounded in the Triune God's renewal of the life of sinners in which God makes them holy. Sanctification also involves Christians' constant repentance and crucifying of sinful desires.

Review Questions

1. What does the term "Christian life" mean in Christian theology? Describe different ways Christians understand the Christian life.

2. How should Christians live out the Christian life in the world? Discuss different ways Christian theologians have answered this question.

3. What roles do the persons of the Trinity play in the formation of the Christian life? What is the church's responsibility in the formation and practice of the Christian life?

Suggestions for Further Reading

Fabella, Virginia, et al. *Asian Christian Spirituality: Reclaiming Traditions*. Maryknoll, NY: Orbis, 1992.

Guder, Darrell L., ed. *Missional Church: A Vision for the Sending of the Church in North America*. Grand Rapids: Eerdmans, 1998.

Merton, Thomas. *Life and Holiness*. Garden City, NY: Image, 1964.

Powell, Samuel M. *A Theology of Christian Spirituality*. Nashville: Abingdon, 2005.

Shorter, Aylward, ed. *African Christian Spirituality*. Maryknoll, NY: Orbis, 1980.

Bibliography

Abasciano, Brian J. "Corporate Election in Romans 9: A Replay to Thomas Schreiner." *Journal of the Evangelical Theological Society* 49 (2006) 351–71.

———. "Does Regeneration Precede Faith? The Use of 1 John 5:1 as a Proof Text." *Evangelical Quarterly* 84 (2012) 307–22.

Abelard, Peter. *Commentary on the Epistle to the Romans.* Translated by Steven R. Cartwright. Fathers of the Church: Mediaeval Continuation 12. Washington, DC: Catholic University of America Press, 2011.

Agang, Sunday. "Breaking Nigerian Fatal Deadlock: Christians and Muslims Will Find Peace if They Work together for Justice." *Christianity Today* 56.54 (2012) 48–51.

Aghiorgoussis, Maximos. *Together in Christ: Studies in Ecclesiology and Ecumenism.* Brookline, MA: Holy Cross Orthodox Press, 2012.

Allen, Prudence. "Integral Sex Complementarity and the Theology of Communion." *Communio* 17 (1990) 523–44.

Allison, Gregg R. *Historical Theology: An Introduction to Christian Doctrine.* Grand Rapids: Zondervan, 2011.

Anderson, Allan Heaton. *To the Ends of the Earth: Pentecostalism and the Transformation of World Christianity.* New York: Oxford University Press, 2013.

Anderson, Gary A. *Sin: A History.* New Haven: Yale University Press, 2009.

Archer, Gleason L., et al. *Three Views on the Rapture: Pre-, Mid-, or Post-Tribulation?* Grand Rapids: Zondervan, 1996.

Arminius, James. *The Writings of James Arminius.* Translated by James Nichols and W. R. Bagnall. 3 vols. Grand Rapids: Baker, 1977.

Ateek, Naim. *Justice, and Only Justice: A Palestinian Theology of Liberation.* Maryknoll, NY: Orbis, 1989.

———. "A Palestinian Theology of Jerusalem." *Church and Society* 96 (2005) 88–97.

———. "Who Is My Neighbor?" *Interpretation* 62 (2008) 156–65.

Augustine. *The City of God: An Abridged Version.* Translated by Gerald G. Walsh et al. Edited by Vernon J. Bourke. Garden City, NY: Image, 1958.

Confessions. In vol. 1 of *A Select Library of the Nicene and Post-Nicene Fathers*, Series 1. Edited by Philip Schaff. 1886–1889. 14 vols. Reprint, Grand Rapids: Eerdmans, 1956.

———. *Confessions.* Translated by R. S. Pine-Coffin. Baltimore: Penguin, 1961.

341

Bibliography

————. On the "Proceedings" of Pelagius. In vol. 5 of A Select Library of the Nicene and Post-Nicene Fathers, Series 1. Edited by Philip Schaff. 1886–1889. 14 vols. Reprint, Grand Rapids: Eerdmans, 1956.

Aulén, Gustaf. Christus Victor: An Historical Study of the Three Main Types of the Idea of the Atonement. Translated by A. G. Hebert. New York: Macmillan, 1969.

Avram, Wes, ed. Anxious about Empire: Theological Essays on the New Global Realities. Grand Rapids, Brazos, 2004.

Awad, Najeeb George. "Theology of Religions, Universal Salvation, and the Holy Spirit." Journal of Pentecostal Theology 20 (2011) 252–71.

Backman, Clifford R. The Cultures of the West: A History. Combined volume. New York: Oxford University Press, 2013.

Barr, William R. "Christian Hope: Introducing the Issue." In Constructive Christian Theology in the Worldwide Church, edited by William R. Barr, 475–77. Grand Rapids: Eerdmans, 1997.

Barrett, Lois. "Missional Witness: The Church as Apostle to the World." In Missional Church: A Vision for the Sending of the Church in North America, edited by Darrell Guder, 110–41. Grand Rapids: Eerdmans, 1998.

Barrett, Matthew. "Does Regeneration Precede Faith in 1 John?" Mid-America Journal of Theology 23 (2012) 5–18.

Barth, Karl. Christ and Adam: Man and Humanity in Romans 5. Translated by T. A. Smail. New York: Collier, 1962.

————. The Christian Life. Translated by G. W. Bromiley. Grand Rapids: Eerdmans, 1981.

————. Church Dogmatics I/1: The Doctrine of the Word of God. Translated by G. W. Bromiley. 2nd ed. 1975. Reprint, Peabody, MA: Hendrickson, 2010.

————. Church Dogmatics II/2: The Doctrine of God. Translated by G. W. Bromiley. 2nd ed. 1975. Reprint, Peabody, MA: Hendrickson, 2010.

————. The Epistle to the Romans. Translated by Edwin C. Hoskyns. New York: Oxford University Press, 1968.

————. "No." In Natural Theology: Comprising "Nature and Grace" by Professor Dr. Emil Brunner and the Reply "No!" by Dr. Karl Barth, translated by Peter Fraenkel, 65–128. 1987. Reprint, Eugene, OR: Wipf and Stock, 2002.

————. The Theology of John Calvin. Translated by G. W. Bromiley. Grand Rapids: Eerdmans, 1995.

————. The Word of God and the Word of Man. Translated by Douglas Horton. New York: Harper & Row, 1956.

Bass, Clarence B. Backgrounds to Dispensationalism: Its Historical Genesis and Ecclesiastical Implications. 1960. Reprint, Eugene, OR: Wipf & Stock, 2005.

Beach-Verhey, Tim. Review of American Providence: A Nation with a Mission, by Stephen H. Webb. Political Theology 10 (2009) 376–78.

Belousek, Darrin W. Snyder. Atonement, Justice, and Peace: The Message of the Cross and the Mission of the Church. Grand Rapids: Eerdmans, 2012.

Berding, Kenneth. What Are Spiritual Gifts? Rethinking the Conventional View. Grand Rapids: Kregel, 2006.

Berger, Calinic. "Does the Eucharist Make the Church? An Ecclesiological Comparison of Staniloae and Zizioulas." St. Vladimir's Theological Quarterly 51 (2007) 23–70.

Berkhof, Louis. Systematic Theology. 4th ed. Grand Rapids: Eerdmans, 1941.

Biddle, Mark E. *Missing the Mark: Sin and Its Consequences in Biblical Theology*. Nashville: Abingdon, 2005.

Blocher, Henri. *Original Sin: Illuminating the Riddle*. Grand Rapids: Eerdmans, 1999.

Blomberg, Craig L. *Matthew*. New American Commentary 22. Nashville: Broadman, 1992.

Boettner, Loraine. "A Postmillennial Response." In *The Meaning of Millennium*, edited by Robert G. Clouse, 47–54. Downers Grove, IL: InterVarsity, 1977.

Bohm, David. *On Dialogue*. New York: Routledge Classics, 2004.

Bonhoeffer, Dietrich. *The Communion of Saints: A Dogmatic Inquiry into the Sociology of the Church*. New York: Harper & Row, 1963.

———. *The Cost of Discipleship*. Translated by R. H. Fuller, with some revision by Irmgard Booth. Rev. ed. New York: Macmillan, 1959.

———. *Creation and Fall*. Translated by John C. Fletcher. New York: Touchstone, 1997.

Borland, James A. "Women in the Life and Teaching of Jesus." In *Recovering Biblical Manhood and Womanhood: A Response to Evangelical Feminism*, edited by John Piper and Wayne Grudem, 113–23. Wheaton, IL: Crossway, 1991.

Bouteneff, Peter C. "Ecclesiology and Ecumenism." In *The Orthodox Christian World*, edited by Augustine Casiday, 369–82. New York: Routledge, 2012.

Boyd, Gregory A. "Christus Victor View." In *The Nature of the Atonement: Four Views*, edited by James Beilby and Paul R. Eddy, 23–49. Downers Grove, IL: IVP Academic, 2006.

Braaten, Carl E. *The Apostolic Imperative: Nature and Aim of the Church's Mission and Ministry*. Minneapolis: Augsburg, 1985.

———. *Mother Church: Ecclesiology and Ecumenism*. Minneapolis: Fortress, 1998.

———. *That All May Believe: A Theology of the Gospel and the Mission of the Church*. Grand Rapids: Eerdmans, 2008.

Braaten, Carl E., and Robert W. Jenson, eds. *Union with Christ: The New Finnish Interpretation of Luther*. Grand Rapids: Eerdmans, 1998.

Brock, Rita Nakashima. *Journeys by Heart: A Christology of Erotic Power*. New York: Crossroad, 1988.

Brown, Colin. *Karl Barth and the Christian Message*. London: Tyndale, 1967.

Brown, Joanne Carlson. "Divine Child Abuse?" *Daughters of Sarah* 18 (1992) 24–28.

Bultmann, Rudolf. "The New Testament and Mythology." In *Kerygma and Myth: A Theological Debate*, edited by Hans Werner Bartsch, 1–44. New York: Harper, 1961.

Calvin, John. *Commentaries*. Vol. 21. Edited by William Pringle. Reprint. Grand Rapids: Baker, 2009.

———. *Institutes of the Christian Religion*. Edited by John T. McNeill. Translated by Ford Lewis Battles. 2 vols. Philadelphia: Westminster, 1960.

Cameron, Nigel M. de S. *Are Christians Human? An Exploration of True Spirituality*. Grand Rapids: Zondervan, 1988.

Canales, Arthur D. "A Rebirth of Being 'Born Again': Theological, Sacramental, and Pastoral Reflection from a Roman Catholic Perspective." *Journal of Pentecostal Theology* 11 (2002) 98–119.

Carr, Anne E. *Transforming Grace: Christian Tradition and Women's Experience*. New York: Continuum, 1996.

Carson, D. A. "Atonement in Romans 3:21–26: 'God Presented Him as a Propitiation.'" In *The Glory of the Atonement*, edited by Charles E. Hill and Frank A. James III, 119–39. Downers Grove, IL: InterVarsity, 2004.

———. *Becoming Conversant with the Emerging Church: Understanding a Movement and Its Implications*. Grand Rapids: Zondervan, 2005.

Chafer, Lewis Sperry. *Systematic Theology*. 8 vols. Dallas: Dallas Seminary Press, 1947–48.

Chan, Simon. *Pentecostal Ecclesiology: An Essay on the Development of Doctrine*. Blandfor Forum, UK: Deo, 2011.

Clark, David K. "Is Special Revelation Necessary for Salvation?" In *Through No Fault of Their Own? The Fate of Those Who Have Never Heard*, edited by William V. Crockett and James G. Sigountos, 35–45. Grand Rapids: Baker, 1991.

Clarke, F. Stuart. *The Ground of Election: Jacobus Arminius' Doctrine of the Work and Person of Christ*. Waynesboro, GA: Paternoster, 2006.

Clarke, W. Norris. *Explorations in Metaphysics: Being-God-Person*. Notre Dame: University of Notre Dame Press, 1994.

Clooney, Francis X. *Comparative Theology: Deep Learning across Religious Borders*. Chichester, UK: Wiley-Blackwell, 2010.

———, ed. *The New Comparative Theology: Interreligious Insights from the Next Generation*. New York: T. & T. Clark, 2010.

Clowney, Edmund P. *The Church*. Downers Grove, IL: InterVarsity, 1995.

Coakley, John W., and Andrea Sterk, eds. *Readings in World Christian History*. Vol. 1, *Earliest Christianity to 1453*. Maryknoll, NY: Orbis, 2004.

Collins Winn, Christian T. "Groaning for the Kingdom of God: Spirituality, Social Justice, and the Witness of the Blumhardts." *Journal of Spiritual Formation & Soul Care* 6 (2013) 56–75.

———. *"Jesus is Victor!": The Significance of the Blumhardts for the Theology of Karl Barth*. Eugene, OR: Pickwick, 2009.

Cone, James H. *A Black Theology of Liberation*. Maryknoll, NY: Orbis, 1986.

Congar, Yves. *The Mystery of the Church*. Translated by A. V. Littedale. 2nd rev. ed. Baltimore: Helicon, 1965.

Conradie, Ernst. "Eschatology in South African Literature from the Struggle Period (1960–1994)." *Journal of Theology for Southern Africa* 107 (2000) 5–22.

Corcoran, Kevin. "Introduction: The Emerging Church." In *Church in the Present Tense: A Candid Look at What's Emerging*, edited by Kevin Corcoran, xi–xx. Grand Rapids: Baker, 2011.

———. "Who's Afraid of Philosophical Realism? Taking Emerging Christianity to Task." In *Church in the Present Tense: A Candid Look at What's Emerging*, edited by Kevin Corcoran, 3–21. Grand Rapids: Baker, 2011.

Costas, Orlando E. *Christ Outside the Gate: Mission Beyond Christendom*. Maryknoll, NY: Orbis, 1982.

Cottrell, Jack W. "Responses to Bruce Ware." In *Perspectives on Election: 5 Views*, edited by Chad Owen Brand, 59–62. Nashville: B & H, 2006.

Cox, Harvey. *Many Mansions: A Christian's Encounter with Other Faiths*. Boston: Beacon, 1988.

Craig, William Lane. "No Other Name: A Middle Knowledge Perspective on the Exclusivity of Salvation through Christ." In *The Philosophical Challenge of Religious*

Diversity, edited by Philip L. Quinn and Kevin Meeker, 38–53. New York: Oxford University Press, 2000.

Cranfield, C. E. B. *A Critical and Exegetical Commentary on the Epistle to the Romans.* Vol. 1. Edinburgh: T. & T. Clark, 1975.

Crisp, Oliver D. "Penal Non-Substitution." *Journal of Theological Studies* 59 (2008) 140–68.

Crossan, John Dominic. *Who Killed Jesus? Exploring the Roots of Anti-Semitism in the Gospel Stories of the Death Jesus.* New York: HarperSanFrancisco, 1995.

Croteau, David A. "Repentance Found? The Concept of Repentance in the Fourth Gospel." *Master's Seminary Journal* 24 (2013) 97–123.

Cullmann, Oskar "Pétros, Kēphás." In *TDNT*, edited by Geoffrey W. Bromiley, 5:100–112. Grand Rapids: Eerdmans, 1968.

Cummings, Charles. *Monastic Practices.* Kalamazoo, MI: Cistercian, 1986.

Cunningham, Lawrence S., and Keith J. Egan. *Christian Spirituality: Themes from the Tradition.* New York: Paulist, 1996.

Cunningham, Mary Kathleen. *What Is Theological Exegesis? Interpretation and the Use of Scripture in Barth's Doctrine of Election.* Valley Forge, PA: Trinity, 1995.

Davidson, Ivor J. *A Public Faith: From Constantine to the Medieval World, A.D. 312–600.* Grand Rapids: Baker, 2005.

Dawkins, Richard. *The God Delusion.* New York: Houghton Mifflin, 2006.

D'Costa, Gavin. *Christianity and World Religions: Disputed Questions in the Theology of Religion.* Chichester, UK: Wiley-Blackwell, 2009.

DeBruyn, Lawrence A. "Preterism and 'This Generation.'" *Bibliotheca Sacra* 167 (2010) 180–200.

De Duve, Christian, with Neil Patterson. *Genetics of Original Sin: The Impact of Natural Selection on the Future of Humanity.* New Haven: Yale University Press, 2010.

De Kadt, Emanuel Jehuda. *Assertive Religion: Religious Intolerance in a Multicultural World.* New Brunswick, NJ: Transaction, 2013.

DeYoung, Curtiss Paul. *Coming Together in the 21st Century: The Bible's Message in the Age of Diversity.* Valley Forge, PA: Judson, 2009.

Duffy, Regis A. "Baptism and Confirmation." In *Systematic Theology: Roman Catholic Perspectives*, edited by Francis Schüssler Fiorenza and John P. Galvin, 2:213–30. Minneapolis: Fortress, 1991.

Dulles, Avery. *Models of the Church.* Expanded ed. New York: Doubleday, 1987.

Ecumenism Among Us: Report of a Cross-Generational Conversation about the Unity of the Church and the Renewal of Human Community, June 4–8, 1994. Collegeville, MN: Institute for Ecumenical and Cultural Research, 1995.

Eddy, Paul R. "John Hick's Monotheistic Shadow." In *Can Only One Religion Be True? Paul Knitter and Harold Netland in Dialogue*, edited by Robert B. Steward, 117–37. Minneapolis: Fortress, 2013.

———. "Religious Pluralism and the Divine: Another Look at John Hick's Neo-Kantian Proposal." In *The Philosophical Challenge of Religious Diversity*, edited by Philip L. Quinn and Kevin Meeker, 126–38. Oxford: Oxford University Press, 2000.

Edwards, David L., and John R. W. Stott. *Evangelical Essentials: A Liberal-Evangelical Dialogue.* Downers Grove, IL: InterVarsity, 1988.

Edwards, Jonathan. *Charity and Its Fruits: Christian Love as Manifested in the Heart and Life.* Edited by Tryon Edwards. London: Banner of Truth Trust, 1969.

Ellul, Jacques. *Violence: Reflections from a Christian Perspective*. Translated by Cecilia Gaul Kings. New York: Seabury, 1969.

Erickson, Millard J. *Christian Theology*. 2nd ed. Grand Rapids: Baker, 1998.

Evans, Abigail Rian. *The Healing Church: Practical Programs for Health Ministries*. Cleveland: United Church Press, 1999.

Evans, Robert F. *Four Letters of Pelagius*. New York: Seabury, 1968.

———. *Pelagius: Inquiries and Reappraisals*. New York: Seabury, 1968.

Ezigbo, Victor I. *Introducing Christian Theologies: Voices from Global Christian Communities*. Vol. 1. Eugene, OR: Cascade, 2013.

———. *Re-imagining African Christologies: Conversing with the Interpretations and Appropriations of Jesus in Contemporary African Christianity*. Eugene, OR: Pickwick, 2010.

Fabella, Virginia, and Mercy Amba Oduyoye, eds. *With Passion and Compassion: Third World Women Doing Theology*. Maryknoll, NY: Orbis, 1988.

Fackenheim, Emil L. *The Jewish Return into History: Reflections in the Age of Auschwitz and a New Jerusalem*. New York: Schocken, 1978.

Fahey, Michael A. "Church." In *Systematic Theology: Roman Catholic Perspectives*, edited by Francis Schüssler Fiorenza and John P. Galvin, 2:3–74. Minneapolis: Fortress, 1991.

———. "Sacraments." In *The Oxford Handbook of Systematic Theology*, edited by John Webster et al., 267–84. New York: Oxford University Press, 2007.

Fairweather, Eugene R., ed. *A Scholastic Miscellany: Anselm to Ockham*. Philadelphia: Westminster, 1956.

Fee, Gordon D. *God's Empowering Presence: The Holy Spirit in the Letters of Paul*. Peabody, MA: Hendrickson, 1994.

Feinberg, John S. *No One Like Him: The Doctrine of God*. Wheaton, IL: Crossway, 2001.

Ferguson, Neil. "Separating Speaking in Tongues from Glossolalia using a Sacramental View." *Colloquium* 43 (2011) 39–58.

Ferguson, Sinclair B. *The Holy Spirit*. Downers Grove, IL: InterVarsity, 1996.

———. *Know Your Christian Life: A Theological Introduction*. Downers Grove, IL: InterVarsity, 1981.

Fergusson, David. "Eschatology." In *The Cambridge Companion to Christian Doctrine*, edited by Colin E. Gunton, 226–44. Cambridge: Cambridge University Press, 1997.

Ferré, Nels F. S. *The Finality of Faith, and Christianity among the World Religions*. New York: Harper & Row, 1963.

Fiddes, Paul S. "Salvation." In *The Oxford Handbook of Systematic Theology*, edited by John Webster et al., 176–96. New York: Oxford University Press, 2007.

Finger, Thomas. "*Christus Victor* as Nonviolence Atonement." In *Atonement and Violence: A Theological Conversation*, edited by John Sanders, 87–111. Nashville: Abingdon, 2006.

Flannery, Austin, ed. *Vatican Council II: The Conciliar and Post Conciliar Documents*. Collegeville, MN: Liturgical, 1975.

Flood, Gavin. "Orthodox Christianity and World Religions." In *The Orthodox Christian World*, edited by Augustine Casiday, 568–81. New York: Routledge, 2012.

Fredericks, James L. *Faith among Faiths: Christian Theology and Non-Christian Religions*. New York: Paulist, 1999.

———. "Introduction." In *The New Comparative Theology: Interreligious Insights from the Next Generation*, edited by Francis X. Clooney, ix–xix. New York: T. & T. Clark, 2010.

Fudge, Edward William. "The Case for Conditionalism." In Edward William Fudge and Robert A. Peterson, *Two Views of Hell: A Biblical and Theological Dialogue*, 18–82. Downers Grove, IL: InterVarsity, 2000.

Gaffin, Richard B. "A Cessationist Response to C. Samuel Storms and Douglas A. Oss." In *Are Miraculous Gifts for Today? Four Views*, edited by Wayne A. Grudem, 284–97. Grand Rapids: Zondervan, 1996.

———. "A Cessationist View." In *Are Miraculous Gifts for Today? Four Views*, edited by Wayne A. Grudem, 25–64. Grand Rapids: Zondervan, 1996.

Gay, Doug. *Remixing the Church: Towards an Emerging Ecclesiology*. London: SCM, 2011.

George, Timothy. *Galatians*. New American Commentary 30. Nashville: Broadman and Holman, 1994.

Gibbs, Eddie, and Ryan K. Bolger. *Emerging Churches: Creating Christian Community in Postmodern Cultures*. Grand Rapids: Baker Academic, 2005.

Gibson, David. *Reading the Decree: Exegesis, Election and Christology in Calvin and Barth*. London: T. & T. Clark, 2009.

Gonzalez, Michelle A. *Created in God's Image: An Introduction to Feminist Theological Anthropology*. Maryknoll, NY: Orbis, 2007.

Greer, Rowan A. *Christian Hope and Christian Life: Raids on the Inarticulate*. New York: Herder and Herder, 2001.

Grenz, Stanley J. *The Millennial Maze: Sorting Out Evangelical Options*. Downers Grove, IL: InterVarsity, 1992.

———. *The Social God and the Relational Self: A Trinitarian Theology of the Imago Dei*. Louisville: Westminster John Knox, 2001.

———. "Theological Foundations for Male-Female Relationships." *Journal of the Evangelical Theological Society* 41 (1998) 616–30.

———. *Theology for the Community of God*. Grand Rapids: Eerdmans, 2000.

Grenz, Stanley J., and Denise Muir Kjesbo. *Women in the Church: A Biblical Theology of Women in Ministry*. Downers Grove, IL: InterVarsity, 1995.

Gritzner, Christian, et al. "The Asteroid and Comet Impact Hazard: Risk Assessment and Mitigation Options." *Naturwissenschaften* 93 (2006) 361–73.

Grotius, Hugo. *A Defense of the Catholic Faith Concerning the Satisfaction of Christ against Faustus Socinus*. Translated by Frank Hugh Foster. Andover: Warren F. Draper, 1889.

Grudem, Wayne, ed. *Are Miraculous Gifts for Today? Four Views*. Grand Rapids: Zondervan, 1996.

———. *Evangelical Feminism: A New Path to Liberalism?* Wheaton: Crossway, 2006.

———. *Systematic Theology: An Introduction to Biblical Doctrine*. Grand Rapids: Zondervan, 1994.

Guder, Darrell L., ed. *Missional Church: A Vision for the Sending of the Church in North America*. Grand Rapids: Eerdmans, 1998.

Gunton, Colin E. *The Christian Faith: An Introduction to Christian Doctrine*. Oxford: Blackwell, 2002.

Guthrie, Donald. *New Testament Theology*. Downers Grove, IL: InterVarsity, 1981.

Gutiérrez, Gustavo. "The Option for the Poor Arises from Faith in Christ." *Theological Studies* 70 (2009) 317–26.

———. *A Theology of Liberation*. Fifteenth anniversary ed. Maryknoll, NY: Orbis, 1988.

Harrison, Carol. *Rethinking Augustine's Early Theology: An Argument for Continuity*. New York: Oxford University Press, 2006.

Harrison, Verna E. F. "Orthodox Arguments against the Ordination of Women as Priests." In *Women and the Priesthood*, edited by Thomas Hopko, 165–87. Crestwood, NY: St. Vladimir's Seminary Press, 1999.

Hayes, Zachary J. "The Purgatorial View." In *Four Views on Hell*, edited by William Crockett, 91–121. Grand Rapids: Zondervan, 1992.

Heard, J. B. *The Tripartite Nature of Man: Spirit, Soul, and Body*. Edinburgh: T. & T. Clark, 1882.

Heath, Elaine A., and Larry Duggins. *Missional, Monastic, Mainline: A Guide to Starting Missional Micro-Communities in Historically Mainline Traditions*. Eugene, OR: Cascade, 2014.

Hellwig, Monika K. "Eschatology." In *Systematic Theology: Roman Catholic Perspectives*, edited by Francis Schüssler Fiorenza and John P. Galvin, 2:349–72. Minneapolis: Fortress, 1991.

Hick, John. *A Christian Theology of Religions: The Rainbow of Faiths*. Louisville: Westminster John Knox, 1995.

Hodge, Charles. *Systematic Theology*. Vol. 2. Reprint, Grand Rapids: Eerdmans, 1968.

Hodges, Zane C. *Absolutely Free: A Biblical Reply to Lordship Salvation*. Grand Rapids: Zondervan, 1989.

Hoekema, Anthony A. "Amillennialism." In *The Meaning of the Millennium: Four Views*, edited by Robert G. Clouse, 155–91. Downers Grove, IL: InterVarsity, 1977.

———. *Created in God's Image*. Grand Rapids: Eerdmans, 1986.

Holten, Wilko van. "Eschatology with a Vengeance: Hell as the Greatest Conceivable Evil." In *The Future as God's Gift: Explorations in Christian Eschatology*, edited by David Fergusson and Marcel Sarot, 181–88. Edinburgh: T. & T. Clark, 2000.

Horowitz, Maryanne Cline. "The Image of God in Man—Is Woman Included?" *Harvard Theological Review* 72.3–4 (1979) 175–206.

Horsley, Richard A. *Jesus and the Empire: The Kingdom of God and the New World Disorder*. Minneapolis: Fortress, 2003.

Horton, Michael. *The Christian Faith: A Systematic Theology for Pilgrims on the Way*. Grand Rapids: Zondervan, 2011.

Hotz, Kendra G., and Matthew T. Matthews. *Shaping the Christian Life: Worship and the Religions Affections*. Louisville: Westminster John Knox, 2006.

Hoyt, Herman A. "A Dispensational Premillennial Response." In *The Meaning of the Millennium: Four Views*, edited by Robert G. Clouse, 144–48. Downers Grove, IL: InterVarsity, 1977.

———. "Dispensational Premillennialism." In *The Meaning of the Millennium: Four Views*, edited by Robert G. Clouse, 163–92. Downers Grove, IL: InterVarsity, 1977.

Hurley, James B. *Man and Woman in Biblical Perspective*. Grand Rapids: Academie, 1981.

Hurtado, Larry W. "Resurrection-Faith and the 'Historical' Jesus." *Journal for the Study of the Historical Jesus* 11 (2013) 35–52.

Ignatius of Loyola. *The Spiritual Exercises of St. Ignatius Loyola*. Translated by Elisabeth Meier Tetlow. Lanham, MD: University Press of America, 1987.

Indian Preparatory Group. "An Indian Search for a Spirituality of Liberation." In *Asian Christian Spirituality: Reclaiming Traditions*, edited by Virginia Fabella et al., 64–84. Maryknoll, NY: Orbis, 1992.

Irenaeus. *Against Heresies*. In vol. 1 of *Ante-Nicene Fathers*. Edited by Alexander Roberts and James Donaldson. 1885–1887. 10 vols. Reprint, Grand Rapids: Eerdmans, 1969.

Jenson, Robert W. "The Bride of Christ." In *Critical Issues in Ecclesiology: Essays in Honor of Carl E. Braaten*, edited by Alberto L. Garcia and Susan K. Wood, 1–5. Grand Rapids: Eerdmans, 2011.

Jewett, Paul K. *Man as Male and Female*. Grand Rapids: Eerdmans, 1975.

Johnson, Elizabeth A. *Quest for the Living God: Mapping Frontiers in the Theology of God*. New York: Continuum, 2007.

Johnson, S. Lewis, Jr. "Role Distinctions in the Church: Galatians 3:28." In *Recovering Biblical Manhood and Womanhood: A Response to Evangelical Feminism*, edited by John Piper and Wayne Grudem, 154–64. Wheaton, IL: Crossway, 1991.

Jones, Serene. *Feminist Theory and Christian Theology: Cartographies of Grace*. Minneapolis: Fortress, 2000.

———. "What's Wrong with Us? Human Nature and Human Sin." In *Essentials of Christian Theology*, edited by William C. Placher, 141–58. Louisville: Westminster John Knox, 2003.

Kalu, Ogbu. *African Pentecostalism: An Introduction*. New York: Oxford University Press, 2008.

Kapic, Kelly M. "Anthropology." In *Mapping Modern Theology: A Thematic and Historical Introduction*, edited by Kelly M. Kapic and Bruce L. McCormack, 121–48. Grand Rapids: Baker, 2012.

Karfíková, Lenka. *Grace and the Will according to Augustine*. Translated by Marketá Janebová. Leiden: Brill, 2012.

Kärkkäinen, Veli-Matti. *Christ and Reconciliation: A Constructive Christian Theology for the Pluralistic World*. Vol. 1. Grand Rapids: Eerdmans, 2013.

———. *Introduction to Ecclesiology: Ecumenical, Historical, and Global Perspectives*. Downers Grove, IL: InterVarsity, 2002.

———. *An Introduction to Theology of Religions: Biblical, Historical, and Contemporary Perspectives*. Downers Grove, IL: InterVarsity, 2003.

Kato, Byang H. *Theological Pitfalls in Africa*. Kisumu: Evangel, 1975.

Kay, William K. "Where the Wind Blows: Pentecostal Christians in Hong Kong and Singapore." *Pentecostal Studies* 11 (2012) 128–48.

Keener, Craig S. *A Commentary on the Gospel of Matthew*. Grand Rapids: Eerdmans, 1999.

———. *1–2 Corinthians*. New York: Cambridge University Press, 2005.

———. "Women in Ministry: Another Egalitarian Perspective." In *Women in Ministry: Two Views*, edited James R. Beck, 205–48. Rev. ed. Grand Rapids: Zondervan, 2005.

Kelsey, David H. *Eccentric Existence: A Theological Anthropology*. 2 vols. Louisville: Westminster John Knox, 2009.

Kidwell, Clara Sue, et al. *A Native American Theology*. Maryknoll, NY: Orbis, 2001.

Kitamori, Kazoh. *Theology of the Pain of God*. Richmond: John Knox, 1965.

Klein, Charlotte L. "From Conversion to Dialogue—the Sisters of Sion and the Jews: A Paradigm of Catholic-Jewish Religions?" *Journal of Ecumenical Studies* 18 (1981) 388–400.

Knitter, Paul F. *One Earth, Many Religions: Multifaith Dialogue and Global Responsibility.* Maryknoll, NY: Orbis, 1995.

Kornblum, William, and Joseph Julian. *Social Problems.* 13th ed. Upper Saddle River, NJ: Pearson/Prentice-Hall, 2009.

Küng, Hans. et al. *Christianity and World Religions: Paths of Dialogue with Islam, Hinduism, and Buddhism.* Translated by Peter Heinegg. 2nd ed. Maryknoll, NY: Orbis, 1993.

Kyle, Richard. "Semi-Pelagianism." In *Evangelical Dictionary of Theology*, edited by Walter A. Elwell, 1000–1001. Grand Rapids: Baker, 1984.

Ladd, George Eldon. "An Historic Premillennial Response." In *The Meaning of the Millennium: Four Views*, edited by Robert G. Clouse, 143. Downers Grove, IL: InterVarsity, 1977.

———. "Historic Premillennialism." In *The Meaning of the Millennium: Four Views*, edited by Robert G. Clouse, 17–40. Downers Grove, IL: InterVarsity, 1977.

———. *A Theology of the New Testament.* Rev ed. Grand Rapids: Eerdmans, 1993.

Le Goff, Jacques. *The Birth of Purgatory.* Translated by Arthur Goldhammer. Chicago: University of Chicago Press, 1984.

Lillback, Peter A. *The Binding of God: Calvin's Role in the Development of Covenant Theology.* Grand Rapids: Baker, 2001.

Lindbeck, George A. *The Nature of Doctrine: Religion and Theology in a Postliberal Age.* Philadelphia: Westminster, 1984.

Longenecker, Richard N. "Authority, Hierarchy, and Leadership: Patterns in the Bible." In *Women, Authority, and the Bible*, edited by Alvera Mickelsen, 66–85. Downers Grove, IL: InterVarsity, 1986.

Lossky, Vladimir. *In the Image and Likeness of God.* Edited by John H. Erickson and Thomas E. Bird. Crestwood, NY: St. Vladimir's Seminary Press, 1974.

Louth, Andrew. "The Place of Theosis in Orthodox Theology." In *Partakers of the Divine Nature: The History and Development of Deification in the Christian Traditions*, edited by Michael J. Christensen and Jeffery A. Wittung, 32–44. Madison, NJ: Fairleigh Dickinson University Press, 2007.

Luther, Martin. *Confession Concerning Christ's Supper—Part III (1528).* In *Martin Luther's Basic Theological Writings*, edited by Timothy F. Lull, 50–62. Minneapolis: Fortress, 1989.

———. *Confession Concerning Christ's Supper—from Part I (1528).* In *Martin Luther's Basic Theological Writings*, edited by Timothy F. Lull, 375–404. Minneapolis: Fortress, 1989.

———. *Heidelberg Disputation.* In *Martin Luther's Basic Theological Writings*, edited by Timothy F. Lull, 30–49. Minneapolis: Fortress, 1989.

———. *The Sacrament of the Body and Blood of Jesus Christ—against the Fanatics.* In *Martin Luther's Basic Theological Writings*, edited by Timothy F. Lull, 314–40. Minneapolis: Fortress, 1989.

———. *Temporal Authority: To What Extent It Should Be Obeyed.* In *Martin Luther's Basic Theological Writings*, edited by Timothy F. Lull, 655–703. Minneapolis: Fortress, 1989.

The Lutheran World Federation and the Roman Catholic Church. *Joint Declaration on the Doctrine of Justification*. Grand Rapids: Eerdmans, 2000.

Ma, Wonsuk. "Pentecostal Eschatology: What Happened When the Wave Hit the West End of the Ocean." *Asian Journal of Pentecostal Studies* 12 (2009) 95–112.

MacArthur, John F. *The Gospel According to Jesus: What Does Jesus Mean when He Says "Follow Me"?* Panorama City, CA: Word of Grace, 1988.

Macquarrie, John. *Principles of Christian Theology*. 2nd ed. New York: Scribner's, 1977.

Mangina, Joseph L. "The Cross-Shaped Church: A Pauline Amendment to the Ecclesiology of *Koinōnia*." In *Critical Issues in Ecclesiology: Essays in Honor of Carl E. Braaten*, edited by Alberto L. García and Susan K. Wood, 68–87. Grand Rapids: Eerdmans, 2011.

Mana, Kä. *Christians and Churches of Africa: Salvation in Christ and Building a New African Society*. Maryknoll, NY: Orbis, 2004.

Mannermaa, Tuomo. "Theosis as a Subject of Finnish Luther Research." *Pro Ecclesia* 4 (1995) 37–47.

Martin, Ralph. *Is Jesus Coming Soon? A Catholic Perspective on the Second Coming*. San Francisco: Ignatius, 1997.

———. *Will Many Be Saved? What Vatican II Actually Teaches and Its Implications for the New Evangelization*. Grand Rapids: Eerdmans, 2012.

Martinez, Jessica. "After South African Pastor Makes Church Members Eat Grass, He Now Forces Them to Drink Petrol." *ChristianPost.com*, September 26, 2014. http://www.christianpost.com/news/after-south-african-pastor-makes-church-members-eat-grass-he-now-forces-them-to-drink-petrol-127099/.

Mbiti, John S. *African Religions and Philosophy*. London: Heinemann, 1969.

———. *New Testament Eschatology in an African Background: A Study of the Encounter between the New Testament Theology and African Traditional Concepts*. Oxford: Oxford University Press, 1971.

McCormack, Bruce L. *Orthodox and Modern: Studies in the Theology of Karl Barth*. Grand Rapids: Baker, 2008.

McDougall, Joy Ann. "Feminist Theology." In *The Oxford Handbook of Systematic Theology*, edited by John Webster et al., 671–87. New York: Oxford University Press, 2007.

McFadyen, Alistair. *Bound to Sin: Abuse, Holocaust, and the Christian Doctrine of Sin*. Cambridge: Cambridge University Press, 2000.

McFarland, Ian A. *Difference and Identity: A Theological Anthropology*. Cleveland: Pilgrim, 2001.

McGrath, Alister E. *Christian Theology: An Introduction*. 3rd ed. Oxford: Blackwell, 2001.

———. "The Origins of a Scientific Theology." *Interdisciplinary Science Reviews* 28 (2003) 259–65.

———. "Response to R. Douglas Geivett and W. Gary Phillips." In *Four Views on Salvation in a Pluralistic World*, edited Dennis L. Okholm and Timothy R. Phillips, 256–58. Grand Rapids: Zondervan, 1996.

McGrath, Alister E., and Joanna Collicutt McGrath. *The Dawkins Delusion? Atheist Fundamentalism and the Denial of the Divine*. London: SPCK, 2007.

McGuckin, John Anthony. *The Orthodox Church: An Introduction to Its History, Doctrine, and Scriptural Culture*. Oxford: Blackwell, 2008.

Merton, Thomas. *Life and Holiness*. Garden City, NY: Image, 1964.

Middleton, J. Richard. *The Liberating Image: Imago Dei in Genesis 1*. Grand Rapids: Brazos, 2005.

Migliore, Daniel L. *Faith Seeking Understanding: An Introduction to Christian Theology*. 2nd ed. Grand Rapids: Eerdmans, 2004.

Moehler, R. Albert Jr. "Modern Theology: The Disappearance of Hell." In *Hell Under Fire*, edited by Christopher W. Morgan and Robert A. Peterson, 15–41. Grand Rapids: Zondervan, 2004.

Moffitt, John. "Interreligious Encounter and the Problem of Salvation." *Christian Century* 93.37 (1976) 1001–7.

Moltmann, Jürgen. *The Coming of God: Christian Eschatology*. Translated by Margaret Kohl. London: SCM, 1996.

———. *The Crucified God*. Translated by R. A. Wilson and John Bowden. Minneapolis: Fortress, 1993.

———. *Experiences in Theology: Ways and Forms of Christian Theology*. Translated by Margaret Kohl. London: SCM, 2000.

———. *Sun of Righteousness, Arise! God's Future for Humanity and the Earth*. Translated by Margaret Kohl. Minneapolis: Fortress, 2010.

———. *The Way of Jesus Christ: Christology in Messianic Dimensions*. Translated by Margaret Kohl. Minneapolis: Fortress, 1993.

Moo, Douglas J. "Paul on Hell." In *Hell Under Fire*, edited by Christopher W. Morgan and Robert A. Peterson, 91–109. Grand Rapids: Zondervan, 2004.

Morgan, Christopher W. "Annihilationism: Will the Unsaved be Punished Forever?" In *Hell Under Fire*, edited by Christopher W. Morgan and Robert A. Peterson, 195–281. Grand Rapids: Zondervan, 2004.

Morris, Leon. *The Cross in the New Testament*. Grand Rapids: Eerdmans, 1965.

Morris, Thomas V. *Our Idea of God: An Introduction to Philosophical Theology*. Vancouver: Regent College, 2002.

Mouw, Richard J. "The *Imago Dei* and Philosophical Anthropology." *Christian Scholar's Review* 41 (2012) 253–66.

Mwasi, Yesaya Zerenji. *My Essential and Paramount Reasons for Working Independently*. Blantyre: Kachere Boos, 2000.

Nash, Ronald H. *Is Jesus the Only Savior?* Grand Rapids: Zondervan, 1994.

Nassif, Bradley. "Orthodox Spirituality: A Quest for Transfigured Humanity." In *Four Views on Christian Spirituality*, edited by Bruce Demarest, 27–55. Grand Rapids: Zondervan, 2012.

Netland, Harold. *Encountering Religious Pluralism: The Challenge to Christian Faith and Mission*. Downers Grove, IL: InterVarsity, 2001.

Niebuhr, H. Richard. *Christ and Culture*. New York: Harper & Row, 1951.

Norman, W. H. H. *An Interim Report on Non-Church Christianity in Japan*. Nishinomiya: Kwansei Gakuin University Annual Studies, 1958.

Norris, Frederick W. "Timothy I of Baghdad, Catholicos of the East Syrian Church, 780–823: Still a Valuable Model." *International Bulletin of Missionary Research* 30 (2006) 133–36.

Northcott, Michael S. *A Political Theology of Climate Change*. Grand Rapids: Eerdmans, 2013.

Nyerere, Julius. "The Christian Rebellion." In *African Christian Spirituality*, edited by Aylward Shorter, 82–88. Maryknoll, NY: Orbis, 1980.

Oakes, Kenneth. *Reading Karl Barth: A Guide to "The Epistle to the Romans".* Eugene, OR: Cascade, 2011.

O'Collins, Gerald. *Christology: A Biblical, Historical, and Systematic Study of Jesus.* New York: Oxford University Press, 2009.

O'Donovan, Oliver. *The Just War Revisited.* New York: Cambridge University Press, 2003.

Oduyoye, Mercy Amba. *Daughters of Anowa: African Women and Patriarchy.* Maryknoll, NY: Orbis, 1995.

————. "Feminist Theology in African Perspective." In *Paths of African Theology,* edited by Rosino Gibellini, 166–81. London: SCM, 1994.

Official Catholic Teachings, Update. Wilmington, NC: McGrath, 1980.

Oikotree. "Mission in the Context of Empire: Putting Justice at the Heart of Faith." *International Review of Mission* 101 (2012) 195–211.

Ojo, Matthew A. "Eschatology and the African Society: The Critical Point of Disjunction." *Ogbomoso Journal of Theology* 11 (2006) 93–100.

Okonkwo, Izunna. "The Sacrament of the Eucharist (as Koinonia) and African Sense of Communalism: Towards a Synthesis." *Journal of Theology for Southern Africa* 137 (2010) 88–103.

Omoyajowo, J. Akin. "Christianity as a Unifying Factor in a Developing Country." In *African Christian Spirituality,* edited by Aylward Shorter, 95–98. Maryknoll, NY: Orbis, 1980.

Orobator, A. E. *The Church as Family: African Ecclesiology in Its Social Context.* Nairobi: Paulines, 2000.

Osburn, Carroll D. *Women in the Church: Reclaiming the Ideal.* 2nd ed. Abilene, TX: Abilene Christian University Press, 2001.

Oss, Douglas A. "A Pentecostal/Charismatic Response to C. Samuel Storms." In *Are Miraculous Gifts for Today? Four Views,* edited by Wayne A. Grudem, 235–36. Grand Rapids: Zondervan, 1996.

————. "A Pentecostal/Charismatic Response to Robert L. Saucy." In *Are Miraculous Gifts for Today? Four Views,* edited by Wayne A. Grudem, 164–71. Grand Rapids: Zondervan, 1996.

————. "A Pentecostal/Charismatic View." In *Are Miraculous Gifts for Today? Four Views,* edited by Wayne A. Grudem, 239–83. Grand Rapids: Zondervan, 1996.

Page, Sydney H. T. "The Assumptions behind Spiritual Gifts Inventories." *Didaskalia* 22 (2011) 39–59.

Pappas, Barbara. *Are You Saved? The Orthodox Christian Process of Salvation.* 4th ed. Westchester, IL: Amnos, 1997.

Peace, Jennifer Howe. "Encountering the Neighbor." In *My Neighbor's Faith: Stories of Interreligious Encounter, Growth, and Transformation,* edited by Jennifer Howe Peace et al., 25–29. Maryknoll, NY: Orbis, 2012.

Peacore, Linda D. *The Role of Women's Experience in Feminist Theologies of Atonement.* Eugene, OR: Pickwick, 2010.

Pelagius. *Pelagius's Commentary on St. Paul's Epistle to the Romans.* Translated by Theodore de Bruyn. Oxford: Clarendon, 1993.

Persoon, Joachim G. "Towards an Ethiopian Eco-Theology with Inspiration from Monastic Spirituality." *Swedish Missiological Themes* 98 (2010) 211–37.

Peters, Ted. *Anticipating Omega: Science, Faith, and Our Ultimate Future.* Gottingen: Vandenhoeck & Ruprecht, 2006.

Bibliography

―――. "Eschatology: Eternal Now or Cosmic Future?" *Zygon* 36 (2001) 349–56.

―――. *God as Trinity: Relationality and Temporality in Divine Life.* Louisville: Westminster John Knox, 1993.

―――. "The Terror of Time." *Dialog* 39 (2000) 56–66.

Peterson, Robert A. "The Case for Traditionalism." In *Two Views of Hell: A Biblical and Theological Dialogue,* by Edward William Fudge and Robert A. Peterson, 115–81. Downers Grove, IL: InterVarsity, 2000.

Phillips, Timothy R., and Dennis L. Okholm. *A Family of Faith: An Introduction to Evangelical Christianity.* Grand Rapids: Baker, 1996.

Phipps, William E. "The Heresiarch: Pelagius or Augustine?" *Anglican Theological Review* 62 (1980) 124–33.

Pinnock, Clark H. "Annihilationism." In *The Oxford Handbook of Eschatology,* edited by Jerry L. Walls, 462–75. New York: Oxford University Press, 2008.

―――. *Flame of Love: A Theology of the Holy Spirit.* Downers Grove, IL: InterVaristy, 1996.

―――. *A Wideness in God's Mercy: The Finality of Jesus Christ in a World of Religions.* Grand Rapids: Zondervan, 1992.

Piper, John. *Bloodlines: Race, Cross, and the Christian.* Wheaton, IL: Crossway, 2011.

―――. "A Vision of Biblical Complementarity: Manhood and Womanhood Defined According to the Bible." In *Recovering Biblical Manhood and Womanhood: A Response to Evangelical Feminism,* edited by John Piper and Wayne Grudem, 31–59. Wheaton, IL: Crossway, 1991.

Polkinghorne, John. "The Continuing Interaction of Science and Religion." *Zygon* 40 (2005) 43–50.

―――. "Eschatology: Some Questions and Some Insights from Science." In *The End of the World and the Ends of God: Science and Theology on Eschatology,* edited by John Polkinghorne and Michael Welker, 29–41. Harrisburg, PA: Trinity, 2000.

―――. *The God of Hope and the End of the World.* London: SPCK, 2002.

―――. "Scripture and an Evolving Creation." *Science and Christian Belief* 21 (2009) 163–73.

Powell, Samuel M. *A Theology of Christian Spirituality.* Nashville: Abingdon, 2005.

Power, David N. "Eucharist." In *Systematic Theology: Roman Catholic Perspectives,* edited by Francis Schüssler Fiorenza and John P. Galvin, 2:261–88. Minneapolis: Fortress, 1991.

Procksch, Otto. "Hágios." In *Theological Dictionary of the New Testament,* 1:88–115. Grand Rapids: Zondervan, 1976.

Race, Allan. *Christians and Religious Pluralism: Patterns in the Christian Theology of Religions.* Maryknoll, NY: Orbis, 1983.

Radano, John A., ed. *Celebrating a Century of Ecumenism: Exploring the Achievements of International Dialogue.* Grand Rapids: Eerdmans, 2012.

Rahner, Karl. "Christianity and the Non-Christian Religions." In vol. 4 of *Theological Investigations,* edited by Karl H. Kruger, 115–34. Baltimore: Helicon, 1966.

Rahner, Karl, and Herbert Vorgrimler. *Dictionary of Theology.* Translated by Richard Strachan et al. 2nd ed. New York: Crossroad, 1981.

Ramm, Bernard L. *An Evangelical Christology: Ecumenic and Historic.* Nashville: Thomas Nelson, 1985.

Ratzinger, Joseph. *Eschatology: Death and Eternal Life.* Translated by Michael Waldstein. 2nd ed. Washington, DC: Catholic University of America Press, 1988.

Raunio, Antti. "Natural Law and Faith: The Forgotten Foundations of Ethics in Luther's Theology." In *Union with Christ: The New Finnish Interpretation of Luther*, edited by Carl E. Braaten and Robert W. Jenson, 96–124. Grand Rapids: Eerdmans, 1998.

Rees, B. R. *Pelagius: Life and Letters*. Vol. 2 Rochester, NY: Boydell, 1991.

Riddlebarger, Kim. *A Case for Amillennialism: Understanding the End Times*. Grand Rapids: Baker, 2003.

Robinson, John A. T. *In the End, God*. Religious Perspectives 20. New York: Harper & Row, 1968.

Rollins, Peter. "The Worldly Theology of Emerging Christianity." In *Church in the Present Tense: A Candid Look at What's Emerging*, edited by Kevin Corcoran, 23–36. Grand Rapids: Baker, 2011.

Rowland, Christopher. "The Eschatology of the New Testament." In *The Oxford Handbook of Eschatology*, edited by Jerry L. Walls, 56–72. New York: Oxford University Press, 2008.

Ruether, Rosemary Radford. *Sexism and God-Talk: Towards a Feminist Theology*. London: SCM, 1983.

Russell, Jeffrey Burton. *A History of Heaven: The Singing Silence*. Princeton: Princeton University Press, 1996.

Russell, Robert John. "Eschatology and Scientific Cosmology: From Deadlock to Interaction." *Zygon* 47 (2012) 997–1014.

Ryrie, Charles C. *Basic Theology: A Popular Systematic Guide to Understanding Biblical Truth*. Chicago: Moody, 1999.

———. *So Great Salvation: What It Means to Believe in Jesus Christ*. Wheaton, IL: Victor, 1989.

Sacred Congregation for the Doctrine of the Faith. "Declaration *Inter Insigniores*: On the Question of Admission of Women to the Ministerial Priesthood." 1976. http://www.vatican.va/roman_curia/congregations/cfaith/documents/rc_con_cfaith_doc_19761015_inter-insigniores_en.html.

Samartha, Stanley J. "The Cross and the Rainbow: Christ in a Multicultural Culture." In *Asian Faces of Jesus*, edited by R. S. Sugirtharajah, 104–23. Maryknoll, NY: Orbis, 1993.

Samartha, Stanley J., and J. B. Taylor, eds. *Christian-Muslim Dialogue: Papers Presented at the Broumana Consultation, 12–18 July 1972*. Geneva: World Council of Churches, 1973.

Sanders, John. *No Other Name: An Investigation into the Destiny of the Unevangelized*. Grand Rapids: Eerdmans, 1992.

Sands, Paul Francis. "The *Imago Dei* as Vocation." *Evangelical Quarterly* 82 (2010) 28–41.

Sanneh, Lamin. *Translating the Message: The Missionary Impact on Culture*. Maryknoll, NY: Orbis, 1989.

Saucy, Robert L. "An Open but Cautious Response to Richard B. Gaffin, Jr." In *Are Miraculous Gifts for Today? Four Views*, edited by Wayne A. Grudem, 65–71. Grand Rapids: Zondervan, 1996.

———. "An Open but Cautious View." In *Are Miraculous Gifts for Today? Four Views*, edited by Wayne A. Grudem, 95–148. Grand Rapids: Zondervan, 1996.

Scanzoni, Letha, and Nancy Hardesty. *All We're Meant to Be: A Biblical Approach to Women's Liberation*. Waco, TX: Word, 1974.

Schaff, Philip. *The Creeds of Christendom: With a History and Critical Notes*. 3 vols. 6th ed. Grand Rapids: Baker, 1988.

Shannon-Missal, Larry. "Americans' Belief in God, Miracles and Heaven Declines." Harris Poll #97, December 16, 2013. http://www.harrisinteractive.com/NewsRoom/HarrisPolls/tabid/447/ctl/ReadCustom%20Default/mid/1508/ArticleId/1353/Default.aspx.

Schmemann, Alexander. "Ecclesiological Notes." *St. Vladimir's Theological Quarterly* 11 (1967) 35–39.

———. "The Missionary Imperative in the Orthodox Church." In *Eastern Orthodox Theology: A Contemporary Reader*, edited by Daniel B. Clendenin, 195–201. Grand Rapids: Baker, 1995.

Schreiner, Thomas R. "Women in Ministry: Another Complementarian Perspective." In *Women in Ministry: Two Views*, edited James R. Beck, 265–322. Rev. ed. Grand Rapids: Zondervan, 2005.

Schüssler Fiorenza, Elisabeth. *Jesus: Miriam's Child, Sophia's Prophet; Critical Issues in Feminist Christology*. New York: Continuum, 1994.

Schweitzer, Albert. *The Quest of the Historical Jesus*. Edited by John Bowden. Minneapolis: Fotress Press, 2001.

Scribner, R. W. *The German Reformation*. Atlantic Highlands, NJ: Humanities Press, 1986.

Sharp, Douglas R. *The Hermeneutics of Election: The Significance of the Doctrine in Barth's "Church Dogmatics"*. Lanham, MD: University Press of America, 1990.

Skinner, John. *A Critical and Exegetical Commentary on Genesis*. New York: Scribner, 1910.

Smith, Gary Scott. *Heaven in the American Imagination*. New York: Oxford University Press, 2011.

Smith, Wilbur M. *The Biblical Doctrine of Heaven*. Chicago: Moody, 1968.

Sobrino, Jon. *Christology at the Crossroads: A Latin American Approach*. Translated by John Drury. Maryknoll, NY: Orbis, 1978.

———. "Jesus and the Kingdom of God." In *Liberation Theology: An Introductory Reader*, edited by Curt Cadorette et al., 104–22. Maryknoll, NY: Orbis, 1992.

Sölle, Dorothee. *Thinking about God: An Introduction to Theology*. Translated by John Bowden. Philadelphia: Trinity, 1990.

Souga, Theresa. "The Christ-Event in the Viewpoint of African Women." In *With Passion and Compassion: Third World Women Doing Theology*, edited by Virginia Fabella and Mercy Amba Oduyoye, 22–34. Maryknoll, NY: Orbis, 1988.

Stăniloae, Dumitru. *The Experience of God*. Translated by Ioan Ionită and Robert Barringer. Brookline, MA: Holy Cross Orthodox Press, 1994.

Stavropoulos, Christoforos. "Partakers of Divine Nature." In *Eastern Orthodox Theology: A Contemporary Reader*, edited by Daniel B. Clendenin, 183–92. Grand Rapids: Eerdmans, 1995.

Stoeger, William R. "Scientific Accounts of Ultimate Catastrophes in our Life-Bearing Universe." In *The End of the World and the Ends of God: Science and Theology on Eschatology*, edited by John Polkinghorne and Michael Welker, 19–28. Harrisburg, PA: Trinity, 2000.

Storms, Sam C. "A Third Wave Response to Robert L. Saucy." In *Are Miraculous Gifts for Today? Four Views*, edited by Wayne A. Grudem, 156–63. Grand Rapids: Zondervan, 1996.

————. "A Third Wave View." In *Are Miraculous Gifts for Today? Four Views*, edited by Wayne A. Grudem, 175–223. Grand Rapids: Zondervan, 1996.

Stott, John R. W. *Authentic Jesus: The Certainty of Christ in a Skeptical World*. Downers Grove, IL: InterVarsity, 1985.

————. *The Cross of Christ*. Downers Grove, IL: InterVarsity, 1986.

————. *The Letters of John*. Grand Rapids: Eerdmans, 1988.

Strong, Augustus Hopkins. *Systematic Theology*. Vol. 3, *The Doctrine of Salvation*. Philadelphia: American Baptist Publication Society, 1909.

Swinburne, Richard. "An Open but Cautious Response to C. Samuel Storms." In *Are Miraculous Gifts for Today? Four Views*, edited by Wayne A. Grudem, 225–34. Grand Rapids: Zondervan, 1996.

————. "An Open but Cautious View." In *Are Miraculous Gifts for Today? Four Views*, edited by Wayne A. Grudem, 97–148. Grand Rapids: Zondervan, 1996.

————. *The Resurrection of God Incarnate*. New York: Oxford University Press, 2003.

Takim, Liyakatali. "From Conversion to Conversation: Interfaith Dialogue in Post 9-11 America." *The Muslin World* 94 (2004) 343–55.

Tanner, Kathryn. "Eschatology with a Future?" In *The End of the World and the Ends of God: Science and Theology on Eschatology*, edited by John Polkinghorne and Michael Welker, 222–37. Harrisburg, PA: Trinity, 2000.

————. "Incarnation, Cross, and Sacrifice: A Feminist-Inspired Reappraisal." *Anglican Theological Review* 86 (2004) 35–56.

Taylor, Charles. *A Secular Age*. Cambridge: Harvard University Press, 2007.

Taylor, John V. *The Primal Vision: Christian Presence amid African Religion*. London: SCM, 1963.

Terrell, JoAnne Marie. *Power in the Blood? The Cross in the African American Experience*. Maryknoll, NY: Orbis, 1998.

Tertullian. *Treatise on the Soul*. In vol. 1 of *Ante-Nicene Fathers*. Edited by Alexander Roberts and James Donaldson. 1885–1887. 10 vols. Reprint, Grand Rapids: Eerdmans, 1969.

Thiel, John E. *Icons of Hope: The "Last Things" in Catholic Imagination*. Notre Dame: University of Notre Dame Press, 2013.

Thomas, Aquinas. *Basic Writings of Saint Thomas Aquinas*. Edited by Anton C. Pegis 2 vols. New York: Random House, 1945.

Thomas, Stephen. *Deification in the Eastern Orthodox Tradition: A Biblical Perspective*. Piscataway, NJ: Gorgias Press, 2007.

Tiessen, Terrance L. *Who Can Be Saved? Reassessing Salvation in Christ and World Religions*. Downers Grove, IL: InterVarsity, 2004.

Tillard, J.-M. R. *I Believe, Despite Everything: Reflections of an Ecumenist*. Translated by William G. Rusch. Collegeville, MN: Liturgical, 2000.

————. "New Roman Catholic Insights on Baptism." *Mid-Stream* 18 (1979) 432–43.

Tillich, Paul. *Systematic Theology*. 3 vols. Chicago: University of Chicago Press, 1963.

Togarasei, Lovemore. "The Conversion of Paul as a Prototype of Conversion in African Christianity." *Svensk Missionstidskrift* 95 (2007) 111–22.

Torrance, Thomas F. "Atonement in the Teaching of St. Paul: Atonement as Justification." In *Atonement: The Person and Work of Christ*, edited by Robert T. Walker, 97–136. Downers Grove, IL: IVP Academic, 2009.

————. *Incarnation: The Person and Life of Jesus Christ*. Edited by Robert T. Walker. Downers Grove, IL: InterVarsity, 2008.

Bibliography

Tracy, David. *On Naming the Present: God, Hermeneutics, and the Church.* Maryknoll, NY: Orbis, 1994.

Turaki, Yusufu. *The Unique Christ for Salvation: The Challenge of the Non-Christian Religions and Culture.* Nairobi: International Bible Society Africa, 2001.

Turner, Max. *The Holy Spirit and Spiritual Gifts: Then and Now.* Carlisle: Paternoster, 1996.

Tutu, Desmond. *God is Not a Christian: And Other Provocations.* edited by John Allen. New York: Harper One, 2011.

Twiss, Richard. *One Church, Many Tribes: Following Jesus the Way God Made You.* Ventura, CA: Regal, 2000.

Uchimura, Kanzō. *The Complete Works of Kanzo Uchimura.* 7 vols. Tokyo: Kyobunkwan, 1971–73.

Vanhoozer, Kevin J. *The Drama of Doctrine: A Canonical Linguistic Approach to Christian Theology.* Louisville: Westminster John Knox, 2005.

Volf, Miroslav. *After Our Likeness: The Church as the Image of the Trinity.* Grand Rapids: Eerdmans, 1998.

———. *Exclusion and Embrace: A Theological Exploration of Identity, Otherness, and Reconciliation.* Nashville: Abingdon, 1996.

———. *A Public Faith: How Followers of Christ Should Serve the Common Good.* Grand Rapids: Brazos, 2011.

———. "The Social Meaning of Reconciliation." *Interpretation* 54 (2000) 158–72.

Wagner, C. Peter. *Your Spiritual Gifts Can Help Your Church Grow.* Ventura, CA: Regal, 1979.

Wagner, C. Peter, and Larry Keefauver. *Your Spiritual Gifts Can Help Your Church Grow: Group Study Guide.* Ventura; CA: Gospel Light, 1995.

Walls, Andrew F. "Converts and Proselytes? The Crises over Conversion in the Early Church." *International Bulletin of Missionary Research* 28 (2004) 2–6.

———. *The Cross-Cultural Process in Christian History.* Maryknoll, NY: Orbis, 2002.

———. *The Missionary Movement in Christian History: Studies in Transmission of Faith.* Maryknoll, NY: Orbis, 1996.

Walls, Jerry L. *Heaven: The Logic of Eternal Joy.* New York: Oxford University Press, 2002.

Walvoord, John F. "Postmillennialism." *Bibliotheca sacra* 106 (1949) 149–68.

Ward, Benedicta. "Anthony the Great." In *The Sayings of the Desert Fathers,* translated by Benedicta Ward, 1–9. Kalamazoo, MI: Cistercian, 1975.

Ware, Bruce A. "Divine Election to Salvation." In *Perspectives on Election: Five Views,* edited by Chad Owen Brand, 1–58. Nashville: Broadman & Holman, 2006.

Ware, Kallistos. *The Inner Kingdom.* Crestwood, NY: St. Vladimir's Seminary Press, 2004.

———. *The Orthodox Way.* Rev. ed. Crestwood, NY: St. Vladimir's Seminary Press, 1995.

Warfield, B. B. *Counterfeit Miracles.* London: Banner of Truth Trust, 1972.

Weaver, Darlene Fozard. "Taking Sin Seriously." *Journal of Religious Ethics* 31 (2003) 45–74.

Weaver, J. Denny. "Narrative *Christus Victor*: The Answer to Anselmian Atonement Violence." In *Atonement and Violence: A Theological Conversation,* edited by John Sanders, 1–29. Nashville: Abingdon, 2006.

———. *The Nonviolent Atonement.* 2nd ed. Grand Rapids: Eerdmans, 2011.

Webb, Stephen. *American Providence: A Nation with a Mission*. New York: Continuum, 2004.

Weber, Timothy P. "Millennialism." In *The Oxford Handbook of Eschatology*, edited by Jerry L. Walls, 365–83. New York: Oxford University Press, 2008.

Wells, David F. "The Future." In *Christian Faith and Practice in the Modern World: Theology from an Evangelical Point of View*, edited by Mark A. Noll and David F. Wells, 285–304. Grand Rapids: Eerdmans, 1988.

Wenham, John W. *The Goodness of God*. Downers Grove, IL: InterVarsity, 1974.

Wesley, John. *The Doctrine of Original Sin: According to Scripture, Reason, and Experience*. In *The Works of John Wesley*, vol. 12, *The Doctrinal and Controversial Treatises I*, edited by Randy L. Maddox, 117–481. Nashville: Abingdon, 2012.

Williams, Delores S. "A Womanist Perspective on Sin." In *A Troubling in My Soul: Womanist Perspectives on Evil and Suffering*, edited by Emilie M. Townes, 130–49. Maryknoll, NY: Orbis, 1993.

Williams, Norman Powell. *The Ideas of the Fall and of Original Sin: A Historical and Critical Study*. London: Longmans, Green, 1927.

Williams, Robert R. "Sin and Evil." In *Christian Theology: An Introduction to Its Traditions and Tasks*, edited by Peter Hodgson and Robert King, 194–221. 3rd ed. Minneapolis: Fortress, 1994.

Williams, Rowan. "A Common Word for the Common God." In *A Common Word Between Us and You*, 187–212. Five-year anniversary ed. Amman: Royal Aal al-Bayt Institute for Islamic Thought, 2012.

———. "The Forgiveness of Sin: Hosea 11:1–9; Matthew 18:23–35." In *Proclaiming the Scandal of the Cross: Contemporary Images of the Atonement*, edited by Mark D. Baker, 77–83. Grand Rapids: Baker Academic, 2006.

———. *On Christian Theology*. Oxford: Blackwell, 2000.

———. *Tokens of Trust: An Introduction to Christian Belief*. Louisville: Westminster John Knox, 2007.

World Council of Churches. *Guidelines on Dialogue with People of Living Faiths and Ideologies*. Geneva: WCC, 1979.

Wright, N. T. *Surprised by Hope: Rethinking Heaven, the Resurrection, and the Mission of the Church*. New York: HarperOne, 2008.

Yarbrough, Robert W. "Jesus on Hell." In *Hell Under Fire*, edited by Christopher W. Morgan and Robert A. Peterson, 67–90. Grand Rapids: Zondervan, 2004.

Yeo, K. K. *Musing with Confucius and Paul: Toward a Chinese Christian Theology*. Eugene, OR: Cascade, 2008.

Yoder, John Howard. *The Politics of Jesus*. 2nd ed. Grand Rapids: Eerdmans, 1994.

Yong, Amos. *Beyond the Impasse: Toward a Pneumatological Theology of Religions*. Grand Rapids: Baker, 2003.

Zagano, Phyllis. "Catholic Women's Ordination: The Ecumenical Implications of Women Deacons in the Armenian Apostolic Church, the Orthodox Church of Greece, and the Union of Ultrecht Old Catholic Churches." *Journal of Ecumenical Studies* 43 (2008) 124–37.

Zizioulas, John D. *Being as Communion: Studies in Personhood and the Church*. Crestwood, NY: St. Vladimir's Seminary Press, 1985.

———. *Eucharist, Bishop, Church: The Unity of the Church in the Divine Eucharist and the Bishop during the First Three Centuries*. Translated by Elizabeth Theokritoff. Brookline, MA: Holy Cross Orthodox Press, 2001.

Bibliography

Zwingli, Ulrich. *Commentary on True and False Religion*. Edited by Samuel Macauley Jackson and Clarence Nevin Heller. Durham, NC: Labyrinth, 1981.

———. *On the Lord's Supper*. In *Zwingli and Bullinger*, edited by G. W. Bromiley, 185–238. Philadelphia: Westminster, 1953.

Index